Mohutangi
NORTHLAND
Opononi • Whangarei
Orewa
Auckland
AUCKLAND
Thames
Hamilton
Cambridge
THE CENTRAL
NORTH ISLAND
Taupo
New Plymouth
Gisborne
Napier
Hastings
WELLINGTON
AND
THE SOUTH
Te Araroa
GH • Wellington
Blenheim

**Wellington and
the South**
Pages 156–189

**Marlborough
and Nelson**
Pages 200–221

**Canterbury and the
West Coast**
Pages 222–257

**Otago and Southland**
Pages 258–295

0 kilometres    100

0 miles         100

EYEWITNESS TRAVEL

# NEW ZEALAND

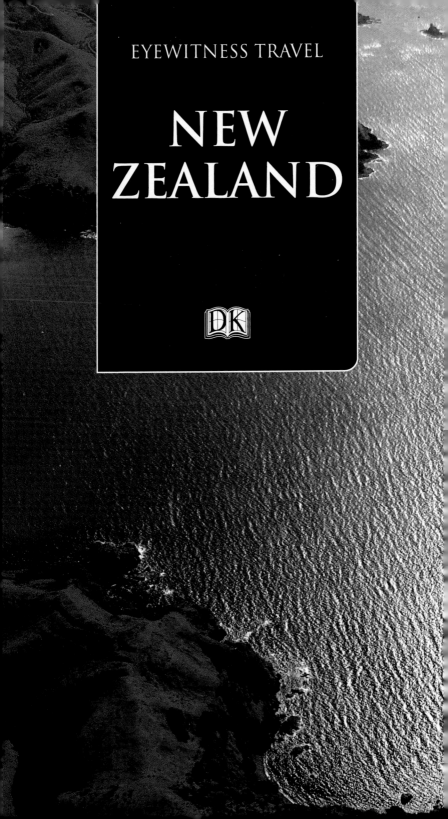

EYEWITNESS TRAVEL

# NEW
# ZEALAND

**DK**

**DK**

LONDON, NEW YORK,
MELBOURNE, MUNICH AND DELHI
www.dk.com

**Produced by** Editions Didier Millet, Kuala Lumpur

**Editorial Director** Timothy Auger

**Project Manager** Noor Azlina Yunus

**Editors** Dianne Buerger, Zuraidah Omar

**Designers** Theivanai Nadaraju, Yong Yoke Lian

**Contributors**

Helen Corrigan, Roef Hopman, Gerard Hutching, Rebecca Macfie, Geoff Mercer,
Simon Noble, Peter Smith, Michael Ward, Mark Wright

**Photographers**

Peter Bush, Gerald Lopez, Lloyd Park, Ron Redfern

**Illustrators**

Yeap Kok Chien, Tan Hong Yew, Denis Chai Kah Yune

**Maps**

ERA-Maptec Ltd, Dublin, Ireland

Printed and bound by South China Printing Co. Ltd., China

First published in Great Britain in 2001
by Dorling Kindersley Limited
80 Strand, London WC2R 0RL
A Penguin Random House Company

13 14 15 16 10 9 8 7 6 5 4 3 2 1

**Reprinted with revisions 2002, 2003, 2005, 2006,
2008, 2010, 2012, 2014**

Copyright 2001, 2014 © Dorling Kindersley Limited, London

A CIP catalogue record is available from the British Library.

ISBN 978 1 40932 901 5

MIX
Paper from
responsible sources
FSC™ C018179
www.fsc.org

Front cover main image: Hooker River, Aoraki/Mount Cook National Park, Canterbury

◀ Aerial view of Tupou Bay, Northland

# Contents

Tamatekapua Maori meeting
house, Rotorua

# Introducing
# New Zealand

Pohutukawa in bloom at Oriental Bay,
Wellington

Punting on the Avon River, Christchurch

Upmarket fish and chips

Club rugby match on the North Island's East Cape

Olveston House, Dunedin

# HOW TO USE THIS GUIDE

This guide helps you to get the most from your visit to New Zealand. *Introducing New Zealand* maps the country and sets it in its historical and cultural context. The seven area chapters in *New Zealand Area by Area* describe the main sights, with photographs, illustrations and maps. Features cover topics relating specifically to the North and South islands as well as subjects of regional interest. Restaurant and hotel recommendations can be found in *Travellers' Needs*. The *Survival Guide* has practical tips on everything from making a telephone call to transport.

## New Zealand Area By Area

New Zealand has been divided into seven main sightseeing areas, coded with a coloured thumb tab for quick reference. A map illustrating how the two main islands have been divided can be found on the inside front cover of this guide. The sights listed within the individual areas are plotted and numbered on a Regional Map.

**1 Introduction**
The landscape, history and character of each region is described here, showing how the area has developed over the years and what it has to offer the visitor today.

**A locator map** shows the region in relation to the other areas of New Zealand.

**Each area** of New Zealand can be identified quickly by its colour coding.

**2 Regional Map**
This gives an illustrated overview of the whole area. All the sights covered in the chapter are numbered and there are useful tips on getting around by car and public transport.

**3 Detailed Information**
All the important towns and other places of interest are described individually. They are listed in order, following the numbering on the Regional Map. Within each entry there is detailed information on the important buildings and other major sights.

**Features and story boxes** highlight special or unique features of an area or sight.

**4 Major Towns**

All the important towns are described individually. Within each entry there is further detailed information on interesting buildings and other sites. The Town Map shows the location of the main sights.

**A Visitors' Checklist** gives you the practical details to plan your visit, including transport information, the address of the tourist office and festivals.

**The Town Map** shows all major and minor roads. The key sights are plotted, along with train and bus stations, parking areas and tourist information offices.

**5 Street-by-Street Map**

Towns or districts of special interest to the visitor are given a bird's-eye view in detailed 3D with photographs and descriptions of the most important sights.

**A suggested route** for a walk covers the most interesting streets in the area.

**Opening hours**, the telephone number and transport details for the sight are given in the Visitors' Checklist.

**6 The Top Sights**

These are given two or more pages. Historic buildings are dissected to reveal their interiors; national parks have maps showing facilities and trails; museums have colour-coded floorplans. Photographs highlight the most interesting features.

**Stars** indicate sights that visitors should not miss.

# INTRODUCING
# NEW ZEALAND

# DISCOVERING NEW ZEALAND

The following itineraries have been designed to take in as many of New Zealand's highlights as possible, while keeping long-distance travel manageable. Ideally you'll want to divide your time evenly between the North Island and the South Island. First comes a one-week tour of the North Island, supplemented by a three-day jaunt around Northland and a couple of days in the capital, Wellington. For those with more time, there are some suggestions for extending these trips, including a few days around the East Cape. The two-week grand tour of the South Island takes in the best on offer, but again, this can be extended with trips to Golden Bay and the country's third major land mass, Stewart Island. Pick, combine and follow your favourite tours, or simply dip in and out and be inspired.

**White-water rafting on Shotover River, Queenstown**
New Zealand's fast-flowing rivers are perfect for white-water rafting. The Oxenbridge Tunnel Rapid on the Shotover River leads through the exhilarating rapids of the Skippers Canyon.

**Key**

— North Island tour

— Northland

— South Island tour

## Two Weeks in the South Island

- Watch whales, swim with dolphins and get close to fur seals at picturesque **Kaikoura**.

- Sip a Marlborough Sauvignon at **Wairau Valley**, then cruise the nearby **Queen Charlotte Sound.**

- Kayak the crystal-clear waters or hike the easy Coast Path in the **Abel Tasman National Park**.

- Go adventure-crazy in **Queenstown** or just appreciate the stunning scenery.

- Thread your way along the bush-cloaked, hairline waterways of remote **Fiordland**.

- Take the slow road along the **Catlins Coast**, with its leaping dolphins, petrified forest and dramatic coastlines.

0 kilometres 100

0 miles 100

Paparoa National Park

SOUTH ISLAND

Westland/Tai Poutini National Park
Franz Josef Glacier
Fox Glacier
Aoraki/Mount Cook National Park
Haast
Christchurch
Lyttelton
Lake Tekapo
Haast Pass
Lake Pukaki
Akaroa
Mount Aspiring National Park
Milford Sound
Wanaka
Fiordland National Park
Arrowtown
Doubtful Sound
Queenstown
Te Anau
Lake Wakatipu
Oamaru
Manapouri
Moeraki
Otago Peninsula
Dunedin
Invercargill
Catlins
Nugget Point
Stewart Island
Curio Bay
Porpoise Bay

◀ The inner city suburb of Oriental Bay, Wellington, ca. 1930

## Three Days in Northland

- Dive or snorkel the **Poor Knights Islands**, New Zealand's prime dive site.

- Pick through the historic locations around the **Bay of Islands**, sites crucial to both Maori and Europeans.

- Take a bus tour or drive to **Cape Reinga** via **Ninety Mile Beach**.

- Relax in the laid-back Hokianga Harbour villages of **Rawene** and **Opononi**.

- Gaze up at the kauri, New Zealand's largest trees, in the **Waipoua Forest**.

**Cathedral Cove**
A natural stone arch separates the two sandy beaches at Cathedral Cove on the Coromandel Peninsula.

## One Week in the North Island

- See the best of Maori, Pacific and wider New Zealand art at the galleries of **Auckland**.

- Explore the beautiful **Coromandel Peninsula** and dig a hot spring hole in the sand at **Hot Water Beach**.

- Smell the sulphur and see geysers, silica terraces and boiling mud pools in and around **Rotorua**.

- Delve into the glowworm-illuminated underworld of **Waitomo**.

- Take a scenic stroll or a full-day tramp through the volcanic wonders of **Tongariro National Park**.

- Admire **Napier's** Art Deco city centre, then sample some superb Syrah and Chardonnay wines in the **Hawke's Bay Vineyards**.

## One Week in the North Island

- **Arriving** Auckland airport is 20 km (12 miles) south of the city centre. Buses and taxis connect it to the city centre.

- **Transport** A car or campervan is the best option, but everywhere can be reached by fairly infrequent bus services.

Lake Rotorua seen from the North Crater on the Tongariro Alpine Crossing

### Day 1: Auckland
Culturally minded visitors should pay visits to the **Voyager Maritime Museum** (p77), the beautifully renovated **Auckland Art Gallery** (p80) and the **Auckland War Memorial Museum** (p82). Altenatively, take a short cruise to **Rangitoto Island** (p93) with its unique pohutukawa forest, unusual lava tubes and great views of the city.

### Day 2: Coromandel Peninsula
Loop around the beautiful Coromandel Peninsula, winding into the hills at **Driving Creek Railway** (p128), soak in the hot pools at **Hot Water Beach** (p129), swim at golden **Cathedral Cove** (p129) and check out the vibrant **arts and crafts scene** (p131).

### Day 3: Rotorua
It is about a 4-hour drive south to Rotorua, a journey best broken at **Waihi** (p130) with its massive gold-mining hole right in the centre of town. Learn about the genesis of New Zealand's first tourist town by

Wood carving at the Maori Meeting House, Auckland War Memorial Museum

visiting the **Rotorua Museum** (p138) and surrounding **Government Gardens** (p138). Next, stroll around the lakeshore to **St Faith's Anglican Church** (p139) in the original Maori village of Ohinemutu. Set aside the evening for a visit to **Tamaki Maori Village** (p141) with its demonstration of Maori customs and a hangi dinner cooked in an earth oven.

### Day 4: Rotorua
Drive out to **Wai-o-tapu Thermal Wonderland** (p144) in time for the clockwork 10:15am geyser eruption. While there, admire pools of boiling mud and wander past the vibrantly coloured Champagne Pool, Primrose Terraces and Artist's Palette. In the afternoon, choose from: historical explorations at the **Buried Village** (p141); madcap laughs on the Shweeb and bungy jumping at **Agroventures** (p140) or **ZORB®** **Rotorua** (p140); or simply soak the afternoon away at the **Polynesian Spa** (p134).

> **To extend your trip...**
> Spend a couple of days (or longer if you have the time) soaking up the relaxed pace of the **East Cape** (p136), New Zealand's remotest populated corner. It feels like you're stepping back in time 30 or even 50 years.

### Day 5: Waitomo Caves
New Zealand's netherworld wonders peak at **Waitomo Caves** (p124) where the

**Glowworm Caves** (p125) combine viewing stalactite formations with a boat ride under a constellation of glowworms. The wetsuit-clad adventure trip **Lost World** (p125) will get you abseiling, cave tubing and jumping into dark pools. Back above ground, take the short but lovely walk to the **Ruakuri Natural Tunnel** (p124).

### Day 6: Tongariro National Park and Taupo
Take a couple of short walks on the slopes of the three occasionally active volcanoes in **Tongariro National Park** (p146), then head north past the **National Trout Centre** (p145) to the fishing mecca of **Taupo** (p145). Its eponymous lake empties down the Waikato River, which plunges spectacularly over **Huka Falls** (p144).

> **To extend your trip...**
> Set aside an extra day to hike the strenuous **Tongariro Alpine Crossing** (p147), one of the finest day walks in the country.

### Day 7: Hawke's Bay
Explore one of the world's finest small-scale Art Deco townscapes at **Napier** (p150) before lunching at a winery and touring the **Hawke's Bay vineyards** (p154). Alternatively, take a tractor tour along a rugged beach to see the nesting gannets at **Cape Kidnappers** (p153): the tours are tide-dependent, so check times online and book ahead.

## Three Days in Northland

- **Arriving** Auckland airport.
- **Transport** Driving is easiest, but bus services do cover these routes.

### Day 1: The Poor Knights and the Bay of Islands

Divers and snorkellers shouldn't miss the **Poor Knights Islands** (*p103*), followed by short visits to the gorgeous coves at **Matapouri** (*p103*) and **Whale Bay** (*p103*). Alternatively, head straight to the Bay of Islands and historic Russell, home to **Pompallier Mission** (*p106*). Across the Bay, the **Waitangi Treaty Grounds** (*p108*) are the birthplace of modern New Zealand, while **Kerikeri's Stone Store** (*p110*) and **Kemp House** (*p110*) formed one of its first European settlements.

### Day 2: Cape Reinga and Ninety Mile Beach

Take a long day-trip to the island's northern tip at **Cape Reinga** (*p112*), including a drive along the sands of **Ninety Mile Beach** (*p112*). Driving the beach is hazardous for the inexperienced, so it's best to take a bus tour: book ahead.

### Day 3: Hokianga Harbour and the Waipoua kauris

Explore the Hokianga Harbour's backwater villages of **Rawene** (*p114*) and **Opononi** (*p114*), admire the sheer majesty of the kauri trees in **Waipoua**

The Beehive, part of New Zealand's Parliament Buildings

**Forest** (*p115*) and spend an hour at the engaging **Kauri Museum** (*p115*) at Matakohe before returning to Auckland.

## Two Days in Wellington

*The nation's compact capital has a great setting, a strong café culture, a vibrant arts scene and many interesting sights.*

- **Arriving** Drive down from Auckland or fly to Wellington airport, 6 km (4 miles) from the city centre.
- **Moving on** Head across Cook Strait to Picton, on the South Island, using the Inter-Island Ferry Services (*p356*), a gorgeous 3-hour journey through the Tory Channel and Queen Charlotte Sound (*p207*).

### Day 1

Kick-start your day with a coffee in one of Wellington's cutting-edge **cafés** (*pp319–21*), then set aside the morning to explore **The Museum of New Zealand Te Papa Tongarewa** (*pp170–71*). Take the **Wellington Cable Car** (*p164*) up to the suburb of Kelburn, then walk through the **Wellington Botanic Garden** (*p164*) towards the **Parliament Buildings** (*p162*), the two **cathedrals** (*p162*) and the **Katherine Mansfield Birthplace** (*p163*).

### Day 2

Bird-watchers should not miss a day-trip to **Kapiti Island Nature Reserve** (*p175*), while *Lord of the Rings* and Peter Jackson fans will love to explore **Weta Workshop** (*p160*). Alternatively, take a lovely Marine Drive Tour (*p172–3*) around the city's wild and windy coast or see the great art at the **City Gallery** (*p168*).

The stunning Whale Bay on the Tutukaka Coast, Northland

## Two Weeks in the South Island

- **Arriving** Fly into Christchurch, or join the tour at Picton (Day 3), the South Island terminus of the Cook Strait ferries from Wellington.

- **Transport** A car will get you around in good time. It is possible do the tour by infrequent buses but you'll probably want to allow a few extra days.

- **Booking ahead** Book the Kaikoura whale watching trip a few days in advance: rough seas often cause trips to be cancelled, so build an extra day into your schedule if you can.

### Day 1: Christchurch

See how Christchurch is rising from the rubble of the devastating earthquakes of 2011. There's a great deal of work still to do – much of the city centre is still rubble – but necessity has pushed the residents to find innovative ways to keep the city going – visit the trasitional **Cardboard Cathedral** (p227) and the **Re:START** shopping mall fashioned from shipping containers (p229). Christchurch's traditional charms haven't all been lost: punting from the **Antigua Boat Sheds** (p231) and strolling through the **Botanic Gardens** (p232) is still a superbly relaxing way to experience the South Island's capital. In the late

Antigua Boat Sheds on the Avon River in Christchurch

Hikers in Abel Tasman National Park

afternoon, head to Kaikoura (a 2-hour drive) for an early start the next day.

### Day 2: Kaikoura

The crack of dawn is the best time to go cetacean-spotting with Whale Watch **Kaikoura** (p213). Top up your marine mammal quota by joining one of the **dolphin swimming** cruises (p213) or by simply walking around the rugged coastline. On the way to Marlborough, pause at **Ohau Point** (p213), where New Zealand fur seals cover the rocks beside the highway.

### Day 3: Marlborough and Queen Charlotte Sound

Spend the morning supping New Zealand's wine gift to the world, Marlborough Sauvignon Blanc, sampled at one of the dozens of wineries around the **Wairau Valley** (p210), some of which serve excellent lunches beside the vines. Continue to **Picton** (p204), where you can take a short water-taxi ride to one of the delightful **waterfront lodges** (p299) beside the **Queen Charlotte Track** (p207).

### Day 4: Nelson

Take a water-taxi back to Picton, then drive the winding, delightful **Queen Charlotte Drive** (p204) past **Havelock** (p205) and the pretty **Pelorous Bridge Scenic Reserve** (p205) to laid-back **Nelson** (pp214–5). Either visit the **Nelson Provincial Museum** (p214) and the **Suter Art Gallery** (p210) or head west to **Höglund Art Glass** (p216) and **McGlashen Pottery** (p216).

### Day 5: Abel Tasman National Park

If it's Saturday, browse in the excellent **Nelson Market** (p215) for an hour. Spend the rest of the day in **Abel Tasman National Park** (p220), either hiking sections of the easy **Coast Track** or **kayaking** from **Marahau** (p129), with easy water-taxi access to avoid retracing your steps or paddle strokes.

> **To extend your trip…**
> Slow the pace in Golden Bay, visiting **Waikoropupu Springs** and **Farewell Spit** (p221) from bohemian **Takaka** (p220).

### Day 6: The West Coast

There's a lot of driving involved on Day 6, so take a quick peek at **Nelson Lakes National Park** (p216) en route to the Pancake Rocks in **Paparoa National Park** (p240). Check out the **greenstone carving** (p241) at Hokitika, then push on to Franz Josef and Fox glaciers in **Westland / Tai Poutini National Park** (p242).

### Day 7: Wanaka

Admire the reflective waters of **Lake Matheson** (p242), then take a long drive through the temperate rain forest towards **Haast** (p277) and through the **Gates of Haast** (p277) to the open rolling countryside around **Wanaka** (p274). Set off early and you'll make it in time to visit **Stuart Landsborough's Puzzling World** (p274) or the dramatically-sited **Rippon Vineyard** (p274).

### Day 8: Queenstown

If you fancy some hiking in magnificent scenery, head up the Matukituki Valley into **Mount Aspiring National Park** (p276). Otherwise, drive over the Crown Range to pretty **Arrowtown** (p278), then continue to **Queenstown** (p280) to catch a late-afternoon cruise aboard the TSS *Earnslaw* on **Lake Wakatipu** (p280), or ride the **Skyline Gondola** (p281) up Bob's Peak, where you can dine overlooking the town.

### Day 9: Queenstown

Experience the **Adventure Capital of New Zealand** (p280). Go bungy jumping, white-water rafting, jet-boating, tandem parapenting or heli-biking, possibly all of them in one day with a combo deal. If this does not appeal, take a lakeside drive to scenic **Glenorchy** (p282), or just relax in the **cafés and bars** (p324–5).

> **To extend your trip…**
> If a multi-day hike sounds appealing, set aside 3 or 4 days to hike in either **Mount Aspiring National Park** (p276) or **Fiordland National Park** (p284) where the Milford, Routeburn and Kepler tracks are the star picks.

### Day 10: Fiordland

The perennial tourist dilemma is whether to visit Milford Sound or Doubtful Sound. Both are dramatic and beautiful but **Milford Sound** (p286) is the most popular, with the widest range of cruises, kayak trips and the most people (though it is hardly crowded). By contrast, **Doubtful Sound** (p288) is remoter and far less visited, and getting there is all part of the adventure.

### Day 11: The Catlins Coast

Pay a short visit to the ancient, lizard-like tuataras at **Invercargill's Southland Museum and Art Gallery** (p290) en route to the sparsely-populated **Catlins** (pp294–5) where the winding roads force

Observers watching a parapenter (paraglider) passing overhead

drivers to adopt a measured pace. Take your time, calling in at the petrified forest in **Curio Bay** (p294), the cute Hector's dolphins at **Porpoise Bay** (p295) and the rugged promontory of **Nugget Point** (p294).

> **To extend your trip…**
> There's a real island-life feel to **Stewart Island** (p292), where you can easily spend 2 or 3 days watching the endangered birds on **Ulva Island** (p292) and walking the **Rakiura Track** (p293).

### Day 12: Dunedin and the Otago Peninsula

The buildings of **Robert Lawson** (p263) provide the focus of a walking exploration of **central Dunedin** (pp262–9), where you should also visit the **Dunedin Railway Station** (p266) and **Olveston House** (p269). Wildlife enthusiasts may prefer to focus on the **Otago**

Peninsula (p270), particularly the **Royal Albatross Centre** (p270) and the **Penguin Place** (p270). A stroll along the **Tunnel Beach Walkway** (p268) is ideal on a long summer evening.

### Day 13: Oamaru and Mt Cook

Make a leisurely start and then spend half an hour at **Moeraki Boulders Scenic Reserve** (p271) before lunching in Moeraki. Walk off your meal around wonderfully preserved mercantile buildings in the "whitestone" town of **Oamaru** (p272) before turning inland to **Aoraki/Mount Cook National Park** (p256). The park's diminutive township centres on **The Hermitage** (p256), a classy hotel with fine views of New Zealand's highest mountain. **Hike the tracks** (p257), take a **flightseeing trip** (p256) or kayak the terminal lake of the **Tasman Glacier** (p256).

### Day 14: Christchurch and Akaroa

Spot black stilts (the world's rarest wading bird) at the **Twizel's Kaki Visitor Hide** (p255), then head through the dry grasslands of the Mackenzie Country, where the opaque-blue waters of **Lake Tekapo** (p254) and **Lake Pukaki** (p254) form part of the monumental **Upper Waitaki Hydro Development Scheme** (p255). Continue to **Christchurch** (pp226–33) and, if you have time, consider a trip to quirky **Lyttelton** (p234) or the French-style harbour village of **Akaroa** (p235).

Nugget Point promontory on the Catlins Coast

# Putting New Zealand on The Map: The North Island

New Zealand lies in the South Pacific Ocean, 1,600 km (990 miles) to the east of Australia, 10,000 km (6,210 miles) from San Francisco and a similar distance from Tokyo. Comprising two large islands and a number of smaller ones, its total land area is 270,530 sq km (104,420 sq miles), making it comparable in size to Japan or the British Isles. The main North and South islands are separated by Cook Strait, 20 km (12 miles) wide at its narrowest point. Two-thirds of the country's population of almost 4.5 million live in the North Island, and of these 1.4 million live in Auckland, the country's largest city and the world's most populous Polynesian centre. New Zealand's capital is Wellington, at the southernmost tip of the North Island.

## New Zealand and its Environs

VIETNAM  
PHILIPPINES  
MALAYSIA  
MARSHALL ISLANDS  
MICRONESIA  
*Pacific Ocean*  
INDONESIA  
PAPUA NEW GUINEA  
SOLOMON ISLANDS  
*Indian Ocean*  
VANUATU  
FIJI  
NEW CALEDONIA  
AUSTRALIA  
NEW ZEALAND  
Wellington

## Key to Colour Coding

**North Island**

- Northland
- Auckland
- Central North Island
- Wellington and the South

Cape Reinga  
North Cape  
Te Kao  
Mohutangi  
Kaitaia  
Kerikeri  
Kaikohe  
Paihia  
Opononi  
Kaihu  
Dargaville  
Ruawai  
North Head  
South Head  

*Tasman Sea*  

North Taranaki Bight  
New Plymouth  
Cape Egmont  
Inglewood  
Eltham  
Hawera  
South Taranaki Bight  
Wanganu  

Farewell Spit  
Collingwood  
Golden Bay  
Takaka  
*Marlborough Sounds*  
Kapiti Island  
Paraparaumu  
Upp Hut  
Karamea  
Motueka  
*Tasman Bay*  
WELLINGTON *see inset below*  
Tapawera  
Nelson  
Granity  
Waimangaroa  
*Wairau*  
Renwick  
Blenheim  
Westport  
Murchison  
Seddon  
Cronadun  
*Awatere*  
Cape Palliser  
Reefton  
*La Wairara*  

0 kilometres 50  
0 miles 50  

**For additional map symbols** *see back flap*

**Key**

Urban area
Motorway
State highway
Main road
Other road
Railway line

**Auckland and Environs**

Hauraki Gulf

To Whangarei & North

Motutapu Island

Takapuna

Rangitoto Channel

Rangitoto Island

Birkenhead

Auckland Harbour Bridge

AUCKLAND CITY

Waitemata Harbour

Henderson

Highland Park

Blockhouse Bay

East Tamaki

Manukau Harbour

Manukau City

Auckland International Airport

To Hamilton & South

0 kilometres 5
0 miles 5

Bay of Islands

Russell

Whangarei

Great Barrier Island

Wellford
Leigh

Hauraki Gulf

Orewa

AUCKLAND see inset below

Coromandel

Whitianga

Coromandel Peninsula

Thames

Hamilton

Tauranga

Cambridge

Bay of Plenty

Lake Rotorua

Otorohanga

Rotorua

Whakatane

Hicks Bay
Te Araroa

East Cape

Te Kuiti

Tokoroa

Opotiki

Taupo

Lake Taupo

Tokomaru Bay

Matawai

Te Karaka

Tolaga Bay

Taumarunui

Pacific Ocean

Lake Waikaremoana

Turangi

Gisborne

Raetihi

Waiouru

Hawke's Bay

Waipukurau

Napier

Hastings

Porangahoa

Palmerston North

Alfredton

evin

Masterton

Martinborough

**Wellington and Environs**

Levin & North

Masterton & East

Porirua

Upper Hutt

Silverstream

Tawa

Lower Hutt

Rimutaka Range

Johnsonville

Homedale

Wellington Harbour

WELLINGTON CITY

Wellington International Airport

0 kilometres 10
0 miles 10

# Putting New Zealand on The Map: The South Island

The South Island, 150,440 sq km (58,070 sq miles) in area, is slightly larger than the North Island. The Southern Alps mountain chain runs almost the length of the island, with 223 named peaks higher than 2,300 m (7,550 ft). The eastern side of the alps is dry and largely non-forested, while the West Coast has high rainfall and magnificent forests, mountains and glaciers. Christchurch, the largest city in the South Island, with 380,000 inhabitants, has good international travel links. To the south, Dunedin is an important university town. Stewart Island, south of Invercargill, is New Zealand's third largest island.

**Key to Colour Coding**

**South Island**

- Marlborough and Nelson
- Canterbury and the West Coast
- Otago and Southland

**For additonal map symbols** *see back flap*

**Christchurch and Environs**

**Dunedin and Environs**

**Key**

- Urban area
- Motorway
- State highway
- Main road
- Other road
- Railway line
- Ferry route

0 kilometres 50
0 miles 50

# A PORTRAIT OF NEW ZEALAND

New Zealand is one of the most isolated countries in the world. Maori, some of the early arrivals from the Pacific, called it Aotearoa, "the land of the long white cloud", the first indication to these canoe voyagers of the islands' presence being the cloud covering their high ranges. New Zealand's island location and spectacular terrain affects its climate, its history and its contemporary character.

Spanning latitudes 34 degrees and 47 degrees South, the islands of New Zealand are in the path of "the roaring forties", the winds that circle this lower part of the globe, and are separated from the nearest landmass, Australia, by 1,600 km (990 miles) of the Tasman Sea. On the International Date Line, opposite the Greenwich Meridian of zero degree, New Zealand claims to be the first country to see the sun rise.

The climate ranges from subantarctic to subtropical. The maritime setting creates regular rainfall and abundant vegetation. There is extensive bird and fish life but other than two bat species, the only land mammals are those introduced by early Maori and Europeans. Comparatively a recent settlement and one of the least populated countries in the world, with a population of almost 4.5 million, New Zealand retains in many areas a clean, natural and untouched environment.

The snow-covered Southern Alps and glacial-formed lakes and fiords provide spectacular scenery, and there is extensive volcanic and thermal activity on the North Island central plateau. The country's coastline provides both sheltered bays and harbours and superb beaches. New Zealand's tourism industry focuses upon this natural environment, the urban aspect being less significant by comparison.

The silver fern, one of New Zealand's symbols

◀ Lake Pukaki and Mount Cook

The coastline as seen from Tunnel Beach, south of Dunedin

## Settlement

Captain James Cook's circumnavigation and charting of the main islands in 1769–70 paved the way for the sealing and whaling industry. The unruly conditions, the concerns of missionaries over friction with the Maori and pressure from Edward Gibbon's Colonising Society prompted the British to pursue a treaty with the Maori establishing sovereignty. At Waitangi in the Bay of Islands, a treaty was signed between the British Crown, represented by Captain William Hobson, and a number of Maori chiefs. Although the Treaty of Waitangi provided for protection of Maori and their natural resources, alienation of Maori land occurred well into the 20th century. Maori leaders pressed for justice and organized land marches. In 1975, the treaty was reconsidered and the Treaty of Waitangi Act passed by parliament set up the Waitangi Tribunal, which still considers land claims today.

Captain James Cook

Planned settlement in the 1840s was mainly by English and Scottish enterprises. Today the character of cities such as Christchurch and Dunedin still reflects those origins. Auckland, the country's former capital and now its commercial centre, remains more cosmopolitan. Wellington's early establishment as the capital contributes to its political character.

Early settlers felled extensive areas of forest for the timber trade and for farmland. The independent spirit of New Zealanders can be said to derive from their determination to succeed in their new land. The people of New Zealand came from a cross section of English, Scottish and Irish society, and all were united in their desire to make their country prosper.

Maori leader Dame Whina Cooper setting out for a land march
(*Hikoi*) in October 1975

## Society

New Zealand is an independent state. New Zealand's parliament, based on the Statute of Westminster, pays allegiance to the British sovereign through its governor-general. Proposals that New Zealand become a republic have some support in the country.

New Zealanders take pride in their history of social reform. The first in the world to give all women the vote in 1893, New Zealand had established compulsory, free primary schooling by 1877, and by 1938 a state-supported health system, universal superannuation and a liberal social welfare structure. The country declared its non-nuclear stance in 1986. This has resulted in non-alignment of its armed forces, though New Zealand troops are used in peace-keeping and training roles.

Although the Waitangi Tribunal has enabled substantial compensation for Maori whose land was confiscated, there are still some grievances to settle. Encouragement of the immigration of Pacific Islanders by the governments of the 1960s seeking to obtain a labour force has created ethnic diversity, as too has the influx of Asian immigrants since the 1990s.

The Beehive, part of the Parliament Buildings in Wellington, which houses the Ministers' offices

Nevertheless, visitors comment on the friendliness and welcoming attitudes of New Zealanders, which may stem from a small population living, by world standards, in good quality housing, in small cities that do not suffer from congestion or widespread crime. All have easy access to a superb natural environment. There is also a curiosity

The Nelson market, selling fresh local produce and regional artisan crafts

New Zealand's All Blacks rugby team playing against Italy

about the world and New Zealanders travel abroad a great deal. The great "OE" (overseas experience) is still popular with the young.

Although there is today evidence of a widening gap between rich and poor, New Zealand remains an egalitarian society. There are some social differences based upon wealth and occupation, but there is no class system in New Zealand based on birth and inheritance. Enterprise and energy can secure good employment and quality of life. Almost 86 per cent of the population is urban, with 75 per cent resident in the North Island. In the last 100 years or so the Maori population has increased and now makes up 16 per cent of the country's total. However, the social and economic status of some Maori is still below average, a situation that will hopefully be corrected in time by affirmative government education, employment and health policies.

Maori youngsters on horseback

### Work and the Economy

Although agriculture is the major industry, with dairy, meat, fish and timber products predominating, a need to compete in the world markets has required diversification. A pioneer in agricultural research, New Zealand is a leader in animal and crop technology. Its wines, particularly whites, are internationally recognized and its quality foodstuffs are exported to many countries. Tourism is important and caters for all tastes. Being a small nation that has to transport its exports long distances to foreign markets, New Zealand is vulnerable to the international economy. It does not possess substantial mineral resources, but it has been able to utilize its own natural gas, oil and coal reserves. It is the world's leading exporter of

Sheep droving on a state highway

dairy products, and signs of an export market in information technology, electronics and shipbuilding are encouraging.

The recession in the 1980s prompted a move from welfare state to "user pays" policies, with privatization of state-owned enterprises. The major political parties are Labour (centre left) and National (centre right), with minor parties influencing the balance of power.

Alfresco dining at Queenstown Marina

## Sport and Culture

New Zealand is a sportsperson's paradise. The successful defence of the America's Cup in 2000 attracted one of the world's largest gatherings of mega-yachts. Rugby is the most popular game (the All Blacks won the Rugby World Cup in 2011 to great fanfare), followed by netball and cricket. A wide range of international entertainers, musicians, artists and dance companies make frequent visits to the country. Festivals of Pacific Island and Maori culture coincide with a resurgence of Maori and Pacific Island art and artists. New Zealanders can claim some notable

Teacher and students studying in a park

firsts. Lord Rutherford from Brightwater was the first to split the atom and Sir Edmund Hillary, with Sherpa Tenzing, was the first to reach the summit of Mount Everest. Others of international reputation are author Katherine Mansfield, opera diva Dame Kiri Te Kanawa, soprano Hayley Westenra, film director Peter Jackson and space scientist Sir William Pickering.

New Zealand is today a vibrant, hospitable, multicultural nation that has forged a unique identity derived from a combination of Maori heritage and colonial culture.

Street buskers providing entertainment in Auckland

# New Zealand's Landscape

New Zealand is an old land with a young landscape: some of the rocks that underlie the country are, at 540 million years old, relatively ancient. However, the landforms that have been created from them are very young. The Southern Alps, for example, began to emerge only three million years ago and volcanic explosions and earthquakes continue to create new forms. The overriding feature of the landscape is its diversity: mountains, lakes, rivers, beaches, hills, plains, volcanoes, rainforests and fiords are all contained in a relatively small area.

**Mount Ruapehu**, like other New Zealand cone volcanoes, erupts frequently. It sits astride one of the world's major volcanic centres *(see pp68–9)*.

**The foothills of the Southern Alps**, the Great Divide between the west and east coasts, shelter the Canterbury Plains from prevailing westerly winds.

**New Zealand's coastline** is roughly 16,000 km (9,900 miles) long. About 80 per cent is exposed to open sea while 20 per cent borders sheltered waters. The coasts harbour marine life and are popular playgrounds for water sports.

## Tectonic Plate Formation

Alpine fault

Oceanic crust

Continental crust

Indo-Australian Plate

Pacific Continental Plate

For the last 20–25 million years, New Zealand has been lying astride two of the world's 15 moving "plates". In the North Island, the Pacific Continental Plate pushes under the Indo-Australian Plate, forming volcanoes in between. In the South Island, the Indo-Australian Plate pushes under the Pacific one, forming an Alpine fault line.

## South Canterbury and Southern Alps

Large-scale farming has transformed tussock plains into a landscape of grasslands dissected by rivers and dotted with livestock. The distant Southern Alps bear testimony to the powerful geological forces which have been shaping the country for the last 600 million years.

**Tussock grasslands** cover about 10 per cent of New Zealand's land area. Much of this area was covered in forest or scrubland before the early Maori burned it while hunting for moa.

**The Bay of Islands** comprises more than 150 offshore islands, all within 50 km (30 miles) of the coast. During glacial periods, when sea levels were lower, the islands were connected to the mainland.

**Braided rivers** *(see p195)* transport shingle and sediments from the Southern Alps to create fertile farmlands.

**Sheep**, farmed for both wool and meat, thrive on South Canterbury's hill country and rolling downs.

**The fiords** of southwest New Zealand, carved out over millions of years by successive Ice Ages – the last 10,000 years ago – are among the most spectacular in the world *(see pp284–5)*. The coastline of the fiords extends 1,000 km (620 miles). Doubtful Sound, at 420 m (1,380 ft) is the deepest of the fiords, while Dusky Sound, which stretches 40 km (25 miles) inland, is the longest.

## The Gondwanaland Connection

Until about 80 million years ago, New Zealand formed part of the great super continent, Gondwanaland, which comprised present-day Antarctica, Australia, India, Africa and South America. Once New Zealand floated off into isolation, many of its plants and animals evolved into forms which were never seen on other landmasses.

**180 million years ago**, New Zealand occupied a corner of Gondwanaland, one of the world's two massive continents; the other is called Laurasia.

**135 million years ago**, Gondwanaland began to split apart into the present-day continents. At this time, New Zealand was still attached to Australia.

**Today**, the Tasman Sea separates New Zealand and Australia, and the continents continue to drift apart. New Zealand is moving northwards towards the equator at the rate of about 30 mm (1.2 inches) a year.

# Flora and Fauna

New Zealand has been a land apart for 80 million years, with the result that it is home to a collection of plants and animals found nowhere else in the world. It has only two land mammals (both bats), although seals, whales and dolphins are found around the coasts. Flightless birds, a diversity of lizards, giant snails, primitive frogs and plants that are as old as the dinosaurs combine to make New Zealand unique. Despite the impact of humans on flora and fauna over the last 1,000 years, much remains to fascinate the visitor.

**The tuatara** is the sole remaining species of an order of reptiles which evolved about 220 million years ago. One good place to see a tuatara is at the tuatarium in Invercargill *(see p290)*.

## Kauri Forests

Northland's forests are dominated by massive, straight-trunked kauri trees interspersed with a mix of subtropical plants. So valuable was the timber for boat building, housing and carving that the forests have been depleted since the 1790s.

**Kiwi** are found in forests on North, South and Stewart islands, where they use their long beaks to dig for food.

**Giant weta**, flightless "crickets" as large as a person's hand, are harmless inhabitants of islands and kauri forests.

**The silver fern** or ponga, widely adopted as a national symbol, takes its name from the silvery underside of the fronds.

## Shrublands

Shrublands consist of short, scrubby plants. They are home to many species of animals and are nurseries for mature forest. Widespread throughout the country, shrublands are often areas that were once logged and are now regenerating.

**The green gecko** lives on the outer branches of shrubs and is a daytime hunter. It bears live young in contrast to other species which lay eggs.

**Kowhai**, New Zealand's official national flower, has striking drooping yellow blooms in spring.

**Manuka** is a key pollen and nectar plant for bees.

## Birds of New Zealand

New Zealand is famed for its unusual birds. Evolving without significant predators, such as rats, cats or dogs, to menace them, they lost any reason to fly. Some not

only became flightless, but also developed into some of the largest birds ever to have lived. When Maori arrived, they discovered the moa, the largest species of which stood 2 m (7 ft) tall to the top of its back. As a result of being hunted, the moa became extinct 300–500 years ago. Today, many of New Zealand's ancient bird species survive in limited numbers, among them the kiwi, kakapo, takahe, black robin and kea, and enormous efforts are being made to ensure their survival.

**The kakapo** is a large, flightless, nocturnal parrot.

**Kokako** are poor fliers but are noted for their singing abilities.

## Alpine Landscape

New Zealand's alpine region begins at about 1,300 m (4,270 ft) above sea level in the North Island but drops to 900 m (2,950 ft) in the South Island. Intense cold, heat, dryness and wind combine to produce tussock and shrubs adapted to cope with the climate.

## Around the Coast

Rocky shores, sandy beaches and muddy estuaries provide a diversity of habitats for coastal flora and fauna. Many native plants thrive in the salty environment, thanks to adaptations such as tough leaves which retain moisture in dry conditons.

**Kea** are South Island mountain parrots. They have a reputation for playfulness and intelligence.

**The royal albatross** breeds at Taiaroa Head on the Otago Peninsula *(see p270)* upon returning from its winter feeding grounds.

**The pohutu-kawa's** crimson flowers along the coasts of the North Island herald the arrival of Christmas.

**The vegetable sheep plant** is a mass of thousands of small, separate plants which together resemble the wool of a sheep.

**Alpine plants** climb above the competition to be noticed by pollinating alpine insects.

**New Zealand fur seals** are commonly seen lolling on rocks around the coastline.

# New Zealand's National Parks and Reserves

From the snow-capped volcanoes of Tongariro National Park to the sheer cliffs of Fiordland, New Zealand's national parks contain an awe-inspiring range of scenery, beautiful walking tracks, and numerous plants and animals found nowhere else in the world. The 14 national parks cover over 30,000 sq km (19,000 sq miles) or about 8 per cent of the country's land surface. There are also over 30 conservation and forest parks, thousands of reserves and over 30 marine reserves. Keep safe when tramping or hiking by being well prepared and equipped, and respect the natural environment by leaving the land undisturbed.

**Abel Tasman National Park's** golden sand beaches fringe bush-clad cliffs. Inland, deep caves and underground rivers are a feature of the limestone landscape (see pp218–19).

**Aoraki/Mount Cook National Park** contains the highest mountain in Australasia, Mount Cook, known as Aoraki or "cloud piercer" by the Ngai Tahu tribe, as well as New Zealand's longest glacier (see pp256–7).

**Paparoa National Park's** limestone landscape gives this area its special flavour. Along the coast, constant pounding by the Tasman Sea has sculpted the limestone into the Pancake Rocks and blowholes (see p240).

**Fiordland National Park** is a vast, remote wilderness, with snow-capped mountains, fiords, glacial valleys and lakes, waterfalls, islands and dense temperate forest (see pp284–5).

0 kilometres 100
0 miles 100

Abel Tasman National Park

Kahurangi National Park

NELSO

Nelson Lakes National Park

Paparoa National Park

Westland / Tai Poutini National Park

Arthur's Pass National Park

Aoraki / Mount Cook National Park

CHRISTCHURCH

Banks Peninsula

Mount Aspiring National Park

QUEENSTOWN

Fiordland National Park

Otago Peninsula

INVERCARGILL

DUNEDIN

Foveaux Strait

Rakiura National Park

Stewart Island

**Key**

National parks

Conservation parks

Reserves

Marine reserves

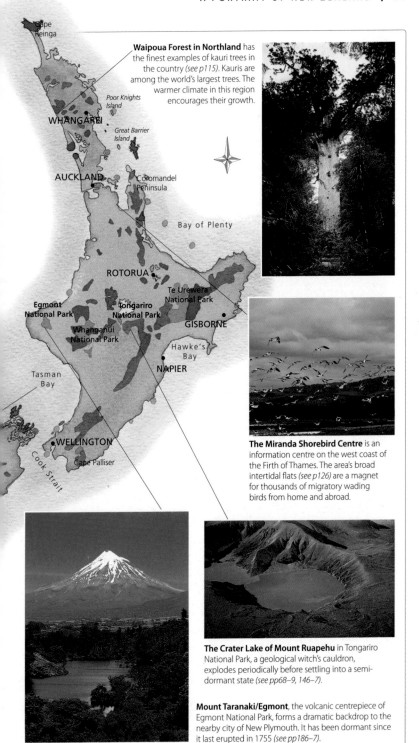

**Waipoua Forest in Northland** has the finest examples of kauri trees in the country *(see p115)*. Kauris are among the world's largest trees. The warmer climate in this region encourages their growth.

**The Miranda Shorebird Centre** is an information centre on the west coast of the Firth of Thames. The area's broad intertidal flats *(see p126)* are a magnet for thousands of migratory wading birds from home and abroad.

**The Crater Lake of Mount Ruapehu** in Tongariro National Park, a geological witch's cauldron, explodes periodically before settling into a semi-dormant state *(see pp68–9, 146–7)*.

**Mount Taranaki/Egmont**, the volcanic centrepiece of Egmont National Park, forms a dramatic backdrop to the nearby city of New Plymouth. It has been dormant since it last erupted in 1755 *(see pp186–7)*.

# Architecture in New Zealand

Earthquake risk in New Zealand has limited the height and structure of buildings, giving towns and cities a somewhat uniform appearance, while abundant space has led to suburban sprawl. Interspersed with the country's ubiquitous wooden houses are gracious historic homes and buildings, well-preserved Maori meeting houses and impressive public and commercial buildings. The latter range from early European-style structures built in stone to modern glass and concrete towers. Contemporary architecture is an eclectic mix of "New Zealand" and imported styles.

Glass and concrete towers in Auckland

## Maori Meeting Houses

Communal meeting houses and storehouses have single gable roofs supported on posts sunk in the ground, and are elaborately carved. The porch bargeboards symbolize the arms of the ancestors, the ridgepole the tribal backbone, and the rafters the ribs of family lineage. Many older houses have been restored and new ones built of modern materials (see p135).

Gable roof
Painted rafters
Carved bargeboard
Plaited reed walls

The figures on wall and roof posts represent ancestors and chieftains

**Te Tokanganui-a-Noho** at Te Kuiti, a well-preserved meeting house built in 1872.

## Homesteads

From the mid-1800s, wealthy sheep or cattle farmers and rich merchants demonstrated their affluence with substantial, architect-designed mansions to which they added rooms as they prospered. Stylistically varied, most mansions reflect a Victorian flavour, and some are romantically nostalgic and grandiose. The interiors are usually richly panelled, with elaborately carved stair rails, balusters, moulded ceilings and cornices (see p269).

High central dormer
Wooden fretwork
Ornate corner turret
Kauri timber walls

**Alberton**, a two-storey residence built for farmer Allen Kerr in 1862, and later extended, now lies within Auckland city.

## Public Buildings

**Otago University** (1878) in Dunedin, built in Gothic style after Scotland's Glasgow University (1870).

By the 1860s, the construction of public buildings reinforced links with "home", reflecting, for example, the Gothic Revival style in Britain. Sometimes timber was substituted for the customary stone. The emphasis is on verticality and repeated ornamentation.

Clock tower
Local grey stonework
Lighter stone facings
Arched windows

## Commercial Buildings

As New Zealand prospered, more permanent commercial buildings replaced temporary shops and warehouses. A wide range of styles, including Classical Renaissance, Edwardian Baroque and Neo-Classical, demonstrated the substance and affluence of successful commercial enterprise. Although façades are often splendid, with Roman or Greek columns, the structure behind uses more modern techniques of steel framing and reinforced concrete. As such techniques allowed varied exterior treatment, there is little consistency of style in city buildings.

Detail of Corinthian column

Arched first-floor windows    Carved capitals    Fluted pilasters

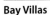

A floriated band of carved stonework marks the level of the first floor

**Bank of New South Wales (Former)** (1882) in Oamaru is Neo-Classical in style, with beautifully carved exterior ornamentation *(see p272)*.

## Bay Villas

In the early 1900s, bay-fronted villas became the standard domestic house, with often a street at a time being built to a stock design. Usually constructed of timber weatherboard with corrugated iron or clay tile roofs, they ranged from single bay villas decorated with crude sawn fretwork to more sophisticated and elaborate multistorey homes for the affluent *(see p165)*.

Gable roof

Pierced wood fretwork decoration

Double-hung sash window

Projecting bays

Corrugated iron roofing

Balustraded verandah

## Contemporary New Zealand Architecture

Although contemporary New Zealand architecture reflects international stylistic diversity, many architects are endeavouring to respond to the natural environment and to utilize ingredients from both Maori and European heritages.

Abstract art design on the exterior glazing

**The Museum of New Zealand Te Papa Tongarewa**, opened in 1998, incorporates elements of the gable forms of Maori meeting houses.

Floating canopy roof    Stylized sail

Precast concrete panels

Entrance porch

# Maori Culture and Art

Maori have developed a complex culture derived from their Pacific Island inheritance. Climatic and seasonal conditions that differed from their former home, and a more extensive land area, permitted independent tribal development and variations in language, customs and art forms. Forests enabled them to build large canoes for transport and warfare, as well as meeting houses. Maori excel in wood, bone and stone carving, and in plaiting and weaving. Oratory, chant, song and dance are the means of passing on ancestral knowledge, and form an essential dimension of the rituals of challenge, welcome and farewell.

**Moko** (tattoo) involves incising lines into the skin and colouring them with pigment. The tradition has been revived and today, some Maori proudly wear moko.

### Carving

The plentiful supply of large, straight-grained and durable timbers, and a variety of hard stones and obsidian that could be shaped into tools, enabled the early Maori to continue the Pacific tradition of carving. Today, an increasing awareness of Maori heritage has brought about a rebirth of traditional crafts. At Te Puia, a Maori arts and crafts centre in Rotorua, students learn to carve wood, bone and greenstone into exquisite and intricate Tiki pendants, combs and ceremonial objects (see p142).

**Carving** in the Maori Affairs Select Committee Room of the Parliament Buildings in Wellington.

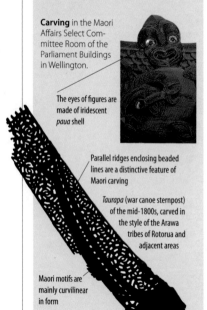

The eyes of figures are made of iridescent *paua* shell

Parallel ridges enclosing beaded lines are a distinctive feature of Maori carving

*Taurapa* (war canoe sternpost) of the mid-1800s, carved in the style of the Arawa tribes of Rotorua and adjacent areas

Maori motifs are mainly curvilinear in form

### Song and Dance

Singing and dancing are an important feature of Maori life. They are performed on various occasions by both men and women. The poi dance, with its graceful movements is, however, restricted to women.

**The *haka*** is a war dance performed by men. Eyes and tongues protrude in a gesture of defiance.

**Plaiting and weaving**, using swamp flax, reeds or bird feathers, are women's arts. This 1880s *kete whakairo*, or decorated bag, was woven from flax.

**Cloaks and capes** are a feature of traditional Maori dress and are made of various materials, including flax, feathers and dogskin. This engraving by Sydney Parkinson (1745–71) depicts a cloaked warrior.

*Poi* **balls** are stuffed with reeds and covered with woven flax fibre.

**Songs** are performed with the whole being; the body, hands, legs, arms and facial expressions all play their part.

**Early Maori weapons** were made of wood, stone and bone. Close hand-to-hand fighting was the main characteristic of Maori warfare. This *wahaika*, or short wooden hand club, from the early 1800s, is an example of a weapon used for striking.

**Skirts** consist of strips of flax hanging from a belt. The green leaves are scraped and dried so that they curl into tubes.

## Contemporary Maori Artist

Very much a part of the remarkable renaissance in contemporary Maori art, artist Cliff Whiting celebrates his ancestral inheritance in this interpretation of the Maori legend of creation. Using a mixture of traditional and modern materials and processes, he depicts Tane Mahuta, God of the Forests, pushing apart Ranginui, his Sky Father, and Papatuanuku, his Earth Mother, to let light enter the world. The mural is in the National Library of New Zealand in Wellington.

Mural by Cliff Whiting (1974), depicting the separation of Ranginui and Papatuanuku

# New Zealand Artists and Writers

From the time of first contact, botanists, navigators, surveyors and amateur painters recorded aspects of New Zealand's flora and fauna, the Maori people and early settlements. There were also many reports, diaries and commentaries in the British press which provided interesting descriptions and accounts of the new land, such as Lady Barker's *Station Life in New Zealand* (1870). The poetry, novels and paintings of the late 19th century were very much in the European tradition, but by the 1900s distinctive national elements began to emerge in writing and art.

Painting of a Maori chief, Charles Frederick Goldie (1870–1947)

## Artists

The pioneer climate in New Zealand was not sympathetic to the arts. "Working class" settlers, struggling to survive in a strange and hostile land, had little knowledge of the arts. For the wealthy, the arts were largely a diversion for gentlewomen. Works of any substance were mainly by artists visiting New Zealand, such as William Hodges, whose work stylised the scenery into Romantic vistas. Italian Girolamo Pieri Nerli and Dutchman Petrus van der Velden, both also had a romantic European view of the untamed land.

A few New Zealanders sought training in European academies, such as Charles Frederick Goldie. By the 1900s art schools and societies had become established in

New Zealand, but many artists, conscious of the Impressionist movement and other developments in Europe, escaped to that more exciting milieu. Frances Hodgkins left in 1901, and although some claim her as an eminent New Zealand artist, she achieved her reputation working in Britain and France.

In the 1920s, British-trained artists, such as Robert Field, Christopher Perkins and Roland Hipkins, came to teach and brought to their students the "radical" ideas of modernism, which were well established in Europe. Expressionist, Cubist and abstract influences began to appear in the works of John Weeks, Rhona Haszard and Louise Henderson, and by the 1940s a number of artists saw in modernism an opportunity to explore the "national"

character of the land and its people. Much of the work of Eric Lee-Johnson, Sir Tosswill Woollaston, Russell Clark, Rita Angus and William Sutton seeks to define the substance or spirit of the land rather than give it superficial description.

In 1954 – late by world standards – the Auckland City Art Gallery presented New Zealand's first show of abstract paintings, "Object and Image", which caused a public outcry. However, artists such as Louise Henderson, Colin McCahon, Don Peebles and Rudy Gopas began to exhibit in the dealer galleries, which had become a feature of the larger cities.

Sculpture lagged behind painting, although Len Lye began his kinetic works as early as 1950. He moved to New York, but New Zealand is fortunate to have a substantial collection of his work at the Govett-Brewster Gallery in New Plymouth *(see p184)*. From the 1960s, significant modern works were commissioned for public places from Jim Allen, Greer Twiss, Marte Szirmay, Terry Stringer, Neil Dawson and Paul Dibble.

Since the 1970s, there has been a substantial increase in the number of full-time professional artists, including outstanding Maori artists such as Ralph Hotere, Para Matchett, Fred Graham and Shona Rapira Davies.

*Dry September* (1949), oil on canvas by William Sutton

*Nga Morehu* (The Survivors; 1988), a sculpture in mixed media by Shona Rapira Davies

## Writers

New Zealand writing began to attract attention by the 1860s, but most of it was published in Britain as New Zealand lacked publishing houses. *Erewhon* (1872) by Samuel Butler is based upon his life in the high country of the South Island. *A History of New Zealand Birds* (1873) by Sir Walter Buller is still highly regarded for its careful documentation and illustrations. William Pember Reeves' *The Long White Cloud*, a romanticized version of New Zealand history, was published in 1898.

Jane Mander's *The Story of a New Zealand River* (1920) attracted some international attention for its depiction of colonial life. *Bliss*, Katherine Mansfield's first collection of short stories, marked the advent of New Zealand writing of originality and substance. Born in Wellington, Mansfield was sent to London to further her education. Although she returned briefly to New Zealand, she spent most of her life in France and England. Though produced abroad, her work, which reveals her sharp observation of human behaviour, is based upon her memories of a New Zealand childhood. Mansfield died in 1923 at the age of 34.

By the 1930s, there emerged a conscious determination by novelists and poets to shape a New Zealand style, using local idioms, references to the raw landscape, and characterization of its settler inhabitants. Time spent overseas in the armed forces during both world wars also gave writers a new perspective of their homeland and added more pungency to their writing. Typical is poet Allen Curnow's *Landfall in Unknown Seas*, a powerful evocation of the visitor confronted by an alien but compelling land.

By the 1950s, Denis Glover, Robin Hyde, Frank Sargeson and Ruth Dallas, among others, ushered in a period of substantial productivity. Novelists such as John Mulgan, Dan Davin, Roderick Finlayson, and poet James K Baxter also cast a sharply critical eye upon what they saw as a conforming and conventional society that concealed disturbing undercurrents.

Historian and poet Keith Sinclair, in his *A History of New Zealand* (1961), was one of the first to question prevailing versions of New Zealand history, which promoted colonial supremacy over "native" primitivism and biased interpretations of land settlement and the subsequent land wars. Dick Scott's research in *Ask that Mountain* (1975) revealed to New Zealanders a truer account of early settlement and relations with Maori. Writers such as Fiona Kidman, C K Stead, Maurice Gee, Fleur Adcock and historian Michael King have demonstrated a new maturity in their commentary upon racial and social issues.

A number of Maori writers are a voice for their people, among them Witi Ihimaera, Patricia Grace and Hone Tuwhare. In 1985, Keri Hulme, of Maori and Pakeha descent, won the British Booker Prize with *The Bone People*. Maori writer Alan Duff's *Once Were Warriors*, later made into a film of the same name, is a powerful exposure of the turbulence within the urban Maori people. Sylvia Ashton-Warner's novel *Spinster*, on provincial attitudes in a rural community, was made into a film in the US, as was Ian Cross's *God Boy*, an insight into adolescence and religion.

**Katherine Mansfield**

Cover of *The Bone People*, a novel by Keri Hulme

THE BONE PEOPLE
KERI HULME

James K Baxter

# Farming and Horticulture

Despite being so urbanized (85 per cent of New Zealanders live in cities or large towns), the country still depends heavily on its agricultural economy. Farming industries utilize around 40 per cent of the total land area of 270,000 sq km (104,247 sq miles) and produce 50 per cent of all export earnings. Traditionally, pastoral farming has centred on sheep and cattle but other types of livestock, such as deer, goats, pigs and poultry, are gaining in importance, with dairy farming being the most prevalent. Pine trees cloak hills too steep to support livestock, while horticulture and other crops now dominate fertile coastal and inland areas.

**Kiwifruit**, grown primarily in the Bay of Plenty *(see p133)*, is successfully marketed in more than 60 countries. New Zealand supplies about a quarter of world production.

**Apples and pears**, New Zealand's main pip fruits, are grown mostly in Hawke's Bay and Marlborough/Nelson. About 17 million cartons are exported annually.

**Plastic sheeting** protects rows of delicate berry fruits from frost.

**Lines of trees** between orchards serve as windbreaks.

**Kiwifruit** grow on vines supported by wooden trellises.

**Peaches** and other stone fruit, such as apricots, nectarines, plums and cherries, are concentrated in Hawke's Bay and Central Otago.

## Horticulture

Although pastoral farming is the major land use in New Zealand, large areas are now planted in crops. The mild, sunny climate and fertile soils of the coastal regions of the Bay of Plenty, Gisborne, Hawke's Bay, Nelson and Otago have created a stunning mosaic of orchards producing a variety of traditional pip and stone fruit as well as citrus, berry and subtropical varieties.

## Pastoral Agriculture

New Zealand's 31 million sheep and 10 million cattle are bred for their meat, wool, dairy produce and hides. Dairy herds are found on the fairly flat land, while sheep and beef cattle are farmed in the rougher hill country. Deer, goats and other livestock are scattered throughout both islands.

**The Romney Cross** is the most common sheep in New Zealand and is bred for both meat and wool production.

**The black and white Holstein-Friesian** is the most common dairy cow, yielding more milk than other breeds.

## Cereal and Other Crops

Fields of traditional cereal crops are found on the plains of the South Island, especially in Canterbury and Southland. Here, wheat and oats are grown for home consumption and for milling, and barley and oats for the manufacture of stock feed; barley is also grown for malting at New Zealand breweries. Large-scale vegetable production has made inroads into fertile coastal regions in both the North and South islands, while new and distinct plant varieties, such as sunflowers, lavender and garlic, add colour and variety to the country's agricultural landscape.

**Sunflowers, grown for their seeds, near Palmerston North**

**Wheat and garlic in Marlborough**

**Sorting and packaging** is done in packhouses.

**Citrus trees** are planted in long, straight lines.

**Other fruits**, such as the citrus grapefuit and subtropical varieties like avocados, tamarillos, persimmons and pepinos (in addition to kiwifruit), are grown in warmer North Island orchards – Northland, around Auckland, the Bay of Plenty and Hawke's Bay -- while berry fruits such as raspberries thrive in the cooler South Island.

**Grapefruit**

**Avocados**

**Pepinos**

**Persimmon**

**Tamarillos**

**Raspberries**

**Grapes** are grown mainly for wine production (see pp40–1). Marlborough, Canterbury, Gisborne and Hawke's Bay are the major grape producing areas. Few table grapes are grown.

**Deer** are bred on some 3,000 farms. Venison fetches premium prices worldwide, while deer velvet is popular in Asia.

**Goats** are farmed both domestically and commercially for their milk, meat and mohair as well as for weed control.

**Ostriches** (as shown here) and emus are among the new livestock breeds gaining in popularity.

# The Wines of New Zealand

Although grapes were first planted in New Zealand as early as the 1830s, it was not until the 1980s when wine makers decided to concentrate on white wines, such as Sauvignon Blanc and Chardonnay, that the country's reputation as an excellent wine producer began. The number of wineries has since grown to almost 700, and export wine sales in 2013 reached 170 million litres (37 million gallons). In less than 20 years, the nation's wine makers went from producing wine of average quality to some of the best in the world. Wine drinking is popular in New Zealand. Many vineyards have restaurants, offer wine tastings and tours, and sell wine at the cellar door.

**A visit to a vineyard** for wine tasting or a meal is a popular weekend leisure activity.

### James Busby

Appointed by the British Government as Resident or government representative to New Zealand in 1833, James Busby (1800–71) became the country's first recorded wine maker. He had earlier studied wine making in France and had also helped to establish a wine industry in the Hunter Valley in Australia. French explorer Dumont D'Urville confirmed the promise of viticulture in the country when he heaped praise on Busby's white wine, which he sampled during an 1840 visit to the Bay of Islands.

**Marlborough** is New Zealand's largest wine-growing region (see pp210–11). The wide, flat Wairau Valley, dry, sunny climate and slow ripening conditions combine to produce the country's finest Sauvignon Blanc.

**French settlers** planted vines on Canterbury's picturesque Banks Peninsula as early as 1840 (see pp234–5). Waipara, north of Christchurch (see pp236–7), has become a more important wine-producing area.

**Christchurch**

**Gibbston Valley Wines** in Central Otago (see p282) produces Pinot Noir, Chardonnay, Pinot Gris and Riesling. It has an underground cellar cut into the rock face behind the winery.

**Central Otago's** growing season is short, but it has become a world leader in Pinot Noir production.

**Dunedin**

0 kilometres 100

0 miles 100

**Dalmatian Croats** living in the Henderson Valley close to downtown Auckland, were the pioneers of the modern wine industry *(see p91)*.

**Mills Reef Winery** in Tauranga, in the Bay of Plenty, sells wines from its Art Deco-style winery building and restaurant.

## Grape Varieties of New Zealand

**Northland's** most notable wines are full-bodied reds, especially Merlot. The **Auckland** area is also primarily a red wine region, concentrating on Cabernet Sauvignon. The most prominent wines in **Waikato**, the **Bay of Plenty** and **Gisborne** are Chardonnays. **Hawke's Bay** has a reputation for high-quality Chardonnays and Cabernet blends. In **Wairarapa**, Pinot Noir is the most widely planted variety. **Marlborough** produces world-class Sauvignon Blanc, some Chardonnay and sparkling wines, while the small **Nelson** vineyards, like those in **Canterbury**, produce Chardonnay, Pinot Noir and Riesling. **Central Otago**, the world's southernmost wine area, produces Pinot Noir and other cold climate varieties.

**Hastings** is the venue for the annual Hawke's Bay Vintners' Charity Wine Auction *(see pp154–5)*.

**Te Mata Estate**, a medium-sized winery using only Hawke's Bay grapes, is New Zealand's oldest winery *(see pp154–5)*. Its Coleraine Cabernet Merlot is of world-class quality.

**Wairarapa** is one of New Zealand's newest wine areas. The original four wineries in 1980 have now grown to about 30.

**Martinborough**, the hub of wine-making in Wairarapa, is a popular weekend destination for people from Wellington. It is also the scene of the annual Martinborough Wine and Food Festival *(see p176)*.

Auckland

Wellington

**Key**

- Northland
- Auckland
- Waikato and Bay of Plenty
- Gisborne
- Hawke's Bay
- Wairarapa
- Marlborough
- Nelson
- Canterbury
- Central Otago

# New Zealand's Sporting Year

Sport has always been an important part of New Zealand cultural life. Maori were fond of running races, wrestling, surfing and canoe competitions, although nothing was formalized. European settlers found the relatively easy climate gave them a chance to play a variety of sports, and sporting events brought together isolated farming communities. The national passion for an active recreational life has contributed to New Zealanders carving out an international reputation for their sporting prowess, producing numerous world-class champions out of all proportion to the size of the country's population.

**The Lake Taupo International Trout Fishing Contest** attracts worldwide participation to this Mecca of trout fishing.

**The NZ Golf Open**, held at a different golf course each year, attracts a world-class field.

**The New Zealand Winter Cup** at Addington, Christchurch, is one of the important harness races on the racing calendar.

| January | February | March | April | May | June |
|---------|----------|-------|-------|-----|------|

**The Auckland Anniversary Regatta**, in which more than 600 yachts take part, is one of the largest yachting events in the world.

**The NZ Rally Championship** attracts overseas competitors to race over some of the country's most difficult roads.

**The Wellington Cup**, like most of horse racing's premier events, is held during summer.

**The National Dragon Boat Championships** take place on Wellington's Lambton Harbour.

**The Provincial Trophy** is cricket's premier event in New Zealand. Cricket is the most popular summer sport and attracts large numbers of spectators.

**The Adventure Racing World Championship**, a race for teams of three to five people, varies its course each year. Teams cycle and use kayaks and rafts to cross lakes and rivers.

**The Air New Zealand Cup**, rugby's top domestic prize, is the climax of the rugby season.

**The NZ Women's Open** *golf championship* is held at a different course each year and attracts keen players from around the world.

| ...ly | August | September | October | November | December |
|---|---|---|---|---|---|

**The World Heli-Challenge**, at Wanaka, is just one of the many adventure sports events in New Zealand.

## Black Magic

No sport has had such an effect on New Zealand life as rugby union. Imported from England in the 1870s, the sport was taken up with alacrity by New Zealanders, especially Maori and, in the last few decades, Polynesian Islanders. The standard bearers for rugby are the famous All Blacks, a name synonymous with the sport. In 1888, the Native team from New Zealand toured Britain, its uniform black with a silver fern on the chest. Known as the Blacks, they were the precursor to the first All Black team which conquered British teams in 1905.

Black attire was later adopted by other New Zealand sporting teams for international events. The national cricket team is dubbed the Black Caps and the basketball team, the Tall Blacks.

Former All Black Jonah Lomu

**Key**

- Cricket
- Golf
- Horse racing
- Lawn bowls
- Netball
- Rugby
- Skiing
- Surf life-saving

# NEW ZEALAND THROUGH THE YEAR

New Zealand's seasons are opposite to those in the northern hemisphere. Spring arrives in September and summer comes in December, autumn is from March to May and the winter months are June, July and August. The South Island's temperatures are slightly lower than those in the North Island. Rain falls heaviest in winter in most areas, with the mid- to late summer months relatively dry. Visitors need to be prepared for sudden weather changes, a feature of the maritime climate. The country's latitudinal position opens it to prevailing westerly winds, ranging from gentle breezes to raging gales.

## Spring

With the onset of finer weather, the rugby posts come down from the playing fields and cricketers start to practise their strokes. Blossom and food festivals, garden and fashion shows begin, and the horse racing season swings into gear.

### September

**Hastings Blossom Festival**
*(mid- to late Sep)*. The country's largest fruit-growing district ushers in a new season. Highlights include concerts and a blossom parade.
**New Zealand Fashion Week**
*(mid-Sep)*, Auckland. The country's top fashion designers showcase their latest collections to local and international buyers, media and guests.
**World of WearableArt Awards (WOW)** *(late Sep)*, Wellington. A choreographed evening in

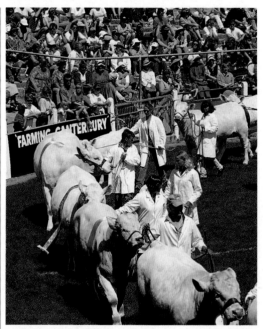
Cattle on parade at Showtime Canterbury

which art designs are worn. The competition began in Nelson where there is a museum of past winners.

### October

**Ngongotaha Trout Festival**
*(early Oct)*. The annual trout fishing tournament and festival open the trout season.
**Dunedin Rhododendron Festival** *(late Oct)*. Displays of rhododendrons set the Dunedin Botanic Garden and other gardens around Otago ablaze with colour in spring.
**Taranaki Rhododendron and Garden Festival** *(last week)*. More than 100 gardens are on view *(see p184)*.

### November

**Showtime Canterbury**, Christchurch. Features the region's main Agricultural & Pastoral Show, horse races, concerts, fashion shows and a diverse range of events.
**F.A.W.C! Food and Wine Classic** *(early Nov)*. Wineries in Hawke's Bay open their doors for this three-day festival. Also held in mid-June.
**Adventure Racing World Championship** *(mid-Nov)*, Buller. An adventure race through some of the toughest terrain in the South Island.
**Toast Martinborough** *(mid-Nov)*, Martinborough Sq, Wairarapa. Showcases

Modelling designs in the World of WearableArt Awards

## Average Daily Hours of Sunshine

Hours

**Sunshine Chart**
The chart gives figures for Wellington, but these are similar to other main centres. Nelson and Blenheim in the South Island, and Tauranga, Napier and Gisborne in the North Island, enjoy more sunshine hours than any other places. The least sunny region is the southern part of the South Island.

the wine and food of the region, with entertainment by local artists.
**Pohutakawa Festival** (end-Nov–mid-Dec), Coromandel. This two-week festival celebrates the music, arts and outdoor culture of Coromandel.

## Summer

Although many New Zealanders head off for their annual visit to the beach, lake or high country during the summer school break, shops no longer "shut down" apart from Christmas and New Year's days. Cities and towns have become increasingly lively places during the holiday season.

### December
**ACICS Kepler Challenge** (early Dec), Te Anau. An annual endurance run that follows the Kepler Track (see p287) over mountains, swamps and rivers, through magnificent scenery.
**TSB Festival of Lights** (Christmas to Feb), New Plymouth. Special festive lighting in Pukekura Park and city streets. There are music and dance performances in the park each evening (see p185).

### January
**Nelson Jazz Festival** (early Jan). A week-long festival featuring local and overseas talent (as part of the Summer in Nelson festival).
**New Zealand Kite Festival** (late Jan). Hosted by various regions, this festival attracts top kite flyers from all over New Zealand as well as from overseas.

Maori performing at the Waitangi Day celebrations

**New Zealand Gliding Grand Prix** (late Jan), Omarama. The world's top glider pilots race head to head.
**World Buskers Festival** (late Jan), Christchurch. Ten days of entertainment featuring street, circus and comedy acts.

Anniversary Day Regatta in Auckland

### February
**Waitangi Day** (6 Feb), Waitangi National Trust. Commemorates the signing of the Treaty of Waitangi (see pp108–9).
**Auckland Anniversary Regatta** (early Feb). Up to 600 yachts take part in one of the world's largest one-day regattas on Waitemata Harbour (see p77).
**Aotearoa Traditional Maori Performing Arts Festival** (early Feb, even years), Waikato. Festival of Maori culture and art by New Zealand's best groups.
**Marlborough Wine & Food Festival** (second Sat), Blenheim. Wines and food under marquees in a vineyard setting (see p212).
**Art Deco Weekend** (third week), Napier. A celebration of Art Deco style with jazz-age dining and dancing, films, house tours, vintage cars and aeroplane rides.
**Garden City Festival of Flowers** (third week), Christchurch. Prestigious festival celebrates the beauty of flowers.

## Average Monthly Rainfall

**Rainfall Chart**
Rainfall is not evenly distributed throughout New Zealand. The west coast of the North Island and South Island is wetter than the east coast. More rain falls in winter and spring than in summer and autumn, in most areas. The figures given here are only for Wellington.

## Autumn

Autumn often brings the most settled weather of the year, a time of mild, calm days still warm enough for most summer activities. This is harvest season, a good time to experience wine and food festivals. Tramping, fishing and hunting are also popular autumnal pursuits.

### March

**New Zealand International Arts Festival** (*Feb to mid-Mar, even years*), Wellington. This prestigious festival features some of the world's best talents (*see pp160–1*).
**National Dragon Boat Championships** (*Chinese New Year*), Wellington. Crews race on Lambton Harbour.
**Golden Shears** (*first week*), Masterton. The world's top shearers are in action at this popular event (*see p177*).
**Pasifika Festival** (*second week*), Auckland. Cultural events and displays by Pacific Islanders (*see p97*).
**Ellerslie Flower Show** (*Mar*), Christchurch. Large floral

Balloons Over Waikato Festival in Hamilton

exhibition located at Hagley Park (*see p231*).
**Hokitika Wildfoods Competition** (*mid-Mar*), Hokitika. Possum stew and huhu grub are some of the delicacies on the menu.
**Round the Bays Run** (*end-Mar*), Auckland. One of the world's largest fun runs with 60,000 people taking part.
**Ngaruawahia Regatta** (*late Mar*), Ngaruawahia. Maori canoes compete on Waikato River in the hometown of the Maori monarch (*see p120*).

### April

**NZ Rally Championship** (*early Apr*), Greater Auckland. Part of the World Rally Championships, in which drivers battle it out on the back country roads.
**Bluff Oyster & Food Festival** (*mid-Apr*). Features an array of

seafood, fine wine and entertainment.
**Royal Easter Show** (*second week*), Auckland. Livestock competitions, art and craft awards, wine awards and the largest equestrian show in the country.
**Balloons Over Waikato** (*mid-Apr*), Hamilton. More than 30 balloons drift over the city and surrounding areas (*see p122*).
**Lake Taupo International Trout Fishing Tournament** (*third week*). Fishermen vie at this fine trout fishing location (*see p145*).
**Warbirds Over Wanaka** (*Easter weekend, even years*). Classic vintage and veteran warplanes take to the skies in this world-class event (*see p274*).

### May

**Rotorua Tagged Trout Competition** (*May*). Rotorua's premier fishing competition has a $10,000 trout waiting to be hooked.

Visitors at a food stall at the Hokitika Wildfoods Competition

## Average Monthly Temperature

**Temperature Chart**
The chart gives the average maximum and minimum tem- peratures for the city of Wellington. The North Island has mild winters and humid summers. The South Island experiences the country's hottest sum- mer temperatures, but in winter these can plunge to below freezing point.

## Winter

Often the most spectacular time of the year to visit, winter also brings reduced rates on airfares, accommodation and activities. On the scenic west coast, rainfall is at its lowest and whales at Kaikoura can virtually be guaranteed to put in an appearance.

### June

**National Agricultural Fieldays** *(mid-Jun)*, Mystery Creek, Hamilton. One of the world's largest agricultural events showcases the best of New Zealand's products, with emphasis on innovative technology *(see p122)*.

### July

**Queenstown Winter Festival** *(mid-Jul)*. One of the highlights of the Queenstown calendar, this 10-day winter festival includes street parties, jazz and

Spectators at the Rally of New Zealand in Auckland

comedy performances, spectacular night skiing and firework displays.
**Christchurch Arts Festival** *(last week, odd years)*. A mid-winter festival of music, theatre, dance, film and the visual arts.

### August

**World Heli-Challenge** *(Aug)*, Wanaka. International snowboarders and skiers take part in three days of heliskiing events.

**Bay of Islands Jazz and Blues Festival** *(mid-Aug)*, Northland. One of the most popular events on the jazz calendar. More than 50 bands from New Zealand and overseas take part.
**Crater to Lake Challenge** *(late Aug)*, Taupo. Multi-sport event featuring skiing, cycling, kayaking, water-skiing and running from the slopes of Mount Ruapehu to Taupo.

### Public Holidays

**New Year's Day** (1 Jan)
**New Year Holiday** (2 Jan)
**Waitangi Day** (6 Feb)
**Good Friday** (varies)
**Easter Monday** (varies)
**Anzac Day** (25 April)
**Queen's Birthday** (first Mon in Jun)
**Labour Day** (varies Oct)
**Christmas Day** (25 Dec)
**Boxing Day** (26 Dec)

Clydesdale horses and wagon at the National Agricultural Fieldays, Mystery Creek, Hamilton

# THE HISTORY OF NEW ZEALAND

The last of the world's significant landmasses to be colonized by people, New Zealand is a nation of immigrants. Maori settled in the country less than 1,000 years ago, while Europeans first arrived in 1642. Together, these two peoples have forged a unique identity out of their common experiences that reflects their Pacific environment.

The date the first Maori arrived in New Zealand has stirred much debate. According to legend, the first explorer to discover New Zealand was the Polynesian Kupe, around AD 950. He then returned to his ancestral homeland, Hawaiki. Four centuries later, a fleet of canoes set sail for New Zealand, guided by Kupe's directions on how to find land.

Basing their findings on radio-carbon dating of Maori middens, archaeologists believe that the first settlement was around AD 1300. Some scientists, however, believe that Maori arrived as long ago as 2,000 years, but these early settlers did not survive for long. Nonetheless, the rats that they brought with them went on to devastate the native bird, lizard and frog populations.

Regardless of when they did arrive, Maori are known to have carried a number of plants and animals with them. The *kiore*, the Polynesian rat, was considered a great delicacy when fattened up on berries. Also known to have survived the journey was the native dog, the *kuri*. Root vegetables Maori brought with them were the yam, *kumara* and *taro*. The *kumara* grew more successfully in the colder climate than the other two, and proved important in the development of Maori culture, enabling permanent settlement.

## Abel Tasman

Since Greek times, there had been talk of a Terra Australis, or "great southern continent", to counterbalance the lands of the northern hemisphere. Such a landmass was necessary, it was argued, to offset the weight of the continents in the north and to balance the Earth on its axis. The mathematician Pythagoras speculated about the existence of such a land, but it was not until almost 2,000 years later that 17th-century Dutch explorers finally sighted Australia.

In 1642, the Dutch East India Company, a trading firm anxious to explore prospects for commerce beyond the East Indies, sent Abel Tasman south from Java in Indonesia. After sailing past Tasmania (then known as Van Diemen's Land), Tasman reached a point off present-day Hokitika on 13 December 1642, noting "a large high elevated land".

*Moa skeleton*

**1400–1500** Maori hunting drives moa to extinction

**1500** Maori develop fortified sites *(pa)* to defend themselves

*Double canoe*

| 1300 | 1400 | 1500 | 1600 |
|---|---|---|---|
| **1300** First Polynesian inhabitants arrive from Cook and Society islands | **1400** Great fires on the South Island east coast destroy swathes of forest | **1531** Map drawn with Terra Australis on it | **1642** Dutch explorer Abel Tasman sights New Zealand |

◀ Detail from *The Signing of the Treaty of Waitangi* by Marcus King (1939)

# Maori Exploration and Voyage

It is now fairly well accepted that Polynesians, ancestors of Maori, made planned voyages to New Zealand rather than simply drifting there by chance. Polynesians were skilled navigators who sailed long distances between the islands in the Pacific in large craft. Driven out of an island by starvation or intertribal warfare, some groups would have deliberately sailed to a far-off land, especially if they had been given directions by someone like Kupe who had been there *(see p49)*. With their vessels laden with plants and small animals, they would have been guided by traditional navigation clues, such as the stars, migrating birds and cloud formations.

**Kupe's Anchor Stone**
A 1912 photograph of a Maori elder standing beside what may be Kupe's anchor stone.

**Canoe Prow**
The prows of Maori waka (canoes), carved in intricate patterns, had forward-thrusting prows to improve the canoes' performance.

**Fishing Net**
Fish, a valuable part of Maori food supply, were caught using a variety of nets. This wood engraving (1840) by Joel Pollack is of a landing net.

## Polynesian Settlement

*Archaeological discoveries indicate that Polynesians came from Southeast Asia to the eastern Pacific islands, settling the lands from Hawaii to Easter Island. In about 1250, expeditions from the islands of central Polynesia reached New Zealand where they established coastal tribal settlements.*

**Kuri**
Maori brought the *kuri* (dog) with them on their migrations. It became extinct soon after European settlement.

**Single Canoe**
The single canoe was used as a coastal vessel. It had decking made of long rods. Thwarts, lashed from one top edge to the other, served as seats.

**Periods of Settlement**

——— 30,000 years ago
——— 3,000 years ago
——— 1,500–2,000 years ago
——— 1,000 years ago
——— 500 years ago

**Double Canoes**
The largest of these craft, depicted here by William Hodges, artist on Cook's 1773 voyage, were capable of carrying up to 200 passengers and crew.

***Taro* Plant**
Few plants taken from Polynesia survived the voyage to New Zealand. *Taro* grew, but because it was not productive, it became a luxury food.

***Kiore***
The kiore or Polynesian rat was introduced from Polynesia. It was a source of food for the early Maori, but killed native birds.

0 kilometres 1,000
0 miles 1,000

**Canoe Regatta**
Maori today celebrate their heritage of exploration and voyage in the annual Ngaruawahia Regatta, held on the Waikato River *(see p120)*.

**Legend of Maui**
An ink drawing (1907) by Wilhelm Dittmer depicts the legend of Maui, who created New Zealand by fishing the North Island out of the ocean.

Abel Tasman's ships, the *Heemskerck* and *Zeehaen*

Abel Tasman and the crews of the *Heemskerck* and *Zeehaen* had sighted the Southern Alps. Tasman wanted to land, but the rolling swell off the coastline convinced him to head north, where he found a relatively calm anchorage in what is now called Golden Bay. However, the provoked Maori rammed a pinnace from the *Zeehaen*, and clubbed four of the Dutch sailors to death. The Dutch named the location Murderers' Bay. Tasman set sail north and left New Zealand waters on 6 January 1643 without further investigation.

### Captain James Cook

There was a lull in European exploration of the New Zealand region for more than 100 years. No good commercial reason encouraged any visits; indeed, the reputation of the hostile Maori discouraged them. Then, in 1769, Englishman Captain James Cook set sail on a scientific expedition of discovery to the South Pacific, to observe the transit of the sun by the planet Venus. After having observed the rare phenomenon

at Tahiti, Cook sailed south until he sighted the east coast of New Zealand, on 9 October 1769.

Cook's ship, the *Endeavour*, was well equipped for its voyage, with botanists and artists on board. Besides documenting new scientific finds, Cook's mission was to assess the potential of the country as a colony. A master mariner, Cook mapped the coastline and the scientists on board made hundreds of discoveries. On this first of three visits to New Zealand, he claimed the country for England. Coincidentally, a French expedition led by explorer Jean de Surville sailed within a few kilometres of Cook at the end of 1769, but neither was aware of the other's presence.

Following Cook, Europeans trickled rather than flooded into New Zealand, working as whalers, sealers and timber traders. Few became permanent immigrants, and as soon as the resource they sought disappeared, so did they. By the early 1800s it had become uneconomic to send sealing gangs to New Zealand because most of the easy prey had been taken; whale numbers, too, plummeted.

Abel Tasman

### The Treaty of Waitangi

The impact of these visitors on the traditional Maori way of life was enormous. Maori were exposed to a disastrous number of diseases, such as measles and smallpox, and their warlike instincts were incited by the purchase of guns. During the 1820s, at least 20,000 Maori were killed in intertribal "musket wars", which changed

---

**1791** First whaling ship sails into Doubtless Bay, Northland

**1814** Samuel Marsden sets up first Anglican mission in the Bay of Islands

**1821** Musket wars begin between Maori tribes

**1831** Whaling stations established around Cook Strait

**1833** James Busby appointed British Resident

**1750**      **1800**      **1820**      **1830**      **1840**

**1769** Captain Cook makes first of three visits to New Zealand

**1815** First Pakeha child born in New Zealand

**1835** Declaration of Independence signed by 34 northern chiefs

**1840** British sovereignty proclaimed. Treaty of Waitangi signed by 50 chiefs

*HMS Endeavour*

*Maori chief*

The Treaty House at Waitangi

the political face of Maori New Zealand as tribes invaded neighbouring territories, sometimes taking them permanently.

Another major influence for change was Christianity. Anglican missionary Samuel Marsden established New Zealand's first mission station in the Bay of Islands in 1814, and although progress was slow in converting Maori to Christianity, the faith had a significant foothold by 1840.

By then Maori numbered about 115,000 and European settlers (Pakeha) 2,000. While some Maori benefitted by trading with the Europeans and growing crops for them, there was concern about increasing lawlessness, the buying up of land by Europeans and the intertribal warfare. Leading chiefs asked Queen Victoria to provide a framework of law and order. Eventually Captain William Hobson obtained the signatures of Maori chiefs on the 1840 Treaty of Waitangi, giving sovereignty to Britain, although the Maori translation gave the chiefs a different understanding of the treaty.

### Treaty of Waitangi

The Treaty of Waitangi is New Zealand's founding document, an agreement between the British Government and Maori that is today the centrepiece of the country's race relations.

In return for giving Queen Victoria the right to buy land, Maori were granted all the rights and privileges of British subjects. A clause also gave them "full exclusive and undisturbed possession of their Lands and Estates Forests Fisheries and other properties". But misunderstanding arose because there were two different versions (Maori and English) which carried different meanings. The crucial difference was what was meant precisely by the word sovereignty, translated by many as *kawanatanga*, suggesting a distant figure of authority. Controversy over the Treaty continues to this day.

Signatures on the Treaty

### The New Zealand Wars

Unlike Australia, where some of the first immigrants were convicts, New Zealand settlers were freemen and many came in family groups. The New Zealand Company was set up in 1837 to transplant a cross-section of English society in the Antipodes. Planned settlements were established at Wellington, Wanganui, Nelson, New Plymouth, Christchurch and Dunedin.

Following the signing of the Treaty of Waitangi, Maori–Pakeha relations were relatively harmonious for some years. If there were conflicts, they were generally over land, and isolated skirmishes occurred until 1860, the year the New Zealand Wars began. The critical point was at Waitara, Taranaki. The cause was a land sale between the government and a minor chief of the Te Ati

**1844** Hone Heke chops down British flagpole and starts "War of the North"

**1848** Dunedin settlement founded by Scottish pioneers

**1850** Canterbury settlement founded by genteel English emigrants

**1854** First session of General Assembly (Parliament)

Gold nugget

**1860** New Zealand Wars begin between Maori and Europeans over land

**1861** First New Zealand gold rush after discovery at Tuapeka, Central Otago

Te Kooti

**1865** Capital moves from Auckland to Wellington

**1867** Four Maori seats established in Parliament

1845　1850　1855　1860　1865

Awa tribe who did not have the tribe's permission to sell, a prerequisite for communal property under Maori custom. When the tribe refused to accept the bogus deal, the government retaliated by marching troops onto the land, seizing it by force.

In response, most central North Island tribes backed the Te Ati Awa, intensifying the rebellion. At the height of hostilities in the mid-1860s, British forces had increased to more than 20,000, against about 5,000 Maori warriors. On the British side were significant numbers of Maori who were either opportunists or had a score to settle with an enemy tribe.

United, Maori would have easily been a match for the Pakeha. Even divided, they came close to persuading many settlers to flee the colony. In 1868, two chiefs, Titikowarau in the west and Te Kooti in the east, won a series of significant battles, but internal squabbles saw them lose the support of the wider Maori population. By 1869, the New Zealand Wars came to a halt as Maori opposition fell away. Land sales escalated, many of them under duress. The wars resulted in the government confiscating

*Passengers from the Cressy Landing at Port Lyttelton* by William Fox (1851)

12,000 sq km (4,630 sq miles) of prime land. Most of it was given to "friendly" Maori tribes, while some was handed to Pakeha settlers. It was a legacy that came back to haunt the country more than a century later, as Maori pursued their legitimate grievances through the Waitangi Tribunal.

## Economic Expansion

The 1861 discovery of gold in Otago, and subsequent finds on the West Coast, set the South Island on its industrial feet. Up until then, the North Island had been outstripping the South economically and in population terms; it was not until 1896 that the North Island reasserted itself.

The late 19th century saw a time of great economic expansion, thanks to large-scale government borrowing. The rail network was established, telegraph lines were installed and emigrants were assisted to the country. During the 1870s, the population doubled. Good export prices for wool (which proved to be the mainstay of the economy for the next 100 years) underpinned the frenzy of economic activity. Technological advances

*Te Henheu's Old Pa of Waitahanui at Lake Taupo* by George F Angas (1847)

**1869** New Zealand Wars end because of Maori disunity

**1879** Vote given to every male over 21

1870

*Maori weapon*

**1882** First refrigerated ship leaves Otago for the UK

1880

**1887** Tongariro National Park, the first in New Zealand, established

**1893** First country in the world to extend the vote to all women

1890

*Early transport*

**1907** New Zealand becomes a Dominion

1900

1910

24c New Zealand

NELSON-HORSE TRAM 1882

also played their part. The first shipload of frozen meat for Britain sailed from Otago in 1882; this technology was also vital later in shipping butter.

New Zealand soon gained a reputation for social innovation. In 1893, the Liberal Government granted the vote to all women, and in 1898 it introduced a means-tested old-age pension, both the first in the world.

## The War Years

As New Zealand's population reached the one million mark in 1907, the country's status as a colony of Great Britain changed to that of the Dominion of New Zealand. In 1917, the title of governor (the representative of the Queen) became that of governor-general.

World War I poster

The Liberal Party, with its progressive tax policies, old-age pensions, votes for women and breaking up of large land holdings, was hailed domestically and externally for making New Zealand "the birthplace of the 20th century". Its hold on power lasted until 1912, by which time it had lost touch with the public. It was replaced by the Reform Party, which was led by Bill Massey and gained most of its suppport from the farmers. The Reform Party remained in power until 1928 and served in a coalition with the Liberals until 1935 when a Labour government was elected.

World War I was a defining moment for the fledgling nation. In 1915, New Zealanders and Australians combined to form the Australian and New Zealand Army Corps (ANZAC). Ordered by the British to attack well-armed and better-placed Turkish defenders on the Gallipoli Peninsula, thousands were killed in eight months of action. The 25th of April (Anzac Day) has since been set aside as a national holiday to remember the soldiers' sacrifice.

For a small country, New Zealand suffered enormously during the war. Out of a total of 110,000 troops, 16,697 died and 41,262 were wounded – a massive casualty rate.

The period between the wars was one of mixed fortunes for New Zealand. While the 1920s were initially positive, the world's

New Zealand Expeditionary Force on the Hutt Road near Petone, Wellington, 1914

**1915** New Zealand troops suffer heavy losses in the Gallipoli campaign against Turkey

**1920** First Anzac Day commemoration

**1933** Elizabeth McCombs first female MP

*Elizabeth McCombs*

**1936** New Zealand pilot Jean Batten flies from England to Australia in world record time

| 1915 | 1920 | 1930 | 1935 | 1938 |

**1914** New Zealand enters World War I on the Allied side

**1918** End of World War I

**1935** First Labour Government elected

**1936** 40-hour week introduced

*Factory workers*

Relief camp for unemployed workers at Akatarawa, Hutt Valley, in the 1930s

and Italy, even though the most serious threat to the country came from Japan. After the attack on Pearl Harbour (1941), troops were increasingly deployed in the Pacific and links were forged with the US. American soldiers spent time in New Zealand during the war and took New Zealand wives back home with them. In 1951, military ties between the US, Australia and New Zealand were formalized with the signing of the ANZUS military pact.

economic woes engulfed the country, and by 1932 it was in the depths of the Depression. The first Labour Government, elected in 1935, spent its way out of the Depression. New Zealand gained further accolades as the social laboratory of the world with its income-related health scheme and extended pension programme.

In 1939, for the second time in the century, New Zealand found itself embroiled in a world war. Prime Minister Michael Joseph Savage was in no doubt where the country's loyalty lay: "Where Britain goes we go, where she stands we stand." New Zealand soldiers served in Greece, the Middle East

## Moving away from Britain

After the war, while New Zealand looked to the US for its military security, its economy still remained firmly wedded to Britain. As Britain's "South Pacific farm", New Zealand had traditionally enjoyed easy access to UK's markets. As late as 1960, 55 per cent of its exports landed there. But the boom times came to an end once "the old country" joined the European Union (EU) in 1973 and its priorities shifted to the European continent. Within 20 years of joining the EU, Britain took only 6 per cent of New Zealand's exports. New markets were found, and Asia became important. Hong Kong, China, Japan, Taiwan and South Korea are now among the top ten countries with which New Zealand trades.

Mirroring countries in the West, New Zealand went through great social changes during the 1960s, as baby-boomers reached adulthood and challenged conservative society. The decision to support the US with a token force in the Vietnam War was vigorously opposed, and in 1972

Interior of a Wellington clothing factory in the 1940s

**1939** New Zealand fights in World War II on Allied side

*Sir Edmund Hillary*

**1953** Sir Edmund Hillary climbs Mount Everest with Sherpa Tenzing

**1965** Combat force sent to Vietnam

**1975** Waitangi Tribunal established to investigate Maori land claims following confiscations and compensate where justified

**1940**    **1950**    **1960**    **1970**

**1947** Statute of Westminster adopted by Parliament

**1948** Protest against exclusion of Maori from All Black rugby tour to South Africa

*Carving at Waitangi Marae*

**1961** Capital punishment abolished

**1973** Frigate sent to French Polynesia to protest French nuclear testing conscription was dropped by the new Labour Government. A year later, the government sent a frigate to French Polynesia to protest against nuclear weapons testing there.

In the mid-1970s, as imported oil price hikes affected the population, New Zealanders returned to the conservative politics of the National Party under the combative Robert Muldoon. Finally, weary of his interventionist economic policies, the electorate voted in a socially leftist but economically rightist Labour Government in 1984, headed by David Lange.

For the next six years, the country experienced a whirlwind of change as Labour floated the exchange rate, deregulated industries, removed tariffs, sold off state assets and made thousands of civil servants redundant in a quest for greater efficiency. At the same time, foreign relations were in upheaval: New Zealand had always maintained a strong anti-nuclear weapons policy, and in 1985 the US was told that nuclear-armed or powered warships were no longer welcome in New Zealand ports. The Americans suspended

The *Rainbow Warrior*, sunk in Auckland Harbour in 1985

ANZUS. In that same year, French saboteurs sank the Greenpeace vessel, the *Rainbow Warrior*, in Auckland.

The National Government, which came to power in 1990 led by Jim Bolger (succeeded in 1997 by Jenny Shipley), continued with economic reforms, albeit at a slower pace. However, many New Zealanders, disillusioned over a succession of unresponsive administrations, voted in a Mixed Member Proportional electoral system based on the German model. The system was first tested in 1997, which resulted in a vastly more representative parliament than before, and the emergence of the country's first directly elected woman prime minister, Helen Clark of the Labour Party, in 1999.

New Zealand society today has changed significantly, from a period when an overwhelming majority of the population was Pakeha to a point where Auckland is now the largest Polynesian city in the world, and an increasing number of Asians have become citizens. With its increasingly diverse cultures, New Zealand is carving out a confident and independent identity as a Pacific nation in the international community.

Representatives of the Ngai Tahu tribe and the government signing the Deed of Settlement in 1997

| 1985 *Rainbow Warrior* sunk | 1987 Maori becomes official language | 2006 Maori Queen Te Atairangikaahu dies after a reign of 40 years | 2008 National Party wins general election | 2016 New Zealand population projected to reach 4.5 million |
|---|---|---|---|---|
| 1984 Lange Government takes power | 1995 Team New Zealand wins America's Cup | 2004 Peter Jackson's *Lord of the Rings* wins 11 Oscars | 2010 Major earthquake hits Christchurch | |

| 0 | 1990 | 2000 | 2010 | 2020 |
|---|---|---|---|---|

| 1981 First Maori language kindergarten opens | 1990 National forms government | 1997 Jenny Shipley first woman prime minister | *Jenny Shipley* | 2011 Christchurch hit by worst earthquake in the country's history, causing widespread damage |
|---|---|---|---|---|
| 1981 Country divided by South African rugby tour with widespread protests | 1990 Dame Catherine Tizard first woman Governor-General | 1997 Government compensation to Ngai Tahu tribe for land confiscations |  | 2011 New Zealand hosts Rugby World Cup |
| | | 1997 First MMP Parliament elected | | |

The beautiful turquoise-coloured Lake Tekapo, Canterbury ▶

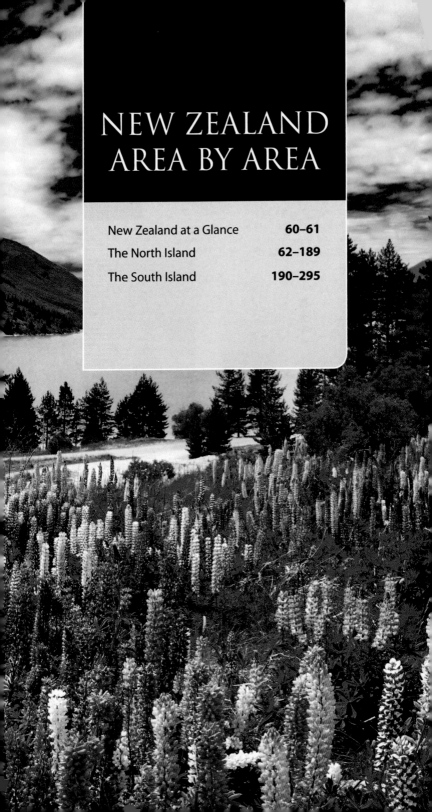

# NEW ZEALAND
# AREA BY AREA

# New Zealand at a Glance

Tucked away in the southwest corner of the Pacific Ocean, New Zealand is one of the most isolated and least populated countries in the world. It is also a land of contrasts: between the subtropical north and the colder south; the wet west and the drier east; the volcanoes of the central North Island and the fiords of the South Island. Powerful geological forces have created a landscape that is dominated by mountains, hills, lakes and rivers. These, in turn, have allowed New Zealand to become a paradise for nature lovers and outdoor enthusiasts. Sheep and cattle farming still cover large areas of the country, but more and more the accent is on diversity. The more populated north is the centre of Maori and Pacific Island culture.

One of the many vineyards in Marlborough (see pp210–11)

The Pancake Rocks and blowholes at Punakaiki in Paparoa National Park (see p240)

The Gothic-style Canterbury Museum in Christchurch (see p230)

Lake Wakatipu from The Remarkables (see p280)

Collingwood
Motueka
Karamea    Nelson
Westport         Blenhe
Murchison
Reefton  MARLBOROU
AND NELSON
Greymouth        (See pp200–221)
Hokitika                Kaikoura
Arthur's
Pass
Fox           Waipara
Glacier    Springfield
CANTERBURY AND
THE WEST COAST      Christchurch
Haast        (See pp222–257)
Twizel   Geraldine    Ashburton
Milford Sound        Timaru
Wanaka
Alexandra     Oamaru
Manapouri   OTAGO AND
SOUTHLAND   Palmerston
(See pp258–295)
Gore
Dunedin
Invercargill   Balclutha
Oban

Larnach Castle, a century-old stone mansion (see p270)

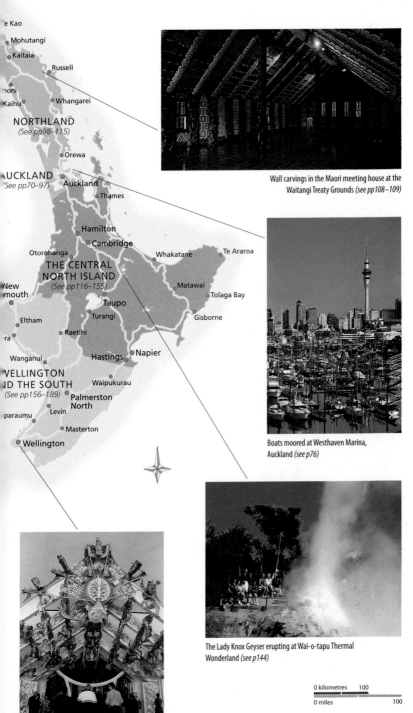

Wall carvings in the Maori meeting house at the
Waitangi Treaty Grounds *(see pp108–109)*

Boats moored at Westhaven Marina,
Auckland *(see p76)*

The Lady Knox Geyser erupting at Wai-o-tapu Thermal
Wonderland *(see p144)*

0 kilometres    100

0 miles    100

Maori meeting house at the Museum of New
Zealand Te Papa Tongarewa *(see pp170–71)*

Marina in Whitianga Harbour, Coromandel Peninsula on North Island ▶

Te Kao
Mohutangi
Kaitaia
Russell
noni
Kaihu
Whangarei

**NORTHLAND**
*(See pp98–115)*

Orewa

**AUCKLAND**
*(See pp70–97)*
Auckland
Thames

Hamilton
Cambridge
Otorohanga
Whakatane
Te Araroa

**THE CENTRAL
NORTH ISLAND**
*(See pp116–155)*
Matawai
Tolaga Bay

New
mouth
Taupo
Turangi
Gisborne
Eltham
Raetihi

ra
Wanganui
Hastings
Napier

**VELLINGTON
ID THE SOUTH**
*(See pp156–189)*
Waipukurau
Palmerston
North
paraumu
Levin
Masterton
Wellington

# THE NORTH ISLAND

# Introducing the North Island

Blessed with a varied landscape, the North Island also offers a range of climates, from the "winterless" north to the snow-bound mountains of the Central Plateau and the blustery winds of the south. From the tip of Northland down to Taranaki on the west and Hawke's Bay on the east, the sea lends a distinct character to each coast. Although best known for its geothermal wonders around Rotorua and the Volcanic Plateau, the North Island is also a fertile land of lush dairy pastures, highly productive orchards and rolling sheep country. The country's largest city, Auckland, and its capital, Wellington, are both located in the North Island.

NORTHLAND
(See pp98–115)

Te Kao

Mohutangi

Kaitaia

Kerikeri

Kaikohe

Opononi

Kaihu

Dargaville

Ruawai

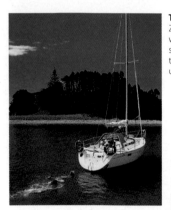

**The Bay of Islands** (see pp106–7) is one of New Zealand's most beautiful and historic areas. The warm, sparkling, aquamarine waters, year-round sunshine, sandy beaches and quiet coves make the area a paradise for deep-sea fishing, underwater diving, swimming and sailing.

**Mount Taranaki/Egmont** (see pp186–7), a dormant, snow-capped volcanic peak, is the centrepiece of the agriculturally rich Taranaki region and the dominant feature of Egmont National Park.

New Plymouth

Inglewood

Eltham

Hawera

Wanganui

**The Parliament buildings** in Wellington (see p162) are interesting for their varied architectural styles. The circular, copper-domed "Beehive", which houses Cabinet offices, is in complete contrast to the square marble Parliament Buildings, home to the House of Representatives.

Collingwood

Takaka

Karamea

Motueka

Paraparaumu

Nelson   Picton

Lower Hutt

Wellington

Murchison

Blenheim

St Arnaud

**Sky Tower** *(see p79)* is Auckland city's dominant landmark. From its four observation decks, visitors enjoy 360-degree views of the city centre, its sprawling suburbs, harbours, and the Hauraki Gulf islands.

**Locator Map**

**The Bath House** in Rotorua *(see p138)*, an elegant Tudor-style building situated in the English-style Government Gardens, is the town's most frequently photographed building. Originally constructed as a thermal bath house in 1908, it is now home to the excellent Rotorua Museum of Art and History.

angarei

ellford
Leigh

Orewa

0 kilometres    50

0 miles    50

Auckland    Coromandel
CKLAND    Whitianga
e pp70–97)

Thames

Hamilton    Tauranga

Cambridge

Otorohanga    Whakatane    Hicks Bay

Kuiti    Tokoroa    Rotorua    Opotiki

Tokomaru Bay

THE CENTRAL    Matawai
NORTH ISLAND
Taupo    *(See pp116–155)*    Te Karaka

Taumarunui

Turangi    Gisborne

Raetihi
Waiouru

Hastings    Napier

WELLINGTON
ND THE SOUTH    Waipukurau
*(See pp156–189)*

Palmerston    Porangahoa
North

Alfredton

Masterton

tinborough

**Napier's Art Deco buildings** *(see pp150–1)*, such as the Rothmans Building, were constructed following a devastating earthquake in 1931.

**Martinborough** *(see p176)* is the hub of wine growing in Wairarapa, and its wineries have gained a reputation as producers of red wines. A good way to experience the area's wineries is to join one of the many vineyard tours that leave from Wellington.

# Historic Northland

Between 700 and 800 years ago, the first Polynesian voyagers are believed to have come ashore on the northern coasts of the North Island. Northland is also sometimes referred to as "the birthplace of the nation". It was at Rangihoua in Northland that Samuel Marsden, the first missionary, set up an Anglican mission in 1814; at Waitangi that the Treaty of Waitangi was signed in 1840 *(see pp52–3)*; and at Russell that New Zealand's first capital was established in 1840 before shifting south. Here, too, were sown the first seeds of Maori rebellion against the British.

**Kemp House**
This Kerikeri Mission House, completed in 1822, is the oldest building in New Zealand. The house is associated with the Kemp family who lived in it for 142 years *(see p110)*.

**Waipoa Bay, Moturoa Island**
Captain Cook (in 1769) and French explorer Marion du Fresne (in 1772) took water on board here. Du Fresne buried in the sand a bottle with a document claiming New Zealand for France.

**Kauri trees** are symbolic of Northland but much of the forest is now gone. Logging was at its height from 1870 to 1910.

### Logging on the Hokianga

Charles Heaphy's painting *View of the Kahu-Kahu, Hokianga River* (1839) depicts the logging industry on the Hokianga River. The giant kauri trees made ideal ships' spars as well as timber for new settlements.

**Hokianga Harbour** was one of the main points of early Maori settlement. Kupe *(see p49)* left for Hawaiki from here.

**Russell, Bay of Islands**
This whaling and sealing town was dubbed the "Hell-hole of the Pacific" in the lawless days of the early 1800s *(see p106)*.

INTRODUCING THE NORTH ISLAND

### Hongi Hika

After Maori chief Hongi Hika met King George IV during a trip to England in 1820, he returned home determined to become king of New Zealand. In the 1820s, he led his Northland tribe, the Ngapuhi, in many conquests of other tribes.

### Maori Kauri Gum

Gum from kauri trees, used in paints and polishes, was an important export product from Northland until World War II.

### Pohutukawa

The pohutukawa has an important place in Maori mythology. Maori believe that the spirits of the dead descend down the roots of a pohutukawa tree at Cape Reinga on their way to the homeland on Hawaiki.

**Kauri logs** being towed to a waiting ship.

### Warrior Chiefs

Hone Heke is shown here with his wife, Harriet, and another chief, Kawiti. Unhappy with the Treaty of Waitangi, he was one of the first chiefs to fight the British.

### Pa Site at Ruapekapeka

This *pa* (fortification) site was one of the most complex ever built. In 1846, British troops stormed it on a Sunday morning, catching the Maori inside by surprise. They did not expect the British to fight on a day traditionally given to rest and prayer.

# Volcanic Heartland

From White Island in the northeast of the North Island to Mount Ruapehu in the centre lies the Taupo Volcanic Zone, which also includes Rotorua's geothermal wonders. Here, where the Pacific "ring of fire" begins, the clash of the Pacific Continental Plate and the Indo-Australian Plate has created the conditions for one of the most active volcanic regions in the world *(see p26)*. Beneath the Taupo Volcanic Zone, great slabs of crust are thrust down into the earth's mantle where they melt to form rhyolite magma. Every few thousand years, this magma reaches the surface, resulting in events like the Lake Taupo eruption of AD 186, when pumice was punched 50 km (30 miles) up into the air.

**Mount Ruapehu**
The North Island's tallest mountain is permanently snow-capped and cloaked by eight glaciers. Eruptions in 1995–6 emptied the crater of its lake and closed the mountain to skiers.

Mount Ruapehu
2,797 m (9,176 ft)

Mount Ngauruhoe
2,290 m (7,513 ft)

Mount Tongariro
1,968 m (6,457 ft)

Lake Rotaira

Turangi

Lake Taupo

Taupo

Tongariro River

Hamilton

Waikato River

Mount Tauhara
1,968 m (6,457 ft)

0 kilometres 25
0 miles 25

## New Zealand's Main Volcanic Types

There are three major types of volcano in New Zealand: volcanic fields, such as Auckland, where each eruption builds a single small volcano at a different place; cone volcanoes, where a succession of eruptions occur close to a vent to form a large cone, which is the volcano itself; and caldera volcanoes, where eruptions are often so large that the ground surface collapses into the hole left behind. The Taupo Volcanic Zone contains three frequently active cone volcanoes (Ruapehu, Ngauruhoe and White Island) and the two most productive caldera in the world (Taupo and Tarawera). Mount Ngauruhoe is the vent for the adjacent Mount Tongariro.

Slightly concave sides

Vent

Cinder

Fine ash

**Cone Volcano**

Caldera (crater)

Old cone

New cone

Ash

**Caldera Volcano**

**Wairakei Geothermal Power Station**
Almost 60 bores tap a vast underground water system, naturally heated by very hot rocks, to produce commercial quantities of steam.

**Locator Map**

**Pohutu Geyser**
One of only 12 geysers in New Zealand, Pohutu Geyser thunders to a height of more than 30 m (98 ft) *(see pp142–3)*.

**White Island**
This is an excellent active volcano to visit, by boat or by helicopter, because of its intense thermal activity *(see p134)*.

Lake Rotoiti

**Tauranga**

Lake Rotorua

**Rotorua**

*Bay of Plenty*

**Whakatane**

Lake Trawera

*Rangitaiki River*

**Taupo Volcanic Zone**
The area from White Island to Ruapehu is by far the most frequently active of the North Island's five volcanic areas. Apart from its volcanoes, it has the greatest variety of volcanic features – geysers, cauldons, mineral pools, mud pools, silica terraces, lakes, rivers and waterfalls – making it one of New Zealand's most fascinating tourist destinations.

**Wai-o-tapu**
The bubbling, hissing Champagne Pool, with its beautiful ochre-coloured petrified edge, is one of the many colourful attractions at Wai-o-tapu *(see p144)*.

**Mount Tarawera**
In a volcanic explosion in 1886, a 6-km (4-mile) long, 250-m (820-ft) deep chasm was formed and the nearby Pink and White Terraces were buried *(see p141)*.

# AUCKLAND

Every third New Zealander lives in the Auckland region, and the city, with its 1.4 million inhabitants, continues to expand faster than any other part of the country. Its population has increased by 20 per cent since 1991, almost double the national rate. Auckland is the place to enjoy city life, but quiet beaches and bush tracks are within an hour's drive of the central business district.

Maori had settled in the Auckland area as early as 1350. Tribal wars and epidemics brought about the destruction of their settlements, and the area was almost deserted when European settlers arrived in 1840. Because of its central position, good harbour and fine soil, the site was chosen as New Zealand's capital, to replace Russell in the north, after the signing of the Treaty of Waitangi in 1840 (see pp52–3). However, in 1865 the capital moved south to Wellington.

Although Auckland was initially not a prosperous settlement, a gold rush in the Coromandel region and increased agricultural production in the late 19th century helped to develop it into what it is today – the largest and fastest growing city in New Zealand. The inner city has become more vibrant since the mid-

1990s, due to the trend among some Aucklanders to trade in the traditional suburban villa for an inner-city apartment. Places such as Vulcan Lane, Viaduct Basin, Parnell and Ponsonby have become gathering points with cafés, bistros and up-market restaurants. The retail trade and performing arts have reaped the benefits of this migration.

Auckland is also attractive to New Zealand's Pacific Island neighbours and it now is the largest Polynesian city in the world. With Europeans, Maori, Polynesians and Asians complementing one another, the city's cultural diversity gives it a very cosmopolitan atmosphere. This is reflected in the variety of ethnic shops and restaurants, and can be observed at the local markets, such as those in Otara and Avondale.

Surfing at Piha, on the coast west of Auckland

◀ The illuminated Auckland Sky Tower at sunset

# Exploring Auckland

Although the Auckland region is spread over more than 1,000 sq km (390 sq miles), many of its inner-city attractions are clustered near the waterfront and around the city's oldest parks. Panoramic views of the city, harbour and outer islands can be enjoyed from a number of extinct volcanic peaks, such as One Tree Hill *(see p90)*, and from the observation decks and restaurants of Sky Tower, the city's most distinctive landmark *(see p79)*. Queen Street, long known as Auckland's "golden mile", is a major business, entertainment and shopping area, complemented by Ponsonby, Parnell and Newmarket on the fringes of the city. Water is an important part of Auckland's magic, and no visit is complete without a trip to Rangitoto or one of the other islands in the Hauraki Gulf *(see pp92–3)*.

Yachts moored at Westhaven Marina, Auckland *(see p76)*

## Sights at a Glance

1. Waitemata Harbour
2. Auckland Harbour Bridge
3. Westhaven Marina
4. Viaduct Harbour
5. Voyager New Zealand Maritime Museum
6. Ferry Building
7. Britomart Transport Centre
8. Old Customhouse
9. SKYCITY Auckland
10. Aotea Square and Aotea Centre at THE EDGE
11. Auckland Town Hall
12. Sky Tower
13. Old Government House
14. Old Arts Building and Clock Tower
15. Auckland Art Gallery
16. Auckland Domain and Winter Gardens
17. Auckland War Memorial Museum

**For keys to symbols** *see back flap*

0 metres          500
0 yards           500

## Getting Around

Auckland's city centre is compact and most places of interest are within walking distance. Alternatively, visitors can take the Auckland Explorer Bus, which leaves the Ferry Building every 30 minutes from 9am (hourly from 10am in winter) and stops at 14 tourist destinations. The tour includes taped commentary in various languages. For drivers, good motorways and internal roads link the northern, southern and western suburbs, which are also serviced by buses. Regular ferry services take visitors to the islands in the Hauraki Gulf.

Rollerblading along Tamaki Drive
(see p86)

# Street-by-Street: The Waterfront

Excellent shops, historic buildings, top restaurants and bars, a superb view – Auckland's waterfront has something for everyone. Yet only 20 years ago, this area was of little interest to residents and visitors, and the inner city, traditionally reserved for offices, was almost deserted after dark. That trend has been reversed and downtown Auckland is now a hive of activity. New apartments, many on the water's edge and others in garden environments, along with numerous trendy bars and restaurants, have made the waterfront a prime living and entertainment area.

**Old Customhouse**
Formerly part of the city's financial district, this 1889 building houses a duty-free store (*see pp77, 94*).

**Britomart Transport Centre**
Auckland's public transport hub is housed in the refurbished Chief Post Office building.

**★ Ferry Building**
At the Ferry Building, visitors can buy tickets for ferries and harbour cruises or dine at its popular ground-floor restaurant (*see p77*).

**Princes Wharf**, the departure point for overseas cruises, also attracts visitors to its restaurants and bars.

**Boat Services**
A variety of harbour cruises and ferry services to Devonport and the Hauraki Gulf islands operate from the back of the Ferry Building.

CUSTOMS STREET EAST

ALBERT ST

QUAY STREET

LOWER

QUAY STREET

QUEEN'S WHARF

WAITEMATA HARBOUR

**Locator Map**

0 metres 100
0 yards 100

## America's Cup

Viaduct Harbour was the home base for the yachts that participated in the 1999–2000 and 2002–2003 America's Cup. New Zealand successfully defended the cup it took off the Young America (USA) team led by Dennis Connor in 1995. In the 2002–2003 event nine challengers took on Team New Zealand and these syndicates came from all over the world, including France, Italy, Sweden, Switzerland, England and the United States. The history of the cup goes back to the 1850s, but the intense emotion surrounding the challenge still remains.

New Zealand's *Black Magic* defeating its Italian challenger in the America's Cup 2000 final

**Tepid Baths**
Built in 1914 and refurbished, the baths now house modern aquatic and fitness facilities.

**Viaduct Harbour**
This former industrial area was developed as an entertainment precinct for the 1999–2000 America's Cup *(see p76)*.

FANSHAWE STREET

STURDEE STREET

HOBSON STREET

MARKET LANE

MARKET PLACE

PAKENHAM STREET

CUSTOMS STREET WEST

VIADUCT HARBOUR

EASTERN VIADUCT

HOBSON
WEST
MARINA

★ **Voyager New Zealand Maritime Museum**
The museum's many fascinating exhibits include historic vessels that take visitors out onto the harbour *(see p77)*.

**Key**

— Suggested route

A forest of masts at Westhaven Marina, viewed from the Auckland Harbour Bridge

# ❶ Waitemata Harbour

This sparkling harbour, with the green volcanic cone of Rangitoto Island in the background, is one of Auckland's most cherished sights. Not only does the harbour add to the city's scenic beauty, it also forms a natural barrier between the central business district and the populous North Shore. Ferries and cruise boats, as well as commercial ships, use the harbour daily.

# ❷ Auckland Harbour Bridge

State Hwy 1.

In the late 19th century, ferries began taking passengers across the water from Auckland City to the north. In 1959, the Auckland Harbour Bridge was built and ten years later, the 43-m (141-ft) high steel bridge was widened, increasing the number of lanes from four to eight. Peak hour traffic across the 1,020-m (3,350-ft) bridge is slow. Concrete barriers marking the traffic lanes are shifted twice daily by a custom-built machine to accommodate the morning flow into the city and the late afternoon return to the northern suburbs. An electronic traffic light system at both ends of the bridge clearly indicates which lanes are accessible to traffic. Despite the traffic jams, the Harbour Bridge offers some of the best views in the city.

The bridge does not only link two large areas of Auckland; State Highway 1 is also the main arterial route for northbound traffic. Southbound travellers driving across the bridge will notice a forest of masts on their left.

# ❸ Westhaven Marina

Westhaven Drive.

Westhaven Marina reflects Aucklanders' passion for yachting. Operating for more than 70 years, it is one of the largest marinas in the southern hemisphere, accommodating 1,980 vessels. Among the facilities are Pier Z (the home of several major charter boat companies), launching ramps for trailer craft and a mast gantry. The premises of prominent yacht clubs are on the northern side of the marina.

# ❹ Viaduct Harbour

Cnr Halsey St and Viaduct Harbour.

Largely a legacy from the 1999–2000 America's Cup, the Viaduct Harbour's up-market apartments, shops and restaurants overlook a marina with mooring facilities for 150 yachts. The harbour is part of an extensive redevelopment of Auckland's waterfront, following the trend in cities such as Sydney, London and San Francisco, and the precinct has a vibrant atmosphere and a variety of restaurants. The Viaduct Events Centre is the focus for large conventions and trade shows, such as New Zealand Fashion Week.

Café at Viaduct Harbour

## ❺ Voyager New Zealand Maritime Museum

Cnr Quay & Hobson sts. **Tel** (09) 373 0800. **Open** daily. **Closed** 25 Dec.

🏛️ ♿ 🎦 🚫 💻 📷

ⓦ **maritimemuseum.co.nz**

Boats have played a pivotal role in New Zealand's history, from those of the early Polynesian navigators who steered their canoes towards the country *(see pp50–1)*, to the whalers who made Russell *(see p106)* the centre of the whaling industry in the 1840s, and the thousands of immigrants who arrived in the 19th and 20th centuries. These aspects of the country's maritime past are highlighted in the museum. In Maori, the museum is called Te Huiteananui-a-Tangaroa, "the legendary house belonging to Tangaroa", god of the sea.

Even those with a limited interest in boats will enjoy the innovative exhibition galleries. One room is fitted out as a ship's interior, complete with a gently swaying floor and appropriate creaking noises. Several of the historic vessels berthed outside the museum take visitors for harbour trips.

Exhibit at the Voyager New Zealand Maritime Museum

## ❻ Ferry Building

Quay St. 🚢 **Open** daily. 🚫 💻

This 1912 Edwardian baroque building is the focal point for commuter ferries. A 10-minute ferry ride to Devonport leaves here, as do boats to Waiheke Island *(see p92)*. Designed by Alex Wiseman, the ornate building is made of sandstone

The Ferry Building, a gateway to the harbour

and brick, with a base of Coromandel granite and is registered with the Historic Places Trust. Not just a transport centre, it is also home to a number of cafés and restaurants with stunning harbour views.

## ❼ Britomart Transport Centre

Queen St.

The Britomart Transport Centre brings together Auckland's train, bus and ferry services in a single complex. The centre was the focus of an urban renewal project completed in 2009, which included the redevelopment of surrounding streets, creating public spaces and Taku Tai Plaza, a precinct of shops and restaurants.

## ❽ Old Customhouse

Cnr Albert & Customs sts.
**Open** daily. 📷

The old Customhouse replaces a building that was burned down in the 1880s. Designed by Thomas Mahoney, the 1889 French Renaissance-style building is said to have been modelled on the present Selfridge's department store in Oxford Street, London. It features intricate plaster-work and kauri joinery.

One of the oldest commercial buildings in the city, the Old Customhouse used to house the Customs Department, Audit Inspector, Sheep Inspector and Native Land Court. It is now home to the city's largest duty-free shop *(see p94)*.

### City of Sails

Auckland is purported to have the greatest number of pleasure boats per capita of any city in the world. The city's temperate climate also means that, on average, these are used more intensively than boats in Europe or on the east coast of America. Yachting has been a popular pastime in Auckland since the 1840s, when the first sailing regattas were held on Waitemata Harbour. Safe harbours and the nearby scenic islands make sailing attractive to overseas visitors as well. Charter company charges depend on the size of the yacht, the time of the year and whether a skipper is hired. The highlight of the nautical year is the Auckland Anniversary Regatta *(see p45)*.

Yacht racing on Waitemata Harbour

Casino in the SKYCITY complex

## ❾ SKYCITY Auckland

Cnr Victoria & Federal sts.
**Tel** 0800 759 2489, (09) 363 6000.
**Open** daily. ♿ 🚻 🖥 📷
**w** skycityauckland.co.nz

Lucky punters can win luxury cars at SKYCITY Auckland, New Zealand's biggest casino. Open 24 hours a day, 7 days a week, the complex offers a wide variety of entertainment and leisure options. More than 1,600 gaming machines feature all the latest stepper reel, video reel, poker and keno games offering cash prizes. The complex boasts 4 casinos and over 100 gaming tables with traditional games such as Caribbean stud poker, craps, blackjack, baccarat, roulette and money wheel. Chinese favourites include tai sai, played with three dice in a clear glass dome, and pai gow, played with 32 domino pieces.

Entertainment at SKYCITY is not limited to gaming. The complex is best known for the country's tallest structure, the Sky Tower, which has viewing levels and restaurants *(see p79)*. There are also two hotels, the four-star SKYCITY Hotel (see p302), with 306 rooms and 38 suites, and the five-star Grand Hotel, which has 316 guest rooms and a spa. In addition, there are bars, cafés, restaurants, conference facilities, and a 700-seat theatre.

## ❿ Aotea Square and Aotea Centre at THE EDGE

Queen St. **Tel** (09) 309 2677.
**w** the-edge.co.nz

In the late 1980s, several New Zealand souvenir shops began stocking a postcard that was entirely black except for a small heading, "Night Life in New Zealand". Things have since changed. Built in 1990, the Aotea Centre was designed by New Zealand architect Ewen Wainscott and is a hub of vibrant nightlife. On its opening night, the centre featured New Zealand-born Dame Kiri Te Kanawa, the world-renowned opera singer. It is a venue for dance, opera, classical music, theatre and shows. It is also used for festivals, such as the Aotearoa Hip Hop Summit.

Aotea Square, in front of the centre, houses a popular market as well as outdoor festivals. The wooden *waharoa* (gateway) at its entrance was created by Maori artist Selwyn Muru. The square is flanked on one side by the Force Entertainment Centre, which includes a 460-seat Imax (widescreen) Cinema *(see p97)*, a games centre, cafés and shops. The Auckland Town Hall is situated on the other side of the square.

Collectively, the locations bordering Aotea Square – the Town Hall, Aotea Centre and Force Entertainment Centre – are known as THE EDGE and promote performing arts, culture and entertainment.

## ⓫ Auckland Town Hall

Queen St. **Tel** (09) 309 2677.
**Open** daily. **Closed** public hols. ♿

The wedge-shaped Edwardian Town Hall, built in 1911, is Auckland's prime historic building. It has been used extensively as an administrative and political centre, as well as a cultural venue. During work to re-store it to its original design, the building was gutted (non-original materials were removed) and strengthened structurally.

The Concert Chamber, Council Chamber and main street foyer were meticulously restored, a process which included using vintage glass to reconstruct windows that had disappeared over the years. The Great Hall, an excellent concert facility, is a replica of the Neues Gewandhaus in Leipzig, Germany, which was destroyed by Allied bombing during World War II.

Auckland Town Hall

# ⑫ Sky Tower

Opened in August 1997, Auckland's 328-m (1,076-ft) Sky Tower, a splendid tourist, broadcasting and telecommunications facility, has taken over from Sydney's AMP Tower as the tallest tower in the southern hemisphere. Part of SKYCITY Auckland, the tower is visited by almost one million people a year. Its three observation levels offer 82-km (50-mile) views while the tower's SkyJump and 360° SkyWalk provide the ultimate in adrenaline adventure.

**Observation Levels**
Visitors enjoy fantastic views of the city of Auckland and its environs from the tower's indoor observation levels.

**The 93-m (305-ft)** high spire weighs 150 tonnes and is the main tele-communications and broadcasting mast in the region.

**The sky deck** offers 360-degree views through seamless glass, and is the country's highest public viewing area.

**Orbit Revolving Restaurant** makes a full revolution every 60 minutes.

**SkyJump** is a 192-m (630-ft) cable controlled base jump.

**The floors** above and below the centre pod house telecommunications facilities.

**The main observation level** offers free multilingual audio guides, live weather forecasts and touch-screen computers.

**The lower observation level** contains the Sky Lounge Café.

**The structure** of the tower has been designed to withstand winds gusting to 200 km/h (125 mph) and earthquakes measuring 8.0 on the Richter Scale.

**Entrance to Tower**
Entry to Sky Tower's lifts is through an underground gallery.

Concrete legs

Paved street level

Lift

Entrance level

**The Sky Tower at Night**
The Sky Tower is an even more visible landmark at night. At various times of year it is lit in different colours to mark a range of activities and celebrations.

Old Government House, New Zealand's first wooden mansion

# ⑬ Old Government House

Cnr Waterloo Quadrant and Princes St. **Closed** to public.

The classical Old Government House was the seat of government until 1865 when the capital was moved to Wellington. It was also the residence of New Zealand's governor-general until 1969. Royalty used to stay here, and Queen Elizabeth II broadcast her Christmas speech from upstairs in 1953. It is now a part of the University of Auckland, housing the staff common room, council reception suite and apartments for visiting academics.

Located within walking distance of the central business district, Old Government House, designed by William Mason and completed in 1856, appears from a distance to be made of stone. Like its British prefabricated predecessor,

however, it is built from wood. A big coral tree and a Norfolk pine at the southern edge of the lawn are said to have been planted by Sir George Grey during his second term as governor from 1861 to 1867.

# ⑭ Old Arts Building and Clock Tower

Princes St. **Closed** to public.

Also part of the university buildings, the Old Arts Building and Clock Tower face Albert Park, a summer gathering place for students. Designed by Chicago-trained architect R A Lippincott, it was completed in 1926. Lippincott's brother-in-law, Walter Burley Griffin, was the designer of Canberra in Australia. The clock tower that crowns the building was inspired by the Tom Tower of Christ Church in Oxford, England, and has come to symbolize the university. The building's octagonal interior is vaulted and galleried with a mosaic floor and piers. A major reconstruction was undertaken between 1985 and 1988, which won an Institute of Architects award.

From the rear of the Old Arts Building, the Barracks Wall runs for 85 m (280 ft) to the back of the Old Choral Hall. Built in 1847, it is the only remnant of the wall which enclosed an area, including Albert Park, where British troops were stationed until 1870. The basalt stone wall was quarried from the slope of Mount Eden, now known as Eden Garden.

# ⑮ Auckland Art Gallery

Cnr Wellesley & Kitchener sts. **Tel** (09) 307 7700. **Open** daily. **Closed** 25 December, Good Friday. some exhibits. **W** **aucklandartgallery.govt.nz**

Visitors interested in art should add the Auckland Art Gallery (Toi o Tamaki) to their itinerary. Designing the 1887 French Renaissance-style building must have been a challenge to the architectural firm of Grainger and D'Ebro, as it occupies a rising corner site. The gallery originally housed civic offices and the public library, but today it is solely a gallery, mainly devoted to showcasing the development of New Zealand art. The collection of around 12,500 works includes international as well as national art. The New Zealand collection contains works from many of the nation's most prominent artists, including Frances Hodgkins, Colin McCahon and Ralph Hotere. The Mackelvie Collection, named after a self-made man who lived in Auckland between 1865 and 1871, is mainly of non-New Zealand paintings, as is the Grey Collection.

The New Gallery, across the road from the Auckland Art Gallery, was a former telephone exchange. It focuses on contemporary art.

A multi-million dollar development next door to the original gallery building has created a space where the gallery can compete with renowned galleries, playing host to international artists.

University of Auckland's Old Arts Building and Clock Tower

Entrance to the New Gallery, Auckland Art Gallery

## ⑯ Auckland Domain and Winter Gardens

Auckland Domain: **Open** daily.
Winter Gardens: **Open** daily.
📷 (War Memorial Museum).

The Sky City Starlight Symphony playing at the Auckland Domain

Central Auckland has been built around a number of extinct volcanoes, including 14 volcanic cones, many of which are now parks. The oldest park is the Auckland Domain, situated within walking distance of both the city centre and the Parnell area. Tuff rings created by volcanic activity thousands of years ago can still be seen in its contours.

Land for the city's 1.35-sq-km (0.50-sq-mile) park was set aside in 1840, in the early years of European settlement. In 1940, a carved Maori memorial palisade was installed around a totara tree on Pukekaroa knoll. This enclosure commemorates Maori leader Potatu Te Whero Whero, who made peace with the neighbouring tribes on the site a hundred years earlier.

Nearby is a sports field where the tuff rings form a natural amphitheatre. The field is used for free outdoor concerts over the summer that attract large crowds.

The large, shady Auckland Domain is also a popular place with walkers and picnickers. Several of the large trees in the park were seedlings from a nursery set up in 1841 to grow and distribute European plants and trees. The formal gardens feature many sculptures. The best known are the three bronze sculptures in the free-form pond. The central, male figure represents Auckland and the two females represent wisdom and fertility of the soil.

**Statue at the Winter Gardens**

The Winter Gardens, a legacy from the Auckland Exhibition of 1913, consist of two glasshouses joined by a courtyard that contains a large water lily and lotus pool. The dome-roofed areas contain a wide variety of plants. The scoria quarry behind the Winter Gardens has been converted into a fernery. Ferns are a dominant feature of the New Zealand landscape and there are more than 100 varieties in the fernery. The gardens are a popular venue for wedding and other photography.

The Domain's best-known structure is the Auckland War Memorial Museum *(see pp82–3)*. Made of reinforced concrete and faced with Portland stone, the museum has bronze detailing. The façade contains plaques that list the battles of World War I, while at the rear of the building, added by RF and M K Draffin in 1960, there are lists of World War II battles.

One of the two glasshouses at the Winter Gardens

# ⑰ Auckland War Memorial Museum

Built in 1929 to commemorate the end of World War I, in which 16,697 New Zealanders died, the museum has a Neo-Classical façade that evokes the Greek temples that many servicemen saw from the decks of warships in the Mediterranean. The design of the cenotaph in front of the museum is based on newsreel footage, shown at the beginning of movies in the 1920s, of the tomb of the unknown soldier in London. Besides providing visitors with an introduction to New Zealand's history, people and landscape, the museum also contains a renowned collection of Maori treasures and Pacific artifacts and holds Maori cultural performances.

Aerial view of the museum, located in the Auckland Domain

**Museum Lobby**
The lobby features tall columns reminiscent of the Parthenon in Greece. Light filters through the stained-glass ceiling above the lobby.

**"Origins"** features the skeletons of extinct animals, such as dinosaurs and moa, many of which were discovered in caves around the country.

Garden

Ground floor

**The museum entrance** evokes the temples of Greece.

**Key to Floorplan**

- ▢ Natural History Galleries
- ▢ Design & Decorative Arts
- ▢ Exhibition Hall
- ▢ Library
- ▢ Maori and Pacific
- ▢ Other exhibits
- ▢ Discovery Centres
- ▢ War exhibits

★ **Maori Treasures**
This gallery showcases a superb collection of Maori artifacts, such as the *waka* (canoe) in the foreground and a traditional carved meeting house.

### Discovery Centres

The two Discovery Centres, "Weird and Wonderful" and "Treasures and Tales", are colourful, interactive areas where children can learn about and explore the natural world.

Top Floor

Auditorium

### "Scars on the Heart"

contains exhibits depicting the two World Wars, including a re-creation of a World War I front trench.

Library

First Floor

### "Oceans"

helps visitors discover marine life with a rock pool and replicas of a beach and the Poor Knights Islands marine reserve.

**Spitfire Gallery**
This area features early fighter planes. A high percentage of Royal Air Force pilots during World War II came from New Zealand, including its Supreme Commander, Keith Park.

### ★ World War I Sanctuary

The stained-glass ceiling above the entrance lobby shows the coat of arms of all British dominions and colonies during World War I. On the balcony are badges of the units, regiments and corps in which New Zealanders served.

## Museum Guide

*The museum's collection is housed on three levels. The ground level is dedicated to the people of New Zealand, both of Maori and European descent, and the Pacific region. The first level provides information on the land and its natural history, while the top level focuses on New Zealand at war and how these experiences have forged the country's identity. The Library is open 1–5pm Mon–Fri (10am–5pm Sat), and offers a dynamic range of resources. The Atrium houses exhibition halls and shops.*

# Further Afield

Beyond central Auckland, visitors are offered a range of places to visit and a variety of things to do. Harbours, beaches and islands are prime attractions, not only for their superb scenic views but also for sea sports, such as kayaking, surfing and sailing. The city is well known for its beautiful parks and gardens which provide peaceful retreats; some offer visitors a chance to walk through bush and wilderness. Families with young children will find Kelly Tarlton's Antarctic Encounter and Underwater World, Rainbow's End and the Auckland Zoo enjoyable. Across the harbour by a short ferry ride, Devonport makes for a pleasant outing for the day, with its many restaurants and art and crafts shops. Its naval history is also of interest.

A view of Auckland City from Tamaki Drive

## ❶ Tamaki Drive

Tamaki Drive, east of the city, shows Auckland at its best. The road crosses Hobson Bay and closely follows the water's edge past Okahu Bay, Mission Bay and St Heliers Bay. The views across Waitemata Harbour towards Rangitoto Island and Devonport are stunning and should not be missed.

Many of the city's most prestigious homes are located on the slopes behind Tamaki Drive. Many tourist buses make a small detour to go through nearby Paritai Drive, which is the most expensive real estate in Auckland. Sandy beaches, such as the one at Mission Bay, are a major attraction along Tamaki Drive. These lovely beaches serve as a base for family outings, swimmers and sunbathers.

Mission Bay got its name from the Melanesian Mission House. Built in 1859, the house was part of Bishop Selwyn's Mission School. When the school was transferred to Norfolk Island in 1867, the house was used for different purposes. It is now an up-market restaurant. Tamaki Drive ends at St Heliers Bay. Instead of turning right

## Sights at a Glance

### Key

Central Auckland
Motorway
State highway
Other road
Airport

Cyclists enjoying the sun on Tamaki Drive

*For hotels and restaurants in this region see pp302–7 and pp314–25*

Rangitoto Island, dominating Auckland's harbour horizon

into St Heliers Bay Road, it is worthwhile to continue along Cliff Road, leading to Ladies Bay. The viewing platform at the top of the cliff offers a superb panorama of the Hauraki Gulf. Directly below the platform, but far enough from viewers not to be intrusive, is one of New Zealand's few nudist beaches. At other beaches along Tamaki Drive, nudity is prohibited.

**Learning to windsurf**

### ❷ Savage Memorial Park

Located off Tamaki Drive, the Savage Memorial Park was named after New Zealand's first Labour prime minister, Michael Joseph Savage (1871–1940). The gardens, which have formal arrangements, also contain concrete fortifications that date from World War II.

The area occupied by the gardens was originally a historic Maori *pa*, and its shoreline was renowned for its plentiful supply of mussels. Originally named

Tokapurewha, Maori for "mussel rocks", the area has since been renamed Bastion Point.

It is best known for a Maori protest staged in 1977 after the government had razed a local Maori village to develop Bastion Point as a prime residential zone. A 506-day occupation was organized to protest against the appropriation of the site, followed by ten years of litigation. In 1990, the land was finally returned to the Ngati Whatua tribe. The nearby 900-sq-m (9,690-sq-ft) Orakei Marae is the tribe's meeting house. Smaller ones can be found around the Kaipara Harbour and at Helensville, on the North Shore.

### ❸ Kelly Tarlton's Antarctic Encounter and Underwater World

23 Tamaki Drive. **Tel** (09) 528 0603 or 0800 805 050. 🚌 Downtown Centre, 757, 767, 769. **Open** daily. 🚫 📷 no flash. ♿ 📷 Antarctic Encounter.

Tamaki Drive's best-known tourist attraction is Kelly Tarlton's Underwater World and Antarctic Encounter. Visitors ride on a moving walkway through a Plexiglas tunnel inside a tank, with fish swimming around the sides. The tunnel winds past two marine aquariums, one devoted to reef fish and the other to sharks and stingrays. The Antarctic Encounter features a replica of the Cape Evans 1910 hut of South Pole explorer Robert F Scott (1868–1912), complete with ice and winds. A highlight is a ride in a heated Snow Cat through a typical subantarctic landscape, past a penguin colony, and under the ice to a subantarctic aquarium.

Riding through the Plexiglas tube at Kelly Tarlton's Underwater World

## ❹ Museum of Transport and Technology

Great North Rd, Western Springs.
📷 Customs St, 45. **Tel** (09) 815 5800,
0800 668 286. **Open** daily. **Closed** 25
Dec. 🅿 ♿ 📷 🅦 **motat.org.nz**

The Museum of Transport and Technology (MOTAT) has a collection of about 300,000 items, 20 per cent of which can be seen in various buildings and halls on two sites within walking distance of Auckland Zoo. Exhibits vary from dental equipment and underwear to 19th-century houses and a pumphouse. An interactive gallery for under-5s offers hands-on play with pulleys, levers, diggers and wheelbarrows.

The focal point is a collection of 30 rare and historic aircraft. These include a replica of a home-made plane by New Zealander Richard Pearse, believed by many to have preceded the Wright brothers in being the first person to fly *(see p252)*. Also of interest is the Solent flying boat ZK-AMO *Aranui*, a luxurious aircraft, the only one in the world of its kind, that flew around the South Pacific from 1949 until 1960. An electric tram runs about every 20 minutes from the entrance of MOTAT to the zoo gates.

Early aircraft at the Museum of Transport and Technology

## ❺ Auckland Zoo

Motions Rd, Western Springs. 📷
Customs St, 45. **Tel** (09) 360 3800.
**Open** daily. **Closed** 25 Dec. 🅿 ♿
📷 📷 📷 🅦 **aucklandzoo.co.nz**

New Zealand's isolated geographical position means that its fauna has developed differently from that of most countries. A lack of predators, for example, has resulted in many flightless birds. With the exception of bats, there are no native mammals. There is no better place to learn about the country's varied and unusual wildlife than at Auckland Zoo. Established as a small private menagerie in 1912, the zoo opened in its current location in 1922. It houses more than 700 animals covering 117 species, including saddlebacks, tui, kaka and kakariki, besides the nocturnal kiwi.

The zoo's population, which is not limited to native animals, is presented in natural settings. Primates such as squirrel monkeys and macaques can be seen at close range in a rainforest. Zebras and giraffes roam on an African savanna with Zulu huts and inter-connected habitats. A wetlands environment features baboons as well as hippopotamuses.

## ❻ One Tree Hill

Manukau Rd.

One Tree Hill (Maungakiekie), a dormant volcanic cone and once the site of the largest prehistoric Maori settlement in the region, was named after the solitary tree which was planted on its summit in 1640. Since then, a succession of single trees have stood on the summit. The last, a Monterey

One Tree Hill (Maungakiekie), formerly the site of a large Maori fortification

pine, was removed in October 2001 by city council workers as it was unstable (its replacement is still the subject of debate). Its most famous predecessor was a native totara tree, cut down in 1852 by a party of work-men angry at the non-arrival of rations.

Surrounding the hill is Cornwall Park, named after the Duke and Duchess of Cornwall, and donated to the city by Sir John Campbell during their royal tour in 1901.

**Acacia Cottage**, Auckland's oldest surviving wooden building, was built in 1841 by Sir John Campbell. It was relocated in 1920 from Shortland Street to Cornwall Park, where Sir John once had a farm.

Near the entrance to the park, is the **Stardome Observatory**. It has telescopes for viewing the stars, and aspects of space and astronomy are shown at the Stardome Planetarium.

**🎦 Acacia Cottage**
Cornwall Park. **Tel** (09) 630 8485. **Open** 10am–4pm daily. **Closed** public hols. 🚌 302, 304, 305.

**🏛 Stardome Observatory**
One Tree Hill Domain (best accessed from Mortimer Pass). **Tel** (09) 624 1246. **Open** daily. **Closed** public hols. 🅿 ♿ ✉ Stardome and telescopes. 📷 🔲 stardome.org.nz

Acacia Cottage, in Cornwall Park

# 🔴 Highwic House

40 Gillies Ave, Epsom. 🚌 Link bus. **Tel** (09) 524 5729. **Open** Wed–Sun. **Closed** Good Fri, 25 Dec. 📷

Built in 1862, Highwic was the home of Alfred Buckland, a stock and station owner. The house was built in stages, with the front part showing more

Water ride at Rainbow's End

detail than the rest. The house, with its elaborate decoration and diamond pane windows, is an example of Carpenter Gothic Revival architecture. The extensive landscaped gardens are also worth a visit.

# 🔴 Auckland Regional Botanic Gardens

Hill Rd, Manukau City. **Tel** (09) 267 1457. **Open** daily. ♿ 📷 🔲 🅦 aucklandbotanicgardens.co.nz

These gardens, which sprawl over 640 sq km (250 sq miles), contain more than 10,000 species of New Zealand native and introduced plants, as well as a large collection of ornamental plants. Guided walks are held regularly. There is an award-winning visitor centre where the Ellerslie Flower Show is held each year.

# 🔴 Rainbow's End

Cnr Great South & Wiri Station rds, Manukau City. 🚌 Central Auckland, 471, 472. **Tel** (09) 262 2030. **Open** daily. **Closed** 25 Dec. 📷 🅦 🔲 📷 🅦 rainbowsend.co.nz

Lots of rides and entertainment are available at this amusement park, which is New Zealand's largest. The most popular attraction is a roller coaster that takes you up more than 30 m (98 ft) in the air, hurls you down through a complete loop, round a corner and through a double corkscrew. Other attractions include the Motion Master Virtual Theatre, featuring dinosaurs, an enchanted forest ride, a minigolf course, family go-karts, water rides and the Goldrush, which takes you on a thrilling ride through an abandoned gold mine in a runaway mining cart. Kidz Kingdom provides indoor amusements for small children.

## Sir John Logan Campbell

Sir John Logan Campbell (1817–1912) was one of New Zealand's pioneering entrepreneurs. On 21 December 1840, he set up a tent at the bottom of Shortland Street that served as Auckland's first shop. When he died at the age of 95, he was the city's most prominent businessman. Apart from trading and farming, he was involved in shipping, brewing, timber, the export of kauri gum, flax and manganese, newspaper publishing and banking. He was also a member of New Zealand's parliament, captain of the militia, and a founding member of the Mechanics Institute and the Northern Club. Today, "the father of Auckland" is best remembered for donating his farm, Cornwall Park (*see p89*), to the city.

Totem pole at the entrance to the Arataki Visitors Centre

# ⑩ Titirangi

**Road map** E2. ⚲ 3,400. ▦

Situated to the west of Auckland city, the small settlement of Titirangi offers superb views of the Waitakere Ranges and the 390-sq-km (150-sq-mile) Manukau Harbour to the south. The village, which is home to a number of artists and writers, has a reputation for being trendy. Its main street is lined with cafés and restaurants. The main landmark is the Spanish-style Lopdell House, opened in 1930, which houses an art gallery, small theatre and restaurant. The square in front of the nearby library is transformed into an art and crafts market on the last Sunday of the month from 9am to noon.

Titirangi is the gateway to the Auckland Centennial Memorial Park in the Waitakere Ranges. Formed by volcanic action about 1.7 million years ago, the park has about 250 km suitable for people of all levels of fitness. It attracts over two million visitors a year.

The **Arataki Visitors Centre**, 5 km (3 miles) beyond Titirangi, has well-organized displays on the area's logging history and attractions, and also stocks detailed maps of the ranges, books, audio tapes and posters. Large timber decks around the building offer good views of the harbour. Across the road from the centre is the Arataki Nature Trail, a self-guided walk, which provides a good introduction to native plants and wildlife.

**ℹ Arataki Visitors Centre**
Scenic Drive. **Tel** (09) 817 0077.
**Open** daily. **Closed** 25 Dec.

# ⑪ Piha

**Road map** E2. ⚲ 2,500. ▦

Prized by locals but not well known to tourists, Auckland's rugged, wind-swept west coast beaches are within easy reach of Auckland and are well worth visiting. Because they are exposed to the Tasman Sea, however, swimmers and surfers need to exercise care as the currents can be treacherous and conditions often change rapidly.

Piha is the most popular of the beaches because of its heavy surf. It is also the most gentrified. Here, many "baches", New Zealand's traditional ramshackle holiday homes, have made way for architect designed mansions. The Piha Surf Life Saving Club serves as a community centre over the summer.

**Environs**
The bleakest, yet perhaps grandest, stretch of coast is at **Whatipu**, south of Piha at the entrance to the Manukau Harbour. A sand bar visible from the beach partly blocks the harbour. It was here that the HMS *Orpheus* was shipwrecked on 7 February 1863. Of the 259 officers and crew of the 1,727-tonne corvette, only 70 survived.

Just south of Piha, **Karekare** has several idyllic picnic spots and a swimming hole at the base of a waterfall. Its beach achieved some fame as the location for the award-winning film *The Piano*.

To the north of Piha is **Bethells Beach**, inhabited by Maoris for several centuries; some 75 sites have been recorded here by archaeologists. Ihumoana Island, just off the beach, is the area's best-preserved island *pa*. Although not as spectacular as Cape Kidnappers (*see p153*), a headland at **Muriwai Beach**, beyond Bethells, is home to a colony of around 2,000 Australasian gannets, which originally nested on offshore Motutara Island. Barriers and viewing platforms allow visitors to observe the birds without disturbing them. The best time to see the gannets is between December and March.

# ⑫ Henderson

**Road map** E2. ⚲ 4,600. ▦

The vineyards at Henderson, many dating back to the early 1900s, are an hour's drive from Auckland city. They have

View of Piha from the lookout at the top of the road

become a popular weekend destination for Aucklanders and visitors alike. Many of the wineries sell food, ranging from a snack to a complete meal, and offer free wine tastings.

Family-owned Babich Wines, founded in 1916, has a picnic and *pétanque* area overlooking its vineyards. The winery has a reputation for award-winning vintages, such as Babich Patriarch, but also produces inexpensive wines. New Zealand's second largest winery, Corbans Wine, established by Lebanese immigrants in 1902, is another popular destination, as is Montana Wines, which produces numerous varieties – half of the country's total output, making it the largest wine producer in New Zealand. Its Deutz Marlborough Cuveé, made under an arrangement with Champagne Deutz, won the 1998 Sparkling Wine of the Year award at the International Wine Challenge in London. Visitors can obtain details of Henderson's vineyards at the Auckland visitor centre.

Locally grown fruit and vegetables for sale at Kumeu

included in every wine safari. Specializing in regionally grown grapes, Kumeu River's Chardonnay has made the top 100 Wines of the World list of the United States *Wine Spectator* magazine five times. The House of Nobilo, with 4,000 tonnes of grapes crushed in 1998, is the country's fourth largest winery. It also sells wines from Selaks Wines, which it purchased in 1998. Soljans Estate Winery

features a pleasant picnic area and offers visitors tours. Its premium varieties include Chardonnay.

Matua Valley Wines produces a broad range of good quality wines. The winery also serves gourmet treats to accompany the wines. These may be enjoyed in the pleasant grounds, which have picnic and barbecue facilities, as well as a children's play area.

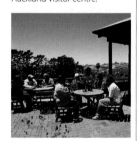

Outdoor eating area at Babich Wines in Henderson

## ⓭ Kumeu

**Road map** E2. 🚗 1,800. 🚌

Another popular weekend pursuit of Aucklanders is lunch at a vineyard restaurant followed by shopping for fresh fruit and vegetables from a roadside stall on the way home. At Kumeu, a wine as well as fruit growing district, where a high percentage of the people involved in the wineries and orchards are from Croatia, visitors are spoilt for choice. Kumeu River Wines should be

### Film Making In New Zealand

New Zealand's coastal scenery has not escaped the notice of location finders in the movie industry. The beach scenes in Jane Campion's *The Piano*, winner of the 1994 Palme d'Or at Cannes and Oscars for Best Original Screenplay and Best Supporting Actress, were shot at Karekare. Bethells Beach features in *Xena: Warrior Princess* and *Hercules: The Legendary Journeys*. Numerous television series, such as *Black Beauty*, movies and commercials have also been filmed along the New Zealand coast. International interest has spawned a burgeoning domestic film industry. Over 120 feature films have been produced in the country since 1940. Lee Tamahori's *Once Were Warriors* was released in 1994 in cinemas around the world. Local director Peter Jackson's Oscar-winning *Lord of The Rings* trilogy eclipsed all previous New Zealand motion pictures in terms of scale and budget.

Shooting a film on a New Zealand beach

Well-preserved Victorian buildings on Devonport's waterfront

# ⑭ Devonport

**Road map** E2. 🏔 18,000. 🚌 ⛴

In comparison to Auckland's less affluent southern and western (except Titirangi) quadrants, the eastern and northern quadrants are seen to be prosperous. Although over-simplified, this view is not a completely inaccurate one. The North Shore, the suburban area north of the Harbour Bridge, is relatively wealthy and blessed with a string of beaches that also function as launching pads for sailing boats and dinghies.

Devonport is a 10-minute ferry ride from Auckland's Ferry Building *(see p75)*. It is the only North Shore suburb with a distinctly historical flavour. With many of its villas found along the waterfront, a stroll along King Edward Parade provides an impression of the suburb's Victorian architecture, as well as views of Auckland's central business district across Waitemata Harbour. From Victoria Wharf, where the ferries arrive, it is a 5-minute walk to the cafés, restaurants and book shops of Victoria Road. Mount Victoria and North Head, both extinct volcanoes, are accessible by car or by walking and offer good views.

Devonport has a long military history. Its association with the Royal New Zealand Navy dates back to 1941 and there are approximately 2,200 staff currently stationed at the local base. Devonport's naval heritage can be viewed at the

Navy Museum which houses a collection of photographs, uniforms, weapons and other related memorabilia.

Further north, **Takapuna** has its own popular beach. Restaurants, cafés and shops are found along Hurstmere Road.

🏛 **Navy Museum**
64 King Edward Parade.
**Tel** (09) 445 5186. **Open** daily.
**Closed** Good Fri, 25 & 26 Dec. 🎟
donation. 🎧 on request. 📷

# ⑮ Orewa

**Road map** E2. 🏔 (including Hibiscus Coast) 28,000. 🚌 ℹ 214A Hibiscus Coast Hwy, (09) 426 0076.

Beach houses and motels line the main road through this small seaside town, 40 minutes' drive north of Auckland. Orewa's main attraction is its beach, a 3-km (2-mile) long stretch of sand. The beach is suitable for swimming, surfing and boating. Easterly winds from the sea also attract windsurfers.

## Environs

Just north of Orewa, a small road off State Highway 1 leads to **Puhoi**, New Zealand's earliest Bohemian settlement. A tiny calvary shrine beside the road leading to the settlement is a reminder of the settlers' background. The local pub also doubles as a museum of the pioneers of the area. The Church of St Peter and St Paul, built in 1881, features a Bohemian painting.

About 48 km (30 miles) north of Auckland, Waiwera is best known for its thermal resort, **Waiwera Infinity Hot Pools**. The complex has nine indoor and outdoor pools, spas, water slides, beauty therapies and picnic areas. The natural springs deliver up to 1 million litres (0.2 million gallons) of water per day.

🏊 **Waiwera Infinity Hot Pools**
State Hwy 1. **Tel** 0800 924 937.
**Open** daily. 🎟 📷 🖥 📷
🌐 waiwera.co.nz

# ⑯ Hauraki Gulf Islands

**Road map** E2. ⛴ ℹ Department of Conservation, 137 Quay St, Auckland, (09) 379 6476.
🌐 doc.govt.nz

The Hauraki Gulf Islands are among the most beautiful in the world. Some of the 65 islands are popular spots for recreational activities. Others, with their rare bird sanctuaries and unspoiled stands of native trees and plants, are protected for conservation. Waiheke is now home to many commuters, while Great Barrier and Kawau are preferred by those who

The beach at Orewa, popular with swimmers and windsurfers

Sir George Grey's historic home, Mansion House, on Kawau Island, Hauraki Gulf

enjoy a somewhat slower lifestyle. **Waiheke Island** has gained an "alternative" reputation because of its organic farms and artisans. Apart from its white sand beaches, its vineyards and olive groves are attractive to visitors.

Electricity on **Great Barrier Island**, the furthermost island in the Hauraki Gulf, is provided by windmills and diesel generators, while some refrigerators still use kerosene. Drinking water comes from rain collected on roofs. The island is dominated by Mount Hobson, standing at 620 m (2,034 ft), and Ruahine, 410 m (1,345 ft). Visitors may spot a kaka, the New Zealand parrot, or a brown teal duck while on a tramping trip.

Regular boats to **Kawau Island** leave from Sandspit at Warkworth. The island is best known for Mansion House, built in 1846, the home of former New Zealand governor and prime minister Sir George Grey. Sir George imported a variety of animal species, such as kookaburras and peacocks. Several, such as the parma wallaby, thought to be extinct in Australia, can still be seen.

Brown kiwi with egg

**Rangitoto** has a highly visible presence in the gulf. The now-extinct volcano erupted about 600–700 years ago to form an island. Now, the 260-m (850-ft) high lava slopes are covered in native trees and shrubs including ferns, mangroves, tree daisies, orchids, coastal pohutukawa, manuka and rewa. There are good walks, including one to the summit. Alternatively, visitors can use a tractor-drawn train.

**Rakino** is popular with weekenders. A hotchpotch of houses sit perched on striking ridges. Its beaches are suitable for swimming and it is a favourite stop for yachts.

**Little Barrier Island**, a wildlife sanctuary, has 30 native and 19 introduced species of birds breeding on it. They include the brown kiwi, kaka and bellbird. Flora includes 370 native species, with 90 ferns. It is prohibited to land on Little Barrier but it is possible to visit the island with a permit obtained from Forest and Bird.

Gazetted in 1975, **Goat Island Marine** Reserve is also known as the Leigh Marine Reserve. The sheltered channel between Goat Island and the mainland provides an opportunity to see red moki, moray eel, snapper and blue cod, as well as marblefish and kelpfish.

The channel is only about 2 to 5 m (7 to 17 ft) deep and diving is possible straight from the beach. Underwater visibility fluctuates from 2 to 15 m (7 to 50 ft) and is at its best from January to June.

**Waiheke Island**
8,000. 118E Ocean View Rd, Oneroa, (09) 372 1234.
w **waiheke.co.nz**

**Great Barrier Island**
1,000. Claris Airport, (09) 367 6009.
w **greatbarrier.co.nz**

**Kawau Island**
200.

Visitors watching birds at the Leigh Marine Reserve

# SHOPPING IN AUCKLAND

Shops in Auckland cater for the needs of most shoppers. However, the city is quite spread out and it pays to do some research first. Shops in downtown Auckland are predominantly European in character; in other areas they have a more Pacific or Asian flavour. Shoppers in search of local items should consider pure wool products, such as hand-knitted sweaters or cuddly toys made from possum fur. The New Zealand fashion scene is lively and creative, and local designers such as Zambesi, Karen Walker, Anne Mardell, and Trelise Cooper have outlets in all the smart shopping areas. Jewellery, pottery, glass and other crafts are of a high standard and are worth buying. Specialized retailers sell items such as crayfish, which they will package for outbound travellers.

## Shopping Hours

Typical business hours are 9am to 6pm, with many stores open on Saturday and Sunday. Most large supermarkets are open until 9pm and some 24 hours. Dairies (convenience stores) are found throughout the suburbs and sell a wide range of groceries and other items, as do most gas stations.

## Duty-Free Shopping

The New Zealand government adds 12.5 per cent Goods and Services Tax (GST) to sales items. Visitors to New Zealand can avoid paying this tax, as well as other government duty, by purchasing duty-free goods on arrival and departure at the airport or at the large duty-free shop, **DFS Galleria**, in the city. This results in savings of 30 per cent on average. Items purchased at the shop have to be collected at the airport. Besides the usual cigarettes and alcohol, sheepskin goods, *paua* shell jewellery, *paua* pearls, and finely crafted woodwork using local timbers are popular items with tourists.

## Shopping Areas

Queen Street is the major banking and commercial centre. However, the restoration of Charles Bohringer's Civic Theatre (1929), the Force Entertainment Centre and shopping complexes such as **Atrium on Elliott**, the **Tower Shopping**

Interior of a Rodd and Gunn outlet in the city

**Centre** and **Westfield Downtown Shopping Centre** have revitalized the central business district as a shopping and entertainment centre. Book stores such as **Whitcoulls**, **Dymocks** and **Unity Books**, CD and record shops such as **Marbecks Classical Shop**, woollen clothing and couture boutiques, and many souvenir stores are also found

The country's largest duty-free shop, DFS Galleria, located at the Old Customhouse

downtown. Nautical-type clothing and souvenirs, sought after since the 2000 America's Cup Regatta, can be bought at the **Voyager New Zealand Maritime Museum Shop**.

Newmarket is Auckland's prime shopping area and has hundreds of stores. Shops along Broadway include **Country Road, Rodd and Gunn**, and **Living and Giving**. Parnell and Ponsonby retailers specialize in luxury goods, such as delicatessen food, clothing, art, ceramics and glassware.

Fresh fruit on sale at one of Auckland's markets

## Markets

Shoppers who are more interested in typically New Zealand goods at lower prices should go to **Victoria Park Market**, a former rubbish destructor building built in 1905. Today, the site houses shops and stalls selling anything from souvenirs to snacks. There are also three licensed restaurants and a food court at the complex. Saturday morning's **Otara Market**, open from 6am to noon, offers yams, green bananas, *hangi* (Maori food cooked on heated stones) and Pacific Island fashion.

# DIRECTORY

## Shopping Centres

**Atrium on Elliott**
21–25 Elliott St.
**Tel** (09) 375 4960.
W atriumonelliott.co.nz

**DFS Galleria**
Old Customhouse, Cnr of Albert & Customs sts.
**Tel** 0800 388 937.

**Dress-Smart Factory Outlet**
151 Arthur St,
Onehunga.
**Tel** (09) 622 2400.

**Queens Arcade**
34–40 Queen St.
**Tel** (09) 358 1777.
W queensarcade.co.nz

**Tower Shopping Centre**
125 Queen St.

**Westfield Downtown Shopping Centre**
11–19 Custom St West.
**Tel** (09) 978 5265.

## Markets

**Otara Market**
Newbury St & Te Puke,
Otara Community Hall.
**Tel** (09) 274 0830.

**Victoria Park Market**
210 Victoria St West.
**Tel** (09) 309 6911.
W victoria-park-market.co.nz

## Food and Wine

**Accent on Wine**
347 Parnell Rd,
Parnell.
**Tel** (09) 358 2552.

**Pandoro Panetteria**
427 Parnell Rd, Parnell.
**Tel** (09) 358 1962.

## Clothes

**Country Road**
164 Queen St.
**Tel** (09) 309 6862.
157 Broadway,
Newmarket.
**Tel** (09) 529 1987.

**Karen Walker**
The Pavillions,
18 Te Ara Tahuhu
Walking St, Britomart.
**Tel** (09) 309 6299.
6 Balm St,
Newmarket.
**Tel** (09) 522 4286.

**Living and Giving**
Westfield St Lukes,
St Lukes Road,
St Lukes.
**Tel** (09) 846 6999.

**Rodd and Gunn**
75 Queen St.
**Tel** (09) 309 6571.
277 Broadway,
Newmarket.
**Tel** (09) 522 0607.

**Voyager New Zealand Maritime Museum Shop**
Viaduct Basin.
**Tel** (09) 373 0800.

**Workshop**
Cnr of Vulcan Lane and High St. **Tel** (09) 303 3735.
18 Morrow St, Newmarket.
**Tel** (09) 524 6844.

## Books and Music

**Dymocks**
246 Queen St.
**Tel** (09) 379 9919.

**Marbecks Classical Shop**
28 Queen's Arcade.
**Tel** (09) 379 0444.
W marbecks.co.nz

**Rare Books**
6 High Street.
**Tel** (09) 379 0379.

**Real Groovy Records**
438 Queen St.
**Tel** (09) 302 3940.

**Unity Books**
19 High St.
**Tel** (09) 307 0731.
W unitybooks.co.nz

**Whitcoulls**
210 Queen St.
**Tel** (09) 984 5400.

**Women's Bookshop**
105 Ponsonby Rd.
**Tel** (09) 376 4399.
W womensbookshop.co.nz

## Souvenirs and Others

**OK Gift Shop**
Downtown Shopping Centre, Cnr of Albert & Customs sts.
**Tel** (09) 303 1951.

**Opal and Jade World**
105 Queens St.
**Tel** (09) 379 3739.

**Smith and Caughey's**
253–261 Queen St.
**Tel** (09) 377 4770.
255 Broadway,
Newmarket.
**Tel** (09) 524 8049.

**The Sheepskin Store**
7A Bassant Ave,
Penrose.
**Tel** (09) 622 2889

# ENTERTAINMENT IN AUCKLAND

Reflecting Auckland's ethnic diversity, events staged in the city range from a Puccini opera to a Maori dance performance. Many of these take place at venues in the central business district. The Aotea Centre, Auckland Town Hall and several cinemas are all on Queen Street. The Civic Theatre Centre is worth a visit for architectural reasons alone. Bordering Queen Street, Fort Street and Karangahape Road, commonly known as K-Road, offer alternative entertainment in the form of strip clubs and massage parlours. K-Road is also known for its funky atmosphere and its many nightclubs. SKYCITY Casino features more than 100 gaming tables and 1,000 machines. In the suburbs, multiplex cinemas, sports parks and nightclubs are the main entertainment venues.

Impressive interior of the Civic Theatre Centre

## Information

The entertainment section of *The New Zealand Herald* should be checked first for events in the city. It carries cinema listings and information about concerts, ballets and theatre performances. Several publications outlining what's on in Auckland are available from visitor information centres which can be found across the city. The country's two main booking agencies, **Ticketmaster** and **Ticketek**, list events on their websites. Reservations can be made online or by phone.

## Theatre

The two main venues, the **Aotea Centre** and the **Auckland Town Hall**, are part of the complex known as THE EDGE *(see p78)*. This is where the biggest musicals and productions are staged. The Great Hall in the Auckland Town Hall *(see p78)* is renowned for its acoustics. Other theatres include the Maidment Theatre at the university and the Silo in Grey's Avenue.

## Dance

New Zealand has a small dance community. Its leading contemporary dance choreographers are Mary Jane O'Reilly, Michael Parmenter, and Douglas Wright.
    At present, the Footnote Dance Company is the country's only full-time contemporary dance company. Based in Wellington, the troupe performs in Auckland, as does the classical Royal New Zealand Ballet, which also has its home in the capital. However, the Black Grace Dance Company is Auckland-based. There are regular tours by overseas dance and ballet companies.

Annabel Reid of the Royal New Zealand Ballet in *Raymonda*

## Music

For classical music, the New Zealand Symphony Orchestra (NZSO) and the Auckland Philharmonia Orchestra (APO) have a good reputation. The 33-member APO is unusual in that the musicians own the orchestra. Most concerts are held in the Auckland Town Hall. Both the NZSO and the APO also perform at the free "Symphony under the Stars" concert at Auckland Domain *(see p81)*. This event attracts huge crowds of more than 100,000 people.
    Many pubs in Auckland have live bands which play most nights, including the Powerstation, King's Arms and The Dogs Bollix, a popular Irish pub.

Fireworks during a symphony performance at the Auckland Domain

A traditional show given by the Manaia Cultural Performance Group

## Cultural Performances

At the Auckland War Memorial Museum *(see pp82–3)*, visitors are able to witness authentic Maori ceremonies and dances. During the shows, which are staged three to four times daily, talented singers and dancers from the Manaia Cultural Performance Group present the *haka*, the fierce war dance of the men, the *poi* dances of the women *(see pp34–5)*, as well as various other traditional songs and dances. Each show lasts about 45 minutes.

Visitors can also get to see Pacific Island culture and events at the Pasifika Festival, held at Western Springs, in March every year *(see p46)*. The festival features the traditional arts and culture of the various Pacific Island communities.

## Clubs

Although theatres throughout the country feature one-off performances by local and visiting comedians, the **Classic Comedy & Bar** claims to be the only venue in the whole of New Zealand that is dedicated to stand-up comedy.

The city's main nightclub strip is on Karangahape Road. Venues that are popular with young people include **Sinners Nightclub**, which can accommodate up to 1,000 people on busy nights, **Fu Bar**, which

features dance music such as hip hop and drum and bass, and **Kiss Bar**, a popular dance club playing mainly house music. Auckland's gay clubs include **Mea Culpa** on Ponsonby Road and **Flesh Nightclub & Lounge Bar** on O'Connell Street, which hosts drag acts and other entertainment evenings.

## Film

Multiplex cinemas are found throughout Auckland. The larger multiplexes, such as the **Village SKYCITY Cinemas**, show blockbuster movies, often before they are seen in Europe. Newmarket's refurbished **Rialto Cinema**, on the other hand, regularly screens foreign titles for more sophisticated movie buffs.

The highlight of the cinematographic year is the New Zealand Film Festival, held in July. Auckland filmgoers get to enjoy a wide selection of local and international films over several days.

Façade of the Village SKYCITY Cinemas

## DIRECTORY

### Booking Tickets

**Ticketek**
Tel (09) 307 5000, 0800 TICKETEK.
w ticketek.com

**Ticketmaster**
Tel (09) 970 9700.
w ticketmaster.co.nz

### Theatres

**Aotea Centre**
Queen St. **Tel** (09) 309 2677.

**Auckland Town Hall**
Queen St. **Tel** (09) 309 2677.

**Civic Theatre Centre**
Cnr Queen and Wellesley sts.

**SKYCITY Theatre**
Cnr Wellesley and Hobson sts.
**Tel** 0800 759 2489.

### Clubs

**Boogie Wonderland**
Cnr Custom & Queen sts.
**Tel** (09) 361 6093.

**Classic Comedy & Bar**
321 Queen St.
**Tel** (09) 373 4321.

**Fu Bar**
174 Queen St.
**Tel** (09) 309 3079.

**Kiss Bar**
309 Karangahape Rd.
**Tel** (09) 303 2726.

**Lolabar**
212 Ponsonby Rd.
**Tel** (09) 360 0396.

**Mea Culpa**
3/175 Ponsonby Rd.
**Tel** (09) 376 4460.

**S P Q R**
150 Ponsonby Rd.
**Tel** (09) 360 1710.

**Spy Bar**
204 Quay St, Viaduct Basin.
**Tel** (09) 377 7811.

### Cinemas

**Rialto Cinema**
169 Broadway, Newmarket.
**Tel** (09) 369 2417.

**Village SKYCITY Cinemas**
**Tel** (09) 972 2800.

# NORTHLAND

Strong Maori roots, early European settlements, a subtropical climate and enchanting scenery – these make Northland both the cradle of the nation and one of its favourite playgrounds. Northland is where Europeans first made their presence felt in New Zealand. It is a region with a history of bloodshed and raw frontier emotions, but is today dominated by holiday fun.

The long history of Maori occupation in Northland is evident in the hillside *pa* sites and shellfishing grounds around the coast. Maori culture *(see pp34–5)* continues to be extensively practised in this region and many Maori tribes live here.

Early post-European history in Northland includes both the licentious whalers, who earned Russell its title of "hell-hole of the Pacific" *(see p106)*, and missionaries, who brought Christianity to the country. The brothels and taverns have now disappeared, but buildings like Pompallier House are reminders of early Christian influences.

Historically, Waitangi Treaty House, where the Treaty of Waitangi was signed *(see pp52–3, 108–9)*, is of major importance. Cape Reinga *(see p112)* is a drawcard, because of its location at the top of the country where the Pacific Ocean and Tasman Sea merge, and also because of its significance in Maori mythology as the place from where the spirits of the dead depart for Hawaiki.

Visitors to Northland will be impressed by its natural beauty: gently rolling farmland, white sand beaches, massive sand dunes and rock formations. In a world where scenic spots are often spoiled due to countless visitors, Northland stands out. In its forests, with gigantic kauris that are around 2,000 years old, it is still possible to walk for hours without encountering a single fellow tramper. The region also offers other activities, such as fishing, diving, kayaking, tobogganing and horseback riding.

Diving near the wreck of the *Rainbow Warrior (see p57)* off Matauri Bay

◀ Matapouri Bay on the stunning Tutukaka Coast

# Exploring Northland

Northland's charm lies in its unspoiled, simple character. The region is blessed with two contrasting coastlines, which offer endless scope for outdoor recreation. As the site of first permanent contact between Maoris and Europeans, the region is also rich in history and has many well-preserved historic sites. There are many areas from which visitors can explore the region: Paihia, which has its own attractions but is close to historic Russell, Waitangi and Kerikeri, and the beautiful Bay of Islands; Kaitaia, which attracts day-trippers to the Aupori Peninsula, Mangonui and Ahipara; and Opononi and Omapere, which have wonderful beaches and are close to Rawene, a historic settlement on Hokianga Harbour.

CAPE REINGA ⑬
North Cape
Te Paki
Parengarenga Harbour
AUPORI PENINSULA TOUR
Te Kao ⑮
Great Exhibition Bay
NINETY MILE BEACH
Ca Karika
Pukenui
⑭
Mohutangi
Waipapakuri
Awar
Abipara Bay
⑫ KAI
Tauroa Point
Ahipara
Broadwoc
Hokian, Harbor
OPONOI
Omape

Pohutukawa trees and bays around Whangarei Heads

0 kilometres        20
0 miles               20

## Top Outdoor Activities

The places shown here have been selected for their recreational activities. Conditions vary depending on the weather and the time of year, so exercise caution and, if in doubt, seek local advice.

| | Cruising | Game Fishing | Kayaking | Sailing | Scuba Diving | Snorkelling | Swimming | Tramping |
|---|---|---|---|---|---|---|---|---|
| Cape Reinga | | | | | | | | ■ |
| Kai-Iwi Lakes | | | ● | ■ | | | ■ | |
| Kaitaia | | | | | | | | ■ |
| Ninety Mile Beach | | | | | | | ● | ■ |
| Omapere | ● | ■ | ● | | | | ● | |
| Opononi | ● | ■ | ● | | | | ● | |
| Paihia | ● | ■ | ● | ■ | ● | ■ | ● | |
| Russell | ● | ■ | ● | ■ | ● | ■ | ● | ■ |
| Tutukaka | ● | ■ | ● | ■ | ● | ■ | ● | |
| Waipoua Forest | | | | | | | | ■ |
| Whangarei | ● | ■ | ● | ■ | ● | ■ | ● | ■ |

Painting an ancestral figure on the meeting house at Waitangi

Fullers tour coach on Ninety Mile Beach

## Sights at a Glance

1. Whangarei
2. Tutukaka
3. Poor Knights Islands
4. Matapouri
5. Russell
6. Paihia
7. *Waitangi Treaty Grounds pp108–9*
8. Kerikeri
9. Waimate North
10. Whangaroa
11. Doubtless Bay
12. Kaitaia
13. Cape Reinga
14. Ninety Mile Beach
16. Kaikohe
17. Rawene
18. Opononi
19. Waipoua Forest
20. Dargaville

**Tour**

15. Aupori Peninsula

## Getting Around

The best way to see Northland is by car. The main road to the Aupori Peninsula is a 21-km (13-mile) section to Cape Reinga. Tour operators usually return via Ninety Mile Beach, a trip that is not recommended for cars. Most visitors travelling north from Auckland prefer to drive up via the east coast and back along the west coast.

### Key

— Major road
═ Minor road
— Scenic route
— Minor railway
— Regional border
— Toll road

**For additional map symbols** *see back flap*

The Town Basin on the waterfront at Whangarei

# ❶ Whangarei

**Road map** E1. 🚏 47,000. ✈ 🚌
ℹ️ Tarewa Park, 92 Otaika Rd, (09) 438
1079. 🔤 **whangareinz.org.nz**

The northernmost city in New
Zealand and the only one in
Northland, Whangarei is a two-
hour drive from Auckland. The
city lies between forested hills
and a deep harbour. The
combination of fertile soil and
temperate climate is reflected
in the city's lush gardens and
in the surrounding farmlands
and orchards.

Whangarei's historic Town
Basin, in the heart of the city, has
been redeveloped in a colonial
theme. Its cafés, restaurants, art
galleries, museums and
speciality shops make it a
popular gathering place for
locals and visitors. It is also one

The picturesque Whangarei Falls

of the most popular destinations
for yacht sailors wandering
the world, who come here
to avoid the cyclonic
storms common in the
South Pacific over the
summer. The Town Basin
and local marinas are often
full with visiting yachts
coming to refit.

A giant sundial marks
the location of the Town
Basin's **Clapham Clock
Museum**, which
houses more than
1,400 items, of which
400 were donated by
A Clapham, who
made many of the
clocks himself. The
oldest, an English lantern clock,
dates from 1690. The collection
also includes Biedermeier wall
clocks, grandfather and Black
Forest clocks, and a
*staartklok* (literally a "tail
clock" after the shape of
its winding mechanism)
from Friesland in the
Netherlands. To avoid the
deafening sound of the
hundreds of time-pieces
marking the hour simul-
taneously, the clocks have
been set at different times.

Just to the west of
Whangarei is the **Quarry
Arts Centre**, offering local
arts and crafts for sale. Set
in a bush-clad quarry the
Trust is home to a number
of artists who live on-site,
some in adobe-style
dwellings. Further out is
the **Museum & Kiwi
House Heritage Park**. The
museum displays a fine

Clapham Clock
Museum exhibit

range of Maori artefacts, and
there is a 1885 homestead. The
Kiwi House provides the chance
to view one of the country's
most endangered birds.

For those looking for more
challenging activities, there are
many tramping opportunities
around Whangarei. The Parahaki
Scenic Reserve, on the eastern
side of the city, has good bush
walks. The war memorial at the
summit of Parahaki Mountain
can be reached via Memorial
Drive or by two tracks from Mair
Park or Dundas Road, for a
superb panoramic view of the
city and harbour. There are Maori
pits and old gum-digging
workings on all the walks, and a
trail leads to a historic Maori *pa*
site nearby. Whangarei Falls,
known as the most
photogenic waterfalls in
New Zealand, lie northeast of
the Parahaki Scenic Reserve in
the suburb of Tikipunga, 5 km
(3 miles) north of the town
centre. The 26-m (86-ft)
high waterfall drops over
basalt cliffs.

There are natural pools
and picnic spots, plus two
viewing platforms that
provide excellent views
of the falls.

🏛 **Clapham Clock Museum**
Town Basin, Dent St.
**Tel** (09) 438 3993. **Open** daily.
**Closed** 25 Dec. 🈺 🅱 🗓 🏠

🏛 **Quarry Arts Centre**
21 Selwyn Ave. **Tel** (09) 438 1215.
**Open** daily. 🏠 🅱

🏛 **Kiwi North (Museum
& Kiwi House)**
Gate 1, 500 State Hwy 14, Heritage
Park, Maunu. Tel (09) 438 9630.
**Open** daily. **Closed** 25 & 26 Dec.
🈺 🅱

# ❷ Tutukaka

**Road map** E1. 🚏 520. 🚌 ℹ️ Dive!
Tutukaka, Marina Rd, (09) 434 3867.

On the coastal loop road, a
short distance from Whangarei,
Tutukaka is a well-known base
for diving trips to the Poor
Knights Islands and for big
game and deep-sea fishing.
Several diving companies are
based here and the sheltered,

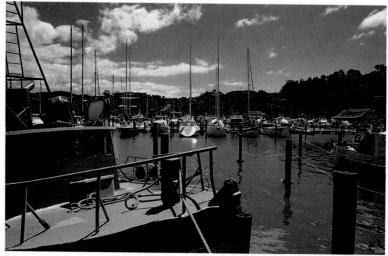

Yachts moored at the marina in Tutukaka's sheltered harbour

natural harbour is alive with yachts and fishing boats.

One of the most popular diving sites off the coast between Tutukaka and Matapouri is an artificial reef created by the sinking of two former naval ships, the *Tui* and the *Waikato*. Several professional diving companies offer their services as guides to this underwater grave. For further information on diving trips available in the area, visit www. diving.co.nz.

### ❸ Poor Knights Islands

**Road map** E1. 🛈 Tarewa Park, 92 Otaika Rd, Whangarei, (09) 438 1079. 🅦 whangareinz.org.nz

About 24 km (15 miles) from the coast at Tutukaka are the Poor Knights Islands. Once a favourite spot for fishermen, the area around these two islands was established as a marine reserve in 1981. Although landing on the islands is prohibited without a special permit from the Department of Conservation, the surrounding waters are accessible to divers. Well-known mariner Jacques Cousteau considered the reserve one of the world's top five diving sites because of its exceptional water clarity and

the variety of its sea life. The area benefits from a subtropical current that makes it warmer than the surrounding coastal waters, and promotes a profusion of tropical and temperate marine life. Eroded volcanic rock has created a seascape of tunnels, arches and caves where divers can view fish and sponges. Scuba diving in this haven can be enjoyed all year round. Boats leave daily from Tutukaka Marina.

Reptiles such as geckos and tuataras can be found on both islands, which are thought to be the world's only nesting spot for Buller's shearwaters.

### ❹ Matapouri

**Road map** E1.

Located a short distance north of Tutukawa on the coastal loop road, Matapouri has one of Northland's most beautiful beaches. Tucked between headlands and dotted with islets, Matapouri's calm waters and white sands make it a popular place for swimming and snorkelling.

A walking track connects the beach with Whale Bay, 2 km (1.2 miles) north. Lookout points on the track offer magnificent views of the coastline and ocean.

Diving in the marine reserve at Poor Knights Islands

Town Basin in Whangarei ▶

The churchyard, Christ Church, Russell

## ❺ Russell

**Road map** E1. 🏔 1,000. 🚌 ⛴
ℹ The Wharf, (09) 403 8020.

At the turn of the 19th century, Russell, then known as Kororareka, served as a shore station for whalers. It became a lawless town, earning the title "Hell-hole of the Pacific". It was renamed Russell in 1844 in honour of the British colonial secretary of the day. Today, the quiet town is involved in tourism, fishing, oyster farming and cottage industries.

Formerly known as the Captain Cook Memorial Museum, the **Russell Museum** features a working model of Captain Cook's *Endeavour* and memorabilia from American author Zane Grey, who helped establish the Bay of Islands as a game fishing centre in the late 1920s. There is also a collection of early settlers' relics.

**Christ Church**, built in 1836, is the country's oldest surviving church. One of the contributors to the church was Charles Darwin, author of *The Origin of Species*, who visited New Zealand in 1835.

Stately **Pompallier Mission** was built on the waterfront between 1841 and 1842 to house the Marist mission's Gaveaux printing press. The building later became much neglected, until it passed to the New Zealand Historic Places Trust in 1968 and was restored to its original state in 1993. The country's oldest standing industrial building, it now houses a printing and bookbinding exhibition, which includes the original printing press.

Flagstaff Hill serves as a reminder of Russell's turbulent past. It was here that Hone Heke (1810–50) cut down the British shipping signal flagpole in 1844 *(see p67)*.

Paihia restaurant sign

🏛 **Russell Museum**
2 York St. **Tel** (09) 403 7701. **Open** daily. **Closed** 25 Dec. 🅿 ♿ 🅷

⛪ **Christ Church**
Church Rd. **Tel** (09) 403 7696.
🕙 10:30am Sun.

🏘 **Pompallier Mission**
The Strand. **Tel** (09) 403 9015.
**Open** daily. **Closed** 25 Dec.
🅿 ♿ garden only. 🎫 🅷

## ❻ Paihia

**Road map** E1. 🏔 1,850. 🚌 ⛴
ℹ Marsden Rd, (09) 402 7345.

Starting life as a mission post in 1823, Paihia now joins places such as Russell and Tutukaka as a base for deep-sea game fishing. To the north of Pahia, on the road to Kerikeri is the **Lily Pond Farm Park**. The park gives visitors the chance to interact with a whole range of farm animals including sheep, pigs and goats. There are also more exotic species of animal, such as eels, alpaca and emus. It is a working farm that will appeal to families with small children.

Located 3 km (2 miles) from Paihia, on the Waitangi River *(see pp108–9)*, are the **Haruru Falls**. There is a track from Waitangi to Haruru Falls. Visitors can also walk to the mangroves to see herons and nesting native shags. An alternative approach to the falls is by kayak along the river. Kayaks can be hired from **Coastal Kayakers**, who also take groups of kayakers on guided tours.

🌾 **Lily Pond Farm Park**
RD1 Puketona Rd. **Tel** (09) 402 6099.
**Open** Fri–Tue. **Closed** 25 Dec. 🅿 ♿

🏞 **Haruru Falls**
Waitangi Treaty Grounds. **Tel** (09) 402 7437. **Open** 9am–5pm daily. **Closed** 25 Dec. 🅿 🎫 Coastal Kayakers: Te Karuwha Pde, Waitangi. **Tel** (09) 402 8105. 🎫 🆆 coastalkayakers.co.nz

# Leisure Activities in the Bay of Islands

A favourable climate, an irregular coastline lapped by the Pacific Ocean and some 150 islands dotted around its aquamarine waters, which are full of marine wildlife, combine to make the Bay of Islands one of New Zealand's most popular playgrounds. The region has been a favourite tourist destination since the 1930s when a road connecting Northland with Auckland to the south was built. The Bay of Islands' reputation is based primarily on deep-sea fishing, but today visitors also have the opportunity to experience other water sports, such as swimming, kayaking, sailing, diving and waterskiing. Tour operators tempt visitors by adding new attractions, such as scenic flights, paragliding and horse trekking.

The Rowe family, keen anglers of the Bay of Islands Swordfish Club, with their prize catch

### Game Fishing

Deep-sea game fishing is a year-round activity in the Bay of Islands. The most prolific game fish is the striped marlin, which may weigh up to 120 kg (265 lb). Many other species, which can be caught using both heavy and light tackle, are abundant in the bay's waters. Deep-sea fishing charters usually include accommodation, food, tackle and bait. No licence is required for ocean fishing.

**Anglers** increasingly are tagging and releasing the fish they catch, such as this striped marlin.

**Swimming with dolphins** in the bay's warm waters is a popular activity. Licensed tour operators ensure that human attention does not scare the dolphins.

**Kayaking** guided tours range from paddling up sheltered waters to kayaking on the open sea.

**Paragliding**, one of several airborne sports introduced in the Bay of Islands, is an excellent way to appreciate the beauty of the bay.

**Leisure cruises** include Paihia's Cream Trip. The boat used to collect cream from outlying dairy farms but now drops off mail and takes visitors on cruises.

# ❼ Waitangi Treaty Grounds

Waitangi earned its pivotal place in New Zealand's history on 6 February 1840 when the Treaty of Waitangi was signed *(see pp22, 52–3)* in front of the house of James Busby (1800–71), the British Resident. The Residency, renamed the Treaty House, became a national memorial in 1932. The house and grounds are a gathering point for Maoris and government leaders each year on 6 February, Waitangi Day. Visitors are recommended to take the guided tours.

**Aerial View of Waitangi Treaty Grounds**
The grounds are surrounded by a beautiful coastline, tidal estuary, mangrove, forest and native bush.

**Visitor Centre**
An audiovisual presentation every half hour describes the events surrounding the signing of the Treaty of Waitangi. There are also displays on the major personalities involved and copies of the Treaty documents. A shop sells souvenirs, Maori carvings and books.

Paihia

Tai Henare Drive

0 metres    200
0 yards     200

Hobson Beach

## KEY

① Café

② Car Park

③ Canoe House

④ **A coastal walk** takes visitors past unusual pillow lava rock, which fractured into hexagonal shapes as it erupted under water.

⑤ Copthorne Hotel and Resort

⑥ Te Tii Marae

⑦ Bay of Islands Yacht Club

⑧ Waitangi Golf Course

⑨ Flagstaff

**★ Maori War Canoe**
Carved from three kauri trees, this 35-m (114-ft) long canoe, named Ngatokimatawhaorua after the canoe in which Kupe discovered New Zealand *(see p49)*, carries up to 120 warriors. It is launched each year on Waitangi Day.

### VISITORS' CHECKLIST

**Practical Information**
Road map E1.
🌐 waitangi.org.nz
ℹ️ 1 Tau Henare Drive, Waitangi,
(09) 402 7437. **Open** 9am–5pm
daily. **Closed** 25 Dec. ♿ ♿

**Transport**
🚌 from Kerikeri.

### Mangrove Forest Boardwalk
A boardwalk takes visitors through a
mature mangrove forest to the Haruru
Falls at the end of the tidal Waitangi River.

### ★ Treaty House
Prefabricated in Australia,
the Treaty House *(see p53)*,
was the home of the first
British Resident, James
Busby. It was the venue
for important political
events up to 1840.

### ★ Maori Meeting House
Opened on 6 February 1940 to
commemorate the centennial
of the Treaty, the meeting house
(Te Whare Runanga) contains
beautiful Maori wall carvings.

### Treaty Grounds
A ceremonial celebration of the signing of
the Treaty of Waitangi is held each year on
the grounds in front of the Treaty House.

The Stone Store, St James Church and Kerikeri Mission House

## ❽ Kerikeri

**Road map** E1. 🚗 4,200. 🚌 🚢

The pretty town of Kerikeri is noted for its subtropical climate, citrus and kiwifruit orchards, historic buildings, and an art and craft trail.

The Kerikeri Basin is home to **Kerikeri Mission Station**, one of New Zealand's earliest settlements. It was the second European mission station to be set up in New Zealand, in 1819, under the protection of Maori chief Hongi Hika *(see p67)*; the first mission was established near the entrance to the Bay of Islands five years earlier. The mission station includes Kerikeri Mission House. Constructed in 1821, the building belonged to the Kemp family in 1832 and was left to the New Zealand Historic Places Trust in 1974. Restored, it looks much as it did in the 1840s. The mission station also encompasses New Zealand's oldest surviving stone building, the Stone Store, built in 1835 as part of the mission house. Intended as a storehouse, it gradually turned into a general store and, from the 1960s, a souvenir shop, selling merchandise such as hand-forged nails and other products in keeping with its history. On the slope behind the mission house is **St James Church**, constructed in 1878 of native timbers such as kauri and puriri. Above the Basin are the remnants of Kororipo Pa, a Maori fortification. The strategic base of Hongi Hika, the *pa* is best known as an assembly point for war parties in the 1820s. Across the river from the *pa* is **Rewa's Village**, a reconstructed pre-European Maori fishing village built from native materials, those used before the missionaries came. It provides an introduction to traditional buildings such as *marae* (gathering place) and *pataka* (communal raised storehouse). There are two ancient canoes at the village and the Discoverers' Garden.

**🏠 Kerikeri Mission Station**
The Basin, 246 Kerikeri Rd.
**Tel** (09) 407 9236. **Open** daily.
**Closed** 25 Dec. 🐾 📷 📷

**⛪ St James Church**
The Basin. 🕆 daily.

**🏛 Rewa's Village**
1 Landing Rd. **Tel** (09) 407 6454.
**Open** daily. **Closed** Good Fri, 25 Dec.
🐾 ♿ 📷 by arrangement. 📷

## ❾ Waimate North

**Road map** E1. 🚗 700.

Not far from Kerikeri is Waimate North, a missionary community in the 1830s. It was also the site of New Zealand's first large English-style farm. It is now best known for **Te Waimate Mission**, the sole survivor of three mission houses built in 1832 and first occupied by the Clarke family. It is furnished with missionary period furniture and early tools.

**🏠 Te Waimate Mission**
Te Ahu Ahu Rd. **Tel** (09) 405 9734.
**Open** May–Oct: Sat–Mon; Nov–Apr: daily. **Closed** 25 Dec. 📷

## ❿ Whangaroa

**Road map** E1. 🚗 530. 🚢

A small, scenic settlement with a beautiful harbour, Whangaroa is best appreciated from the summit of St Paul, a rock formation which dominates the town. The surrounding hills were once covered in huge kauri trees, which have long since been turned into ship masts and timber. Croatians worked the Matauri Bay gum-fields in the late 19th century, extracting resin *(see p114)*.

Today, Whangaroa Harbour has become well known for its big game fishing, cruises, diving and snorkelling.

## ⓫ Doubtless Bay

Road map D1. 🚢

Said to be the first landfall for the explorer Kupe *(see pp49–50)*, Doubtless Bay was an important base for whalers in the early days of European settlement. The bay encompasses a wide crescent of golden beaches, including Cable Bay and Cooper's Beach, popular with swimmers and snorkellers. The fishing village of Mangonui, situated on the bay's estuary, has many historic buildings.

Te Waimate Mission, one of New Zealand's oldest wooden buildings

# Arts and Crafts

Art and crafts are well developed in Northland, often with a strong local flavour in the use of colours and motifs. Ironically, the best-known artist was not a New Zealander but Austrian architect and painter Hundertwasser, who spent much of his time in New Zealand until his death in March 2000. Visitors to Kawakawa, south of Paihia, and Russell can visit a grass-roofed Hundertwasser-designed toilet block. Local artist Chris Booth is known for sculptures that feature large stones – his best-known work is on the headland at Matauri Bay. There are many outlets in the area, however, that offer paintings, prints, bone carvings and traditional greenstone (jade) items. In Kerikeri, an art and craft trail leads visitors through shops selling a variety of individually handcrafted and decorated pieces of high quality.

### Swamp Kauri Carving

Swamp kauri is turned by local artisans into items ranging from small bowls to dining sets. The timber is milled from the remnants of huge trees which fell into swamplands 30,000–50,000 years ago.

**Part of a stone sculpture** by Northland artist Chris Booth, which forms the entrance to Auckland's Albert Park.

**Plaited floor mats, baskets and hats** made from flax, a swamp plant, are popular souvenirs. Flax weaving is a traditional Maori skill.

**Wood, bone or greenstone** are carved by crafts people like Hohepa Renata, who use their own designs or traditional Maori ones.

Carved wooden mask

**Pottery** is produced in a variety of techniques, including glazing methods from Japan.

## ⑫ Kaitaia

**Map** D1. 🏛 5,300. 🚌 ℹ Cnr Matthews Ave and South Rd, (09) 408 0879.

The largest town in the Far North, Kaitaia is a good base for day trips in the area. It is home to the **Te Ahu Centre**, which has the earliest authenticated European artifact left in New Zealand – a 1,500-kg (3,300-lb) wrought-iron anchor, lost in a storm in Doubtless Bay in 1769 by J F M de Surville, the French explorer.

**🏛 Te Ahu Centre**
Cnr Matthews Ave and South Rd.
**Tel** (09) 408 1403. **Open** daily.
**Closed** Good Fri, 25 Dec.
♿ ✉ ♿ 🅿 on request. 📷
**W** farnorthmuseum.co.nz

## ⑬ Cape Reinga

**Map** D1.

Reinga, meaning "under-world", refers to the Maori belief that this is where the spirits of the dead leave for the journey to Hawaiki. The roots of an old pohutukawa tree at the tip of the cape are said to be the departure point for these spirits. Looking out from Cape Reinga over the Columbia Bank, visitors can see the Tasman Sea converge with the Pacific Ocean. The cape is not the very end of the country; the northernmost point is on North Cape.

## ⑭ Ninety Mile Beach

**Map** D1.

A misnomer, Ninety Mile Beach is, in fact, only 96 km (60 miles) long. The longest beach in the country, this area is almost like a desert, with sand dunes that can reach 143 m (470 ft) high fringing the beach. It was once a forested region, but the kauri trees were destroyed by inundations of water during successive Ice Ages. Pine trees have been planted to stabilize the dunes. Surf fishing and digging for shellfish are popular activities.

## ⑮ Aupori Peninsula Driving Tour

Called "The Tail of The Fish" by Maori, Aupori Peninsula is a thin strip of land no more than 12 km (7 miles) wide between Ninety Mile Beach on the west coast and a number of beaches and bays along the east coast. The unspoilt beaches and coastline, together with high year-round temperatures, make this region an appealing holiday destination. The peninsula offers swimming, walking, sand tobogganing and fishing.

**⑥ Ninety Mile Beach**
The hard sand on the beach makes it a popular area for farm biking and coach tours, as well as for cycling and marathons.

0 kilometres 6
0 miles 6

**Key**
▬ Tour route
▬ Scenic route
═ Other roads

**⑤ Cape Reinga Lighthouse**
Visible from a distance of 48 km (26 nautical miles) offshore, the solitary, whitewashed Cape Reinga Lighthouse is New Zealand's northernmost lighthouse.

③ **Spirits Bay**
This sacred Maori area is the starting point for the 28-km (17-mile) walking track to Cape Reinga.

*North Cape*

② **Rarawa Beach**
Sparkling white silica sand makes Rarawa Beach one of the most attractive beaches on the east coast.

*Great Exhibition Bay*

① **Gumdiggers Park**
Take a walk around this park and learn about the ecology of the Manuka regrowth forest and its inhabitants.

*Henderson Bay*

**Pukenui**

**Houhora Heads**

**Mohutangi**

**Hukatere**

*Waipapakauri Beach*

## Digging for Shellfish

Gathering *kai moana* (seafood) is not just a Maori tradition. Many other New Zealanders fish from boats or the shore, dive for fish, or dig in the sand for shellfish to supplement their diet. At Ninety Mile Beach, people are likely to be searching for *tuatua*, a shellfish that occurs in large quantities in the area. The daily limit a person can collect is 150 and each shellfish must be at least 125 mm (5 inches) long. More difficult to find, *paua* (abalone) are also gathered along the beach. The daily limit per person is ten.

Digging for *tuatua* at Ninety Mile Beach

④ **Te Paki Reserve**
Tobogganing off the massive sand dunes is the main attraction here but there is also a pleasant 40-minute walk to the beach.

## Tips for Drivers

**Length:** 210 km (130 miles).
**Stopping-off points:** There are places to stay and eat between Kaitaia and Waitaki Landing. There is a further 21-km (13-mile) drive to the lighthouse. As an alternative to returning on State Hwy 1, 4WD vehicles can access Ninety Mile Beach at Te Paki, 16 km (10 miles) south of Cape Reinga Lighthouse, and exit near Waipapakauri Beach. Trips should be made two hours before or after high tide. Visitors are advised to take a coach tour, as rental cars are not allowed on the beach.

Boatshed Café and Gallery at Rawene

## ⓰ Kaikohe

**Road map** E1. 🗻 4,100. 🚌

A service centre for farms in the area, Kaikohe is best known for the **Ngawha Hot Springs** (Waiaraki Pools). While such hot springs have been turned into major tourist attractions in places such as Rotorua *(see pp140–41)*, they are mainly a local feature in Kaikohe, where most visitors and the attendant are on first-name terms. Outsiders are welcome, and if they can accept the springs' unadorned character, they will enjoy the hot spring waters with temperatures between 32 and 42 °C (90 and 108 °F).

Kaikohe's **Heritage Kaikohe** indoor and outdoor museum is a collection of houses and artifacts related to the district's early Maori and European history. A conducted tour takes visitors to attractions from the 1862 Old Courthouse to Maioha Cottage (1875), Utakura Settlers Hall (1891) and Alexander's Sawmill (1913). There are also vintage vehicles, a fire station, a bush railway and a small railway station. From a hillside monument to Chief Hone Heke (grand-nephew of the old chief), there are fine views of both coasts.

🏠 **Ngawha Hot Springs**
Ngawha Springs Rd, off SH 12.
**Tel** (09) 405 2245. **Open** daily.
**Closed** public hols. 🅿️

🏛 **Heritage Kaikohe**
1a Recreation Rd. **Tel** (09) 401 0816.
**Open** daily. **Closed** 1 Jan, Good Fri,
25 & 26 Dec. 🅿️ ♿ 📷 🏠

## ⓱ Rawene

**Road map** D1. 🗻 520. 🚌
ℹ️ Boatshed Café and Gallery, Clendon Esplanade, (09) 405 7728.

This quaint village, which has shops jutting out over the water, was home to James Reddy Clendon (1800–72), the first US Consul in New Zealand. He later became Hokianga's Resident Magistrate. **Clendon House**, now owned by the New Zealand Historic Places Trust, was probably built after 1866.

The ferry across Hokianga Harbour links with an alternative route to Kaitaia, via Broadwood and Herekino.

🏛 **Clendon House**
Clendon Esplanade. **Tel** (09) 405 7874.
**Open** Sat–Mon. **Closed** May–Oct & 25 Dec. 🅿️ 🔲 **historic.org.nz**

## ⓲ Opononi

**Road map** D1. 🗻 600. 🚌 🚌
ℹ️ Hokianga i-SITE, State Hwy 12, (09) 405 8869.

In the minds of many New Zealanders, the small beach town of Opononi is forever linked to that of its most famous visitor, Opo. This dolphin became a national celebrity when it spent the summer of 1955 playing with children and performing tricks with beach balls. Sadly, it was killed by unknown dynamite fishers. A sculpture by Christchurch artist Russell Clark marks the dolphin's grave outside Opononi's pub. A video of Opo can be viewed at the Hokianga i-SITE information centre.

Diagonally across the road from Opo's statue is the wharf, which is the starting point for a short boat trip to see, at close range, the giant sand dunes on the far side of Hokianga Harbour.

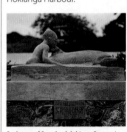

Sculpture of Opo the dolphin at Opononi

### The Early Kauri Gum Industry

As the immigrants of the 19th century rapidly depleted the country's native forests of kauri trees, a new industry began to emerge. Resin, exuded by the trees, became a valuable commodity in the production of varnish. To reveal the location of lumps of resin, long rods were poked into the ground near dead trees, a job mostly carried out by Yugoslav immigrants. By 1885, 2,000 people were employed in this trade. Many of these people later turned to growing vegetables and to viticulture near Auckland.

Today, lumps of kauri gum, known as amber, are popular souvenir items. The gum is carved and polished and made into pendants and other small items. Sometimes insects or fern fragments can be seen trapped inside the finished items.

Polished kauri gum

Tane Mahuta, New Zealand's largest kauri tree

range from old photos of the local Yugoslav Social Club to memorabilia from the Northern Wairoa Scottish Society and a pig skull from New Mexico.

**Dargaville Museum**
32 Mt Wesley Coast Rd, Harding Park.
**Tel** (09) 439 7555. **Open** daily.
**Closed** 25 Dec.

**Environs**

Located 45 km (28 miles) south of Dargaville, the **Kauri Museum** in Matakohe gives visitors an insight into kauri trees, especially after a trip through Waipoua Forest Park. The museum illustrates the role these mammoth trees played in New Zealand's pioneering history. A steam sawmill, with mannequins representing local settler families, shows how the logs were milled.

Within the main museum there is also kauri furniture, carvings and timber panels as well as an extensive collection of carved and polished kauri gum. Outside is a kauri post office from 1909, a 6-room fully furnished early 20th-century home and an 1867 pioneer church.

The **Kai-Iwi Lakes**, 34 km (21 miles) north of Dargaville, may lack the excitement of west coast beaches, but they are well frequented by locals and visitors. Comprising the Waikere, Taharoa and Kai-Iwi, these brilliant blue lakes are popular with swimmers, water-skiers, fishermen, picnickers and campers.

**Kauri Museum**
5 Church Rd, Matakohe. **Tel** (09) 431 7417. **Open** daily. **Closed** 25 Dec.
by arrangement.
**W** kaurimuseum.com

## ⑲ Waipoua Forest

**Road map** D1. 🛈 Waipoua Visitors' Centre, (09) 439 6445. **Open** daily.

Waipoua Forest is well worth a visit because of its magnificent kauri trees. Being in the presence of a tree that has entered its third millennium is a memorable experience, as photos seldom capture the grandeur of these trees. Local Maori have christened the country's largest living kauri Tane Mahuta, "the god of the forest". Reached by an easy 5-minute walk from the road through the park, the tree is 51 m (168 ft) high, has a girth of 14 m (46 ft) and a volume of 244.5 cu m (8,635 cu ft). Department of Conservation experts estimate the tree to be about 1,500 years old. Four other known giant trees in the forest are at least 1,000 years old. The forest also contains around 300 species of trees, palms and ferns.

## ⑳ Dargaville

**Road map** E1. 🛦 4,900. 🚍 🛈 4 Murdoch St, (09) 439 4975. **W** kauriinfocentre.co.nz

Dargaville is the nation's *kumara* capital and many road stalls with honesty boxes offer the opportunity to buy these sweet potatoes. The **Dargaville Museum** is not just of interest to sailors. Apart from Maori canoes, ship models and other nautical items, the displays

Boat exhibit in the Dargaville Museum

# THE CENTRAL NORTH ISLAND

Stretching from Auckland down to Taranaki, Manawatu and Hawkes Bay, this area includes beautiful and varied natural and man-made sights: snow-capped volcanoes, geothermal features, trout-filled lakes and rivers, mountain ranges, sandy beaches, fertile farmlands, prolific orchards and vineyards, and extensive forests. It is also a major centre of Maori history and culture.

Cutting a swathe from White Island in the north to Mount Ruapehu in the south, the Taupo Volcanic Zone *(see pp68–9)*, is testimony to underground forces that have fashioned the central plateau. Rotorua has a range of thermal attractions: geysers, bubbling mud pools, multi-coloured silica terraces, steaming lakes and streams and hot mineral pools. Lakes dotting the plateau offer excellent fishing, while rivers flowing from them are used for white-water rafting and jet-boating. In winter there is downhill skiing on the slopes of Mount Ruapehu in Tongariro National Park.

Steep, rugged, bush-clad ranges stretch 300 km (186 miles) from the volcanic plateau to the East Cape, separating the temperate area to the west from the warm, dry east coast region. Farming and forestry are well established in the Bay of

Plenty, King Country and Waikato. Dairy farmers compete with horticulturists for the best land, while sheep, cattle and deer roam larger paddocks on hills clear-felled of their native forest in the 19th and early 20th centuries. The Coromandel Peninsula, gripped by gold fever in the latter half of the 19th century, is now home to alternative lifestylers and artists inspired by its natural beauty. The curving Bay of Plenty, the scenic East Cape and the beaches of Gisborne offer excellent swimming, fishing and surfing.

The entire region is rich in Maori history, and Rotorua is the main centre for Maori cultural experiences. The Waikato-based Maori King Movement *(see p121)* began here in 1858, shortly before battles waged between the government and Maori over land.

Maori cultural performance at Rotorua

◄ Geothermal vents and stream at Waimangu, Rotorua

# Exploring the Central North Island

The Central North Island contains a wide range of landscapes and activities. Hamilton, the region's metropolitan hub, is set among lush farmland close to the western surf beaches of Raglan and the magical Waitomo Caves. North of Hamilton, the rugged Coromandel Peninsula flows into sandy, unspoilt Bay of Plenty beaches, the East Cape and the east coast, all popular spots for fishing and water sports. Hawke's Bay is famous for its Art Deco buildings, orchards and vineyards. Geothermal attractions stretch from lunar-landscaped White Island to the volcano Ruapehu, the North Island's best skiing location. At the bottom of the region, Tongariro National Park offers a wilderness experience.

Hawke's Bay vineyard

## Top Outdoor Activities

The places shown here have been selected for their recreational activities. Conditions vary depending on the weather and the time of year, so exercise caution and, if in doubt, seek local advice.

| | Game Fishing | Golf | Scuba Diving/ Snorkelling | Skiing | Surfing | Swimming | Tramping | Trout Fishing |
|---|---|---|---|---|---|---|---|---|
| Coromandel | | ▪ | ● | | ● | ▪ | ● | |
| Gisborne | ● | ▪ | ● | | ● | ▪ | | ▪ |
| Mayor Island | ● | | ● | | | ▪ | ● | |
| Mount Maunganui/Tauranga | ● | ▪ | | | ● | ▪ | ● | |
| Opotiki | | ▪ | | | ● | ▪ | ● | ▪ |
| Raglan | | ▪ | ● | | ● | ▪ | ● | |
| Rotorua | | ▪ | | | | ▪ | ● | ▪ |
| Taupo | | ▪ | | | | ▪ | ● | ▪ |
| Te Urewera National Park | | | | | | ▪ | ● | ▪ |
| Tongariro National Park | | ▪ | | ▪ | | ▪ | ● | ▪ |
| Turangi | | ▪ | | | | ▪ | ● | ▪ |
| Whitianga | ● | ▪ | ● | | ● | ▪ | ● | |

**For additional map symbols** *see back flap*

### Key

— Major road
═ Minor road
— Scenic route
— Major railway
— Minor railway
— Regional border
▲ Summit

## Sights at a Glance

1. Ngaruawahia
2. Raglan
3. Pirongia Forest Park
4. Kawhia
5. Hamilton
6. Cambridge
7. Otorohanga
8. *Waitomo Caves pp124–5*
9. Thames
10. Coromandel Forest Park
11. Coromandel
12. Port Jackson
13. Whitianga
14. Hahei
15. Whangamata

16. Waihi
17. Katikati
18. Tauranga
19. Mount Maunganui
20. Mayor Island
21. Te Puke
22. Whakatane
23. White Island
24. Opotiki
26. Te Urewera National Park
27. Gisborne
28. *Rotorua pp138–43*
29. Waimangu Volcanic Valley
30. Wai-o-tapu Thermal Wonderland

31. Orakei Korako Geyserland
32. Wairakei Park
33. Taupo
34. Turangi
35. *Tongariro National Park pp146–7*
36. *Napier pp150–51*
37. Hastings
38. Cape Kidnappers

### Tours

25. East Cape
39. Hawke's Bay Vineyards

Maori meeting house at
Te Kaha, Bay of Plenty

### Getting Around

The best way to tour the Central North Island is by car.
State Hwy 1 bisects the region, while the scenic Pacific
Coast and Thermal Explorer highways hug the
Coromandel Peninsula, Bay of Plenty and East Cape.
Roads are usually in good repair, but in winter snow may
close roads near Tongariro National Park. A passenger
train service links Auckland with Wellington, with
stops at Hamilton and other main towns. Local buses
and tour companies operate throughout the region.

0 kilometres    40

0 miles    40

# ● Ngaruawahia

**Road map** E2. 🚗 6,500. 🚌
ℹ️ 156 Great South Rd, Huntly,
(07) 828 6406. 🎪 Ngaruawahia
Regatta (third Sat in March).
**w hamiltonwaikato.com**

Situated where the Waikato and
Waipa rivers meet at the edge
of the central Waikato Basin,
Ngaruawahia is one of the oldest
and most historic settlements in
Waikato and an important
centre of Maori culture. On the
northeastern bank of the river,
off River Road, is one of the
Maori people's most important
locations – Turangawaewae
Marae, "the footstool" or home
of the Waikato Tainui tribe.
Turongo House, located within
the *marae*, is the official
residence of the reigning Maori
monarch, Tuheitia Paki. Although
Turangawaewae Marae is
considered too sacred for
tourism, and visitors are likely
to be referred to Rotorua where
Maori cultural experiences are
widely available, the *marae* is
open to the public for the annual
Ngaruawahia Regatta on the
river, which features *waka* (canoe)
racing, *iwi* dance competitions
and other activities (see p46).

The 1863–64 Waikato War
was a pivotal moment in New
Zealand's history. Maori united
to protect their land and formed
a resistance movement known
as Te Kingitanga. Take a look at
the Waikato War Driving Tour on
www.thewaikatowar.co.nz to
learn how this war unfolded and
relive the events at these sites.

The single-plume Bridal Veil Falls in Raglan

In the Hakarimata Scenic
Reserve on the slopes of the
Hakarimata Range to the north
of Ngaruawahia, native rimu
and kauri trees grow beside
three well-marked tracks, which
offer excellent tramping and
views of the Waikato Basin.

## Environs
**Waingaro Hot Springs**, 30 km
(19 miles) west of Ngaruawahia,
features four open-air mineral
water pools ranging in
temperature from 32 to 42 °C
(89 to 107 °F) as well as private
spa pools. New Zealand's
longest hot water hydroslide as
well as bumper boats offer
plenty of excitement. A range
of accommodation options is
available at the springs.

🏨 **Waingaro Hot Springs**
Waingaro Rd. **Tel** (07) 825 4761.
**Open** daily. 🅿️

# ● Raglan

**Road map** E2. 🚗 3,100. 🚌
ℹ️ 13 Wainui Rd, (07) 825 0556.
🎪 Raglan Surf Classic (Nov).

Waikato's only seaside resort on
the west coast, Raglan is a laid-
back coastal town with friendly
locals and a thriving arts scene.
Raglan fills with visitors during
summer, drawn to the water
sports available in its tranquil
harbour, its good swimming
beaches and its excellent
surfing. Te Kopua Beach and Te
Aro Aro Bay, close to Raglan, are
popular for swimming, while
Whale Bay, a ten-minute drive
south along the coast, is famous
worldwide among surfers for its
left-hand break.

The 25-km (15-mile) drive
south along Raglan's narrow
coastal Whaanga Road provides
fantastic views of the coastline
and the swells of the Tasman Sea.

Turangawaewae Marae, Ngaruawahia, home of the Maori king

About 21 km (13 miles) southeast of Raglan, on the road to Kawhia, an easy ten-minute walk through dense bush leads to the Bridal Veil Falls. The 55-m (180-ft) waterfall plunges in a single plume from a rock cleft to a deep pool below. A stepped track continues to the base of the falls and an even more dramatic vantage point with views across the pool and up at the falls.

Mount Pirongia, an extinct volcanic peak

Whale Bay, Raglan, world famous for its surfing

## ❸ Pirongia Forest Park

**Road map** E3. 🛈 Pirongia Heritage and Information Centre, 798 Franklin St, Pirongia, (07) 871 9018.

This park, comprising four separate forest areas south and southeast of Raglan, contains an extensive network of trails, from easy walks on the lower peaks to more strenuous hikes higher up. At 959 m (3,146 ft),

Mount Pirongia, an ancient volcano lying southeast of Raglan, is the most obvious landmark in the park; its dramatic skyline and dark green forest contrast strongly with the surrounding farmland. Closer to Raglan, 756-m (2,480-ft) Mt Karioi rises sharply from the coastline. Tracks lead to both peaks.

During the summer months it is advisable to carry drinking water when walking on the tracks. A number of native birds can be seen along the tracks and around the park's margins. Several native fish species and a huge variety of aquatic invertebrates can be found in the park's streams.

A hut on Mount Pirongia – Pahautea – sleeps six to eight people. Hut tickets are available from the Department of Conservation in Hamilton. There are picnic areas at the end of both Corcoran and Grey roads and a camping area alongside trout-filled Kaniwhaniwha Stream.

## ❹ Kawhia

**Road map** E3. 🚹 550. 🛈 Kawhia Museum & Information Centre, Kaora St, (07) 871 0161.

Located on the coast 55 km (34 miles) to the south of Raglan, along winding but scenic back roads, the small settlement of Kawhia comprises a jumble of cottages on the north side of Kawhia Harbour, 5 km (3 miles) from the Tasman Sea. The harbour is remote, splendid and huge, its shoreline twisting and turning for 57 km (35 miles).

In former times, Maori prized the harbour and the fertile valleys running down to it and fought over rights to the area. The Maori migration canoe Tainui, which plied the coastline eight centuries ago, is buried on the slopes behind the Makatu meeting house. Stones placed 23 m (75 ft) apart above the bow and stern mark its position. The canoe was once moored to a pohutukawa tree, Tangi te Korowhiti, on the shore at the end of Karewa Street. Now a large clump of pohutukawas, the tree is still revered by the Tainui people as signifying the beginning of their association with Aotearoa.

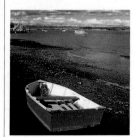

The large Kawhia harbour on the west coast

## Maori King Movement

Queen Te Atairangikaahu

This movement grew in the 1850s out of a realization among Maoris that intertribal feuding assisted the Pakeha (Europeans) to acquire Maori land. In 1858, several tribes chose a paramount king in the hope that the dignity and *mana* (respect) that would accrue to him would promote peaceful co-existence with the government and settle land conflicts. Instead, the government interpreted the Maori King Movement as a form of rebellion. Attitudes hardened and spawned the Waikato land wars of the 1860s *(see pp53–4)*. In 1966, Te Atairangikaahu was proclaimed queen. She was succeeded by King Tuheitia Paki in 2006, the seventh monarch. His role is mainly cultural and spiritual, though this is becoming more important as the place of Maori in New Zealand society is reassessed.

# ❺ Hamilton

**Road map** E2. 🗺 118,000. ✈ 10 km (6 miles) S of city. 🚌 ℹ Cnr Aro and Alexandra Sts, Garden Place, (07) 839 3580. 🎈 Balloons Over Waikato (Apr); National Agricultural Fieldays (Jun). 🌐 **hamiltonwaikato.com**

New Zealand's fourth largest metropolitan area and largest inland city, Hamilton straddles a meandering section of the mighty Waikato River, at 425 km (264 miles) the longest in the country. The city has grown from a 19th-century military settlement into a bustling centre servicing the Waikato region, a huge undulating plain. Attractive parks and gardens, dissected by footpaths, border the river, and bridges connect the east and west banks. The **Waikato River Explorer** cruises the river from its landing at Hamilton Gardens Jetty, offering the best views of the area.

Perched on five levels above the river, the **Waikato Museum of Art and History** features a large collection of New Zealand art, Waikato history and history of the local Tainui people. On permanent display is an impressive war canoe, Te Winika.

The **Hamilton Gardens**, located at the southern end of the city, are Hamilton's most popular visitor attraction. Set along a scenic stretch of the Waikato River, they include pavilions showcasing Japanese, Chinese and English gardens as well as seasonal attractions.

Hamilton hosts Balloons Over Waikato, a fiesta which attracts balloonists from around the world, and the National Agricultural Fieldays at nearby Mystery Creek, one of Austra-lasia's largest agricultural trade shows (*see p47*).

🚢 **Waikato River Explorer**
Hamilton Gardens Jetty. **Tel** (0800) 139 756. **Open** Oct–May: Sat–Sun; Jun–Sep: Sat. 🧩 🚻 🌐 **waikatoexplorer.co.nz**

🏛 **Waikato Museum of Art and History**
1 Grantham St. **Tel** (07) 838 6606. **Open** daily. **Closed** 25 Dec. 📷 🚻 🌐 **waikatomuseum.org.nz**

🌿 **Hamilton Gardens**
Cobham Drive. **Tel** (07) 856 3200. **Open** daily. 🚻 🚻

# ❻ Cambridge

**Road map** E3. 🗺 13,500. ✈ 15 km (9 miles) E of city. ℹ Cnr Queen & Victoria sts, (07) 823 3456.

Fifteen minutes' drive south of Hamilton, Cambridge lies amid farmland, home to New Zealand's thoroughbred horse industry. Known as "the town of trees" because of its avenues of oak and elm, the town has a charming village green and pretty gardens. The domain around Lake Koutu, fringed by exotic trees and native bush, is a popular place for walks and picnics.

Cambridge is also known for its contemporary art and crafts outlets; one, the large, award-winning **Cambridge Country**

Items for sale at the Cambridge Country Store

**Store**, is located in a church built in 1898. The town's numerous antique shops and galleries are another major attraction.

Visitors can also view a pot-pourri of architectural styles at St. Andrew's church and the public buildings along and adjacent to Victoria Street.

🏪 **Cambridge Country Store**
92 Victoria St. **Tel** (07) 827 8715. **Open** daily. **Closed** 25 Dec. 🚻 🚻 🌐 **cambridgecountrystore.co.nz**

# ❼ Otorohanga

**Road map** E3. 🗺 2,600. 🚉 🚌 ℹ 27 Turonga St, (07) 873 8951.

Fifty kilometres (31 miles) south of Hamilton lies Otorohanga, a small provincial town whose main attraction is the **Otorohanga Kiwi House**. Three kiwi species are bred at the zoological park and 300 birds, representing 29 species, many of which can be viewed in a massive walk-through aviary. In addition to kiwi, these include native pigeons, tui, silvereyes, parakeets and saddlebacks. Geckos, weta, and tuataras (an ancient reptile) are also on display.

Otorohanga is regarded as the gateway to the Waitomo Caves (*see pp124–5*).

🥝 **Otorohanga Kiwi House**
20 Alex Telfer Drive. **Tel** (07) 873 7391. **Open** daily. **Closed** 25 Dec. 🦎 🚻 🦉 Nocturnal House. 🚻 🌐 **kiwihouse.org.nz**

Glassware at the Cambridge Country Store

The *Waikato River Explorer* cruising on the Waikato River

# Stock–Stud Heartland

One of the most fascinating sights on the drive between Hamilton and Cambridge is the wooden-railed fences behind which young thoroughbred horses cavort, growing strong on the best pasture and supplementary feed their owners can provide. Set back from the road are sign-posted stud stables where the horses are housed and trained. Black and white cows grazing on dappled green fields can also be seen. New Zealand's thoroughbred racehorse and dairy cattle stud industries are concentrated in the Waikato region. Here a mild, wet climate produces lush cattle pasture and the rolling plains that are ideal for exercising and training racehorses.

Thoroughbred yearlings and foals on a Waikato stud farm

### Thoroughbred Horses

Waikato is renowned internationally for its racing progeny, and the yearling export industry earns the country more than NZ$120 million annually. Some 60 stallions are available for breeding purposes at 18 Waikato commercial thoroughbred studs, the most sought after of these sires mating 100–150 mares.

**New Zealand Horse Magic**, 6 km (4 miles) south of Cambridge, showcases a collection of horse breeds and features an informative hour-long show. Thoroughbred stud tours are also available at other stud farms in the area.

**Waikato**-bred horses have won Australia's Melbourne Cup, the pinnacle of the Australasian racing season, 18 times.

**New Zealand's main dairy breeds** – Holstein-Friesian, Jersey and Ayrshire – can be found in Waikato, although the Holstein-Friesian predominates. The average New Zealand cow produces 3,420 litres (752 imperial gallons) of milk a year.

**New Zealand's** thoroughbred industry is showcased to the world each February at the yearling sale held at Karaka on the southern outskirts of Auckland.

# ❽ Waitomo Caves

The area known as Waitomo consists of a 45-km (28-mile) network of underground limestone caves and grottoes linked to the Waitomo Caves River. A chamber of the Waitomo Glowworm Caves was first explored in 1887, but most caves remain the domain of cavers and speleologists. Apart from touring the Waitomo Glowworm and Aranui caves, famous for their glowworm grottoes and fantastic limestone formations, visitors can enjoy a range of cave-based adventure activities, including abseiling into a limestone shaft and cave system, and black-water rafting, an adventure sport unique to New Zealand. The 2.5 km (1.5 miles) of caves accessible to the public have superb lighting, good paths, handrails and informative local guides.

**Waitomo Walkway**
A 5-km (3-mile) walk over farmland and through native bush takes visitors past typical limestone karst features such as outcrops, small caves and sinkholes.

**Black-water Rafting**
Equipped with wet suits, lights and "cave rafts" (inner tubes), these black-water rafters drift in darkness, beneath millions of glowworms, along an underground river in the Ruakuri Cave.

## KEY

① **The Ruakuri Natural Tunnel**, a large U-shaped tunnel, is reached by a 30-minute walk up the Ruakuri Gorge. Ruakuri Cave is accessible to wheelchairs and guided tours are available.

② **The Tokikarpu meeting house**, off Te Anga Road, serves the needs of the local Maori people.

③ **The Waitomo Caves Hotel**, built in 1908, nestles among trees on a hill above Waitomo village. It has rooms to suit every traveller.

④ **Kiwi Paka YHA Waitomo hostel**

⑤ **The Museum of Caves**, which includes the Waitomo i-SITE Visitor Centre, has excellent displays on caves and natural history as well as a multi-media show about the New Zealand glowworms.

⑥ **Waitomo Top Ten Holiday Park camping ground**

⑦ **Woodlyn Park** hosts the pioneer heritage show, held daily, where visitors can help shear a sheep and train a farm dog.

**Key**
```
=== Road
━━ River
━━ Walking track
```

0 metres — 500
0 yards — 500

**★ Aranui Cave**
The high chambers, magnificent formations and pale brown, pink and white shades of the huge stalactites are the finest to be seen in Waitomo's caves.

★ **Waitomo Glowworm Caves**
A walk through the three levels of the caves – the Banquet Chamber, Pipe Organ and Cathedral – is capped by a tranquil boat ride through the magical Glowworm Grotto.

State Highway 3
and Lost world

**Lost World**
The Lost World involves a 100-m (330-ft) abseil descent into a huge limestone shaft followed by an amazing caving expedition through the Mangapu Cave system.

## Formation of the Waitomo Caves

Caves are formed through the erosion of layers of limestone by water flowing underground. The cave systems in the Waitomo area have developed in fractured limestone, up to 100 m (330 ft) thick, along or adjacent to major fault lines *(see p24)* where percolation of groundwater is particularly high. Surface water flowing down cracks in the limestone created an underground drainage system which gradually increased in size and complexity. Inside the Waitomo caves, dripping water containing dissolved limestone has formed stalactites on the cave roofs, stalagmites on the floors, and other fascinating formations.

Sinkhole
Volcanic ash
Upper cave entrance
Fault
Shaft
Stream
Limestone
Cavern
Stream bed

Karaka Bird Hide on the Firth of Thames

## ❾ Thames

**Road Map** E2. 🖼 10,000. ✈ 2 km
(1.2 miles) S of town. 🚌
ℹ 206 Pollen St, (07) 868 7284.
🎭 Pohutakawa Festival (Nov–Dec).
🌐 **thamesinfo.co.nz**

Located at the southeastern
corner of the Firth of Thames,
against hills that 100 years ago
rang to the sound of battery
stamps pounding quartz ore
to extract gold, Thames is the
principal town of the
Coromandel region. It services
surrounding farmland and a
swelling coastal population.
It is the gateway to the
Coromandel Peninsula and
an ideal base from which to
explore the Coromandel Forest
Park wilderness area. Many
buildings in the town owe their
grandeur to wealth created
during the gold-mining era.

The **Thames Historical
Museum** features relics from
the town's past, including the
pioneering foundries that
sprang up to support the
mining industry, while the
**Thames School of Mines
and Mineralogical Museum**
features 5,000 mineral samples
and equipment used to process
quartz ore and extract gold.
Mine managers were taught in
the school's classroom from
1885 to 1954.

A large World War I memorial,
off Waiotahi Creek Road, stands
on a hill above the town to the
north, and affords panoramic
views of the town, the Firth of
Thames, and the Hauraki Gulf

beyond. At the small Karaka Bird
Hide, built among mangroves
off Brown Street on the edge of
town, migratory wading birds
can be seen, especially between
high and low tides.

🏛 **Thames Historical Museum**
Cnr Pollen & Cochrane sts.
**Tel** (07) 868 8509. **Open** 1–4pm daily.
🚫 🅿 ♿ 🏠

🏛 **Thames School of Mines and
Mineralogical Museum**
101 Cochrane St. **Tel** (07) 868 6227.
**Open** Jan–Feb: daily; Mar–Dec: Wed–
Sun. **Closed** Good Fri, 25 Dec. 🅿
🅿 🏠

### Environs

Along the Firth of Thames'
southern edge, 85 sq km (33 sq
miles) of rich, intertidal mud
flats provide another excellent
habitat for migratory wading
birds, such as gulls, shags,
oystercatchers and pied stilts,
and opportunities to observe
them. The **Miranda Shorebird**

Trampers in the Kauaeranga Valley,
Coromandel Forest Park

**Centre**, established by the
Miranda Naturalists' Trust, can
arrange tours to see the birds as
well as accommodation. Nearby
is the Miranda Hot Springs, a
thermal pool complex.

🦅 **Miranda Shorebird Centre**
285 East Coast Rd, Pokeno.
**Tel** (09) 232 2781. **Open** daily.
**Closed** 25 Dec. 🅿 donation. ♿ 🏠
🌐 **miranda-shorebird.org.nz**

## ❿ Coromandel
Forest Park

**Road map** E2. ℹ Kauaeranga Valley,
Thames, (07) 867 9080.

This park stretches for 100 km
(62 miles) along the peninsula's
interior, but the most accessible
part is the forested Kauaeranga
Valley, with its well-developed
network of short walks, longer
tramps and picnic areas.

The valley was a major source
of kauri timber from the 1870s
to the 1920s. Remains of dams,
trestle bridges and river booms,
used to flush kauri logs into the
Kauaeranga River, are evident.

Anglers can fish for trout in
the valley's streams where the
keen-eyed may also find gemstones. A rocky ridge known as
the Pinnacles offers fine views of
both coastlines. The Kauaeranga
Visitor Centre, 13 km (8 miles)
northeast of Thames, provides
details of walks and tramps
that comprise the Kauaerang
a Kauri Trail, a pack track made
by kauri bushmen, as well as
park accommodation.

# Gold Fever in the Coromandel

The first significant gold find on the Coromandel Peninsula occurred in October 1852 near Coromandel Town. Three hundred diggers rushed to the area. Further discoveries near Thames in 1867 attracted 5,000 men into the surrounding hills. Soon Thames became a boom town and its population mushroomed to 18,000. Miners thronged the town on Saturdays, three live theatres were seldom closed, and more than 100 hotels sold liquor. However, by the 1870s the Thames goldfields were in decline and interest had shifted southeast to Karangahake Mountain and to Waihi. By 1912, Waihi's Martha Mine had become one of the world's largest *(see p130)*. The mines all closed eventually, but new goldbearing zones found within old fields prompted large-scale mining operations to begin once more at the open mining pit at Waihi from 1988 to 2007.

Candles provided light and indicated the presence of gas.

**A mallet and pick** were used to loosen gold-bearing rock.

### Gold-Mining Relics

Old gold mines, shafts, mine dumps and abandoned mining machinery are dotted around Thames. The mining school and mineralogical museum, as well as the gold mine tours on offer, are further reminders of the town's gold-mining history. Coromandel gold had to be laboriously extracted from the ground with pick and shovel.

**Canvas bags** held any nuggets that were extracted.

Model of a miner at the Thames Gold Mine and Stamper Battery

Orange calcite    Goodlitite    Amethyst

Stitchtite

Pink tourmoline

**Coromandel** is also rich in semi-precious gemstones. It is still possible to stumble across agate on some of the beaches north of Thames.

**This classroom** in the Thames School of Mines provided practical instruction for gold-miners working the quartz fields.

**Fossicking for gold** in the old gold mines is a popular pastime but care must be taken when entering old mines that they are structurally safe.

**The Imperial Hotel**, one of a number of fine colonial hotels in Thames built at the height of the town's gold-rush prosperity.

# ⓫ Coromandel

**Road map** E2. 🏔 1,500. ✈ 3 km
(2 miles) S of town. 🚌 ℹ 355
Kapanga Rd, (07) 866 8598.
🅦 **coromandeltown.co.nz**

Coromandel town, as it is
referred to by those wishing to
distinguish it from the peninsula
itself, is a quiet fishing and crafts
town about an hour's drive
north of Thames. It owes its
name to the 1820 visit of HMS
*Coromandel*, which called to
load kauri spars for the British
Royal Navy. Mining featured
prominently in the town's
formative years *(see p127)*, and
fine examples of Victorian and
colonial architecture are a
legacy of that era. The laid-back
atmosphere and beauty of the
area make it a haven for artists
and crafts people, and an ideal
place in which to tramp, swim,
fish, sail or simply relax.

One of Coromandel's most
popular attractions is the
**Driving Creek Railway and
Potteries**, built by New Zealand
potter Barry Brickell to convey
clay and wood to his kiln, and to
service a kauri forest replanting
project. The narrow-gauge
mountain railway takes visitors
in specially designed carriages
on a one-hour round trip
through native forest and tunnels
and across bridges to a viewpoint
high above Coromandel.

The **Coromandel Gold
Stamper Battery** and a 100-year-
old gold-processing museum,
featuring a working water
wheel, lie at the end of Buffalo
Road to the north of the town.
The **Coromandel School of**

Water-powered bicycle at the Waterworks,
a fun-park set in lovely gardens

**Mines and Historical Museum**
has displays of early gold-
mining and kauri logging,
and an old jailhouse.

🚉 **Driving Creek Railway
and Potteries**
380 Driving Creek Rd. **Tel** (07) 866
8703. **Open** daily. **Closed** 25 April,
25 Dec. 🖼 🖼 🖼
🅦 **drivingcreekrailway.co.nz**

🏭 **Coromandel Gold
Stamper Battery**
Buffalo Rd. **Tel** (07) 866 7933.
**Open** summer: daily; winter: Thu–
Mon. **Closed** 25 Dec. 🖼 🖼

🏛 **Coromandel School of Mines
and Historical Museum**
841 Rings Rd. **Tel** (07) 866 8039.
**Open** summer: daily; winter: Sat &
Sun. **Closed** 25 Dec. 🖼 🖼

## Environs
The delightful **Waterworks**,
9 km (5.5 miles) from
Coromandel Town, showcase
artist Chris Ogilvie's genius for
inventing water-powered art
forms and gadgets that amaze

both children and adults. One
of Coromandel's most nnovative
attractions, the waterworks is
set in park-like gardens.

Just east of the waterworks is a
turn-off to Castle Rock. At 525 m
(1,722 ft), it is the core of an old
volcano on the "back-bone" of
the peninsula. A drive through
pine forest takes visitors to the
start of a 45-minute walk. The
last few metres are a strenuous
climb, but panoramic views
make it worthwhile. Further
along the road is the Waiau
Kauri Grove where magnificent
kauris, protected for more than
100 years, can be seen ten
minutes' walk along a track
on the left side of the road.

🌿 **The Waterworks**
471 The 309 Rd. **Tel** (07) 866 7191.
**Open** daily. 🖼 🖼 🖼
🅦 **waiauwaterworks.co.nz**

Coastline between Coromandel Town and
Port Jackson

# ⓬ Port Jackson

**Road map** E2. 🏔 10. ℹ 355
Kapanga Rd, Coromandel Town,
(07) 866 8598.

At the tip of the peninsula,
56 km (35 miles) north of
Coromandel, Port Jackson's
long, lupin-backed beach comes
as a surprise. The road, which is
unsealed from the small
settlement of Colville, the last
supply point, ends at Fletcher's
Bay, 6 km (4 miles) further on,
a pretty pohutukawa-shaded
cove with good fishing.

The Coromandel Walkway,
a 7-km (4.5-mile) track, leads
from Fletcher's Bay to Stony Bay
and takes about three hours to
complete. Port Jackson, Fletcher's
Bay and Stony Bay all have
camping grounds with toilets,
cold showers and barbecue pits.

The unique Driving Creek Railway

Boats at sheltered Whitianga harbour

## ⑬ Whitianga

**Road map** E2. ⛰ 3,500. ✈ 3 km (2 miles) SW of town. 🚌 ℹ 66 Albert St, (07) 866 5555. 🅦 whitianga.co.nz

Whitianga sits on the innermost recess of Mercury Bay which was named by Captain Cook *(see p52)* when he observed a transit of the planet Mercury on his 1769 visit to the area. Whitianga provides safe boat launching, ideal during the big game fishing season from November to April. Major fishing contests occur in February and March. The tiny Mercury Bay Boating Club, at the west end of Buffalo Beach, earned world fame when it spearheaded Auckland financier Michael Fay's unsuccessful 1988 challenge to the San Diego Yacht Club for the America's Cup.

The **Mercury Bay Museum** occupies a disused dairy factory opposite the wharf on The Esplanade. It documents the Polynesian chief Kupe *(see p50)*,

Boating club logo

whose descendants are said to have occupied the town for more than 1,000 years. A short ferry ride across the narrow harbour entrance takes visitors to Ferry Landing, the original site of Whitianga, where there are walks, lookouts and craft outlets. Whitianga Rock, upstream of Ferry Landing, was formerly a *pa* site of the Ngati Hei tribe. Whitianga's Buffalo Beach is named after an 1840 shipwreck. The British ship *Buffalo*, which had delivered convicts to Australia and was to return to Britain with kauri spars, was blown by a storm onto the beach and destroyed. A cannon from the ship is mounted at the RSA Memorial Park in Albert Street.

At the northeast tip of the headland, 1.5 km (1 mile) from Ferry Landing, is Shakespeare Lookout, named after the bard. Here also, a memorial to Cook stands above Lonely Bay and Cooks Beach. Wave action at Flaxmill Bay, at the southwest

end of Front Bay, has undercut the rock to form a natural soundshell.

The **Te Whanganui-A-Hei Marine Reserve** at Cathedral Cove covers 9 sq km (4 sq miles) and extends from Cooks Bluff to Hahei Beach. It was established in 1992 to restore the area's marine environment to its former rich and varied condition. No fishing or gathering of shellfish is allowed, although visitors may swim, dive and sail in the reserve.

🏛 **Mercury Bay Museum**
11A The Esplanade. **Tel** (07) 866 0730. **Open** daily. **Closed** 25 Dec. 🅿 ♿
🅦 mercurybaymuseum.co.nz

## ⑭ Hahei

**Road map** E2. ⛰ 200. 🚌 General Store, Hahei Beach Rd.

Hahei is the start of a two-hour return walk to Cathedral Cove, where a dramatic, cathedral-shaped cavern, accessible at low tide, cuts through a white headland. Reasonable fitness is required to reach the cove but panoramic cliff-top views make the effort worthwhile. Hahei's beach is sheltered by offshore islands and tinged pink with broken shells. The area is popular with divers.

At Hot Water Beach, 6 km (4 miles) south of Hahei, visitors can dig their own thermal spa in the sand between low and mid-tides. Spades are available for hire.

Visitors soaking in hot springs in the sand at Hot Water Beach, south of Hahei

Whangamata Beach, one of New Zealand's best surf beaches

## ⑮ Whangamata

**Road map** E2. ⚐ 4,100. 🚌 ℹ 616
Port Rd, (07) 865 8340.
Ⓦ whangamatainfo.co.nz

The town of Whangamata, meaning "obsidian harbour", was named after the dark, glass-like volcanic rock that has washed ashore from Mayor Island, 30 km (19 miles) from the mainland. The town is often referred to as "the surfing capital of New Zealand" because of the size of the waves in the area, particularly its sandbank surf break known as "the bar". Its surf is also popular with swimmers who enjoy large waves and with surf-fishers. Other superb surfing beaches in the vicinity include Onemana and Opoutere to the north of the town and Whiritoa on the coast to the south.

The hills and valleys behind Whangamata, a short drive from the town, offer many outdoor activities. Within the Tairua Forest lie the Wentworth Valley, Taungatara Recreation Reserve and Parakiwai Valley. These are crisscrossed with walking tracks that make the most of stony streams and pockets of native bush. A popular walk takes in the "Luck at Last" gold mine and the remains of ore processors, water races, buildings and even a baker's oven. Walk details are available from the Whangamata information centre and forestry company Matariki Forests, which may close access when it is conducting forestry operations. Wharekawa Wildlife Refuge, 15 km (10 miles) north of Whangamata, is a conservation area based on the Opoutere sandspit. It is home to oyster-catchers and dotterels.

## ⑯ Waihi

**Road map** E2. ⚐ 4,500. 🚌
ℹ Seddon St, (07) 863 6715.
Ⓦ waihi.org.nz

The history of Waihi has been linked with gold since Robert Lee and John McCrombie discovered a gold-bearing quartz reef in 1878. The **Martha Mine**, established on the site in 1882 and worked continuously until 1952, was the most important and successful of many in the district (see pp126–7). In 1988, the Martha Mine reopened, with concessions to operate until 2007, and substantial amounts of gold were extracted from the mine during that period of time. The mine is undergoing further exploration, with a likelihood that mining will resume in the future.

The **Goldfields Railway** operates vintage diesel and steam trains on 7 km (4 miles) of track between Waihi and Waikino, gateway to the Karangahake gold fields. The

Karangahake Gorge Historic Walkway, a 5-km (3-mile) loop along the gorge past old bridges, abandoned mining equipment and mining shafts, is signposted from the road. Waihi Beach, 11 km (7 miles) east of the town, is one of the most popular along the coast.

🚂 **Goldfields Railway**
30 Wrigley St. **Tel** (07) 863 9020. **Open** daily. **Closed** 25 Dec. 🦽 ♿ 💻 📷

## ⑰ Katikati

**Road map** E2. ⚐ 4,000. ℹ 34 Main Rd, (07) 549 1658. Ⓦ katikati.co.nz

Enthusiastic Irish colonizer George Vesey Stewart bought Katikati and its surrounding land in the 1870s and sold it to 406 "refined and educated" Ulster families. Unfamiliar with the hard work needed to break in their land, these immigrants initially resented Stewart, but the district has since proved itself ideal for horticulture and dairy farming. Today, Katikati is thought of as an open-air "art gallery". More than 30 murals and other art decorate its buildings, streets and parks, all produced by local artists. **Sapphire Springs & Motor Camp**, set in a bush reserve 6 km (4 miles) from the town, has freshwater thermal springs for swimming or soaking.

Street sculpture, Katikati

🏕 **Sapphire Springs & Motor Camp**
Hot Springs Rd. **Tel** (07) 549 0768. **Open** daily. 🦽 📷

Mural on a building at Katikati

# Coromandel's Artisan Lifestyle

The ever-changing sea, beautiful valleys and rugged forest interior of the Coromandel Peninsula not only offer a quiet alternative to city life but provide constant inspiration to a large number of artists and crafts people. Here painters farm, potters paint and raise silkworms, and weavers rear their own sheep for wool. Since their arrival in the early 1960s, many of these "alternative lifestylers" have turned to art and crafts to support their nature-based lifestyle, honing their talents to produce a large number of items for sale in retail outlets throughout New Zealand. The Coromandel Craft Trail leaflet, available at visitor centres, directs visitors to tucked-away studios where they can see artists at work and buy items direct at studio prices.

**Bone and greenstone** are popular materials for carving pendants with Maori designs.

**Retail outlets** in Thames and Coromandel Town, such as Weta Art, sell a wide range of Coromandel and other New Zealand–made crafts.

Barry Brickell at Driving Creek Potteries

**Pottery items** are either thrown on a wheel or, like these pieces, hand-sculpted and glazed in a multitude of colours.

## Coromandel's Crafts

*Although the initial surge of artistic pursuits on the peninsula in the early 1960s focused on clay, crafts quickly diversified to include carving (in wood, bone and greenstone), kauri furniture, weaving, knitting, jewellery, leadlight glass work, hand-made knives and garden décor.*

**Colville Store**, one of the peninsula's most unusual retail outlets, 26 km (16 miles) north of Coromandel Town, is owned by an 80-member co-operative.

**Alternative lifestylers** often choose to raise young children in supportive community environments where they grow organic produce, paint, sculpt and make crafts.

# ⑱ Tauranga

**Road map** E2. 🗺 including
Mount Maunganui, 100,000.
✈ 3 km (2 miles) E of town. 🚌
ℹ 95 Willow St, (07) 578 8103.
🌐 bayofplentynz.com

The largest city in the western
Bay of Plenty and an important
commercial centre and port,
Tauranga lies along a section of
the sprawling Tauranga Harbour,
a plain thought to have been
flooded at the end of the last
Ice Age. On its seaward side, the
city is sheltered by Matakana
Island and to the west by the
Kaimai Ranges.

Tauranga is a popular city.
Its benign climate and coastal
location are attractive to retired
New Zealanders and to anyone
who enjoys year-round outdoor
activities. Recreational and
competitive boating, surfing
and deep-sea fishing are among
its major attractions. It is also a
popular venue for jet-skiing,
water-skiing, windsurfing,
parasailing and diving. The
Strand, in the centre of town,
is the main shopping and
restaurant area.

Originally a flax-trading and
missionary town, Tauranga was
the scene of fierce fighting
during the New Zealand land
wars in the 1860s (see pp53–4).
Many of the troops involved in
a significant battle at Gate Pa,

5 km (3 miles) south of the city,
were stationed at Monmouth
Redoubt, a military camp built
by British troops in 1864 to stop
supplies reaching the Waikato
Maori King Movement (see p121).
Well-preserved earthworks and
heavy artillery, are still in place.

**The Elms Mission Station**,
built in stages between 1838
and 1847 by the Reverend
Alfred Brown, is one of New
Zealand's oldest homes. The
grounds contain gardens and
several buildings, including an
1839 free-standing library.

Tauranga's other attractions
include 50 km (31 miles) of
beach and foreshore reserve
and 27 km (17 miles) of public
walkways around the coast,
estuary and inland reserves.

🏠 **The Elms Mission Station**
Cnr Mission & Chapel sts. **Tel** (07) 577
9772. **Open** grounds: daily; house &
library: 2–4pm Wed, Sat, Sun & public
hols (tours by arrangement). 🅿
house & library. 🌐 **theelms.org.nz**

## Environs

**McLaren Falls Park**, off State
Highway 29 on the road to
Hamilton, has walks through
picturesque native bush
interspersed with thousands
of introduced trees. A river and
Lake McLaren offer swimming.
On scheduled days throughout
the year, top white-water action

occurs downstream on the
Wairoa River when floodgates
on the hydro-controlled waterway are opened. The park has
three backpacker hostels.

🌲 **McLaren Falls Park**
McLaren Falls Rd. **Tel** Tauranga
District Council, (07) 577 7000.
**Open** daily. ♿

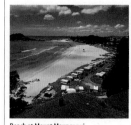

Beach at Mount Maunganui
from "The Mount"

# ⑲ Mount Maunganui

**Road map** E2. 🗺 including Tauranga,
100,000. ✈ 3 km (2 miles) S of town.
🚌 ℹ Salisbury Ave, (07) 575 5099.

The town of Mount Maunganui,
built on a narrow peninsula at
the mouth of Tauranga Harbour,
is the main port for the central
North Island timber industry.
Overshadowing the town is the
232-m (761-ft) cone-shaped
Mount Maunganui. A walk
to the summit and back takes
90 minutes and provides views
of Maori fortifications dating
from when "The Mount", as it is
commonly called, was a pa site.
At the top, unobstructed views
up and down the coast can be
seen. At the bottom are the
**Mount Salt Water Pools**, which
are heated by natural thermal
water and make a great way
to relax after a walk.

Magnificent Ocean Beach
extends east from The Mount to
Papamoa and beyond, creating
an ideal summer playground for
surfers and swimmers. In high
seas, a blowhole at Moturiki
Island, off Marine Parade, shoots
spray skywards.

🏊 **Mount Salt Water Pools**
Adams Ave. **Tel** (07) 575 0868.
**Open** daily. 🅿 ♿ 📷

Game fishing competition, Tauranga

## ⑳ Mayor Island

**Road map** F2. 35 km (22 miles) from Tauranga Harbour. 🚤 from Tauranga or Whangamata. ℹ️ 95 Willow St, Tauranga, (07) 578 8103.

Mayor Island (Tuhua) is rather hilly and bush-clad and there are very few landing places around its steep cliffs. The highest peak, Opauhau, reaches 354 m (1,161 ft) above a roughly circular island 4 km (3 miles) across. Two lakes lie within a crater crowning the summit of what is a dormant volcano rising from the sea floor.

The island's most striking feature is black obsidian, a natural glass formed by rapid cooling of silica-rich lava. In pre-European times, Maori prized obsidian and fought battles over the island.

An 18-km (11-mile) walking track circles the island while other paths cross the interior. All sea life is protected within a marine reserve on the northern coastline. A camping ground and cabins provide accommodation, but visitors must take adequate food and water as supplies on the island are limited. Game fish in the vicinity of the island include tuna, marlin, kingfish and mako sharks. Several companies run diving and sightseeing trips to the island.

Tour in kiwi-carts through Kiwi360

## ㉑ Te Puke

**Road map** F3. 🏘️ 6,800. 🚌 ℹ️ 130 Jellicoe St, (07) 573 6772. 🌐 **tepuke.co.nz**

Te Puke is another town originally settled with Irish folk by Ulsterman George Vesey Stewart (see p130) in the 1880s. Early farming of sheep and cattle in the area was hampered by "bush sickness," a cobalt deficiency that dogged farming in many central North Island regions until it was identified in the 1930s and corrected with cobaltized fertilizers. With an ideal climate for sheep, cattle

Entrance to Kiwi360

and dairy farming, these land uses predominated until interest in horticulture strengthened in the 1960s.

Pioneering horticulturists experimented with what was then known as the Chinese gooseberry, and developed an international market for it under a new name – kiwifruit.

Since then Te Puke has been hailed as "the kiwifruit capital of the world". All aspects of the industry are displayed at the export kiwifruit orchard and horticultural park **Kiwi360**, 6 km (4 miles) southeast of Te Puke.

**Spring Loaded Fun Park**, 8 km (5 miles) south of Te Puke, is a large farm designed to show the diversity of New Zealand farming. There are sheep and pigs, as well as groves of avocado, kiwifruit and pine trees. Children can get up close to young animals and hand-feed 60-year-old eels. Visitors can also explore the stunning natural beauty of the bush-clad Kaituna River during a 30-minute jet-boat ride.

🎟️ **Kiwi360**
35 Young Rd. **Tel** (07) 573 6340. **Open** daily. **Closed** 25 Dec. 🏛️ 👿 ⏱️ obligatory. 🚫 🅿️ 🏛️ 🌐 **kiwi360.com**

🎟️ **Spring Loaded Fun Park**
316 State Hwy 33, Te Puke. **Tel** (07) 533 1515. **Open** summer: daily; winter: Wed–Sun. **Closed** 25 Dec. 🏛️ rides. 👿 ⏱️ obligatory. 🅿️ 🏛️

---

### Kiwifruit

Before kiwifruit (*Actinidia chinensis*) became an international marketing success, it was known in New Zealand as the Chinese gooseberry after its country of origin. The first plant was grown in Te Puke in 1918, but it was not until the mid-1930s that Te Puke grower Jim McLoughlin planted the first orchard and sold fruit on the local

Kiwifruit from Te Puke

market. Offshore markets were sought as more kiwifruit were grown. In the late 1960s, the industry was propelled to success by a combination of good marketing and the discovery that refrigerated kiwifruit remains in good condition for up to six months. In the late 1970s, many horticulturists became millionaires almost overnight. Since 1998, the yellow-fleshed, tropical-flavoured Zespri Gold variety has supplemented the traditional emerald green-centred Hayward variety.

Fishing at the mouth of the
Whakatane River

## ㉒ Whakatane

**Road map** F3. 🏛 17,000. 🚌 🛈 Cnr
Quay St & Kakahoroa Dr, (07) 306 2030,
0800 942 528. **W** whakatane.com

Resting in the coastal heart
of the eastern Bay of Plenty,
Whakatane is one of New
Zealand's sunniest locations. The
town enjoys more than 2,500
sunshine hours a year, making it
ideal for a wide range of marine
activities. These include fishing
and viewing and swimming
with dolphins. Whales and
Dolphin Watch NZ takes visitors
on a voyage out into the Bay of
Plenty to swim with dolphins.

The **Whakatane District
Museum and Gallery** gives an
insight into the lifestyles of early
Maori and European settlers. It
contains a pictorial history of
the district as well as displays
of Maori artifacts.

There are several excellent
local walkways. One, the Nga
Tapuwae O Toi Walkway,
provides beautiful views of the
sea and coastal pohutukawa
trees. Access to the route, which
takes seven hours to complete,
is from Seaview Road above the

town. The first landmark is Kapu
te Rangi ("ridge of heaven"),
with some of the country's
oldest earthworks.

🏛 **Whakatane District Museum
and Gallery**
51–55 Boon St. **Tel** (07) 306 0505.
**Open** daily. **Closed** 1 Jan, Good Fri,
25 & 26 Dec. 🗲 donation. 🚻
**W** whakatanemuseum.org.nz

**Environs**
**Whale Island**, 10 km (6 miles)
north of the harbour entrance,
is a wildlife refuge. Excursions
are organized by the Wha-
katane Coastguard over the
Christmas–New Year period.
Bookings can be made at the
Whakatane Visitor Centre.

East of Whakatane, idyllic
**Ohope Beach** stretches 12 km
(7.5 miles) from Otarawairere, its
western extremity, to the mouth
of tidal Ohiwa Harbour.

## ㉓ White Island

**Road map** F2. 50 km (31 miles) from
Whakatane.

New Zealand's most active
volcano, White Island lies at the
northern end of the Taupo–
Rotorua volcanic fault line (see
pp68–9). It can be reached by
boat or helicopter or simply
viewed from the air. The island's
terrain is likened to that of the
moon or Mars and many visitors
rate it as one of the country's
best attractions. The island was
mined for sulphur until 1914,
when a night-time eruption
killed all the miners. Remains of
mining activities can be seen.
There is a large gannet colony

on the island and it suffers
no ill-effects from the ash
fall-out. The island also offers
excellent diving.

Old sulphur mining equipment on
White Island

## ㉔ Opotiki

**Road map** F3. 🏛 4,150. 🚌
🛈 70 Bridge St, (07) 315 3031.
**W** opotikinz.com

Situated at the confluence of
the Waioeka and Otara rivers,
Opotiki is the gateway to the
East Cape and the last major
town before Gisborne. In 1865,
at Opotiki, the Reverend Carl
Sylvius Völkner was hanged
and then decapitated by
Maori convinced he passed
information about their
movements and fortifications to
Governor George Grey (see p80).
Hiona St Stephen's Anglican
Church, where the incident took
place, lies at the northern end
of the Church Street business
area. A key is held across the
road at the **Opotiki Museum**,
which is full of early settlers'
items and has a separate
grocery and hardware store
museum nearby.

An excellent example of a
warm, temperate rainforest is
Hukutaia Domain, which can
be reached from the western
end of Waioeka Bridge along
Woodlands Road. The reserve is
home to more than 2,000 native
tree species, including a
2,000-year-old hollow puriri
(Vitex lucens) where the
bodies of important Maori
were once exposed.

🏛 **Opotiki Museum**
123 Church St. **Tel** (07) 315 5193.
**Open** Mon–Sat. **Closed** Good Fri,
25 Dec. 🗲 🚻 📷

Ohope Beach, Whakatane's best surf beach

# Maori Migration and Settlement

According to legend, three migration canoes travelling from Hawaiki landed in the eastern Bay of Plenty in the 14th century *(see p49)*: the Mataatua at Whakatane, the Arawa at Maketu and Tainui at Whangaparaoa Bay, west of East Cape. Muriwai's Cave at Whakatane is testament to Muriwai's arrival on the Mataatua: she is believed to have had supernatural powers and lived hermit-like in the cave. Mild weather and abundant seafood encouraged Maori to settle along the coastal margins. Maori continue to form a high proportion of the population in the Bay of Plenty area, and red-framed Maori meeting houses, important spiritually and as decision-making centres, dot the countryside.

## Maori Art And Culture

*The meeting houses and other Maori works of art seen along the coast reflect Maori history, belief in gods and ancestral spirits, and a hierarchical, tribal social structure. Maori culture was primarily a wood culture. Wood was crafted into objects for economic, social and religious purposes, and embellished with symbols and motifs (see pp34–5).*

**Meeting houses**, like the beautifully carved Tukaki at Te Kaha, are usually symbolic of a male tribal ancestor. His head is represented by the mask below the gable figure, while the wide, sloping bargeboards represent his arms.

**Elements of Maori artistry** have been incorporated into Christian churches, such as the intricate woven panels, carved wooden wall panels and rafter patterns at St Mary's Church at Tikitiki.

**The *haka*,** a vigorous rhythmic posture dance formerly performed by warriors to steel their resolve for war, is taught in schools along the coast.

**This ornately carved gateway** guards the entrance to coastal Omaio Marae.

**A prominent carving** in the main street of Opotiki is indicative of a renaissance in Maori arts, culture and traditions that took hold in the 1980s and 1990s.

# ❷ East Cape Tour

Skirting the rugged hills of the East Cape peninsula, this section of the Pacific Coast Highway offers exceptional scenery. From Opotiki northeast to East Cape, the road clings to rocky coastline cloaked with pohutukawa trees. The second part of the route heads south to Gisborne along an inland farming route with secondary roads providing access to the coast. Most beaches and bays are suit-able for swimming, fishing and diving. There are also opportunities for jet-boating, horse trekking and tramping. Maori *marae* and churches dot the route.

**③ Te Araroa Pohutukawa**
On the foreshore at Te Araroa grows Te Waha-o-Rerekohu ("the mouth of Rerekohu"), believed to be the largest pohutukawa tree in the country. It has 22 trunks.

**② Raukokore Church**
Built in 1894, this small, wooden Anglican church, with its distinctive roofline, stands lonely sentinel between road and sea.

**① Motu River**
The Motu River, banked by steep hills and forest, is a magnificent setting for rafting and jet-boating. There is also excellent fishing at its mouth.

**⑧ Tolaga Bay**
The site of New Zealand's longest wharf, Tolaga Bay is excellent for swimming and fishing. A 5-km (3-mile) walk leads to Cooks Cove and a fascinating rock archway.

**⑦ Tokomaru Bay**
This attractive, cliff-framed bay is popular with swimmers and surfers. Old buildings at the bay house crayfishermen and crafts people.

Cape Runaway

Hicks Bay

Te Kaha

*Raukumara Ranges*

Bay of Plenty

Motu River

Mata River

Hikuwai River

Opotiki

35

Waioeka River

Waimata River

2

Gisborne

0 kilometres 20
0 miles 20

Poverty Bay

**For additional map symbols** *see back flap*

**Tips for Drivers**

**Length:** 334 km (207 miles)
**Stopping-off points:** There is a spectacular view from the Maraenui Hill Lookout 36 km (22 miles) from Opotiki. Towns on the route are small, but most offer food. Accommodation is available at Hicks Bay. Permission to climb Mount Hikurangi must be obtained from Ngati Porou Outdoor Pursuits, Gisborne (06) 876 9960. Bookings for jet-boating on the Motu River can be made at the Opotiki Information Centre (see p134).

#### ④ East Cape Lighthouse
A gravel road along a picturesque coastline leads to New Zealand's most easterly lighthouse. The view from the lighthouse is well worth the climb up the 700 steps to reach it.

#### ⑤ Tikitiki's St Mary's Church
Built in 1924 to commemorate Maori servicemen killed in World War I, St Mary's Church at Tikitiki is one of the most ornate Maori churches in the country (see p135).

#### ⑥ Mount Hikurangi
The first place in mainland New Zealand to see the sun each day, Mount Hikurangi is sacred to Maori and permission must be obtained to climb it.

#### Key
▬ Tour route
═ Other roads
═ River

*Star of Canada* wheelhouse, Gisborne Museum

## ㉖ Te Urewera National Park

**Road map** F3. 🚌 *i* Aniwaniwa Visitor Centre, State Hwy 38, Wairoa, (06) 837 3803. **w** doc.govt.nz

This is New Zealand's fourth largest national park and the biggest tract of untouched native forest remaining in the North Island. For centuries its dense rainforest sheltered the industrious and resilient Tuhoe people. At the centre of Te Urewera lies the 243-m (797-ft) deep Lake Waikaremoana ("the lake of rippling waters"), formed 2,200 years ago by a landslide. A 46-km (28-mile) track around the lake, one of the country's Great Walks (see p334), takes three to four days to complete. Booking through the Aniwaniwa Visitor Centre is essential. There are also many beautiful short walks into the park from the main road, which is partly gravel.

## ㉗ Gisborne

**Road map** F3. 🏙 35,000. ✈ 4 km (2.5 miles) NW of town. 🚌 *i* 209 Grey St, (06) 868 6139. 🎏 Wine and Food Festival (last week of Oct). **w** gisbornenz.com

Gisborne is renowned for its warm summers, its farming, viticulture and horticulture, its surf beaches at Midway, Wainui and Makorori, and its history. A monument and reserve on Kaiti Hill are named in honour of Captain James Cook who made his first New Zealand landfall at Gisborne's Kaiti Beach (see p52) on 9 October 1769.

The **Gisborne Museum**, also known as the **Tairawhiti Museum and Arts Centre**, houses fine Maori and European artifacts and an extensive photographic collection. On the bank of the Taruheru River, but part of the museum complex, rests the salvaged wheelhouse from the *Star of Canada*, which sank off Kaiti Beach in 1912. Statues of Captain Cook and Young Nick, at the mouth of the Turanganui River, commemorate cabin boy Nicholas Young, the first crewman on board Cook's ship, the *Endeavour*, to sight New Zealand.

#### 🏛 Gisborne/Tairawhiti Museum and Arts Centre
Kelvin Park, Stout St. **Tel** (06) 867 3832. **Open** daily. **Closed** Good Fri, 25 & 26 Dec. 🚻 except in Star of Canada. 🖵 📷 **w** tairawhitimuseum.org.nz

#### Environs
**Eastwoodhill Arboretum**, 35 km (22 miles) west of Gisborne, contains a world-renowned collection of exotic trees and shrubs. Set among lush native bush and abundant birdlife, **Morere Hot Springs**, 60 km (37 miles) south of Gisborne, has both hot and cold pools.

#### 🌳 Eastwoodhill Arboretum
2392 Wharekopae Rd. **Tel** (06) 863 9003. **Open** daily. **Closed** 25 Dec. 🚻 📷 by arrangement.

#### ♨ Morere Hot Springs
State Hwy 2, Morere. **Tel** (06) 837 8856. **Open** daily. **Closed** 24 & 25 Dec. 🚻 📷

Tall trees in the Eastwoodhill Arboretum, Gisborne

# ㉘ Rotorua

Situated on the southern shore of a lake of the same name, Rotorua is the North Island's most popular tourist destination. The city's hot and steamy thermal activity (evident from countless bores and fissures), healing mineral pools, adventure activities and surrounding lakes, rivers and crystal springs are major attractions. Rotorua is known as the heartland of Maori culture and offers visitors the chance to experience Maori art, architecture, song and dance and cultural performances.

Government Gardens and the Rotorua Museum of Art and History

### 🞉 Government Gardens
Queens Drive.

The formal Government Gardens are laid out in front of the stately Tudor-style Rotorua Museum of Art and History. They comprise a series of trimmed croquet and bowling greens and formal flower gardens dotted with steaming thermal pools. The 1927 Arawa Soldiers' Memorial, a short distance north of the museum, symbolizes the history of contact between Pakeha and local tribes. At its base is the Arawa migration canoe, from which Rotorua's Te Arawa people trace their descent.

### 🏛 Rotorua Museum of Art and History
Government Gardens, Queens Drive. **Tel** (07) 349 4350. **Open** daily. **Closed** 25 Dec. 🞉 🞉 ground level. 🞉 🞉 **w** rotoruamuseum.co.nz

Maori artifacts are plentiful in Rotorua's museum, situated within a magnificent building that opened as the Great Spa of the South Pacific in 1908. Some of the most important of these are bargeboards from Rotoiti's

Houmaitawhiti meeting house, carved in 1860. Also on display is 19th-century palisading from the Maori settlement of Ohinemutu and a female pumice figure, Pani, a *kumara* goddess depicted in the act of giving birth; most Maori fertility gods are male.

The story of the building itself is shown in "Taking the Cure", in a section of the building painstakingly restored to its original condition. History, mythology and geology are

combined in a dramatic 15-minute film to explain Rotorua's geothermal activity and Maori history. The film also shows a re-enactment of the 1886 Tarawera eruption.

### 🞉 The Blue Baths
Queens Drive. **Tel** (07) 350 2119. **Open** daily. **Closed** 25 Dec. 🞉 🞉

These heated pools were built in the 1930s and offered the then-novel attraction of mixed bathing. Housed in a Spanish mission-style building, they were once a symbol of New Zealand's ambitions to become the premier spa of the British Empire. A museum documents the social history associated with the construction and use of the baths.

### 🞉 Polynesian Spa
Hinemoa St. **Tel** (07) 348 1328. **Open** daily. 🞉 🞉 🞉
**w** polynesianspa.co.nz

People from around the world visit the Polynesian Spa's mineral waters, which vary in temperature from 33 °C (92 °F) to 42 °C (107 °F). Radium and Priest waters, both acidic and cloudy, are sourced from an underground spring while alkaline Rachel water is piped to the spa from nearby. Adults have access to a mineral pool overlooking a large, heated, freshwater pool, with a shallow end for toddlers. Users can regulate the temperature in the spa's private pools. Aix massage (under jets of water) and other therapies are available in the luxury spa area.

## Spa City

"Cripples throw away their crutches and the gouty man regains his health," a government report proclaimed in 1903, referring to Rotorua's mineral waters. Two mineral waters were used in a succession of 19th-century and early 20th-century spas, the largest being the Bath House, opened in 1908. The waters were considered "stimulating and tonic in reaction". Today, on the shores of Lake Rotorua, QE Health uses hot mineral waters to relieve pain, relax muscles and stimulate joint movement.

Mineral pool at Polynesian Spa complex

*For hotels and restaurants in this region see pp302–7 and pp314–25*

St Faith's Anglican Church

### 🏛 St Faith's Anglican Church
Ohinemutu. **Open** daily. 🕘 9am Sun.
Built in 1910, the Tudor-
style St Faith's is
the second church
built at Ohinemutu, a
Maori village on the
shores of the lake
around which Rotorua
grew. An etched-glass
window in the chapel
at the far end of the
church depicts Christ
dressed in a *korowai*
(chief's cloak) and
appearing to walk on the
waters of Lake Rotorua.
The interior is richly
embellished with Maori
carvings, woven wall
panels and painted
scrollwork. There are
several graves of
interest next to the
church, including that
of Seymour Mills
Spencer (1810–98)
who preached to the
Arawa for 50 years, and
Captain Gilbert Mair
(1843–1923) of the
Arawa Flying Column,
a guerilla unit of
local Maori who fought for
the British army in the New
Zealand wars.

### 🏛 Tamatekapua
Ohinemutu.
The magnificent Tamate-
kapua meeting house,
built in 1873, is the main
gathering place of the
Arawa tribe. Located
opposite St Faith's, it was
named for an earlier house
that stood on Mokoia
Island and the captain
of the *Arawa*, one of the
canoes that brought the
ancestors of Maori to New
Zealand. The figure at the
base of the centre post is
Ngatoroirangi, the

Carving at
Tamatekapua

canoe's navigator, whom
mythology credits with bringing
thermal activity to the region.

### 🏕 Kuirau Park
Kuirau Rd.
Within Kuirau Park there are a
number of boiling mud pools,
steam vents and small geysers.
Free thermal foot pools, picnic
areas, well-kept gardens, a
children's playground and
a small, warm lake are other
attractions within the domain.
Visitors will also appreciate a
scented garden in the park.

## VISITORS' CHECKLIST

**Practical Information**
**Road map** E3. 🚊 68,000.
🌐 **rotoruanz.com** ℹ 1167
Fenton St, (07) 348 5179.
**Open** 8am–6pm daily.
**Closed** 25 Dec. 🎭 Biennial
Rotorua Festival of the Arts (Jan/
Feb, odd years); New Zealand
International Two-Day Walk (Mar);
Rotorua Marathon (May).

**Transport**
✈ State Hwy 30, 10 km (6 miles)
NE of city. 🚌

## Rotorua City Centre

① Government Gardens
② Rotorua Museum of Art
   and History
③ The Blue Baths
④ Polynesian Spa
⑤ St Faith's Anglican Church
⑥ Tamatekapua
⑦ Kuirau Park

| 0 metres | | 500 |
| 0 yards | | 500 |

**For keys to map symbols** see back flap

# Greater Rotorua

Many of Rotorua's best attractions lie outside the city centre, around Lake Rotorua and the 17 other magnificent bush-fringed lakes that make up the Rotorua Lakes district. Complementing the lakes are geothermal wonders, bubbling springs, crystal-clear trout streams and unspoiled native forests. The rivers and lakes are renowned for their trout, and make a beautiful setting for boating, camping and tramping. Thrill-seekers can take four-wheel drive tours and ride horses to remote forest locations. Visitors can also enjoy Maori cultural experiences and observe the farming and livestock displays.

Visitors viewing trout at Rainbow Springs Kiwi Wildlife Park

Lake Rotorua and Mokoia Island from Mount Ngongotaha

## ✂ Lake Rotorua

This nearly circular lake is the largest of the lakes around Rotorua and is a popular venue for fishing, windsurfing and kayaking. It can be enjoyed by paddle steamer, kayak, jetboat or water scooter. Mokoia Island, in the centre of the lake, is famous for the love story of Hinemoa, who defied her family's wishes and swam at night to the island to be with the chief Tutanekai, who played his flute to guide her. The island is rich in native bird life and offers 4 km (2.5 miles) of walking tracks as well as Hinemoa's thermal pool.

## 🏛 Skyline Skyrides

185 Fairy Springs Rd. **Tel** (07) 347 0027. **Open** daily. 🚹 🚻 🚻 🚻
Ⓦ skylineskyrides.co.nz

Mount Ngongotaha towers 778 m (2,552 ft) above the city and lake. The Skyline lookout, at 487 m (1,598 ft), can be reached by gondola, and gives unmatched views of the city, lakes and countryside. An exciting way to

descend the mountain, by day or night, is by luge (a short, raised toboggan on wheels). A 2-km (1.2-mile) scenic ride suits most people, while two shorter and steeper rides provide an adrenalin rush. Chairlifts return riders to the start.

## ✂ Rainbow Springs Kiwi Wildlife Park

Fairy Springs Rd. **Tel** (07) 350 0440. **Open** daily. 🚹 🚻 🚻 🚻 🚻
Ⓦ rainbownz.co.nz

Visitors can feed some of the thousands of rainbow, brown, brook and tiger trout in the crystal-clear freshwater streams and fern-fringed pools here,

and view tuataras and kiwi in a walk-through aviary. Rainbow Springs is also home to Kiwi Encounter, a conservation-in-action attraction, combining natural history with wildlife conservation. Staff prepare, incubate and hand-raise kiwi chicks taken as eggs from the wild. Once at maximum weight, they are returned to the wild.

## 🔲 The Agrodome and Agroventures

Western Rd, Ngongotaha. **Tel** (07) 357 1050. **Open** daily. 🚹 🚻 🚻 🚻 🚻
Ⓦ agrodome.co.nz

Founded in 1972, this family business offers a broad range of farming-related and adventure activities. There are three live sheep shows daily, at which champion rams are introduced on stage, and sheep shearing and sheep dog trials are demonstrated. Visitors can also tour the organic farm and feed the animals. The shop specializes in quality woollen clothing and sheepskin rugs. Adventure activities include the Shweeb (the world's first human-powered monorail racetrack, consisting of two overhead rail circuits from which hang high performance pedal-powered vehicles), bungy jumping, and jet-boating.

Live sheep show at the Agrodome Agricultural Theme Park

Nearby, though separate from the Agrodome, is ZORB® Rotorua, which offers a chance to roll downhill inside a large plastic ball.

### 🏠 Hells Gate

State Hwy 33. **Tel** (07) 345 3151.
**Open** daily. 🌀 🔥 🍴 🍴 🏪 🏧 ☕
W **hellsgate.co.nz**

Sixteen km (10 miles) from Rotorua, at Tikitere, Hells Gate is famous for its ferocious volcanic activity. Drifting, wraith-like mists part to reveal a fierce and spectacular thermal valley that includes the Kakahi Falls, the largest hot waterfall in the southern hemisphere, and New Zealand's largest boiling whirlpool. Another cauldron of water, the Sulphur Bath, is purported to cure septic cuts, bites and skin ailments. The area is well signposted, with good pathways and barriers. Traditional Maori massage is on offer at the Wai Ora Spa.

Horse riding in Whakarewarewa Forest Park

### 🌳 Whakarewarewa Forest Park

Off State Hwy 5.

This 40-sq km (15-sq mile) multipurpose forest adjoining the Whakarewarewa thermal area *(see pp142–3)* contains majestic groves of redwoods, firs and other plantation trees. Forest walks can take from 30 minutes to all day. There are also mountain biking and horse tracks, a nature trail and picnic area.

### 🏠 Tamaki Maori Village

State Hwy 5. **Tel** (07) 349 2999.
**Open** daily. **Closed** 25 Dec. 🦽 ♿
☕ 🏪 🏧

Visitors are introduced to Maori customs and traditions at this replica of a pre-European Maori

A Maori "warrior" greets visitors at the Tamaki Maori Village

village. Sampling a full *hangi* feast, in which selected foods are cooked on hot rocks in an authentic earth oven, is part of the cultural experience. This daily highlight starts at 6:30pm to 10pm. Education workshops are also held regularly on traditional Maori carving and weaving, performing arts, weaponry and warfare, and Maori food and health.

### 🏠 Blue and Green Lakes

Tarawera Rd.

Eleven km (7 miles) southeast of Rotorua are the stunning Blue and Green Lakes (Tikitapu and Rotokakahi). The narrow isthmus that divides the lakes provides a good vantage point to compare their contrasting hues. Lake Rotokakahi is sacred to Maori and is not accessible, but Lake Tikitapu is the scene of many summer activities.

### 🏠 Buried Village

Tarawera Rd. **Tel** (07) 362 8287.
**Open** daily. **Closed** 25 Dec. 🦽 ♿
🍴 🏪 🏧 W **buriedvillage.co.nz**

Fifteen minutes' drive from Rotorua and 2.5 km (1.5 miles) from Lake Tarawera is what remains of the village of Te Wairoa, devastated by the eruption of Mount Tarawera in 1886. A walk through parkland takes in the excavations of several sites and an interactive museum explains the eruption. A bush walk leads to the Te Wairoa waterfalls, while a walkway offers clifftop views.

### Tarawera Eruption

Months of underground rumbling culminated early in the morning of 10 June 1886 with the eruption of Mount Tarawera, which left a deep crater *(see pp68–9)*. Lasting about three hours, the blast spread along a 17-km (10-mile) rift and killed 153 people. The eruption hurled red-hot volcanic bombs and pieces of solidified lava 14 km (8.5 miles), and the Maori villages of Te Ariki, Te Wairoa and Moura were buried under 20 m (65 ft) of mud. The explosion's roar was heard in Christchurch and Auckland. The famous Pink and White Terraces, massive fan-like silica terraces, acknowledged as the eighth wonder of the world, were completely obliterated. Information on guided walks and 4WD tours to the crater, and on scenic flights over it, can be obtained from the Rotorua information centre *(see p139)*.

Painting by Charles Blomfield of the Pink Terraces, around 1890

# Whakarewarewa Thermal Area

The geothermal area at Rotorua's southern edge, commonly referred to as Whaka, comprises two separate areas – Te Puia, once known as the New Zealand Maori Arts and Crafts Institute, and Whakarewarewa Thermal Village. Te Puia's attractions include Maori carving and weaving, cultural performances, examples of Maori buildings and fortifications, and the geysers Pohutu and Prince of Wales Feathers. At the Thermal Village, visitors can see a meeting house, cooking and bathing pools and a cemetery. At both venues, guides take visitors on an educational journey that unravels the mystery of Maori ways.

★ **Te Aronui-a-Rua Meeting House**
Visitors are greeted with a Maori "challenge" at Te Aronui-a-Rua meeting house at Te Puia.

★ **Carving School**
Ancient carving skills are passed to younger generations at Te Puia's carving school.

HEMO ROAD

Te Puia

**Pataka**
Storehouses like this were used by pre-European Maori to store food. However, *kumara* (sweet potato), their staple carbohydrate, was stored in pits in the ground.

## VISITORS' CHECKLIST

**Practical Information**
Te Puia: Hemo Rd. **Tel** (07) 348 9047. **W** tepuia.com
**Open** 8am–6pm daily (5pm winter). Maori concerts: 10:15am, 12:15pm, 3:15pm. Cultural show: 6:15pm. Whakarewarewa Thermal Village: 17 Tryon St. **Tel** (07) 349 3463. **W** whakarewarewa.com
**Open** 8:30am–5pm daily. **Closed** 25 Dec. Cultural show: 11:15am & 2pm.

**Transport**
No. 2 CityRide bus from main depot in Rotorua.

**★ Pohutu Geyser**
Pohutu ("Big Splash") is the largest geyser and typically erupts 10–25 times a day up to 30 m (98 ft) high, depending on wind strength and direction.

TRYON ST

**★ Wahiao Meeting House**
Tourists, including children, join in a cultural performance outside Wahiao meeting house.

| 0 metres | 100 |
| 0 yards | 100 |

## KEY

① **Lake Waikaukau**

② **Cooking Pool**

③ **At the Weaving House**, broad native flax is transformed into functional items.

④ **Kiwi House**

⑤ **Leaping Frog Mud Pool**

⑥ **At Puarenga Stream**, village children dive for coins thrown from a bridge by tourists.

⑦ **Whakarewarewa Thermal Village**

⑧ **Prince of Wales Feathers Geyser**

⑨ **Geyser Flat**, a 1-sq-km (0.4-sq-mile) silica terrace, is home to more than 500 thermal features, including seven geysers.

⑩ **At the Cemetery** at Whakarewarewa Thermal Village, the dead are buried above ground in vaults to keep the remains out of the steaming earth.

⑪ **The Brainpot**, a symmetrical silica basin, is said to have been used to cook the heads of enemies.

## Volcanic Features

The volcanic activity at Whakarewarewa is a reminder of how the earth is still changing and how the pressure of volcanic gases and heat below the surface can break through in spectacular and often dangerous ways. Here, superheated steam escapes from a vast chamber of boiling water through narrow vents in roaring towers of spray; mud pools boil and heave as gas and hot water seek to escape through the surface, and steam and gases are discharged in hot pools beside mineral-coloured silica flats.

Water heated by hot rocks | Steam jet

**Geyser**

Hot water | Mud mixed with hot water

**Mud pool**

Steam | Superheated water

**Fumarole**

## ㉙ Waimangu Volcanic Valley

**Road map** E3. **Tel** (07) 366 6137.
**Open** daily. 🅿️ ♿ to bus stop & boat cruise (assisted). 🚻 📷
🌐 waimangu.co.nz

Created on 10 June 1886 as a result of the Tarawera Eruption *(see p141)*, Waimangu is the only hydrothermal system in the world wholly formed within historic times. It offers an easy, mostly downhill, 90-minute walk past a succession of geothermal features at the southern end of the 17-km (10-mile) rift created by the eruption.

The 38,000-sq-m (409,032-sq-ft) Frying Pan Lake, claimed to be the world's largest hot water spring, emits steam over its entire area and is dominated by the red-streaked Cathedral Rocks. The lake was formed by an eruption in 1917 that buried a nearby tourist hotel.

The pale blue steaming water and delicate silica clay terracing of the Inferno Crater should not be missed, even though it requires a short detour from the main path. The water reaches 80 °C (176 °F) in the lake and rises and falls 8 m (26 ft) over a 38-day cycle.

At the end of the walk lies Lake Rotomahana, submerging what remains of the Pink and White Terraces *(see p141)*. Across the water stands Mount Tarawera. A boat excursion follows a shoreline scarred by craters, fumaroles and geysers. Unusual thermal plants grow along the lake's edge. Visitors need to allow two to three hours for the volcanic valley walk and the boat cruise.

Champagne Pool at Wai-o-tapu Thermal Wonderland

## ㉚ Wai-o-tapu Thermal Wonderland

**Road map** E3. **Tel** (07) 366 6333.
**Open** daily. 🅿️ main area. 🚻 📷
📷 🌐 geyserland.co.nz

This is the country's most colourful and diverse geothermal area and is home to the reliable Lady Knox Geyser, named in 1904 after Governor-General Lord Ranfurly's daughter. The geyser shoots water and steam up to 21 m (69 ft) into the air at 10:15am daily.

Other main attractions include the Artist's Palette, a panorama of hot and cold pools, boiling mud pools and hissing fumaroles in a variety of ever-changing colours, and the Champagne Pool, with its ochre-coloured petrified edge. The Primrose Terraces are also naturally tinted and have delicately formed lacework patterns. Walks through the geothermal area, over boardwalks and along signposted paths, take 30 to 75 minutes.

## ㉛ Orakei Korako Geyserland

**Road map** E3. **Tel** (07) 378 3131.
**Open** daily. 🅿️ 📷 🚻 (includes boat ride). 🌐 orakeikorako.co.nz

Orakei Korako, or "The Hidden Valley", as it is known, lies at the southern end of Lake Ohakuri, fed by the Waikato River as it flows northward from Lake Taupo. Reaching the valley's geothermal attractions requires a boat trip across the lake to the imposing Emerald Terrace, the largest silica feature of its kind in the country. Beyond is a 60-minute walk taking in a geyser, more silica terraces, hot springs, a cave and mud pools. A café with a large deck overlooking the lake serves snacks and drinks.

Jet-boating rapids on the Waikato River

## ㉜ Wairakei Park

**Road map** E3.

Ten kilometres (6 miles) north of Taupo is the area loosely referred to as Wairakei Park. The star attraction is the Huka ("foam") Falls, where the Waikato River is channelled through a narrow rock chute before hurtling over an 11-m (36-ft) bluff to a foaming cauldron below. Access down the Waikato River from Taupo to the Huka Falls is possible by

Inferno Crater at Waimangu Volcanic Valley

jet-boat, or by the more sedate paddlewheeler, built in 1908. A 7-km (4-mile) path leads from the falls down the right-hand side of the river to the Aratiatia Rapids, also accessible by road. Floodgates to the dam above the rapids are opened several times a day to allow kayaking and jet-boating.

At **Craters of the Moon**, at the end of Karapiti Road, 2 km (1.2 miles) south of Wairakei, steaming craters and boiling mud pits can be viewed free of charge among a bush-covered landscape.

The country's only prawn farm, off Huka Falls Road, uses geothermally heated river water to raise giant prawns for its restaurant, Huka Prawn Park Restaurant. Tours of the farm are conducted hourly.

## ㉝ Taupo

**Road map** E3. 🏔 21,300. ✈ 8 km (5 miles) S of town. 🚌 Gascoigne St Travel Centre. **Tel** (07) 378 9005.
ℹ 30 Tongariro St, (07) 376 0027.
🎣 Lake Taupo International Fishing Tournament (late Apr).
🌐 **laketauponz.com**

The town of Taupo lies at the northeastern end of Lake Taupo, New Zealand's largest lake, formed by a volcanic explosion in AD 186 (see pp68–9). White pumice beaches and sheltered rocky coves surround the lake, which covers 619 sq km (239 sq miles). On a clear day, the distant volcanic peaks of Mounts Tongariro and Ngauruhoe and the snow-capped Ruapehu provide a spectacular backdrop to the lake.

Taupo services surrounding farms and forests and an important tourist industry. All year round the town attracts large numbers of holiday-makers who come for its excellent lake and river fishing, sailing and water sports, and local geothermal attractions. There is a wealth of accommodation in the town, much of it with lakeside views, and good dining and shopping. Many hotels have their own hot pools.

The wide selection of outdoor activities includes bungy jumping, boating and rafting, horse riding, mountain biking, tandem skydiving, flightseeing and golf. The bungy, set in majestic surroundings above the Waikato River off Spa Road, is a big draw. Details of the operators offering outdoor recreation may be obtained from the information centre in Taupo.

## ㉞ Turangi

**Road map** E3. 🏔 5,500. 🚌 ℹ
Ngwaka Place, (07) 386 8999.

Located at the southeastern end of Lake Taupo on the banks of the Tongariro River, Turangi was a small fishing retreat until it was developed into a town in 1964 to accommodate workers for the Tongariro Hydro-Electricity Scheme. It remains an excellent resort area for anglers, and is also a popular base for trampers, white-water rafters, kayakers and skiers.

South of Turangi is the **Tongariro National Trout Centre**, a hatchery and research facility. Ova collected from wild female trout are fertilized to

Trimming pine trees in a pine forest near Turangi

breed trout for research purposes and to release into the lake. A self-guided 15-minute walk takes you through the hatchery and by a stream to an under-water viewing chamber to see trout in their natural environment.

🏞 **Tongariro National Trout Centre**
State Hwy 1. **Tel** (07) 386 9254.
**Open** 10am–3pm daily.
**Closed** 1 Jan, 25 Dec. ♿

### Trout Fishing Paradise

World-famous Lake Taupo and its surrounding lakes – Kuratau, Hinemaia, Rotoaira and Otamangakau – are fed by numerous rivers and streams well-stocked with rainbow and brown trout. Fishermen frequently stand shoulder to shoulder at the mouth of the Waitahanui River to form the "picket fence" fishing phenomenon. Line fishing from boats on Lake Taupo or from the shore is effective from November until March, as trout feed upon smelt spawning close to shore. In late summer, trout congregate after dark where streams flow into the lake, providing excellent fly-fishing. River fishing is best from May till October. A special fishing licence, available from sports shops and information centres, is required in the Taupo Fishing District.

Fishing at the mouth of the Waitahanui River

# ㉟ Tongariro National Park

At the southern end of Lake Taupo lies the magnificent 7,600-sq-km (2,930-sq-mile) Tongariro National Park. The peaks of the three active volcanic mountains which form its nucleus, Ruapehu, Ngauruhoe and Tongariro *(see pp68–9)*, were a gift to the government in 1887 by Tukino Te Heuheu IV, a Ngati Tuwharetoa chief. The park, which is surrounded by access roads, is a winter playground for skiers and snowboarders and a year-round wilderness walking, tramping and mountain climbing area. The park was the first in the world to achieve UNESCO World Heritage status for both its natural (1990) and Maori spiritual and cultural (1993) value.

**★ Whakapapa Ski Area**
The largest developed ski area in New Zealand, Whakapapa has a sophisticated chairlift system and more than 30 groomed trails catering to all levels of skiers and snowboarders.

**Chateau Tongariro**
This luxury hotel, built in 1929 on the lower slopes of Mount Ruapehu, offers outstanding mountain and valley views.

**★ Mount Ruapehu**
In summer, visitors can climb to the crater of Mount Ruapehu, the North Island's tallest mountain, from the highest Whakapapa chairlift.

National Park

Whakapapa Village

*Makatote River*

Mount Ruapehu
2,797 m (9,174 ft)

Round the Mountain Track

*Mangawhero River*

Ohakune Mountain Road

Mangawhero Falls

Ohakune

Rangataua Forest

Dreadnought

## KEY

① **The Turoa Ski Area** is renowned for its expansive ski areas, long runs and vertical drops.

② **Mountain biking** is prohibited in the park but is allowed in the Rangataua, Erua and Tongariro Forest Areas.

③ **Round the Mountain** is a four- to five-day tramp around Ruapehu for those seeking solitude, magnificent mountain views and a back-country experience.

④ **Ketetahi Hot Springs**, consisting of 40 fumaroles, boiling springs and

mud pools, is located on private property but can be viewed from the walking track.

⑤ **Lake Rotopounamu**, "the greenstone lake", is a picturesque lake on the side of Mount Pihanga, 20 minutes' walk from State Highway 47.

⑥ **Mount Ngauruhoe** is the youngest of the three volcanoes, and is a vent of Tongariro.

⑦ **Tukino Skifield**, accessible by 4WD from the Desert Road, is a small club-run field which operates rope tows only.

### Key

━━━ State highway
━━━ Minor road
～～～ River
– – 4 WD track
▪ ▪ Walking track
━ ━ Park boundary
— — Restricted area

**For additional map symbols** *see back flap*

## VISITORS' CHECKLIST

**Practical Information**
Road map E3. Ohakune W doc.
govt.nz i 54 Clyde St, (06) 385
8427. **Open** 9am–5pm daily.
Whakapapa i behind Bayview
Chateau Tongariro, (07) 892 3729.
**Open** 8am–5pm daily.

**Transport**
National Park. National
Park Store, Carroll St.

### ★ Emerald Lakes
The uneven summit of Mount Tongariro, the
lowest of the three volcanoes, comprises a maze
of craters, including the beautiful, mineral-tinted
Emerald Lakes.

### Tongariro Alpine Crossing
The Tongariro Alpine Crossing, from
Mangatepopo to Ketetahi, covers 18.5 km
(11.5 miles) of varied and spectacular
volcanic terrain and is often described as
the best one-day trek in New Zealand.

### Volcanic Hazards
The volcanoes of Tongariro
National Park are unique because
of the frequency of eruptions,
their highly explosive nature and
the high density of active vents.
Volcanic activity can occur in the
park at any time and with little or
no warning. Anyone intending to
tramp or climb on the upper
slopes of the volcanoes needs to
check the current volcanic alert
status and exclusion zones with
the nearest visitor centre and
read any recommended safety
information for the area before
starting out.

### Rangipo Desert
Temperature extremes on the eastern side of the
volcanoes have produced a desolate landscape of
gravel fields and hardy alpine vegetation. The area
is used mainly for army training.

# ㊱ Street-by-Street: Napier

Perched on the edge of the Pacific Ocean, this elegant
city is a memorial to a 1931 earthquake and fire that
destroyed most buildings and killed many people. The
quake raised marshland and the harbour bed, providing
new farmland and room for urban development. During
rebuilding, an earthquake-proof building code was
enforced and architects adopted the then fashionable
Art Deco style. Today, the city's Art Deco buildings, with
their pastel colours, bold lines and elaborate motifs, are
internationally renowned.

**Napier Mall**
Traffic bollards and seats topped
with Art Deco motifs enhance
pedestrian-friendly Emerson Street

★ **Deco Centre**
Purpose-built in 1922 as Napier's Central
Fire Station, and refurbished in Art Deco
style after the earthquake, it now houses
the Art Deco Trust and Art Deco Shop.

**The Municipal Theatre**, built in
1938, is noted for its Egyptian-style
columns and door lintels, and for
the leaping nude wall panels
flanking the stage in the
auditorium.

**The Public Trust Building's**
massive columns and internal
oak fittings escaped
earthquake damage.

**Countrywide Bank**
This 1932 building has charming
balcony windows framed by
angular arches decorated with
sunbursts and zigzags.

## Art Deco Trust

The Art Deco Trust is responsible for protecting, enhancing and
promoting Napier's Art Deco
buildings, keeping a register of
them and maintaining worldwide
links with other Art Deco groups. It
also organizes Art Deco walks and
publishes information on tours. A
highlight is the annual Art Deco
Weekend. Held in February, this
celebration of Art Deco style
attracts more than 40,000 visitors.

**A couple dressed for an
Art Deco Weekend**

0 metres          50
0 yards            50

**Key**

— Suggested route

**The Napier Antique Centre**, built in 1932, is one of four buildings in Napier ornamented with Maori designs.

**Daily Telegraph Building**
Built in 1932, this building is well endowed with Art Deco details – sunbursts, zigzags, ziggurats and fountain-like flowers.

**Criterion Hotel**
Leadlight glass was a favourite form of decoration in the 1930s, as shown in the window in the hotel's stairwell.

**The ASB Bank's** interior features fine examples of Maori carving and rafter patterns.

**Masonic Hotel**
Completed in 1932, the hotel features an unusual first-floor loggia built over the street.

CATHEDRAL LANE

HASTINGS STREET

BROWNING STREET

HERSCHELL ST

MARINE PARADE

**★ The Dome**
This Napier landmark, built in 1936 to house the Silver Slipper Nightclub, has a beautifully restored elevator.

# Exploring Napier

Within easy walking distance of Napier's inner-city Art Deco buildings is the ocean front Marine Parade, fringed by Norfolk pines. The floral clock, Tom Parker Fountain, statue of Pania (a maiden of local legend), Soundshell, Colonnade and Sunken Gardens, all on the seaward side of Marine Parade, add considerably to the city's charm. To the north, Bluff Hill, notable for its steep, tortuous roads and lovely old wooden homes, is the city's only high ground. Beyond it, the bustling port of Ahuriri is the site of the first European settlement in the area.

Visitors at the National Aquarium of New Zealand

### 🏊 Ocean Spa

42 Marine Parade. **Tel** (06) 835 8553.
**Open** daily. **Closed** 25 Dec. 🚗 ♿
💻 📷 🌐 oceanspa.co.nz

This attractively landscaped open-air pool and spa complex has vast ocean views and is a great place to relax and recharge. Visitors can enjoy heated saltwater pools at various temperatures, a lap pool, two leisure pools, a toddler pool, outdoor and indoor private spas, as well as a sauna, steam room, massage facility and the well-equipped Ocean Club gym.

### 🐟 The National Aquarium of New Zealand

Marine Parade. **Tel** (06) 834 1404.
**Open** daily. **Closed** 25 Dec.
🚗 💻 📷 🌐 nationalaquarium.co.nz

The aquarium is located in a stingray-shaped building on Napier's foreshore, and its proximity to the ocean means that fresh seawater can be pumped directly to its tanks and enclosures. The ground floor has native marine life and other species such as the tuatara (the New Zealand lizard), while the upper floor is dedicated to creatures from different parts of the world. The Oceanarium is viewed from an underwater tunnel, and is home to sharks, stingrays, seahorses and east coast native fish. Visitors can watch divers hand-feed the fish at 10am and 2pm every day, and there are even daily opportunities to take part in a supervised swim with the sharks. The aquarium is also involved in many conservation programmes and was the first to hatch a turtle egg in 1975.

## Napier City Centre

① Aquarium
② Hawke's Bay Museum and Art Gallery
③ Ocean Spa
④ Bluff Hill Domain
⑤ Port Ahuriri
⑥ Botanical Gardens

**Key**

▩ Street-by-Street: Napier pp150–51

0 metres 500
0 yards 500

### 🏛 Hawke's Bay Museum and Art Gallery

65 Marine Parade/9 Herschell St.
**Tel** (06) 835 7781. **Open** daily.
**Closed** 25 Dec. 🎨 ♿ 🎫 📷

Housed in an Art Deco building, the museum has extensive collections of Maori treasures, fine art, applied and decorative arts and textiles, as well as artifacts relating to the daily lives of Hawke's Bay's early settlers. Through audiovisual displays and ephemera, visitors can also experience the devastation of the 1931 earthquake.

### 🏰 Bluff Hill Domain

Lighthouse Rd.

Prior to the 1931 earthquake, Napier comprised an oblong mass of hills (Scinde Island) surrounded almost entirely by water. A stroll or drive to the 102-m (335-ft) high lookout within Bluff Hill Domain will recreate this feeling if visitors imagine much of the low-lying area south of the hill covered in water. What were gun emplacements are now vantage points from which to view the Kaweka and Ruahine ranges to the west, the Mahia Peninsula to the northeast, and Cape Kidnappers to the southeast, as well as the spectacular sight of the commercial port below.

### ⚓ Port Ahuriri

At Port Ahuriri, 4 km (2.5 miles) from Napier's centre, visitors can watch boys fishing and fishing fleets being unloaded or enjoy the port's many lively bars and restaurants, which are among the finest in Napier. A beach boardwalk meand-ers to the harbour entrance at Perfume Point. The Roth-mans Building, one of the most beautiful Art Deco buildings in Napier, is in nearby Ossian Street.

### 🌳 Botanical Gardens

Spencer Rd.

Located on a hill in the middle of the city, the gardens form a charming oasis. Apart from a spacious aviary, there are well-kept lawns bordered by flower beds, groves of stately trees, and a stream with ornamental bridges.

View north towards Napier from Te Mata Peak

### ㊲ Hastings

**Road map** F4. 🏔 28,400. ✈ 25 km (15 miles) N of town. 🚉 🚌 Caroline Rd. 🛈 Cnr Russel St North & Heretaunga St, (06) 873 5526. 🎉 Hawke's Bay Wine and Food Festival (first weekend of Feb); Hastings Blossom Festival (Sep).

Situated on the Heretaunga Plains, 20 km (12 miles) south of Napier, Hastings is the centre of a large fruit growing and processing industry, including wine making (see pp154–5). Rebuilt after the 1931 earthquake, it is the only city in New Zealand with streets laid out on the American block system. It has some fine Spanish Mission buildings, the most notable being the Hawke's Bay Opera House.

Hawke's Bay apples

Between Hastings and the eastern coastline, Te Mata Peak rises 399 m (1,309 ft). Maori legend describes the Te Mata ridgeline as the body of chief Te Mata O Rongokako, who choked and died eating his way through the hill, a task set him by the beautiful daughter of another chief. From Hastings the "bite" that killed him can be clearly seen, as can his body, which forms the skyline.

### ㊳ Cape Kidnappers

**Road map** F4.

Maoris believe that the crescent-shaped bay and jagged promontory of Cape Kidnappers, 30 km (19 miles) south of Napier, represent the magical jawbone hook used by Maui to pull the North Island from the sea like a fish. In October 1769, Captain Cook anchored off the headland (see p52) naming it Cape Kidnappers after some Maori attempted to carry off his Tahitian translator.

At the cape, up to 20,000 young and mature yellow-headed Australasian gannets surf wind currents metres from onlookers. The best time to see them is from early November to late February. Access is closed during the early nesting phase between July and October. At low tide, visitors can walk 8 km (5 miles) along the beach to the colony – check walking times with the local i-SITE Visitor Centre. Guided tours by coach and tractor-trailer are also available.

Australasian gannets at Cape Kidnappers Gannet Reserve

# ㊴ Hawke's Bay Vineyard Tour

Hawke's Bay's long sunshine hours, wide range of growing microclimates, and variety of soil types have allowed more than 70 wineries to develop all the classical grape varieties to a high standard. Traditionally a fruit-growing area, Hawke's Bay's fruit is sourced from varied vineyard and orchard sites, and wines are made using both modern and traditional techniques. The success of the region's wine is not only evident in its international awards, but in one of New Zealand's most important wine events, the Hawke's Bay F.A.W.C! Food and Wine Classic festival, held every November and June.

**① Mission Estate Winery**
Established in 1851 by a group of French Catholic missionaries, early vintages were produced for sacramental purposes. Today, New Zealand's oldest winery, nestled on a hill overlooking sweeping vineyards, offers wine sales, winery tours, a gourmet restaurant and a craft gallery.

**⑨ Clearview Estate Winery**
Established in 1989 by Tim Turvey and Helma van den Berg, this gently sloping coastal vineyard produces small quantities of hand-made wines sold only from the winery or by mail order.

**⑧ Te Mata Estate Winery**
One of the oldest wineries operating in New Zealand (vines were planted on the lower slopes of Te Mata peak in 1892) and one of its most prestigious and successful, Te Mata produces mainly red wines, which can be bought at its winery or by mail order.

*Tutaekuri River*

*Ngaruroro River*

*Omahu Road*

50

*Maraekakaho Road*

**⑦ Vidal Wines**
Anthony Vidal, an immigrant from Spain, established his winery in a stable in 1905. Urban development has encompassed the site but Vidals continues to produce good wines. Sales, tastings and a brasserie are available.

↓ *Palmerston North*

2

**⑥ Sileni Estates**
Located within an area of red-metal soils, massive investment has produced a showcase winery incorporating a gourmet food store, wine education centre and restaurant/café.

| 0 kilometres | 4 |
|---|---|
| 0 miles | |

**Key**

▬ Tour route
═ Other roads
▬ River

**For additional map symbols** *see back flap*

## ② Park Estate Winery

Formerly a traditional orchard, Park Estate has established niche markets for three very different beverages: grape wines, fruit wines from feijoa, boysenberry, kiwifruit and apple, and natural fruit juices. Orchard and winery tours, wine tasting and dining are available. A shop sells fresh fruit and homemade produce.

### Fruitbowl of New Zealand

Hawke's Bay's warm, sunny summers and crisp winter frosts have been exploited by generations of horticulturists, who have earned the region its unofficial title of "fruitbowl of New Zealand". While apples are the largest crop, pears, kiwifruit, peaches and other stone fruits are also important. However, increased world production of apples and falling prices have begun to affect export levels.

At Pernel Fruitworld, a large orchard on the outskirts of Hastings with its own packhouse, some 85 varieties of pip and stone fruits are grown. Tours are conducted hourly, fruit is available to taste, and a museum traces the history of the fruit industry.

Orchard tour at Pernel Fruitworld

### ③ C J Pask Winery

This Mediterranean-style winery, located in a stony, silt-covered river bed, produces grapes with very ripe fruit flavours across a range of premium varieties. It is one of the region's best wineries.

### ④ Te Awa Winery

Named "River of God" for the enormous aquifer beneath the Hawke's Bay plains that is tapped to irrigate crops, Te Awa makes fine Bordeaux-blend red wines, which can be savoured at its restaurant.

### Tips for Drivers

Visiting three or four wineries in one day will allow time to taste and discuss the wines. Many wineries offer tours and most offer tastings and sales. Some have indoor and outdoor eating facilities, although booking is advisable. Information on the facilities at each listed winery can be obtained at the Napier Visitor Information centre (see p151).

Visitors planning to visit a greater number of wineries and make the most of tasting opportunities may prefer to take one of the many tours available.

### ⑤ Ngatarawa Wines

A large rectangular lily pond and stable buildings housing the winery make an attractive setting that is more than matched by Ngatarawa's wines. The vineyard also has a pleasant picnic area and a pétanque court.

# WELLINGTON AND THE SOUTH

European settlers arriving in the mid-1800s and making their way north of Wellington, New Zealand's capital city from 1865, quickly found themselves in the middle of virgin rainforest. The recent history of much of the area covered by Wellington and the South is linked to the massive clearance of the land through milling and burning of forest during the late 19th and early 20th centuries.

In their thousands, ancient giant trees covered potentially rich pastoral land acquired from the Maori. Between the 1870s and 1910s, the area became the site of the country's biggest forest clearance programme as settlers poured in from overseas and demand for farmland grew. Sawmills, closely linked with the new rail network, sprang up throughout the district. Small towns along the railway enjoyed periods of importance before the sawmillers moved on. By 1907, however, milling output in the lower half of the North Island had passed its peak, to be superseded by the rich, rolling farmlands and rural lifestyles that have been a feature of the area ever since.

Although Taranaki, Wanganui and Manawatu are among the most productive and intensively farmed areas in New Zealand, these days diversity is the rule rather than the exception for the lower North Island. The exploitation of natural gas fields off the Taranaki coast, for example, has put an additional string to the region's economic bow.

Tourists are drawn to the compact lower North Island because of its mild climate, wild coastline, stunning beaches, scenic rivers, national parks, mountain ranges, ski fields, vineyards, and rich Maori heritage.

Harbour-fringed Wellington, situated at the bottom of the North Island, is the area's main city, and the centre of government, business, and the performing arts. The numerous small towns that radiate from it to the north, servicing local farms, are charming, friendly stopover points for travellers.

The Beehive and Parliament Buildings in Wellington, New Zealand's capital city

◄ Coastal landscape, Wellington

# Exploring Wellington and the South

Wairarapa, the Kapiti Coast, Horowhenua, Manawatu, Wanganui and Taranaki are all within a day's drive of Wellington. The contrast between the arty, political capital city and the areas immediately to its north is striking. Within an hour, the country's rural heartland reveals itself with the numerous small, sleepy towns. Dairy and sheep farms continue to feature strongly in the region, but visitors can also see newer forms of land use, such as ostrich farms and vineyards. The Egmont and Whanganui national parks await the more adventurous.

Sheep farm near Martinborough

## Sights at a Glance

## Top Outdoor Activities

The places shown here have been selected for their recreational activities. Conditions vary depending on the weather and the time of year, so exercise caution and, if in doubt, seek local advice.

| | Golf | Jet-Boating | Kayaking | Sailing | Surfing | Swimming | Tramping | Windsurfing |
|---|---|---|---|---|---|---|---|---|
| Egmont National Park | | | | | | ● | ● | |
| Manawatu Gorge | | ● | | | | | ● | |
| Masterton | ● | ● | | | | ● | ● | |
| New Plymouth | ● | ● | ● | ● | ● | ● | ● | ● |
| Oakura | | | | | ● | ● | | ● |
| Opunake | | | | | ● | ● | | ● |
| Palmerston North | ● | | | | | ● | | |
| Paraparaumu | ● | ● | ● | ● | ● | ● | ● | ● |
| Sugarloaf Islands | | | | | | ● | | |
| Waikanae | ● | ● | ● | | | ● | ● | |
| Wanganui | ● | ● | ● | | | ● | | |
| Wellington | ● | | ● | ● | ● | | ● | ● |
| Whanganui National Park | | ● | | | | ● | ● | |
| Whanganui River | | ● | ● | | | ● | ● | |

## Key

- ▬ Motorway
- ▬ Major road
- ═══ Minor road
- ═══ Major railway
- ─── Minor railway
- ▬ Regional border
- △ Summit

**For additional map symbols** *see back flap*

## Getting Around

The area is well served by rail, bus and air services, and an extensive, well-maintained road network. The country's mild climate ensures roads in the region are usually passable throughout the year. Wellington's state-of-the-art airport serves both international and domestic travellers, while international cruise liners make use of the city's port. Several times a day, ferries, including those carrying cars, trucks and railway carriages, take travellers from Wellington across Cook Strait to the South Island and back again.

Chaffers Marina in Lambton Harbour, Wellington

# Wellington: Cultural Capital

Known primarily as the home of New Zealand's parliament and its public servant population, Wellington transformed itself during the 1980s and 1990s into a vibrant, culture-driven hot spot. Tucked around one of the world's most picturesque harbours, the capital city is intimate, sophisticated, arty and packed with national treasures. It is home to the Museum of New Zealand Te Papa Tongarewa (see pp170–1), the Royal New Zealand Ballet, the New Zealand Symphony Orchestra, the New Zealand Opera, the Chamber Music New Zealand and the New Zealand School of Dance. The city's strong arts scene combines an international flavour with an intrinsic Pacific identity.

**Professional theatre**, strongly supported by Wellingtonians, can be enjoyed at several venues, including Downtown, Circa and Bats

**The numerous public and private galleries** in Wellington are well patronized and exhibit local and international works of art. Dealer galleries, such as the Peter McLeavey Gallery, play a significant role in bringing the best of New Zealand art onto the market.

**The kiwi and the fern**, both symbols of New Zealand, form the logo for the New Zealand International Arts Festival.

## New Zealand's Film Industry

Film making in New Zealand began on a large scale only in the 1960s and 1970s. Today, film production is a multimillion dollar industry in New Zealand, with much of it based in studios around Wellington. The International Film Festival, held every July, attracts large crowds.

Wellington is home to Sir Peter Jackson (director of *The Lord of the Rings* and *The Hobbit*) and to Weta Workshop, which created many of the special effects and props for these films. Behind-the-scenes tours, starting every 30 minutes from 10am to 5pm, give an opportunity to see the props and models created by the workshop. Tickets can be purchased in the Weta Cave on the corner of Camperdown Road and Weka Street in Miramar (www.wetanz.com).

**Film making at one of the many locations around the city**

**The New Zealand Symphony Orchestra**, based in Wellington, performs regularly throughout the country. The orchestra accompanied New Zealand-born diva, Dame Kiri Te Kanawa, to welcome the dawn of the new millennium at Gisborne.

**Percussion instruments**, including assorted percussive junk, are drummed in a high-energy performance of rhythmic power.

## Books and Writers

The emphasis on formal education, especially by Scottish immigrants who settled in Dunedin in the late 1800s, resulted in the demand that education in the new country be "free, secular and compulsory". Today, the early value placed on book learning by those settlers, many of them barely literate, has resulted in a national literacy rate of around 99 per cent. New Zealand-based reading programmes and books for children are exported around the world.

In Wellington, annual literary festivals, writers and readers programmes, and readings by local and visiting authors, are able to attract sponsorship as well as big audiences. Internationally recognized writers from Wellington include UK-based poet Fleur Adcock and novelists Maurice Gee, Elizabeth Knox and Vincent O'Sullivan (*see p37*).

Author Linda Burgess at her book launch

**A scaffold "cube"** formed the setting for the band's players and instruments.

## International Arts Festival

*Held biennially in Wellington in early autumn, the New Zealand International Arts Festival is the country's largest performing arts festival. The New Zealand percussion group, Strike, is among the local and international artistes who have performed at the festival.*

**The Royal New Zealand Ballet** conducts national and international tours from its base in the capital city. Stephen Wellington and Nadine Tyson are shown here in a pas de deux from *Raymonda*.

**The Westpac Stadium** is the leading venue for one of the mainstays of New Zealand culture – sport. Rugby, cricket and soccer, as well as concerts, are held in the 40,000-seat state-of-the-art stadium.

# ① Wellington

Wellington's compact central business district lies between the city's foothills and its mountain-encircled harbour. Partly built on land developed during reclamation projects begun in the mid-19th century, the area today is the working environment of the country's politicians and the national government infrastructure. Foreign embassies, the Court of Appeal, National Archives, National Library, Museum of New Zealand Te Papa Tongarewa and the head offices of local and international businesses are among the institutions and organizations in its precincts. The city is known for its stylish shops, café culture, restaurants and galleries, with an atmosphere that is both stimulating and unhurried.

Lunching outdoors at Astoria Café on Lambton Quay

### 🚌 Lambton Quay

Wellington's premier shopping street, Lambton Quay runs through the heart of New Zealand's political and commercial life. Its lively 1,100-m (3,600-ft) route is lined with arcades, plazas and elevated walkways. Most of Lambton Quay and its seaward parts are sited on reclaimed land. Plaques set at intervals along its footpaths identify the lay of the shoreline before the mid-1800s. While steep steps lead up to the slopes on the west, side streets on the east offer flat access to the redeveloped harbourfront (see pp166–7).

### ⛪ Cathedral Church of St Paul

34 Mulgrave St. **Tel** (04) 473 6722. **Open** daily. **Closed** to tourists Good Fri, 25 Dec. ♿ 📷 📱 donation welcomed. 🆆 oldsaintpauls.co.nz

Known as Old St Paul's, the Cathedral Church of St Paul is an outstanding example of an early English Gothic-style cathedral adapted to colonial conditions and materials. Consecrated in 1866, it is made entirely of native timber, including its nails.

### ⛪ Wellington Cathedral of St Paul

Cnr Molesworth and Hill Sts. **Tel** (04) 472 0286. **Open** daily. 📷 📱 behind church. 📷

After a building programme spread over several decades, including a number of exterior and interior design changes and reversals, the Wellington Cathedral of St Paul was finally completed in 1998. Standing in the parliamentary precinct opposite the Law Courts and the National Library, the Romanesque-style cathedral houses unique etched and stained-glass windows, memorials to historic events, and a 4,000-pipe organ. The Lady Chapel, formerly a parish church on the Kapiti coast north of Wellington, was relocated to the site in 1998 to complete the cathedral complex.

Art in the Galleria of the Parliament Buildings

### 🏛 Parliament Buildings

Molesworth St. **Tel** (04) 817 9503. **Open** daily. **Closed** 1 & 2 Jan, 6 Feb, Good Fri, 25 & 26 Dec. ♿ 📷 📱 📷 🆆 parliament.govt.nz

New Zealand's Parliament is made up of three main buildings: the Edwardian Neo-Classical style Parliament Building (1922); the Parliamentary Library (1899); and the Beehive, occupied since 1979. Free guided tours take in all three buildings. They stand next to each other on the site that has housed the country's parliament since 1865, 400 m (1,300 ft) away from the earthquake fault line which runs through Wellington. Historic trees have been retained in the grounds, which also feature a rose garden.

Bolton St Memorial

Lady Norwood Rose Garden

Begonia House

⑦ Wellington Botanic Garden

Carter Observatory

Cable Car Museum 🚠 P

Kelburn Park

⑧ Victoria University

| 0 metres | 500 |
| 0 yards | 500 |

### Key

◼ Street-by-Street: The Harbourfront pp166–7

Old Government Buildings

## Wellington City Centre

1. Cathedral Church of St Paul
2. Wellington Cathedral of St Paul
3. Parliament Buildings
4. Old Government Buildings
5. Lambton Quay
6. Wellington Cable Car
7. Wellington Botanic Garden
8. Victoria University
9. Katherine Mansfield Birthplace

### Old Government Buildings

15 Lambton Quay. **Tel** (04) 472 7356.
**Open** daily. **Closed** 1 & 2 Jan, Easter
Sun, 25 Apr, 25 & 26 Dec.

The largest wooden building
in the southern hemisphere,
and one of the largest such
buildings in the world, the Old
Government Buildings was built
in the 1870s in a style imitating
stone. Used in the early 20th
century by New Zealand's
parliamentary cabinet and then
by government departments
until 1990, the restored buildings
are now filled with law school
students. The original cabinet
room on the first floor and
historic displays on the ground
floor are open to the public.

Items for sale in the Katherine Mansfield
Birthplace

### Katherine Mansfield Birthplace

25 Tinakori Rd. **Tel** (04) 473 7268.
**Open** 10am–4pm Tue–Sun.
**Closed** Good Fri, 25 Dec.
by appt.

This 1888 villa is the birthplace
and childhood home of the
famous author Katherine
Mansfield (see p37). It contains
period photographs, excerpts
from Mansfield's writing, and
antique furniture.

For keys to map symbols see back flap

# Exploring Wellington

A vibrant, inner-city area bordered to the north by a green belt, central Wellington encompasses late Victorian mansions, student flats, tiny former workers' cottages, the Prime Minister's residence, an historic cemetery and the main motorway in and out of the city. At the end of the 19th century, as the number of overseas settlers increased, land near the foreshore became scarce, and steeper, less accessible land above the city was utilized for housing. Today, a walk around the suburb of Thorndon to higher points shows how a community has spread onwards and upwards from its original concentration in the port area.

Cable car climbing to the top of the Botanic Garden

### 🚠 Wellington Cable Car

Cable Car Lane, 280 Lambton Quay.
**Tel** (04) 472 2199. Museum:
**Open** daily. **Closed** 25 Dec. 🅿️
🌐 wellingtoncablecar.co.nz

Opened in 1902 to link the hill suburbs with the city, the cable cars used on the route have been electrically powered since 1933. Stops on the way include Victoria University, with access to the Botanic Garden and Carter Observatory at the top. The Kelburn terminus has fine views over the city and harbour.

### 🌷 Wellington Botanic Garden

Tinakori Rd. **Tel** (04) 499 1400.
**Open** daily. 🅿️ 📷 📖
🌐 wellington.govt.nz

Established in 1868, the garden is a mix of protected native forest, conifer plantings and plant collections. A major seasonal bedding programme includes a massed display of 30,000 tulips in spring and early summer. The Lady Norwood Rose Garden has 106 formal beds, including recent introductions and old favourites. The Begonia House features tropical and temperate plants, a lily pond, seasonal displays of orchids, and a collection of epiphytic and carnivorous plants. The garden's information hub, the Treehouse Visitor Centre, can be accessed via a tower lift. The more hardy can get to the centre via a steep path.

The **Carter Observatory**, New Zealand's national observatory, stands in the Botanic Garden complex near the terminus of the cable car. Astronomical displays, audiovisual shows and a planetarium are special features.

### 🔭 Carter Observatory

40 Salamanca Rd, Kelburn.
**Tel** (04) 472 8167. **Open** daily. 🅿️
🌐 carterobservatory.co.nz

The ivy-covered Hunter Building at Victoria University

### 🎓 Victoria University

Kelburn Parade. **Tel** (04) 472 1000.
With 21,000 students enrolled in over 50 departments and schools, Victoria University is the fourth largest of New Zealand's eight universities. Opened in 1897, Victoria University's main campus has occupied its Kelburn site overlooking downtown Wellington since 1904. The Faculties of Law and Commerce, as well as the School of Architecture and Design, are among the campuses located in the city.

Lady Norwood Rose Garden in the Wellington Botanic Garden

# Suburban Hillside Villas

Often appearing to cling precariously to the sides of hills, accessible only by cable car or long flights of steep steps, hillside villas are a striking feature of Wellington's older city suburbs such as Oriental Bay, Mount Victoria, Thorndon and Kelburn. These ubiquitous New Zealand homes evolved during the late 19th and early 20th centuries from simple, flat-fronted single-storey colonial cottages with verandahs running across the front, to two-storey houses with projecting faceted bay windows. The villas were traditionally made of timber from New Zealand's kauri forests, roofed with corrugated iron, and decorated with mass-produced components ordered from catalogues. Other features included the use of stained glass, large double-hung sash windows and balustraded porches or verandahs.

### Harbourfront Suburbs

*Wellington's early settlers were forced by a shortage of flat land to build on the hills bordering the harbour. Many original villas, as well as those restored and adapted as family homes, can be seen during a walk or drive through Wellington's harbourfront suburbs.*

Wooden villas on the hillside overlooking Oriental Bay

Corrugated iron hip roof

Flat timber facade

Bull-nosed verandah

Double-hung sash window

Timber fretwork

Bay window

Stained-glass window

Finial

Gable roof

Cast-iron fretwork

*Flat-fronted, hip-roofed villa* with long verandah

*Gabled hip-roofed villa* with faceted bay window

*Gable-roofed villa* with ornate cast-iron decoration

**Late 19th-century villas** constructed for middle-income families usually had a living area (the "parlour"), three or four bedrooms and a central hallway, with a single bathroom and kitchen area to the rear. The toilet (often referred to as the "long drop") and laundry ("wash house") facilities were usually located at the back of the house.

Parlour at the 1888 villa in Thorndon where Katherine Mansfield was born *(see p163)*

# Street-by-Street: The Harbourfront

The area between Lambton Harbour and Clyde Quay Wharf on Wellington's harbourfront stands entirely on reclaimed land. It covers a site once central to Wellington's waterfront industry, and can be covered on foot within an hour. Echoes of the commercial sailing ships and liners that once dominated the area remain in the Museum of Wellington City & Sea. In spring and summer, dragon boat competitions are held opposite the Museum of New Zealand Te Papa Tongarewa. The Civic Square, with its open spaces and nearby public buildings, such as the Town Hall, is a favourite meeting place for Wellingtonians and visitors alike.

**Courtenay Place**
Lined with bars, clubs, restaurants and theatres, Courtenay Place provides a taste of the city's nightlife *(see p169)*.

**Key**

— Suggested route

**Circa Theatre**
This refurbished building is one of the focal points of the city's contemporary theatre scene *(see p160)*.

**Waitangi Park**, next to Te Papa Tongarewa, is an award-winning urban park with a beach and boardwalk promenade – a popular spot on a summer's day.

**The Overseas Terminal** provides berths for yachts and other small vessels. It also houses facilities for conferences and exhibitions.

★ **Museum of New Zealand Te Papa Tongarewa**
The museum offers visitors interactive experiences of New Zealand's Maori heritage, national history and natural environment as well as art treasures *(see pp170–1)*.

| 0 metres | | 100 |
| --- | --- | --- |
| 0 yards | | 100 |

*For hotels and restaurants in this region see pp302–7 and pp314–25*

**City-to-Sea Bridge**
Linking Civic Square and Frank Kitts Park, the bridge is decorated with large, Pacific-style woodcarvings.

**The Civic Square** is an open space bounded by the Michael Fowler Centre, Town Hall and City Gallery *(see p168)*.

**Frank Kitts Park** contains a children's playground with lighthouse and slide. An overhead bridge beside the park provides access to the city's business district.

★ **Museum of Wellington City & Sea**
Housed in an 1892 building, the museum focuses on Wellington's social and maritime history *(see p169)*.

VICTORIA ST

EFIELD ST

WILLESTON ST

JERVOIS QUAY

HUNTER ST

LAMBTON HARBOUR

**Town Hall**
A mainstay of entertainment for decades, the Town Hall is one of several international standard concert venues in the city *(see p169)*.

**Queens Wharf**
The complex of cafés, restaurants and bars on Queens Wharf is a popular entertainment hub for nearby office workers.

# The Harbourfront

The Harbourfront is dominated by the City-to-Sea bridge, a pedestrian-only right of way above one of Wellington's main roads. Bordered on one side by Wellington's wharves and on the other by office blocks, the bridge leads from steps within the Civic Square complex to Frank Kitts Park and the waterfront, a lagoon and further on to the Museum of New Zealand Te Papa Tongarewa *(see pp170–1)*. The bridge is a public art space in its own right, featuring works by leading New Zealand sculptors.

Contemporary exhibit at the City Gallery

### 🔲 Civic Square

Wakefield St. **Tel** (04) 802 4860.
**Open** daily. ♿

The heart of the city's cultural scene, this extensive paved, plaza-style courtyard was opened in the early 1990s, making use of an area that was previously a busy street. The pink and beige square is an open space that features various sculptures and provides a link to a number of institutions bordering it. These include the Public Library, Visitor Information Centre, City Council Buildings, City Gallery and the capital's main concert venues, the Town Hall and Michael Fowler Centre.

The square harkens back to its previous role as a thoroughfare. It brings together Wellington's central business district with the city's cultural and social side: the

Museum of New Zealand Te Papa Tongarewa, the Opera House, theatres, cinemas and shops, as well as the bars and restaurants of the city's main night-time entertainment area, Courtenay Place. The square has become a well-used and central meeting place for Wellingtonians. Visitors to the square will often find themselves among street theatre performers and at outdoor concerts, exhibitions and rallies of all kinds.

### 🏛 City Gallery

Civic Square. **Tel** (04) 801 3021. **Open** 10am–5pm daily. **Closed** 25 Dec. 📷 international exhibitions. ♿ 📷
**w** citygallery.org.nz

Housed in a striking Art Deco building fitted with original kauri doors, marble finishes, handrails and steel windows, the building that for decades

served as the city's Public Library is now home to the country's leading, and often most controversial, art gallery.

Primarily an exhibition space, with no permanent collection of its own, the gallery has nonetheless developed a distinctive character, specializing in bringing to Wellington the best contemporary art and design shows from within New Zealand and around the world. Exhibitions held at the gallery have covered a diverse range of media and subjects, including painting, sculpture, film and video, industrial and graphic design and architecture.

The building has been expanded to include an auditorium, a gallery of Maori and Pacific art, and an enlarged Michael Hirschfield Gallery, which is dedicated to exhibiting works by Wellington artists.

Neil Dawson's ferns sculpture suspended in the Civic Square

### Michael Fowler Centre
Wakefield St. **Tel** (04) 801 4231.
**Open** daily. 🎵 for concerts. ♿
🛗 by arrangement. 💻

Designed by Christchurch's
Sir Miles Warren and named
after a former mayor and
prominent architect, the
semicircular complex is internationally renowned for its
ability to distribute sound
throughout its 2,550-plus seat
concert chamber. Rock
concerts, conventions and even
political rallies are staged in
what has become the city's
premier concert hall. Many
events associated with the
increasingly popular biennial
New Zealand International Arts
Festival *(see pp46, 160–1)*, which
attracts thousands of local and
overseas visitors to Wellington,
are held here.

The Victorian-tiled lobby of the
Town Hall

### Town Hall
Wakefield St. **Tel** (04) 801 4231.
**Open** daily. 🎵 for concerts.
♿ 📷 by arrangement. 💻

Restoration of the Town Hall,
a sedate 1904 Edwardian brick
building with a Roman-style
portico, has returned the hall
to much of its former glory.
Restoration work included
seismic strengthening of the
building, restoring the floor's
Victorian tiles, uncovering
wrought-iron balustrades,
manufacturing lights and
fittings from original samples,
and repairing the auditorium's
pressed zinc ceiling. The hall's
magnificent main staircase is
now a major attraction. The
2,000-seat "shoe box" auditorium
is regarded as one of the world's
leading venues for the performance of classical music.

Courtenay Place, a prime night-time entertainment area

### Courtenay Place
Lined with a concentrated strip
of sophisticated night-clubs,
trendy cafés and restaurants,
and professional theatres,
Courtenay Place and the
streets leading from it form
the night-time entertainment
heart of the city.

With nearly every cuisine style
and price range available, from
budget eating outlets to award-
winning restaurants, Courtenay
Place is the venue to meet
visitors, mix with locals, and eat
and dance the night away.
Live music inside cafés and bars
is matched by a lively street
scene, where crowds thread
their way through buskers and
performers that add to the
area's relaxed atmosphere.

### Museum of Wellington City & Sea
Queens Wharf. **Tel** (04) 472 8904.
**Open** 10am–5pm daily.
**Closed** 25 Dec. ♿ 📷 📷
🌐 museumofwellington.
co.nz

Housed in the former
customs house which
was constructed in 1892,
the Museum of
Wellington City & Sea
gives an insight into the
capital's rich cultural and
social history. The
museum uses model
ships, ships' instruments,
relics from wrecks,
maritime paintings, old
maps and sea journals, as
well as holographic
re-creations and videos

to tell the story of Wellington in
the context of its harbour and
surrounding coast. One of the
most interesting exhibits in the
museum's collection of ship
models is the inter-island ferry,
the *Wahine*. This sank off the
Wellington suburb of Seatoun
in April 1968 during a storm.
A photograph exhibit documents
the tragedy. The Plimmer's Ark
Gallery displays part of the
excavated remains of the ship
*Inconstant*, built in 1848.

The museum also features
a 12-minute show on Maori
creation legends and looks at
early Maori and European
settlement. A 20th century
gallery explores how the city
has changed. There is also an
education room for children.

Façade of the Museum of Wellington City & Sea
on the city's waterfront

# Museum of New Zealand Te Papa Tongarewa

With exhibition space equivalent to three football fields, the Museum of New Zealand Te Papa Tongarewa ("Our Place") is one of the largest museums in the world. Committed to telling the stories of all cultures in New Zealand, home to the National Art Collection, and with ample gallery space for touring international exhibitions, the museum opened on its waterfront site in 1998. Te Papa's collections include a number of significant Maori works of art and treasures, as well as a unique 21st-century carved meeting house.

**Mountains to Sea**
The amazing variety of New Zealand's animals and plants, from kiwis to kauris and a colossal squid, are revealed in exhibits featuring the natural world.

**"Awesome Forces"** help visitors experience the powerful forces shaping the country's landscape.

Level 2

**Earthquake House**
In this simulation of the 1987 Edgecumbe earthquake, you can hear the roar of the earthquake and feel it shake the building.

Level 1

**OurSpace** is an interactive multimedia zone.

**Bush City**
Visitors step into the open air to experience native bush, wetlands, a volcanic landscape, a waterfall and a lagoon right in the centre of the city. They can also explore a glowworm cave.

*For hotels and restaurants in this region see pp302–7 and pp314–25*

## VISITORS' CHECKLIST

**Practical Information**
Cable St. **Tel** (04) 381 7000.
🌐 tepapa.govt.nz
**Open** 10am–6pm daily
(10am–9pm Thu). 🎫 some
temporary exhibitions. ♿ 🅿️
🚻 📷 🎁

**Transport**
🚌 Courtney Place.

**★ Mākōtukutuku Wharepuni**
Go back 600 years on entering this
wharepuni (sleeping house)
reconstructed using traditional
methods and tools.

Ngā Toi/Arts
Te Papa

Level 6

Level 5

Level 4

Level 3

**Level 6** holds short-term
exhibitions on art and
visual culture.

**★ The Marae**
The contemporary meeting house is the focal
point of a Maori *marae*. Named Te Hono ki
Hawaiki ("the link back to Hawaiki"), Te Papa's
*marae* recalls the ancestral land of Maori.

**Key to Floorplan**
- 🟦 Art
- 🟦 History
- 🟦 Maori
- 🟦 Nature

## Gallery Guide

*The first of the high-tech interactive exhibitions begins on Level 2,
which also provides access to Bush City. Level 3 features Blood,
Earth, Fire, telling of the transformation of New Zealand since
human impact. Maori, Pacific Island and European cultural exhibits
are concentrated on Level 4. Level 5 contains Ngā Toi/Arts Te Papa,
works from the national art collection, which are spread throughout
the museum. A small gallery and outdoor terrace with city and
harbour views are on Level 6.*

# ❷ Marine Drive Tour

Hugging the coastline from Oriental Bay, south-east of the city centre on the inner harbour, to Owhiro Bay on the outer shoreline facing Cook Strait, this route is one of New Zealand's great coastal drives. It is both picturesque on cloudless days and awe-inspiring when Wellington's famous southerly gales whip up pounding waves. The route takes visitors past numerous small bays and sheltered, sandy beaches. It also passes through several suburbs where wooden villas *(see p165)* perch on what seem precarious sites high above the road, and around steep, uninhabited hillsides covered with trees that come down to the water's edge.

**⑩ Owhiro Bay**
Tourers can turn right at this bay and return to the city via Happy Valley Road or continue onto the 4-km (2.5-mile) Red Rocks Coastal Walk, where 80–150 male seals take up residence each year.

**⑨ Island Bay**
Descendants of Italian immigrants, who settled here in the early 20th century, are among those seen fishing in Cook Strait and beyond.

**⑧ Lyall Bay**
Bordered by Wellington's airport, this bay is used all year round by surfers and swimmers. On a clear day, the South Island's snow-covered mountain ranges can be seen.

**Key**

▬ Tour route

═ Other road

| 0 kilometres | 1 |
| 0 miles | 1 |

*City Centre*

*Cambridge*

*Governmt Hous*

Adelaide Road

*Wellington Zoo*

*Municipal Golf Links*

*Happy Valley Road*

*Lyall*

Queen's Drive

The Esplanade

⑩

⑨

### ① Oriental Bay
This is an area of cafés and fashionable restaurants and a favourite spot for joggers and swimmers. Across from the sandy beach, stately Victorian villas share the hillside with modern apartment blocks.

### Tips for Drivers

**Length:** 30 km (19 miles).
**Stopping-off points:** There are glorious views at all points along the route. Several parking areas allow visitors to leave their cars and stroll along the bays. Eating places include Scorch-O-Rama at Scorching Bay, whose staff have permission to serve customers seated across the road on the waterfront.

### ③ Mahanga Bay
One of the smallest and most sheltered bays along the route, Mahanga Bay is fringed with pine trees.

### ② Evans Bay
This sheltered bay is a popular spot for yachting. It also contains a marina.

Oriental Parade

unt oria

Parade

Massey Road

Karaka Bay Road

Shelly Bay Road

Marine Parade

Calabar Rd

Broadway

*Miramar Golf Course*

Breaker Bay Road

**Wellington International Airport**

Moa Point Road

### ④ Scorching Bay
Popular with swimmers, this beach allows good views towards Somes and Ward islands and Cook Strait. The seaside suburb of Eastbourne is opposite.

### ⑤ Karaka Bay
This bay is named after the native orange-berried karaka trees found along its edge. It has a pier and a number of wooden summer houses built in the early 20th century by wealthy people from out of town.

### ⑥ Worser Bay
The eastern suburbs are home to the city's thriving film industry, including Peter Jackson's workshops *(see p160).*

### ⑦ Breaker Bay
Little blue penguins can sometimes be seen crossing the road here to nest noisily under nearby houses.

SLOW DOWN!
PENGUINS CROSSING
KIA TUPATO!
HE KORORĀ E WHITI A...

Old trams at the Tram Museum, Paekakariki

## ❸ Paekakariki

**Road map** E4. 🗺 1,700. 🚉 🚌
ℹ️ i-SITE, Rimu Rd, Paraparaumu, (04)
298 8195. 🖥 naturecoast.co.nz

Situated on the Kapiti Coast,
40 minutes' drive north of
Wellington on State
Highway 1, Paekakariki is
the first of four townships
on 40 km (25 miles) of
sandy coast-line known
as the "nature coast".
A main attraction at
Paekakariki is Queen
Elizabeth Park, which
encompasses a stunning
coastline, sand dunes,
streams, peat swamps and
bush walks. A tram ride from
MacKays Crossing north of
Paekakariki takes in the
6.4-sq km (2.5-sq mile) park.
    At the **Wellington Tramway
Museum** in the park, visitors
can view displays of some of
the forerunners of the trolley
buses that still run on
Wellington's streets.

Boy with calf at
Lindale

🏛 **Wellington Tramway Museum**
Queen Elizabeth Park. **Tel** (04) 292
8361. **Open** summer: daily; winter:
Sat & Sun. **Closed** 25 Dec. 🅿️ ♿

## ❹ Paraparaumu

**Road map** E4. 🗺 12,000. 🚉 🚌
🚌 ℹ️ Coastlands, (04) 298 8195.

The main centre on the Kapiti
Coast, Paraparaumu has
shorefront shops, cafés and
restaurants. It also has a
developed beach, with a park
and playgrounds. The town is
the departure point for boat
trips to Kapiti Island.

The area's major attraction is the
**Southward Car Museum**, which
holds the largest collection of
vintage and veteran vehicles in
the southern hemisphere.
The collection of bicycles
includes an 1863 bone shaker.
Marlene Dietrich's limousine
is one of more than 250
classic and quirky vehicles
dating from 1895.
    Racing boats, home-
made vehicles,
motor cycles, early
motoring curios and
traction engines are
also housed on the
site. A highlight is a
1950 Cadillac Gangster
Special, once owned by an
employee of Al Capone and

Lucky Luciano. It boasts a
bomb-proof floor, armour-
plated doors, bullet-proof
windows, and a hinged
windscreen to enable firing
from inside.
    The **Lindale Tourist Centre**,
set around a New Zealand farm,
is a good place to bring children.
The centre offers sheep shearing
demonstrations as well as hands-
on opportunities to milk a cow,
bottle-feed lambs and goats,
play with chickens and baby
deer, and observe exotic species
like llama and emu. There are
farm walks taking in the animal
barn, where visitors can handle
and feed smaller animals.
    A shop showcasing the
award-winning gourmet Kapiti
Cheese and Kapiti Ice Cream, is
located on the site, along with
galleries, shops and eating
places. There are also places to
picnic and have a barbecue.

🏛 **Southward Car Museum**
Otaihanga Rd, Paraparaumu. **Tel** (04)
297 1221. **Open** daily. **Closed** Good
Fri, 25 Apr, 25 Dec. 🅿️ ♿ 🎁 📷 🛒 📷
📷 🖥 southward.org.nz

🏛 **Lindale Tourist Centre**
State Hwy 1, Paraparaumu. **Tel** (04)
297 0916. **Open** daily. **Closed** Good
Fri, 25 Dec. 🅿️ ♿ 🎁 📷 🛒 📷 📷
🖥 lindale.co.nz

Vintage cars at the Southward Car Museum

## ❺ Waikanae

**Road map** E4. � 8,600. 🚉 🚌
ℹ️ i-SITE, Rimu Rd, Paraparaumu (04)
298 8195. 🌐 **naturecoast.co.nz**

Nestled between the foot- hills of the Tararua Range and the Kapiti Coast, Waikanae is primarily a retirement centre, known for its craft shops and magnificent gardens. Burnard Gardens, recognized as one of New Zealand's most formally designed English-style gardens, is located here and viewings can be arranged.

The **Waikanae Estuary Scientific Reserve** is home to over 63 species of birds (though some are migratory), such as shags, dabchicks, Caspian terns, royal spoonbills and pukeko. Fires, hunting and mountain and trail biking are forbidden.

View of the unspoilt Kapiti Island from the mainland

## ❻ Kapiti Island Nature Reserve

**Road map** E4. 🚌 Paraparaumu.
ℹ️ Department of Conservation, Waikanae Field Centre, 10 Parata St, Waikanae, (04) 296 1112.

Kapiti Island, lying about 6 km (4 miles) from the mainland, dominates the Kapiti Coast. The 10-km (6-mile) long island has been a protected wildlife reserve since 1897. Access to the island is very limited although a permit to visit by charter boat can be obtained from the Department of Conservation in Wellington. All parties are met by the resident ranger. Trips around the island, and diving or fishing in the surrounding waters can be done at any time. Making their

home on the island are birds rare or absent from the mainland, such as saddlebacks and takahe. Less rare, but twice as cheeky, are the wekas, which are likely to steal anything unattended.

## ❼ Otaki

**Road map** E4. 🚶 7,600. 🚉 🚌 🚌
ℹ️ State Hwy 1, (06) 364 7620.

Before the European settlers' arrival in 1840, Otaki was heavily populated by Maori. It had the finest Maori church, Rangiatea Church, in New Zealand. Built in 1851, it was destroyed by fire in 1995. A replica of the Maori church has been open to visitors here since 2003.

### Environs

Just south of Otaki is the **Hyde Park Museum**. The museum has Maori artifacts from pre-European days, colonial memorabilia and exhibits from present-day New Zealand. Included are a Royal Room with displays from the 1953 visit of Queen Elizabeth and Prince Phillip, old farm machinery and a grocery shop with over 3,000 items marked at 1937 prices.

South of the town, the 19-km (12-mile) Gorge Road leads to Otaki Forks and the Tararua Forest Park. Along the way are walking tracks.

Entrance to the Hyde Park Museum, Otaki, which houses heritage displays

🏛️ **Hyde Park Museum**
State Hwy 1, Te Horo. **Tel** (04) 298 4515. **Open** Tue–Sun.
🎟️ donation. ♿

## ❽ Levin

**Road map** E4. 🚶 15,400. 🚉 🚌 🚌

Levin sits on a fertile plain that is one of the largest vegetable-producing areas in the country. Its main street, lined with shops that service its farming hinterland, epitomizes much of traditional small town New Zealand. Owner-operated outlets on the outskirts of the town offer "pick-your-own" freshly grown produce direct from the fields and orchards.

---

### Te Rauparaha

Kapiti Island was once the base of Te Rauparaha (1768–1849), chief of the Ngati Toa tribe and one of the greatest Maori generals of his era. After years of warfare in the Waikato and Taranaki areas, he moved to Kapiti Island in the 1820s, dominating the southwestern part of the North Island and the north of the South Island until the 1840s. He is credited with composing the well-known *haka* (war chant) often performed by the All Blacks before international rugby matches.

Watercolour (1840) by Isaac Coates

*Kamate. Kamate.*
*Ka Ora. Ka Ora.*
*Tenei te tangata*
*    puhuruhuru*
*Nana nei i tiki mai*
*I whakawhiti te ra.*
*Upane. Upane.*
*Whiti te ra.*

It is death. It is death.
It is life. It is life.
This is the hairy person
Who caused the sun to
shine.
Abreast. Keep abreast.
The rank. Hold fast.
Into the sun that shines.

Hay rolled into bales, ready for storing, on a farm near Martinborough

# ❾ Featherston

**Road map** E4. 🚗 2,600. 🚉 🚌 *i*
Old Courthouse, Main St, (06) 308 8051,
10am–1pm. **W** wairarapanz.com

Situated at the foot of the
Rimutaka Range, Featherston is
the southern gateway to the
Wairarapa area for those arriving
from the Wellington side of the
divide. Known for its antique
shops and colonial buildings, it
also houses the **Fell Locomotive
Museum**, home to the world's
only surviving Fell engine.
Running on three rails, these
ingenious locomotives used
to climb up and over the
Rimutaka Range.

🏛 **Fell Locomotive Museum**
Cnr Fitzherbert and Lyon sts. **Tel** (06)
308 9379. **Open** daily. **Closed** Anzac
Day (am only), 25 Dec. 🅿 📷 ♿

**Environs**
On the right side of the road
from Wellington, before
reaching Featherston, a signpost
points the way to a lookout.
There are also terrific walks that
enable visitors to enjoy splendid
views across **Lake Wairarapa**
to the ranges of Haurangi
(Aorangi) Forest Park and Palliser
Bay. The lake is home to
internationally recognized
wetlands that are the third
largest in New Zealand. Both
native and migratory breeds of
bird gather at the lake.
 Southeast of the lake is **Cape
Palliser** where, next to a public
road, visitors can find one of the

country's largest breeding
colonies for the New Zealand
fur seal, one of nine fur seal
species found worldwide. Seals
can be seen throughout the
year, with breeding from
November to January.
 Another spectacular sight in
the area is the **Putangirua
Pinnacles**, formed in the past
120,000 years by heavy rain
eroding an ancient gravel
deposit. Some of the pinnacles
may be 1,000 years old.

# ❿ Martinborough

**Road map** E5. 🚗 1,500. *i* 18 Kit-
chener St, (06) 306 5010. 🍷 Toast
Martinborough (Nov), Martinborough
Country Fair (Feb & Mar).
**W** wairarapanz.com

Established in 1881 by Irish
immigrant John Martin,
Martinborough was once reliant
for its prosperity on the

surrounding farming
community. Since the late
1970s, the town has become
internationally known for its
grape growing and wine making
*(see pp40–1)*. It is now a
fashionable weekend
destination for those attracted
by its premium wines, vineyard
cafés, boutique stores, quality
accommodation, olive groves
and award-winning restaurants.
Most of the town's boutique
wineries are within walking or
cycling distance of its
picturesque town square.

**Environs**
New Zealand's first commercial
wind farm, **Hau Hei Wind Farm**,
is 21 km (13 miles) southeast of
Martinborough. Operated by
Wairarapa Electricity, the farm's
turbines are ranged along a
540-m (1,770-ft) ridge. Although
on private land, they can be
seen from a public viewing area.

Visitors enjoying the wine at the Grapevine in Martinborough

*For hotels and restaurants in this region see pp302–7 and pp314–25*

# ⓫ Masterton

Road map E4. 🚆 22,800. 🚗 🚌 🚌
🏢 Cnr Dixon & Bruce sts (at Aratoi),
06) 370 0900. 🎪 Golden Shears
(Mar). 🖥 wairarapanz.com

Ninety minutes' drive from both
Wellington and Palmerston
North, Masterton is Wairarapa's
largest town. It hosts a number
of events during the summer,
including a biennial air show
and also a traditional shearing
competition known as the
Golden Shears which is held
every year.

Masterton is home to **The
Wool Shed**, a national museum
dedicated to New Zealand's
shearing heritage with live
shearing displays for groups of
ten or more. The town also
has a recreation centre with
swimming pools, and the
region's art and history musem,
**Aratoi. Queen Elizabeth Park**
has a children's playground, a
miniature train, mini-golf and a
skatepark.

### 🏛 The Wool Shed

12 Dixon St. **Tel** (06) 378 8008.
**Open** 10am–4pm daily. **Closed** Anzac
Day, Good Friday, 25 Dec. 🚗 🛴 🏠
🖥 thewoolshednz.com

### Environs

Masterton is close to the beach
resorts of **Castlepoint** and
**Riversdale**, which are popular
for surfing, fishing and walking.
State Highway 2 runs through
the village of **Greytown**. Settled
in 1854, it is the oldest town in

Agricultural implements at the
Cobblestones Museum

Wairarapa and has a restored
Victorian main street. It is home
to the **Cobblestones Museum**.
Located on the site of coach
stables built in 1856 for the
Wellington mail service, the
museum houses colonial
buildings, vehicles, agricultural
equipment and a working
print shop. It has relocated
and restored buildings,
complete with
memorabilia of
the days of the
early settlers.

The **Tararua Forest
Park**, located within the
rugged Tararua Range,
can be accessed at Holdsworth,
15 km (9 miles) from State
Highway 2, via Norfolk Road just
south of Masterton. The park

has bush walks ranging from
easy to difficult, while Grassy
flats beside the Atiwhakatu
Stream are ideal for picnics and
barbecues.

### 🏛 Cobblestones Museum

169 Main St, Greytown. **Tel** (06) 304
9687. **Open** daily. 🚗 🛴 🏠

# ⓬ Pukaha Mount Bruce National Wildlife Centre

Road map E4. **Tel** (06) 375 8004. **Open**
9am–4:30pm daily. **Closed** 25 Dec. 🚗
🛴 🖥 🏠 🖥 pukaha.org.nz

Located 30 km (19 miles) north
of Masterton, this centre
conserves some of New
Zealand's most rare and
endangered wildlife. Most
famously, it is home to three
white kiwi and features a Kiwi
House where the birds are
hatched, hand-raised and fed
from October to
April. Other bird
species include the
stitchbird, kokako and
takahe. Visitors can take
a walking tour through
native bush, including a last
remnant of forest once
known as "Forty Mile
Bush", containing native
rimu, rata and kamahi
trees, nocturnal kiwi and
tuatara. It is also possible to
watch eels being fed near the
centre's river bridge and kaka
being fed each afternoon.

Kokako at
Mount Bruce

Sheep shearer in competition

# ⑬ Palmerston North

Manawatu's largest city, Palmerston North lies in the centre of a broad, fertile coastal plain that stretches from the Tasman Sea across to the Tararua and Ruahine ranges and encompasses a varied landscape of valleys, plateaus and rivers. The city is a growing hub for the lower North Island, with three main roads converging near it. New Zealand's largest university, Massey University, and several colleges and research institutes are based here, giving Palmerston North a pleasant and diverse university city atmosphere.

1926 poster in the New Zealand Rugby Museum

### 🌿 The Square

ℹ️ (06) 350 1922.

Laid out in 1866, this tranquil, leafy garden zone at the heart of the city provides welcome relief to the busy commercial centre. Originally bisected by New Zealand's main trunk railway, The Square's clipped lawns, flower beds, trees and shrubs, ornamental ponds and fountains, war memorial and chiming clock tower attract large numbers of visitors all year round. The shops and buildings surrounding The Square reflect the diversity of styles in New Zealand's architectural history.

### 🏛️ Te Manawa Art Gallery

326 Main St. **Tel** (06) 355 5000. **Open** 10am–5pm daily. **Closed** 1 Jan, Good Fri, 25 & 26 Dec. 🌐 temanawa.co.nz

First opened in 1959 as the Palmerston North Art Gallery, the gallery was renamed and rehoused in a modern, spacious building near The Square in 1977. Visitors are greeted at the entrance by local artist Paul Dibble's striking sculpture, *Pacific Monarch*, reputedly the largest bronze work cast in New Zealand.

The gallery's strength lies in its collection of contemporary art, particularly that from the 1970s, but it also houses a permanent collection of paintings, sculpture, prints, drawings, photographs and ceramics by prominent New Zealand artists. There is a regularly changing programme of exhibitions of New Zealand and international art and crafts. The gallery is part of the Te Manawa complex, which also includes a museum and science centre.

### 🏛️ New Zealand Rugby Museum

326 Main St. **Tel** (06) 358 6974. **Open** 10am–5pm daily. **Closed** 1 Jan, Good Fri, 25 & 26 Dec. ♿ 📷 phone to book. 🌐 rugbymuseum.co.nz

Founded in 1968, the museum relocated to the Te Manawa complex in 2011. It contains exhibits and memorabilia relating to the history of rugby in New Zealand from the first game played in the country, at Nelson in 1870, to the present. There are also exhibits from other rugby-playing countries. The paraphernalia on display includes caps, jerseys, trophies, badges, autographed balls, ties, posters and photographs. Interactive exhibits allow visitors to explore the aspects of rugby that interest them most, and famous international games can be watched on screen. Also on display is a broken protestor's shield, a legacy of the bitter 1981 tour to New Zealand by the South African Springbok rugby team. The tour divided the country and caused bloody protests.

### 🏫 Massey University

Tennant Drive. **Tel** (06) 350 5701. ♿ 🌐 massey.ac.nz

Five km (3 miles) south of the city, the eclectic mixture of old homesteads and modern buildings that make up Massey University are set in superb countryside. On the Massey History Walk, part of the City Heritage Trail, visitors can look at these and some of the city's older sites and buildings. The world's first university-based Institute of Rugby and New Zealand's only university aviation school are both located here.

### Environs

East of the city, the Manawatu River runs through the imposing **Manawatu Gorge**. The river defies geographical logic by rising on the eastern slopes of the Tararua Range, then turning back on itself to reach the Tasman Sea to the west. The gorge is popular with jet-boaters, kayakers, walkers and campers.

There are a number of beautiful gardens around the city. One, the Cross Hill Gardens, a 45-minute drive north, has one of New Zealand's largest and most varied collections of rhododendrons.

Sculpture by Paul Dibble in front of Te Manawa Art Gallery

*For hotels and restaurants in this region see pp302–7 and pp314–25*

# Te Manawa

At the heart of the Manawatu region, Te Manawa is the only institution of its kind in New Zealand to unite a museum, art gallery *(see p178)* and interactive science centre. The constantly changing exhibition programme features nationally significant collections as well as innovative hands-on shows. The museum forms the heart of the complex and recalls the long occupation of the region by Maori, as well as exploring the history of the Manawatu. The interactive science centre features changing exhibitions that are popular with children. The New Zealand Rugby Museum *(see p178)* is also part of the Te Manawa complex.

**VISITORS' CHECKLIST**

**Practical Information**
326 Main St. **Tel** (06) 355 5000.
W temanawa.co.nz
**Open** 10am–5pm daily
(including some public hols).
**Closed** 1 Jan, Good Fri, 25,
26 Dec. ♿ 🎥 📷

**Manawatu Journeys**
The area's history is explored via domestic items.

Level 1

Ground floor

**Key to Floorplan**
▨ Kids TM
▨ Museum Galleries

Entrance

**★ Te Awa – The River**
Live cave weta insects are among the creatures in an exhibition on the impact of the Manawatu River.

**AgResearch Conservatory** features samples of exotic and native plant species.

**Kids TM**
This exciting area for the under-8s lets children explore and learn about the world through dressing up and role play.

**★ Tangata Whenua Gallery**
These 19th-century carved palisade posts are among the Maori treasures exhibited in the gallery.

Lush hills in front of Mount Egmont ▶

# ⑭ Wanganui

The area around Wanganui was first settled by Maori about AD 1100. By 1840 the New Zealand Company, unable to provide sufficient land in the Wellington district for the steady flow of new colonists, began to negotiate with Maori for land in Wanganui. The town became a distribution centre for the area extending to Waitotara in the west, Marton in the east and up the Whanganui River Valley in the north. Less than an hour by road to Palmerston North and only two and a half hours to Wellington, Wanganui's thriving arts scene sits alongside a variety of export-oriented industries.

View of Wanganui and the city bridge from Durie Hill

### 🏛 Victoria Avenue

The preserved buildings, cinema, gaslights, wrought-iron street furniture and palm trees make Victoria Avenue, Wanganui's central city shopping area, a charming spot for visitors. From December to March, around 1,000 floral baskets are hung on streetlights and verandahs to celebrate the Wanganui in Bloom festival.

### 🏛 Durie Hill

2 Blyth St, via Anzac Parade.
**Tel** (06) 345 8525. **Open** daily. 🅿
Located opposite the city bridge at the end of Victoria Avenue, Durie Hill is known for an historic elevator, which rises 66 m (216 ft) inside the hill to

the summit. Opened in 1919, it is one of several such elevators in the world. A pedestrian tunnel leads to the elevator. It takes about a minute to rise to the summit.

A climb up the 176 steps of the spiral staircase inside the 34-m (110-ft) Durie Hill Memorial Tower, a short distance from the top of the elevator, allows panoramic views of Wanganui, Mount Taranaki/Egmont to the northwest (see pp186–7), Mount Ruapehu to the east (see pp147–8) and the Tasman Sea. The World War I memorial, opened in 1925, is constructed from blocks of fossilized seashell rock taken from quarries up the river.

### 🏛 Whanganui Regional Museum

Queens Park. **Tel** (06) 349 1110.
**Open** daily. **Closed** Good Fri, 25 Dec.
🅿 🚫 🅰 🏠 🌐 wanganui-museum.org.nz

Among the treasures displayed in the Whanganui Regional Museum, visitors will find paintings of the Maori by Gottfried Lindauer (1839–1926), who managed to avoid service in the Austro-Hungarian army by settling in New Zealand, and Te Mata-o-Hoturoa, a *waka* (Maori war canoe) carved from a single totara tree. Established in 1895, the museum is concerned with the geology, natural and social history of the city and surrounding region.

## Wanganui City Centre

① Cooks Gardens
② Victoria Avenue
③ Whanganui Regional Museum
④ Sarjeant Gallery
⑤ Moutoa Gardens
⑥ Whanganui Riverboat Centre
⑦ Durie Hill

0 metres    500
0 yards     500

    **For keys to map symbols** *see back flap*

The *Waimarie* on the Whanganui River

## 🏛 Sarjeant Gallery

Queens Park. **Tel** (06) 349 0506.
**Open** daily. **Closed** Good Fri, 25 Dec.
🚻 📷 W sarjeant.org.nz

This gallery features a highly
regarded collection of New
Zealand oil paintings, water-
colours and prints from the
19th and 20th centuries. It
houses the Denton photo-
graphy collection and World
War I posters and cartoons.

## 🌳 Moutoa Gardens

Market Place.

Located at the site of the
settling of Wanganui as
a town, the beautiful
Moutoa Gardens feature
monuments set within
mature specimen trees
and flower beds. Since
the early 1990s, the
gardens have been a
political rallying point. In
1995, Maori tribes
protesting about land
and river rights occupied
the gardens for 79 days.

Moutoa
Gardens statue

## 🌳 Cooks Gardens

Maria Place.

A leading outdoor venue, Cooks
Gardens contain a wooden velo-
drome and an attractive old bell
tower. It was here, in 1962, that
New Zealander Peter Snell ran
the mile in under four minutes,
breaking the record held by
Roger Bannister of Great Britain.

## 🚢 Whanganui Riverboat Centre

Taupo Quay. **Tel** (06) 347 1863.
**Open** daily. 📷 📹 inside. 🚻 📷
W riverboats.co.nz

This centre houses the salvaged
and restored paddle steamer
*Waimarie*. Built in London in
1899, it plied the Whanganui
River for 50 years. Cruises on the
restored steamer leave from here.

## ⑮ Whanganui River

Road map E3–E4. i Wanganui
Department of Conservation,
Taupo Quay, (06) 349 2100.
W whanganuiriver.co.nz

The Whanganui River is the
longest navigable and the third
longest river in New Zealand.
The 290-km (180-mile) river
begins its journey high up on
Mount Tongariro in the centre
of the North Island, and
meanders its way down
through the Whanganui
National Park to Wanganui
and the Tasman Sea.

Up until the 1920s
a regular river boat service
carried passengers, mail
and freight into the interior,
and a thriving tourist trade
operated between Mount
Ruapehu and Wanganui.
Today, the river, with its
deep gorges, sheer cliffs
and 239 listed rapids, is
New Zealand's most canoed
waterway. The main entry
and exit points for journeys
on the river by canoe,
raft or jet-boat are
Taumarunui, Pipiriki and
Wanganui. The 145-km
(90-mile) journey from
Taumarunui to Pipiriki
takes about five days by
canoe. From October to
April, visitors must obtain
hut and campsite passes
from the local Depart-
ment of Conservation or
other sales outlets.

The river can also be
followed by road from
Wanganui to Pipiriki.
Good side tracks lead
to historic sites, early
Maori villages, waterfalls
and lookouts.

## ⑯ Whanganui National Park

Road map E3. i Department of
Conservation, 74 Ingestre St,
Wanganui, (06) 349 2100.

Established in 1987, the three
main sections of the park lie
within the catchment of the
Whanganui River, which eroded
through mudstone to form
striking gorges, bluffs, ridges
and valleys. Broadleaf podocarp
forest surrounding the river
forms the heart of the park.
Tree ferns and riverside plants
are also a feature, as is the
birdlife. The river is rich in fish
and contains 18 native species,
as well as non-native fish.

Visitors can choose from
a variety of energetic activities,
including canoeing, kayaking,
rafting, jet-boating, mountain
biking and tramping. There is
also fishing and hunting for
deer and goats. For a more
leisurely trip, visitors can enjoy
a cruise on the 19th-century
paddle steamer *Waimarie*.

The Whanganui River flowing through
Whanganui National Park

# ⑰ New Plymouth

The principal centre of the Taranaki region, New Plymouth is situated around the only deep-water port on New Zealand's west coast, surrounded by surfing beaches along the North Taranaki Bight. The massive cone of Mount Taranaki/Egmont towers behind the city. Agriculture, with a strong emphasis on dairying, as well as heavy engineering, the marine industry and forestry are among the mainstays of the local economy. The area is also the base for the country's major oil, gas and petrochemical industries. New Plymouth is recognized for its many beautiful parks, gardens and reserves, and is an ideal base from which to explore Egmont National Park *(see pp186–7)*.

Altar and stained-glass window in Taranaki Cathedral Church of St Mary

### ⟰ Taranaki Cathedral Church of St Mary

37 Vivian St. **Tel** (06) 758 3111.
**Open** daily. ⟰ most days. ⭑
Consecrated in 1848, this Anglican church is the oldest stone church in New Zealand. It is a fine example of 19th-century architecture, and has some outstanding stained-glass windows, an impressive vaulted timber ceiling and historic artifacts. In the grounds, headstones of children, settlers and soldiers, who died in the Taranaki Land Wars, poignantly recall the difficulties faced by early settlers. Several Maori chiefs are also buried there.

### 🏛 Puke Ariki

1 Ariki St. **Tel** (06) 759 6060. **Open** daily. ⭑ 🏠 🖵 🅦 pukeariki.com
Built on what was originally the most significant Maori site in Taranaki, Puke Ariki is an integrated library, museum and i-SITE. The centre provides a venue for the display of the museum's heritage collection, including 6000 nationally important Maori taonga (treasures), such as objects, paintings, photographs, cartoons, maps and coins. Puke Ariki overlooks a 7-km (4-mile) coastal walkway.

### 🏠 Richmond Cottage

Ariki St. **Tel** (06) 759 6060.
**Open** 11am–3:30pm weekends and public hols. 🏠 ⭑
Richmond Cottage, constructed in 1853 of stone instead of the customary timber, was the residence of the Richmond family. Many of the artifacts and furnishings on display in the beautifully restored cottage belonged to these former owners. During the 1880s, the cottage offered accommodation to seaside holiday-makers.

### ⟐ Pukeariki Landing

Ariki St. **Open** daily.
An oasis of green in the central city, Pukeariki Landing opened in 1990 when train tracks previously fronting the coastline were removed. This attractive park stands where surfboats, which carried people and supplies from ships, used to come ashore.

### 🏛 Govett-Brewster Art Gallery

40 Queen St. **Tel** (06) 759 6060.
**Open** 10am–5pm daily.
**Closed** 25 Dec. 🏛 specific exhibits.
⭑ 🖵 🏠 🅦 govettbrewster.com
Opened in 1970 as a contemporary art museum – a novel concept in New Zealand and the Asia-Pacific region at the time – the Govett-Brewster Art Gallery was the gift of local benefactor Monica Brewster. She stipulated in her deed of gift that the gallery must always have a director of national standing and the ability to acquire art works with "minimal influence from local politicians".

Its main strengths lie in its collection of abstract art from the 1970s and 1980s, including works by Patrick Hanly, Michael Illingworth and Colin McCahon, and in its contemporary sculpture. The gallery is the site of the Len Lye Archive and contains the kinetic sculptures, paintings and films of this internationally renowned New Zealand artist, painter and film-maker (1901–80). The gallery also holds 20 exhibitions a year, conducts frequent art lectures and has a comprehensive research library.

## Taranaki's Gardens and Parks

Taranaki's parks, reserves and gardens are a highlight of the district and a drawcard for visitors. Long hours of sunshine, high rainfall, a mild climate, rich volcanic soils and shelter from prevailing winds combine to create ideal gardening conditions. Rhododendrons, azaleas and camellias suit Taranaki's conditions perfectly, and this is reflected in the large numbers of such species grown successfully throughout the region, along with roses, magnolias, irises and various native plants. From the end of October until the end of the first week of November, about 100 home gardens, both small and large, open their gates for public viewing in the annual Taranaki Rhododendron Festival. Visitors may enjoy tea at some of these gardens and buy plants. Visit www.gardens.org.nz for more information.

Rhododendrons in bloom

Fernery at Pukekura Park

### 🏞 Pukekura Park

Liardet St. **Open** daily. ♿

Opened in 1876 and only a ten-minute walk from the city centre, the dominant theme of Pukekura Park is water. Paths lead through dense native bushland, native and exotic trees, and fern gullies beside freshwater lakes and streams. A fernery, fountain, waterfall, water wheel, playground and boats for hire are other attractions. From the Tea House there is a dramatic view of Mount Taranaki/Egmont. During the Festival of Lights, held from Christmas to early February, Pukekura Park is transformed at night into a fairyland by thousands of coloured lights strung through its walkways and plantings.

### 🏞 Brooklands Park

Brooklands Park Drive. **Open** daily. ♿

Adjoining Pukekura Park, Brooklands is an English-style park with sweeping lawns and formal gardens. Originally a private family estate, it was bequeathed to the city in 1934. Highlights include an enormous 2,000-year-old puriri tree, 300 varieties of rhododendron, and a children's zoo. The Bowl of Brooklands, an outdoor soundshell in a bush and lake setting, is the site of concerts and other entertainment.

The park also contains a colonial hospital, the Gables, built in 1847. The beautiful beach stone building failed as a hospital, attracting only 55 patients, and is now an art gallery and medical museum.

## New Plymouth City Centre

① Govett-Brewster Art
   Gallery
② Richmond Cottage
③ Pukeariki Landing

④ Puke Ariki
⑤ Taranaki Cathedral
   Church of St Mary
⑥ Pukekura Park

For keys to map symbols *see back flap*

# ⓲ Egmont National Park

Egmont National Park is one of the most easily accessed parks in New Zealand. The centrepiece is the solitary 2,518-m (8,261-ft) Mount Taranaki/Egmont, a dormant volcano. Ice and snow permanently cover the peak and upper slopes of this almost symmetrical mountain. The park's 193-km (119-mile) network of tracks offers excellent climbing, skiing and tramping for the fit and well prepared. Many tracks are suitable for the average walker. Weather conditions can change rapidly so trampers should be prepared for all conditions.

**Huts**
Walking tracks link the huts in the park. Hut passes can be bought from information centres and Department of Conservation offices

**Native trees**
The wet mountain climate, combined with periods of dry, hot weather, promote luxurious vegetation. Native trees are abundant on the lower slopes.

0 kilometres 3

0 miles 3

*Oakura River*

*Dover Track*

*Pouakai Range*

*Stony River*

*Puniho Track*

🏕 Kahui

*Kahui Track*

*Oaonui Track*

*Waiaua Gorge* 🏕

*Ihaia Track*

*Brames F*

*Waiaua River*

*Taungatara Track*

## KEY

① **The North Egmont Visitor Centre** has interesting displays on the park and the mountain, an audiovisual show and café.

② **The Dawson Falls/Te Rere O Noke Visitor Centre** has exhibits on the park's flora and fauna, and a model of its volcanic features.

## Walks in Egmont National Park

The park includes an extensive network of walking tracks leading to the summit or around the mountain. Shorter tracks start off from the three roads heading up the mountain. These range from easy to difficult and take from 30 minutes to several hours. The popular two-day Pouaki circuit offers walkers a taste of what Egmont has to offer: rainforest, tussock land, an alpine swamp and volcanic features. This track can be accessed from North Egmont. Vegetation in the park ranges from tall rimu and kamahi trees at lower altitudes, to dense subalpine shrubs and an alpine herbfield complete with plants unique to the park.

*Tramper on one of the park's tracks*

**Key**

▬ Minor road

〜 River

–·– Park boundary

– – Walking track

### Mount Taranaki/Egmont

Mount Taranaki/Egmont is believed to have formed after
a volcanic eruption more than 70,000 years ago. Sacred
to local Maori, the mountain last erupted in 1775.

**Egmont Road**
Signs at Egmont Village point to the 16-km
(10-mile) Egmont Road which brings visitors
into the northern area of the park. There are
picnic areas along the way within the park.

**Winter Climbing**
Several ice and snow routes lead to the
summit from the northern slopes. Climbers
must always be properly equipped.

**Dawson Falls/ Te Rere O Noke**
Dropping 18 m (60 ft) down an ancient
lava flow, the waterfall is a 20-minute
walk from the visitor centre.

**For additional map symbols** see back flap

View of one of the Sugar Loaf Islands

# ⑲ Oakura

**Road map** D3. ▲ 1,000.

Situated on a beautiful stretch of Taranaki coastline 15 km (9 miles) west of New Plymouth, Oakura is one of a number of small, scenic towns typifying the rural aspect of New Zealand. It has the traditional fixtures of such towns – the main street row of shops, service station, recreation grounds, churches, pubs and a war memorial. A train carriage restaurant in the main street is a novelty. The Crafty Fox, a neighbouring shop, sells works by the many artists and crafts people who live in the area.

The beach at Oakura is well known for its beautiful sunsets (in Maori, Oakura means "the place of flashing redness"). It is also a prime spot for swimming, windsurfing and surfboarding.

# ⑳ Sugar Loaf Islands Marine Park

**Road map** D3. 🚢 from Lee Breakwater, New Plymouth.

Established as a marine protected area in 1991, the Sugar Loaf Islands lie between 700 m (2,300 ft) and 1.5 km (1 mile) off New Plymouth's Port Taranaki breakwater. The stacks and spectacular reefs that make up the islands are the oldest volcanic features in Taranaki. They consist of eroded andesitic domes produced around 1.75 million years ago, lying at depths of between 5 m (16 ft) and 30 m (98 ft). Of the eleven islands, or groupings of islands,

the two largest are Motumahanga and Moturoa, located at the northern end of the park. They are often referred to as the "outer islands". Four rocky islets close to the mainland at Paritutu are known as the "inner islands".

The islands support a wealth of wildlife and plants. Among them are 80 recorded types of fish, at least 19 species of birdlife, rare and endangered native and introduced plants and 33 species of sponge. Fur seals are present on the islands all year round, with common and Maui's dolphins and killer, pilot and humpback whales also seen at times.

Although the best way to explore the islands is by charter boat, Round Rock, one of the "inner islands", can be accessed on foot from the beach during mid- to low tide. Snapper Rock, another "inner island", is accessible from the shore only when the spring tides are very low.

The relatively deep water, wide variety of marine life and spectacular underwater scenery make the park a popular venue for divers. Visibility often reaches 20 m (65 ft) during the summer and autumn months. Recreational fishing is also very popular in the park, although there are fishing restrictions. Blue cod, kingfish and snapper are among the most frequently caught species. Game fishing further offshore for tuna, marlin and mako shark usually takes place during summer and early autumn.

# ㉑ Cape Egmont

**Road map** D3.

Taranaki's most westerly point, Cape Egmont is characterized by strong winds and choppy seas. The solitary landmark is the Cape Egmont lighthouse, transferred from Mana Island near Wellington in 1881. Powered by diesel generators until 1951, it now operates on electricity.

Located 30 km (19 miles) offshore from the cape, the Maui field produces gas, which is processed at Oaonui, 9 km (6 miles) northwest of the town of Opunake. At the site of the processing plant, a visitor centre provides details of the history of oil exploration in the Taranaki region. There are also scale models of ships and oil rigs. Visitors can use the binoculars at the centre to get a good view of one of the platforms, Maui A, 35 km (21.5 miles) offshore.

Steps leading up to the Cape Egmont lighthouse

# ㉒ Opunake

**Road map** D3. ▲ 1,600. 🚌 ℹ 55 High St, (06) 278 8599. 🎭 Opunake Beach Carnival (Jan).

The thriving centre of a rich dairying district, Opunake is the largest town on the west side of Mount Taranaki/Egmont. The beach at Opunake, situated along the small, sheltered Middleton Bay, is regarded as Taranaki's best beach. It teems with tourists attracted to its safe swimming and its surfing during the summer months. The Opunake Walkway takes visitors

Opunake Beach, a picturesque swimming spot on the Taranaki coast

around the beautiful coastline and beach front, as well as around the nearby Opunake Lake, an excellent spot for canoeing, yachting and other water sports. Other points along the way include two old cemeteries. The 7-km (4-mile) route can be accessed from a number of points along the way.

## ㉓ Hawera

**Road map** D3. 9,000.
55 High St, (06) 278 8599.

Part of Taranaki's rural heartland, Hawera boasts a number of interesting places. The 38,000-sq-m (409,000-sq-ft) **Hollard Gardens** were laid out in the late 1920s by farmer Bernard Hollard and presented to the Queen Elizabeth II National Trust in 1982. The gardens are at their most colourful from September to November.

Perhaps the best way to appreciate this beautiful region is from the air by taking a helicopter flight organized by **Heliview Taranaki**. They can arrange pick ups and drop offs from any local hotel, motel and campsite using a local mini bus firm. Fly over the city, the coastline, over the summit of Mount Taranaki or the Pouakai Ranges. The best option is one of their 30-minute flights which can include a landing to allow visitors to enjoy one of the sights close up, for example, Mount Damper Falls. "Port to Peak" is another popular 60-minute flight from Port Taranaki to Mount Taranaki.

Near Hawera is the Fontera Dairy Factory, which is the world's largest single-site, multi-product milk processing plant. It is closed to the public.

Hawera and its surroundings can be viewed from the top of the town's water tower, built after a series of fires in the 1880s, one of which razed most of the main street. In 1914, a month after the tower was erected, an earthquake caused it to list 0.75 m (2.5 ft) to the south. The fault has now been reduced to 8 cm (3 inches).

The **Tawhiti Museum**, claimed to be the best private museum in the country, re-creates many aspects of early life in South Taranaki. Exhibits range from the early land wars to the development of the fledgling dairy industry, and there is a traders and whalers experience. The life-like figures in the exhibits, modelled on the faces of local volunteers, were cast at

Cow statue outside Fontera Dairy

the museum's on-site workshops. A bush railway takes passengers on a reconstruction of the logging railways that used to operate in Taranaki.

**Hollard Gardens**
Manaia Road, N of Kaponga.
**Tel** (06) 765 7127. **Open** daily.
donation

**Heliview Taranaki**
Port Taranaki Heliport, Ocean View Parade. **Tel** 0800 435 426, (06) 753 0123. **W** heliview.co.nz

**Tawhiti Museum**
401 Ohangai Rd. **Tel** (06) 278 6837.
**Open** variable. by arrangement.

## ㉔ Stratford

**Road map** D3. 5,700.
61–63 Miranda St, (06) 765 6708.

Lying to the east of Mount Taranaki/Egmont, 40 km (25 miles) south of New Plymouth, Stratford is named after Shakespeare's birthplace, Stratford-upon-Avon, and many of its streets are named after Shakespearean characters. The **Taranaki Pioneer Village** in the town comprises restored or re-created buildings, including a school house, jail, railway station and about 50 other buildings that relate the area's local and provincial history.

**Taranaki Pioneer Village**
State Hwy 3, Stratford South. **Tel** (06) 765 5399. **Open** daily. **Closed** 25 Dec. some exhibits only.
**W** pioneervillage.co.nz

Life-size exhibits in the Tawhiti Museum, Hawera

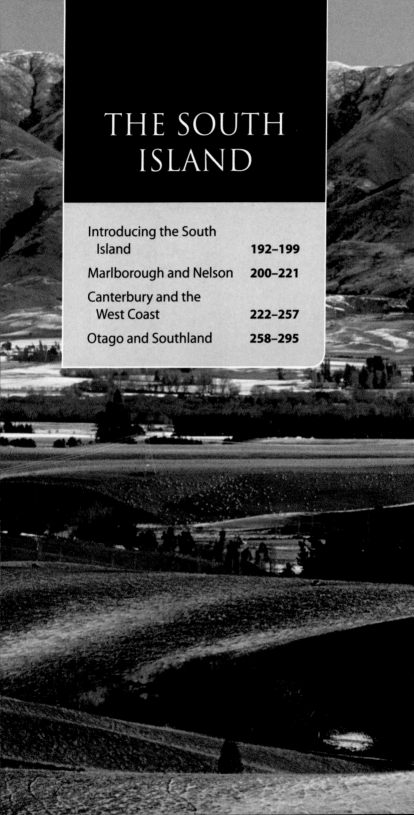

# THE SOUTH ISLAND

# Introducing the South Island

Unparalleled scenic variety awaits the visitor to the South Island. The snow-capped Southern Alps dominate the island, dividing it in two and creating a vast adventure playground of mountains, glaciers, lakes, rivers and fiords. Golden sand beaches, waterways and vineyards dominate the sun-soaked north. Along the narrow West Coast, waves from the Tasman Sea pound wild beaches. To the east is the patchwork Canterbury Plains and the rich, rolling farmland of Otago and Southland. Christchurch, New Zealand's elegant "garden city", and Picton in the picturesque Marlborough Sounds, are the two main entry points to the South Island.

**Locator Map**

**In Aoraki/Mount Cook National Park** *(see pp256–7)*, the highest peaks in New Zealand soar above the crest of the Southern Alps and over the surrounding subalpine park. The park is one of the country's most popular centres for walkers, climbers and photographers.

**Lake Te Anau** *(see p285)*, facing the glacier-carved mountains of Fiordland National Park, is one of the longest lakes in New Zealand and is popular with trout and salmon anglers.

Fox Glacier

Mount Cook

Haast

Twizel

Omarama

Milford Sound

Wanaka

Queenstown

Cromwell

Te Anau

Alexandra

Manapouri

OTAGO AND SOUTHLAND *(See pp258–295)*

Lumsden

P

Wai

Dunedin

Gore

Invercargill

Balclutha

Bluff

Oban

**The Octagon** *(see pp262 & 265)*, an attractive eight-sided garden area in the centre of Dunedin, is surrounded by imposing public buildings and a statue of the Scottish poet Robert Burns.

◄ Canterbury Plains with snow-covered mountains in the background

**Nelson Lakes National Park** *(see p216)*, at the northern tip of the Southern Alps, is dominated by the twin glacier-formed lakes, Rotoiti and Rotoroa.

| 0 kilometres | 50 |
| 0 miles | 50 |

**The Kaikoura coast** *(see pp212–13)* is the only place in New Zealand where a pod of sperm whales can be seen throughout the year. Eco-tourism companies take visitors out to sea in boats to spot the whales and other marine life.

**The Provincial Council Buildings** in Christchurch *(see p230)* are considered the finest example of secular Gothic architecture in New Zealand and are the city's most historic buildings. They were damaged in the earthquake of 2011, but are being repaired and rebuilt.

**The Moeraki Boulders** *(see p271)*, a group of perfectly round, smooth, grey boulders of various sizes, are scattered haphazardly along the seashore and near the cliffs behind the beach.

# Southern Splendour

The overwhelming impression a visitor has of the South Island is its scenic diversity: the bush-clad inlets of the Marlborough Sounds, golden sand beaches of Nelson, sweeping plains of Canterbury, snow-covered mountains of the alpine chain, dripping rainforests of the West Coast, rugged tussocklands and rolling farmland of Otago and Southland and the fiords of the southwest. No less varied is the climate. Only three hours of driving separate the wetter west coast and the drier east coast.

**Mitre Peak**, the centrepiece of Fiordland National Park, is the world's highest sea cliff.

**Abel Tasman National Park's** golden sand beaches contrast with the deep green of the forest *(see pp218–19)*. The coastal walk in this park is one of the most popular in New Zealand.

**Sheep** need supplementary feed, such as hay, during the coldest winter months.

**The West Coast**, occupying a narrow strip of land between the Tasman Sea and the Southern Alps, has the highest rainfall in New Zealand. It also has some of the best examples of untouched rainforest, as shown here on the Milford Track *(see p287)*.

## Southern Alps

*Stretching almost the entire length of the South Island, the mighty Southern Alps and its various alpine environments were formed by the upward thrust of the Pacific Continental Plate (see p26).*

**On Banks Peninsula**, the craters of past volcanoes, created by lava flows, are today's harbours of Lyttelton and Akaroa.

**The Marlborough Sounds**, in the north of the South Island, were produced by the drowning of an extensive river system *(see pp206–7)*.

**Mountains and glaciers** combine to produce spectacular scenery and numerous opportunites for outdoor activities.

**The rocks** of the Southern Alps, folded and raised by titanic forces, and eroded by wind, rain and ice, are a striking sight from the air or road.

**The Sutherland Falls** in Fiordland, once thought to be the highest in the world, plunge 580 m (1,900 ft) in three cascades.

**The lakes** on the eastern side of the Alps, such as Lake Ohau shown here, are the direct result of glacial gouging.

**Lake Tekapo** and other eastern lakes are a milky blue, caused by ice rasping against rocks to produce fine powder.

## Braided Rivers

Weaving sinuous strands of water from the mountains to the sea, the braided rivers of the South Island's east coast are, globally, rare ecosystems. Over thousands of years the largest rivers, among them the Rakaia, Waimakariri, Rangitata and Waitaki, have carried rocks and shingle from the Southern Alps and deposited this debris to create the fertile Canterbury Plains. On the river flats lives the wrybill, the only bird in the world with a sideways turning beak. The world's rarest wader, the black stilt, breeds on shingle "islands" in the rivers of the Mackenzie Basin *(see p255)*.

The sinuous strands of the Waimakariri River cross the Canterbury Plains

# Wildlife Colonies

With a smaller population, there is less human pressure on wildlife in the South Island than in the North Island, and this is reflected in the number of wildlife colonies scattered around the mainland which are accessible to tourists. New Zealand has been described as "the seabird capital of the world" because of the number of species that either visit or breed along its coasts. A lack of predators has also led inland birds to be more fearless, and therefore more visible, than birds in most other countries. Marine mammals abound and tour operators guarantee an almost 100 per cent chance of seeing these animals in their natural habitat.

**The white heron** breeds only in a coastal swamp near Okarito in September–October but is often seen in other estuaries along the coast.

**The royal albatross** has one of the greatest wingspans – up to 3 m (10 ft) – of any seabird. The world's only mainland breeding colony is at Taiaroa Head on the Otago Peninsula (see p270). Here a four-month-old chick is being weighed.

**The kaki/black stilt**, an endangered wader, can be seen along the braided rivers of the Mackenzie Basin and at visitor hides (see p255).

**The blue penguin**, the smallest of all penguins, can survive near populated areas, such as Oamaru (see p273), feeding on fish close to shore.

**Bottlenose dolphins**, known to swim as fast as 40 km/h (25 mph), prey on inshore bottom-dwelling species. A pod has taken up year-round residence in Doubtful Sound (see p288).

**The Fiordland crested penguin**, a rare native species, has a yellow crest over each eye. It comes ashore each June to build nests in caves beneath the roots of trees in coastal rainforests.

*Okarito Lagoon*

*Haast*

*Milford Sound*

*Lake Wanaka*

*Lake Hawea*

*Twiz...*

*Queenstown*

*Doubtful Sound*

*Lake Wakatipu*

*Oam...*

*DU...*

*O...*

*Pe...*

*Invercargill*

STEWART ISLAND

**The kiwi**, although primarily nocturnal, can be seen during twilight hours foraging in the forest on Stewart Island (see pp292–3).

**The yellow-eyed penguin**, the world's rarest species, is mostly concentrated on the Otago Peninsula (see p271). In the evening, they can be seen patrolling the beach.

**Fur seals** haul out on rocky shorelines at several sites. At Cape Foulwind *(see p238)* there is a breeding colony where pups can be seen in spring and summer.

**Wading birds**, such as pied stilts (shown here), congregate in large numbers to methodically feed on rich tidal mud flats around the coastline.

Farewell Spit

Marlborough Sounds

Nelson

Westport

Blenheim •

Kaikoura •

HRISTCHURCH •

Akaroa •

Banks Peninsula

**Sperm whales**, which can be viewed off the Kaikoura coast *(see p213)*, are specialized for hunting the deep sea, diving to depths of 1,000 m (3,280 ft) to feed mainly on large squid.

**Hector's dolphin**, a small species found exclusively in New Zealand, spends most of its time close to the shore, in pairs or small groups.

### Wildlife Watching

It is important to cause as little disturbance as possible, especially when animals are breeding, and to be very patient. Seals can attack if people get between them and the sea, yellow-eyed penguins will not come ashore to feed their young if disturbed, and dolphins do not always welcome people swimming with them. It is best to view wildlife with an experienced guide who is well versed in wildlife etiquette, skilled at finding the animals and who can provide interesting and informative commentary.

kilometres    75

miles                    75

# Adventure Sports Paradise

Queenstown is tagged as New Zealand's top adventure tourism destination because of the many adrenaline-pumping sports on offer in and around the town. The area's mountains, lakes and rivers and generally dry climate combine to create conditions ideal for outdoor pursuits, while daredevil New Zealanders continue to pioneer ever more thrilling sports for the enjoyment of visitors. Strict regulations and highly trained operators reduce the risks involved in speeding through inches of water, leaping off bridges, skiing at remote sites and free-falling from airplanes, and explain New Zealand's excellent safety record.

**Jet-boats** – propellerless power boats specially designed in New Zealand for use in 10-cm (4-inch) deep water – take visitors at breakneck speed down narrow river gorges.

## Queenstown and Surroundings

## Adventure Sports Around Queenstown

These places are all within 115 km (70 miles) of Queenstown and offer a range of activities. Adventure sports tour operators provide transport, equipment and qualified instructors.

| | Bungy Jumping | Hang-Gliding | Jet Boating | Mountain Biking | Skiing | Tandem Parapenting | Tandem skydiving | White-Water Rafting |
|---|---|---|---|---|---|---|---|---|
| Cardrona Alpine Resort | | | | ● | ● | | | |
| Coronet Peak | | ● | | | ● | | | |
| Kawarau Bridge | ● | | ● | | | | | |
| Kawarau River | | | ● | | | | | ● |
| Queenstown (see pp280–81) | ● | | | ● | | ● | ● | |
| Remarkables | | ● | | ● | ● | ● | ● | |
| Shotover River | | | ● | | | | | ● |
| Skippers Canyon | ● | ● | | | | | | |
| Trebble Cone | | | | | ● | ● | | |
| Waiorau Snow Farm | | | | | ● | | | |
| Wanaka (see pp274–5) | | | | ● | | ● | ● | ● |

### Key

— State highway
— Minor road
≈ River

**Downhill skiing** at the commercial ski fields near Queenstown is rated some of the best in the country.

**Mountain biking** allows riders, either independently or as part of a guided tour, to explore off-road routes that were traditionally walked.

**Queenstown**, Lake Wakatipu and the Remarkables from the Skyline Gondola lookout on Bob's Peak.

**White-water rafting** through the narrow gorges and thundering rapids of the Kawarau and Shotover rivers is a heart-pounding, exhilarating and drenching experience.

**The preparation area** where ankles are strapped and adjustments made to the length of the cord to suit the weight of the bungy jumper.

### Bungy Jumping

*This was made famous by New Zealander A J Hackett, who dived from the Eiffel Tower in 1986 suspended by a rubber cord strapped to his ankles. Bungy jumping options now range from plummeting 134 m (440 ft) from a suspended "jump pod" over a gorge, dipping in at Kawarau Bridge, to hurtling earthward from "The Ledge" on Bob's Peak above Queenstown.*

**A jumper** dives off the platform before soaring upwards again at the end of the bungy cord.

**Cross-country skiing** is a speciality of the Waiorau Snow Farm in the Pisa Range near Wanaka, which also hosts cross-country racing and ski-jumping competitions during the ski season.

**Tandem parapenting** (or paragliding) – plunging off a hill with a guide, strapped to a rectangular parachute – is a safer option than the "ultimate" tandem activity, tandem skydiving – jumping out of an airplane with an instructor attached to one's back followed by a parachute descent to ground.

# MARLBOROUGH AND NELSON

The warm climate of the Marlborough and Nelson region has always attracted visitors. Landscapes vary from wild coast, golden beaches, drowned valleys and dry inland mountains to lush, forested ranges. Known for its horticulture, the area is also a major source of fresh seafood. Along with heritage sites, its national parks are an added attraction. Marlborough is New Zealand's largest wine producer.

Archaeological evidence dates Maori occupation of the region to at least AD 1250. Early Polynesian navigators, Kupe *(see p49)* and Rakaihautu, are also known to have spent time here. In 1642, Dutch explorer Abel Tasman sailed into Golden Bay *(see p52)*. A confused and ultimately fatal confrontation with Maori that left four of the crew dead, made the Dutch reluctant to revisit the area. James Cook's later visits to Queen Charlotte Sound in the 1770s fortunately proved more successful *(see p52)*.

Following the signing of the Treaty of Waitangi in 1840 *(see pp52–3)*, the New Zealand Company established its Nelson settlement in 1842 *(see pp214–15)*. In 1858, Nelson was declared New Zealand's second city, a year before Marlborough

gained identity as a separate province. The region splits neatly into halves, Marlborough in the east and Nelson in the west. Marlborough's contrasts are perhaps greater, from the sinuous waterways of the Marlborough Sounds in the north, to the sheep farms and grape-growing region around Blenheim. Further south is the coastal area of Kaikoura.

In northern Nelson is the Golden Bay region, sheltered from the open sea by Farewell Spit and isolated behind the national parks of Abel Tasman and Kahurangi. Nelson city and Motueka sit on the shores of Tasman Bay. The rich hinterland, peopled by artists, vintners and horticulturists, extends south to the Southern Alps and the region's third national park, Nelson Lakes.

The weekend market at Nelson

◀ Montana Brancott Estate Vineyard, Marlborough

# Exploring Marlborough and Nelson

The northern region of the South Island beckons visitors with its sunny climate, inviting coastline, food, wines, marine reserves and three national parks: Nelson Lakes, Abel Tasman and Kahurangi. Marine life watching at Kaikoura *(see p213)*, winery tours *(see pp210–11)* and Nelson's Suter Art Gallery *(see p214)* are well-known attractions. Nelson is home to craft artisans and is an excellent base for boating and adventure tours. Walking, tramping and cycling tracks are spread throughout the national parks and other areas, including the Marlborough Sounds, a unique geographical feature of the region *(see pp206–7)*.

Kaiteriteri Beach near Motueka, a popular beach resort

**Cape Farewell**
Puponga
**FAREWELL SPIT** 19

**COLLINGWOOD** 18 *Golden Bay*
60
**WAIKOROPUPU SPRINGS RESERVE** 17
**TAKAKA** 16
**ABEL TASMAN NP**
Marahau
**TAKAKA HILL** 15
*Cobb Reservoir*
**MOTUEKA** 12

**KAHURANGI** 13
Karamea
*Karamea*
Woodstock
Motueka
**NATIONAL PARK**

*Mount Kendall 1810m*
Tapawera

**WEST COAST**
*Mount Owen 1875m*

**TASMAN**
Owen River

Westport
*Buller*
63
**ST ARNAUD** 10
Murchison
Inangahua
*Lake Rotoroa*
11
**NELSON LAKES NATIONAL PARK**
*St Arnaud Range*

*Martula*
65
*Mount Travers 2338m*

*Mount Una 2301m*

Springs Junction

*Clarence*

Hanmer Springs

## Sights at a Glance

## Key

— Major road
=== Minor road
— Scenic route
— Major railway
— Minor railway
— Regional border
△ Summit

0 kilometres 20
0 miles 20

**For additional map symbols** *see back flap*

## Getting Around

Beyond the highways of the Marlborough and Nelson region many roads are narrow and unsealed, particularly those into Marlborough Sounds and Molesworth Station *(see p212)*. A scenic journey by rail follows the east coast from Picton to Kaikoura and on to Christchurch, but there are no rail services to Nelson. Domestic airlines fly to Nelson city and Blenheim and private companies operate services from Wellington to Golden Bay and some locations in the Sounds. Bus and boat services at Nelson, Motueka, Marahau and Kaiteriteri provide access to all three national parks.

Vineyards at Blenheim in the Wairau Valley, New Zealand's largest wine producing area

## Top Outdoor Activities

The places shown here have been selected for their recreational activities. Conditions vary depending on the weather and the time of year, so exercise caution and, if in doubt, seek local advice.

| | Birdwatching | Boating | Marine Life Watching | Mountain Biking | Sea Kayaking | Swimming | Tramping/Walking |
|---|---|---|---|---|---|---|---|
| **Abel Tasman National Park** | ● | | ● | ● | ● | ● | ● |
| **Blenheim** | ● | | | ● | | | ● |
| **Collingwood** | ● | | | ● | | | ● |
| **Farewell Spit** | | ● | | | ● | | ● |
| **Havelock** | | ● | | | | ● | ● |
| **Kahurangi National Park** | ● | | | | | | ● |
| **Kaikoura** | ● | ● | ● | | ● | ● | ● |
| **Marlborough Sounds** | ● | ● | ● | ● | ● | ● | ● |
| **Motueka** | ● | | | | | ● | ● |
| **Nelson** | | ● | | ● | | ● | ● |
| **Nelson Lakes National Park** | ● | ● | | | | ● | ● |
| **Picton** | | ● | | ● | ● | ● | ● |
| **Queen Charlotte Drive** | | | | | | ● | ● |
| **St Arnaud** | ● | ● | | ● | ● | ● | ● |

# ❶ Picton

**Road map** D4. 🏚 4,000.
✈ Koromiko, 9 km (6 miles) S of
town. 🚗 🚌 🚢 **i** The
Foreshore, (03) 520 3113.
**w** www.lovemarlborough.com

Set in the upper reaches of
Queen Charlotte Sound, Picton
is the South Island terminus for
the ferries that cross Cook Strait.
The buzz of port and railway
activity dominates this pretty
town nestled between the sea
and the hills. Ferries and water
taxis mingle with pleasure boats
in the region, popular for its safe
anchorages.

Picton's wide streets and
historic buildings along the
waterfront reflect the town's
European beginnings. Formerly
known as Waitohi, Picton was
chosen to become the port for
the Wairau district, and in 1859
became the capital of the newly
formed province of
Marlborough. That
status shifted to
Blenheim in 1866. An
inter-island ferry service
was first mooted in 1899
and the first rail and car ferry
began operating in 1962.

Picton is a good base to
explore the history of the
Marlborough region. The
**Picton Museum** tells
stories of the whaling era,
beginning in the 1820s,
and of the 1770s visit of
Captain James Cook to
Queen Charlotte Sound.

At each end of the foreshore,
the scow **Echo** and the sailing
ship **Edwin Fox** provide a
fascinating look at New Zealand's

The *Edwin Fox*, formerly a convict
transport ship

Whaling exhibits at Picton Museum

shipping history. Built in 1905,
the *Echo* is an old cargo scow
that shipped around 14,000
tonnes of freight per year
between Blenheim and
Wellington. The *Edwin Fox* is the
last Australian convict ship and
the last East Indiaman clipper
in existence. It is therefore an
internationally significant
link to the era of colonial
settlement, having
brought convicts to
Australia and migrants
to New Zealand. Built
in 1853, the ship is
now being preserved
in a dry dock beside
a purpose-built
museum. Along the
Picton Waterfront is **EcoWorld
Aquarium and Terrarium**,
featuring the local species
to be seen throughout
Marlborough Sounds.

A number of walks and
cycling tracks in Picton begin
near the *Echo* or at Shelly Beach
on Picton Harbour where a
lookout affords excellent views
of the town. A short uphill walk
from the *Echo* leads to Victoria
Domain, a bushy reserve named
after Queen Victoria. A longer
walk past Bob's Bay passes a
panoramic view of Queen
Charlotte Sound and leads to
The Snout, the headland
between Picton and Waikawa
bays. Maori know the Snout as
Te Ihumoeoneihu (nose of the
sand worm). The Tirohanga
and Essons Valley tracks allow
exploration of the forest
behind the town.

Maori club, Picton
Museum

**📷 EcoWorld Aquarium and
Terrarium**
Picton Waterfront. **Tel** (03) 573 6030.
**Open** daily. **Closed** 25 Dec. 🦆 🏚

**🏛 Picton Museum**
London Quay. **Tel** (03) 573 8283.
**Open** daily. **Closed** 25 Dec. 🦆

**🏛 Echo**
Shelly Beach. **Tel** (03) 573 7498. **Open**
summer: daily; winter: by appointment.
**Closed** 25 Dec. 🦆 🖥 🏚

**🏛 Edwin Fox**
Dunbar Wharf. **Tel** (03) 573 6868.
**Open** daily. **Closed** Good Fri, 25 Dec.
🦆 🏚

### Environs
A 20-minute drive northeast
of Picton leads to Karaka Point,
a narrow peninsula once
occupied by a *pa*. A short walk
leads down to the water with
signs explaining the earthworks
encountered on the way.

# ❷ Marlborough Sounds

*See pp206–7.*

# ❸ Queen Charlotte Drive

**Road map** D4.

The best-known road in the
Marlborough Sounds, Queen
Charlotte Drive is a scenic route
connecting Picton and
Havelock. With stopovers, it can
take up to half a day to
complete the 35-km (21.5-mile)
journey on the sealed but narrow and winding road. Leaving

Picton, the Queen Charlotte Drive passes lookout points above the town and at Governors Bay, 8 km (5 miles) from Picton, with excellent views up and down Queen Charlotte Sound. Beaches and pleasant picnic and swimming areas can be found along the route that passes through the picturesque settlements of Ngakuta and Momorangi bays. At Ngakuta Bay, **Sirpa Alalääkkölä's Art Studio** showcases her large, bright paintings, many of them inspired by the Sounds.

Continuing west, a turn-off 12 km (8 miles) from Governors Bay leads to historic Anakiwa, where the Queen Charlotte Track begins (see pp206–7). A shelter and picnic area are provided and an easy stroll along the track leads through beech forest to Davies Bay.

The Queen Charlotte Drive route continues through Linkwater with the road following the waters of the Mahakipawa Arm, the innermost reaches of Pelorus Sound. The walking tracks and viewpoint at Cullen Point provide another perspective on the waterways below, before the road's final descent into Havelock.

🏛 **Sirpa Alalääkkölä Art Studio**
Phillips Rd, Ngakuta Bay. **Tel** (03) 573 7775. **Open** by appointment.

## ❹ Havelock

**Road map** D4. 🚹 500. 🚌 🚆
🛈 46 Main Rd, (03) 574 2104.
📧 havelockinfocentre.co.nz

The self-styled green lip mussel capital of the world, the village of Havelock receives a growing number of visitors attracted by its history and the success of its mussel farming industry. Havelock was established in the 1850s on the Nelson–Blenheim track near the uppermost navigable reaches of Pelorus Sound. Timber milling and gold mining were its first industries,

A restaurant in Havelock advertising green lip mussels

while today fishing and aquaculture (the cultivation of shellfish) are major industries. The main street still retains something of its pioneer character. Highlights of a walk around the waterfront are the stately 1880s home of timber miller William Brownlee, the stone St Peter's Church, and the old primary school (now a hostel) attended by Lord Ernest Rutherford (see pp25, 216) in the 1870s. A number of cafés can be found in town along with many interesting shops selling antiques, jewellery, carvings, crafts, and Maori art.

**Greenstone carved in Havelock**

Tours and activities such as sea kayaking begin in Havelock, with the scenic mail run (where mail is delivered by boat) being perhaps the easiest and most popular way to get to the outer sounds. The **Havelock Museum** preserves relics from the pioneer era and Rutherford's time. The annual Mussel Festival takes place in March.

🏛 **Havelock Museum**
Main St. **Tel** (03) 574 2176. **Open** daily. 🚫 donation.

### Environs
**Canvastown**, 9 km (6 miles) west of Havelock, was established in 1864 following the region's first gold rush.

A tent city grew here, attracting several thousand miners. Flood-prone fields and severe over-crowding meant many miners left shortly after the gold fields in the West Coast were opened.

A further 11 km (7.5 miles) west, along State Highway 6, the road crosses the Pelorus River at **Pelorus Bridge Scenic Reserve**. Spared destruction after development of a town failed to proceed, the reserve is the last remnant of riverplain forest that formerly covered much of lowland Marlborough. A network of tracks allows visitors to explore the rich forest and river banks, with a suspension bridge, swimming holes and waterfalls. Other facilities include a shop, café, cabins and caravan park with electric powered sites. River cruises and nature tours are also available. Some of the walks are accessible by wheelchair.

Pelorus Bridge Scenic Reserve, a popular swimming and picnic area

# ❷ Marlborough Sounds

The Marlborough Sounds region is a mass of bays, inlets and hidden coves with numerous walking tracks, wildlife, historical sites and unsurpassed views. Picton and Havelock are the Sounds' main towns *(see pp204–5)*. Launch services from these two towns provide the best access to the secluded bays and accommodation by the sea. The best ways to explore the Sounds are by bicycle, sea kayak, or on foot.

Cyclists on the road exploring the Sounds

**D'Urville Island**
Accessible by water taxi, the island was once an important source of argillite, a hard sand-stone used in tool making by Maori. Today, farming is the main occupation with fishing, diving, kayaking and mountain biking popular pursuits.

**French Pass**
This picturesque fishing and farming village takes its name from the narrow and treacherous strait between the mainland and D'Urville Island.

## How the Sounds were Formed

The Sounds region appears as a series of ridges rising above the water but is, in fact, a series of valleys drowned by the ocean. A combination of changing sea levels (due to world climate changes), movement along faults in the region, and

tilting of the landmass downwards and towards the northeast has caused inundation by the sea. The last significant surge in sea level was at the end of an Ice Age about 12,000 years ago, and gives the area its current sinuous coastline.

**Drowned valleys at Elaine Bay, Tennyson Inlet**

### Kenepuru Sound
Numerous accom-
modation styles are
available in this quiet
waterway where
walking, fishing and
camping are popular.

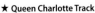

### ★ Queen Charlotte Track
This 71-km (44-mile) scenic
walk (or mountain bike ride),
begins at Ship Cove and ends
at Anakiwa. A well-marked
track, it is suitable for
moderately fit people.
Stout shoes are necessary.

### ★ Motuara Island
The open sanctuary of Motuara
Island Scenic and Historic Reserve is
host to myriad birdlife and can be
explored on a walkway.

### ★ Outer Queen Charlotte Sound
The outer sound provides an enticing
combination of open water, islands
and wildlife. It is best visited by water
taxi, sea kayak or wildlife tour.

### KEY

① **Tennyson Inlet** is cloaked in
native forest. Natural beauty
abounds in this quiet inlet where
picnic areas and campsites are found
along the shoreline.

② **Titirangi Bay**, one of the few
bays in the Sounds with a sandy
beach, has a recreation reserve and
farm park.

③ **Tory Channel** was the site of
New Zealand's first shore-based
whaling stations, beginning in 1827.
Closed in 1964, the remnants of the
last station, Perano's, can still be seen.

④ **Port Underwood** was a strategic
whaling station in the 1830s. Today,
its main attraction is White's Bay,
with its swimming beach and old
cable station.

**Key**

▬ State highway
▬ Minor road
- - Walking track

# ❺ Wairau Valley Vineyard Tour

Well known for its Sauvignon Blanc, the Wairau valley is
New Zealand's largest and best known wine region. In the
early 1970s, grape planting was begun by Montana Wines
*(see p212)*. Now, 130 wineries operate in the area. The wines
of the Wairau are celebrated with the annual Marlborough
Wine and Food Festival each February. South of Blenheim,
at the Montana winery, is the Montana Brancott Visitor
Centre covering all aspects of the wine experience.

Vineyards in the Blenheim region backed
by the Richmond Range

### ⑨ Cloudy Bay
This is one of Marlborough's
most successful exporting
wineries, with a reputation
for fine Sauvignon Blanc,
Chardonnay and Pinot Noir.
Tastings and sales are
available daily.

### ⑧ Allan Scott Wines and Estates
One of the pioneers
of grape growing in
Marlborough, this
vineyard offers wines
characteristic of the
region: Chardonnay,
Sauvignon Blanc
and Riesling.

### ⑦ Stoneleigh Vineyards
Built on a former riverbed, the vineyard is
named after the stones covering the area.
Sunlight reflected from the stones speeds the
ripening process of the grapes. Chardonnay,
Riesling, Sauvignon Blanc and Pinot Noir
wines are produced here.

### ⑥ Hunters Wines
This is one of the region's most
awarded wineries. Red, white and
sparkling wines are available,
including Sauvignon Blanc, Pinot
Noir, Cabernet/Merlot, sparkling
Brut and Chardonnay.

**Key**

- ■ Tour route
- ▭ Other roads
- ▭ River

### ① Ponder Estate

Producing award-winning Sauvignon Blanc and Chardonnay wines, the owners of Ponder Estate are also pioneers of olive growing in New Zealand. The white wines and olive oil are for sale in the estate's Shed Gallery. Mike Ponder's well-known works of art are also on display.

### ② Highfield Estate

Visitors can get an excellent overview of the vineyard district from the Tuscan-styled tower of Highfield Estate. Tours of the winery and tastings are available.

### ③ Te Whare Ra

Sweet wines are the speciality at this small, exclusive winery. Its Gewürztraminer is gaining a reputation as one of New Zealand's best.

### ④ Wairau River Wines

The attractive cob-construction building (mud and clay mixed with straw and horse hair) at Wairau River includes a restaurant and gift shop. Sauvignon Blanc, Chardonnay, Riesling and botrytised Riesling are specialities. Sales and tastings are offered.

0 kilometres  2

0 miles  2

### Tips for Drivers

**Tour length:** 34 km (21 miles). Although a small area, more than one day is needed to taste the wines at a leisurely pace. Remember New Zealand's strict drink driving laws, something which makes a guided tour a wise choice. Enquire about these at the Blenheim Visitor Centre (*see p212*).

**Starting point:** Blenheim is a logical choice to begin and end the tour, which is a circle with a short side trip. Road conditions are good throughout.

**Stopping-off points:** Besides restaurants at the wineries, Renwick and Blenheim offer many eating choices. Fruit stalls abound in summer, with December a good time for cherries.

### ⑤ Cellier Le Brun

is winery specializes méthode traditionelle arkling wines. Tours of the winery and underground cellar available. Wine can be purchased at the wine shop.

The Clock Tower in Seymour Square, Blenheim

# ❻ Blenheim

**Road map** D5. 🗠 20,500. ✈ 6 km (4 miles) W of city. 🚌 🚌 ℹ️ Railway Station, Sinclair St, (03) 577 8080. 🎭 Marlborough Wine and Food Festival (2nd Sat of Feb); Classic Fighters Air Show (Easter); Hunters Garden Marlborough (2nd weekend of Nov).

The largest town in the Marlborough region, Blenheim's importance in the Wairau Valley has grown along with the development of the wine industry in Marlborough *(see pp210–11)*. The annual food and wine festival is a major draw. A number of art and crafts people live and work in Blenheim and its environs.

In the city centre, Seymour Square has a fountain, pretty gardens and the Clock Tower. Blenheim's only public art gallery, the **Millennium Art Gallery** houses works by local artists and sculptors, while the **Marlborough Museum** is set beside the heritage streetscape of Brayshaw Park on the southern edge of town. The park has a miniature railway, boating pond and reconstructed colonial village, giving some insight into the way of life in Blenheim during that period. Nearby is **Wither Hills Farm Park** where a network of foot and cycling tracks have been developed for visitors within the working farm. The tracks are well marked and require average fitness.

🏛 **Millennium Art Gallery**
Cnr Seymour and Alfred sts. **Tel** (03) 579 2001. **Open** 1–4pm Sat & Sun. **Closed** public holidays. 🎨 donation. ♿ 📷

🏛 **Marlborough Museum**
Brayshaw Park, 26 Arthur Baker Place. **Tel** (03) 578 1712. **Open** daily (archive Tue & Thu only). **Closed** 25 Dec. 📷 ♿

🐦 **Wither Hills Farm Park**
Redwood St. **Tel** Blenheim i-SITE Visitor Centre, (03) 577 8080. **Open** daily.

## Environs
South of Blenheim is the **Montana Brancott Visitor Centre**. One-hour tours include insights into the wine process, tastings, audio-visual shows, views of two barrel halls and an interactive "aroma wheel".

Further south, in the Awatere valley, **Molesworth Station**, New Zealand's largest farm, can be explored when the road through it opens each summer. The 59-km (37-mile) road journey through high country, passes historic cob houses, wide river valleys and mountains.

🍷 **Montana Brancott Visitor Centre**
State Hwy 1. **Tel** (03) 520 6975. **Open** daily. **Closed** Good Fri, 25 Apr, 25 Dec. ♿ 📷 📷 📷 📷

🏞 **Molesworth Station**
ℹ️ Department of Conservation, (03) 572 9100. **Open** Dec–Feb. 🎨

# ❼ Kaikoura

**Road map** D5. 🗠 3,700. 🚌 🚌 ℹ️ Westend, (03) 319 5641. 🎭 Kaikoura Seafest (first Sat in Oct); Kaikoura Races (Mon after Labour Day).

The name Kaikoura means "meal of crayfish" and reflects the importance of the sea throughout the area. Captain Cook sailed past the Kaikoura Peninsula in 1770, naming the

place "Lookers On" because of the reticence of local Maori.

The first European settlers and whalers arrived in 1842. The town's current tourism boom is also based on whales and other marine wildlife. The visitor centre has extensive displays and an audiovisual show. Whale tooth carvings can be seen at historic **Fyffe House**, a colonial cottage from the whaling days and Kaikoura's oldest dwelling. Nearby, at the beachfront, is the Garden of Memories with a walkway encased with pairs of whale ribs. Above town Scarborough Street has a lookout point, a remnant *pa* and the Gold Gallery with wall sculptures gilded with gold leaf.

On the southern edge of town, guided tours can be taken at the **Kaikoura Winery** and at **Maori Leap Cave**, a limestone cave full of stalagmites. Six km (4 miles) south of town is Fyffe Country Lodge which has pleasant gardens. Inland roads lead to Mount Fyffe, where superb views can be obtained from the walking tracks through the forest and mountains.

Whale tooth carving

🏛 **Fyffe House**
62 Avoca St. **Tel** (03) 319 5835. **Open** summer: daily; winter: Thu–Mon. **Closed** Good Fri, 25 Dec. 🎨 Adults.

🍷 **Kaikoura Winery**
State Hwy 1. **Tel** (03) 319 7966. **Open** daily. **Closed** Good Fri, 25 Dec. 📷

🦷 **Maori Leap Cave**
State Hwy 1. **Tel** (03) 319 5023. **Open** daily. **Closed** 25 Dec. 📷 📷 obligatory. 📷 📷

Picnickers on the Kaikoura coast

# Marine Life Watching at Kaikoura

In the late 1980s, the popularity of observing marine life in Kaikoura led to a tourism boom that transformed the town into one of New Zealand's premier visitor destinations. The main attraction is sperm whales, seen as they rest on the surface between dives, as well as orca and numerous dolphin species. Through the services of several eco-tourism companies in Kaikoura, the habits of whales and seals and the antics of the acrobatic dusky dolphins can be observed from the shore or air and both in and on the water. The special richness of Kaikoura's marine life is explained by the presence of very deep water and the mixing of warm and cold ocean currents there, which forces nutrients to the surface. Species of seabirds found in Kaikoura include the royal albatross, wandering albatross, grey petrel, Antarctic fulmer, and black-browed mollymawk.

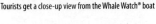

### Whale Watching

*Most whales seen at Kaikoura are toothed whales, quite often sperm whales. Unlike baleen whales, which feed by filtering plankton, toothed whales hunt their prey, including fish, krill and giant squid, sometimes at great depths.*

Tourists get a close-up view from the Whale Watch® boat

**Tour operators** offer opportunities to visitors to get close to the marine life.

**Swimming with dusky dolphins**, inquisitve, playful creatures, is a memorable experience.

**New Zealand fur seals** can be observed at a colony at Ohau Point, 23 km (14 miles) north of Kaikoura.

**Fresh seafood** is a speciality of Kaikoura's restaurants. The abundance of scallops, fish, crayfish and prawns is celebrated annually in October with the Kaikoura Seafest.

**Mollymawks** are one of the marine bird species to be seen within easy reach of the shores of Kaikoura.

# ⓭ Nelson

Nelson was the second settlement developed by the New Zealand Company. The first settlers arrived in February 1842, but in 1844 the company failed. Some settlers persisted, and in 1853 Nelson became the capital of a province of the same name. A royal decree in 1858 made the small town New Zealand's second city. Today, Nelson is renowned as a vibrant art, crafts and festival centre with a superb climate and boutique hotels. The compact city centre includes many galleries, craft shops and heritage attractions. A memorial to Dutch navigator Abel Tasman can be seen at Tahunanui, a popular swimming beach close to the centre of the city.

View of Nelson from Auckland Point

### 🔲 Anzac Park

Cnr Rutherford and Halifax sts.

The beautifully landscaped Anzac Park, with its pretty flowerbeds, tall palms and cenotaph, is Nelson's main war memorial. A horse-drawn passenger carriage ran alongside the park until 1901, using a section of New Zealand's first railway line. Auckland Point nearby was once the site of Matangi Awhio Pa, a fortification. The site is now being revegetated and a winding track to the summit provides excellent views over the city.

### 🏛 The Nelson Provincial Museum

Cnr Trafalgar & Hardy sts. **Tel** (03) 548 9588. **Open** daily. **Closed** Good Fri, 25 Dec. 🎫 donation; charge for special exhibitions.

The lower gallery focuses on the natural and social history of the Nelson and Tasman region. Maori artifacts and *taonga* (treasures such as weapons and ornaments) form a large part of the collection, along with photographs, ceramics, glass and silverware, and textiles from colonial times to the present. The upper gallery hosts special exhibitions.

### 🔲 Centre of New Zealand

Cnr Milton & Hardy sts.

An easy walk beginning at the Botanical Reserve – where the country's first rugby game was played in 1870 – leads up Botanical Hill to a lookout known locally as "the centre of New Zealand". The hill provides good views of the city, harbour, Maitai Valley and the Maitai River, which flows through the city into the harbour. A path follows the river downstream through a pleasant park and past Riverside Pool, a modern heated pool with a historic façade.

### 🏛 Suter Art Gallery

208 Bridge St. **Tel** (03) 548 4699. **Open** daily. **Closed** 1 Jan, Good Fri, 25 Dec. 🎫 ♿ 📷 🖥 🆆 **thesuter.org.nz**

One of New Zealand's oldest galleries (1899), the Suter Art Gallery holds a nationally important permanent collection, including paintings by Sir Tosswill Woollaston (one of the founders of New Zealand modern art), Frances Hodgkins, Colin McCahon, *(see p36)* and contemporary Nelson painter, Jane Evans. It also houses the collection of Andrew Suter, the city's bishop from 1866 to 1891. He donated early colonial paintings, including many by the colonial watercolourist John Gully, to the people of Nelson.

### 🔲 Queens Gardens and Albion Square

One of the city's heritage precincts, the main focus is the Queens Gardens. Some of the trees date back to the 1850s although the gardens were formally established in 1887. Albion Square borders the gardens and was once the political centre of Nelson when provincial government buildings dominated the square. Some historic buildings remain, such as a powder magazine, trout hatchery and fire station. A still-in-service 1864 post box and surveyors' test chain complete the picture.

### 🏛 Church Hill

Trafalgar Square.

Church Hill is dominated by the Anglican Christ Church Cathedral, the third church built on a site which has also been a survey base, *pa*, fort and immigration barracks. Church Hill is linked to Trafalgar Street by the impressive granite Cathedral Steps, one of many gifts to the city by Thomas Cawthron, a philanthropist. Panels explain the history of Church Hill and some

Christ Church Cathedral on Church Hill

resh flowers at the Nelson
weekend market

f its notable trees, while the
remains of the old fort are visible
near the cathedral entrance.

### 🔲 Nelson Market

Montgomery Square. **Tel** (03) 546-
454. **Open** 8am–1pm Sat, 9am–1pm
un. **Closed** 1 Jan, 25 Dec. ♿ ▣

On weekends the car park at
Montgomery Square is trans-
ormed into a colourful market-
place. Vendors of plants, toys,
crafts, organic produce and
oods, ranging from sushi to

Dutch cheeses, set up their
stalls. Shoppers and buskers
bring the market to life, creating a busy spectacle that has
become a key part of life in
Nelson and of visits there.

### 🔲 Trafalgar Street South

Nelson's main street, Trafalgar,
extends south of the cathedral
to Trafalgar Street South. It leads
to Fairfield Park and a small
cemetery with graves of some
early settlers.

Close by are two colonial era
houses, Melrose and Fairfield.
Melrose House (around 1878) is a
truly grand home in the Italianate
style. A feature of Fairfield House
(1873) is its viewing tower, a
replica of one used by its original
owner, Arthur Atkinson, for astro-
logical purposes. The garden
contains some plantings made
by the Dalai Lama during his
1996 visit to New Zealand.

### 🔲 South Street

To the west of Church Hill is the
historic precinct of South Street
comprising a collection of

workers' cottages built between
1863 and about 1867. Sixteen
cottages remain intact and
many have been restored for
use as accommodation or to
house craft galleries.

Former workers' cottages in the historic
South Street precinct

### Nelson City Centre

① Anzac Park
② Nelson Market
③ The Nelson Provincial Museum
④ Suter Art Gallery
⑤ Queens Gardens and Albion
   Square
⑥ Centre of New Zealand
⑦ Church Hill
⑧ South Street
⑨ Trafalgar Street South

For keys to map symbols *see back flap*

# ❾ Richmond

**Road map** D4.  11,000.
Nelson, 8 km (5 miles) W of town.
22 Gladstone Rd, (03) 543 9521.

This busy town serves the productive horticultural lands to its south and west. Highlights are the Wash-bourne Gardens, complete with 1862 jailhouse, and the Redwood Stables restaurant, built using bricks from New Zealand's first racing stables. Visitors can observe the art of glass making at **Höglund Art Glass** where Ola and Marie Höglund create their renowned colourful glassware, including goblets, birds and jewellery.

### Environs

Six km (4 miles) southwest of Richmond, at Brightwater, is a memorial to New Zealand's best known scientist, Lord Ernest Rutherford *(see p25)*, born here in 1871. Also at Brightwater is the **McGlashen Pottery**. Continuing southwest to Wakefield is a historic church, St John's (1846).

🏛 **Höglund Art Glass**
Lansdowne Rd. **Tel** (03) 544 6500.
**Open** daily. **Closed** Good Fri, 25 Dec.

🏛 **McGlashen Pottery**
128 Ellis St, Brightwater. **Tel** (03) 542 3585. **Open** daily. **Closed** 1 Jan, Good Fri, 25 Apr, 25 Dec.

The South Island's oldest church, St John's, at Wakefield

# ❿ St Arnaud

**Road map** D5. 200. View Rd, (03) 521 1806. Antique & Classic Boat Show (Mar); Rainbow Mountain Bike Race (Mar).

Approximately 90 minutes' drive from Blenheim or Nelson is the small town of St Arnaud, nestled on the shore of Lake Rotoiti, a trout fishing, boating and water-

Lake Rotoiti in Nelson Lakes National Park

skiing paradise. The nearby Lake Rotoroa also has good trout fishing but is more secluded and quiet. St Arnaud is the gateway to Nelson Lakes National Park and the closest town to the **Rainbow Ski Area**, where the terrain is suitable for novice and inter-mediate snowboarders and skiers. In summer, the ski field road continues through to Hanmer Springs *(see p237)*.

🎿 **Rainbow Ski Area**
Wairau Valley. **Tel** (03) 521 1861.
**Open** June–Oct daily.

# ⓫ Nelson Lakes National Park

**Road map** C5. View Rd, (03) 521 1806.

The twin, glacier-formed lakes Rotoiti and Rotoroa dominate the 1017 hectares of this park at the northern tip of the Southern Alps. A water taxi is the easiest form of access to the area of high passes, forests, valleys and basins. The lakes and rivers are popular for kayaking, sailing, boating, swimming and trout fishing. Winter pastimes include ski touring. There are many trails for trampers and walkers, including the well-known 80-km (50-mile) Travers–Sabine Circuit that includes two major valleys, an alpine pass, the wetland Speargrass area and both main lakes. The two-day return walk along Robert Ridge to the beautiful Lake Angelus is also very pleasant but with high altitudes, caution is advised.

# ⓬ Motueka

**Road map** D4. 6,600. 20 Wallace St, (03) 528 6543.

Motueka has a diverse horti-cultural industry and is the country's most prolific orcharding area. Kiwifruit, apples, berries, hops, pears, and grapes are some of the produce grown here. The town is also a base for trips to the Abel Tasman and Kahurangi national parks.

### Environs

**Kaiteriteri**, 14 km (9 miles) north of Motueka, is known for its stunning golden beaches. South of Motueka are the coastal villages of Tasman and Mapua. Inland is Upper Moutere village, established in the 1840s by German settlers. Each village has its own artists, shops, wineries, eating places and boutique accommodation.

# ⓭ Kahurangi National Park

**Road map** C4. 20 Wallace St, Motueka, (03) 528 6543.

A great variety of native animals and plants live in the 4,510 sq-km (1,740 sq-mile) park. A highlight is the Heaphy Track, a four- to five-day walking track. Kayaking, hunting, caving, tramping, raft-ing and fishing are all popular activities here. Alpine plants can be seen growing near the Cobb Reservoir. The major gateway is Motueka, but access is also possible from Karamea *(see p238)*.

# The Nelson Arts Scene

A combination of a warm climate and a relaxed environment has attracted many artists to Nelson, making it one of New Zealand's most vibrant arts regions. Its history of artistic endeavour is long. Today, Nelson abounds with opportunities to explore art in the many galleries and studios of glass-blowers, painters, jewellers, textile artists, woodworkers and ceramic artists. The Suter Art Gallery *(see p214)* is noted for its extensive collection of historical and contemporary works. The Nelson region is also becoming known for music and performance events, such as the Nelson Jazz Festival and the Nelson School of Music Winter Festival. Nelson's Tasman Regional Museum houses a photographic display chronicling Nelson and New Zealand's early colonial beginnings.

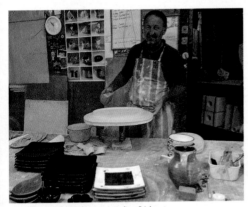

## Ceramics

A variety of fine raw clays and glaze materials has long attracted ceramic artists to Nelson. A large number of pottery outlets showcase the work of talented potters, and many nationally recognized crafts people choose Nelson as a living and working base.

Ron McGlashen at work in his ceramic studio at Brightwater

Handmade tiles adorn the doorway of a tile shop in Mapua

**Glassware** in Nelson is made by combining modern design ideas with traditional glass-blowing methods *(see p216)*. The result is colourful creations, each one hand-crafted and unique.

Art and craft galleries are a common sight in the region

**Artists** in Nelson have long been inspired by their surroundings. A nationally important collection can be seen at The Suter Art Gallery *(see p214)*.

**Three-dimensional art**, designed to be viewed from many sides, is popular in Nelson. Some pieces are practical, others whimsical. Local sculptors have been commissioned to provide works for public areas.

# ⑭ Abel Tasman National Park

New Zealand's smallest national park, at 225 sq km (87 sq miles), Abel Tasman has a mild climate, golden beaches and sandy estuaries fringed by natural forest. The park is best known for its coast track which can be walked one way, with the return trip made on a launch or water taxi. There are huts and a large number of campsites on the coast track to break the journey. Due to the park's popularity, it is necessary to book walks and huts before visiting. Abel Tasman is also one of New Zealand's better sea kayaking destinations and a day spent drifting in a slowly filling stuary or watching seals, penguins, dolphins or birdlife from these quiet craft will not be forgotten.

Aerial view of Abel Tasman National Park

★ **Wainui Falls**
Nelson's finest accessible falls are reached via an easy 30-minute walk from a small car park on the road to Totaranui.

★ **Harwoods Hole**
A 1-hour walk from Canaan car park (*see p220*) leads to the entrance of the 176-m (577-ft) vertical marble shaft known as Harwoods Hole. It is dangerous to get too close to the chasm as the sides may be unstable.

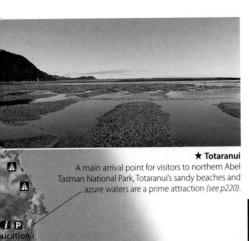

**★ Totaranui**
A main arrival point for visitors to northern Abel Tasman National Park, Totaranui's sandy beaches and azure waters are a prime attraction *(see p220)*.

## VISITORS' CHECKLIST

**Practical Information**
Road map D4. **W doc.govt.nz**
**i** 79 Trafalgar St, Nelson, (03) 546 9339.

**Transport**
to Marahau and Totaranui daily from Nelson and Motueka.
water taxi and launch services from Kaiteriteri and Marahau.

**Coast Track**
The 51-km (32-mile) long Coast Track from Marahau to Wainui crosses four estuaries, two negotiable only at low tide. Two have high tide tracks and a bridge is planned for Onetahuti.

## KEY

① **The Inland Track**, more rugged than its coastal counterpart, is a three-day walk from Tinline Bay to Wainui Bay. Drinking water should be carried on the track.

② **The Tonga Island Marine Reserve** covers 12 km (8 miles) of coastline. Established to restore the marine environment to its natural state, all animals, plants and sea life here are completely protected.

③ **Granite Rocks** are a common feature of the park, and were once extracted at Tonga Quarry.

④ **Falls River** is about a 1-hour walk from Torrent Bay. The track follows Tregidga Stream and passes Cascade Falls before ending at Falls River. A further 15-minute walk up rocks leads to the main falls.

**Key**
— State highway
— Minor road
— River
···· Walking track
---- Park boundary
•••• Marine Reserve boundary

**Marahau**
The southern gateway to Abel Tasman National Park, Marahau is the base for water taxis serving the coast. Outdoor pursuits available at Marahau include sea kayaking, walking and swimming with seals.

**For additional map symbols** *see back flap*

View from Takaka Hill looking towards Motueka and Nelson

## ⓯ Takaka Hill

**Road map** D4.

Takaka Hill is commonly referred to as "the marble mountain" because of its large marble deposits that contrast sharply with the granite hills of adjoining Abel Tasman National Park. There are many caves and sinkholes to explore in the area, including **Ngarua Caves** near the summit of Takaka Hill, where a lookout offers views north to D'Urville Island and east towards Nelson city. Tours of the only cave open to visitors are available and bones of moa (see p29) can be seen. Visible below the caves is Marahau's golden beach (see p219), where marble from a local quarry was shipped to Wellington for use in New Zealand's Parliament Building.

To the west of Ngarua Caves, Canaan Road leads to Canaan car park, the starting point for walking tracks, including the Rameka Track, one of Nelson's better mountain bike rides. An easy walk leads to the impressive Harwoods Hole (see p218), a 176-m (577-ft) vertical shaft. A short steep side track leads to the Harwood Lookout with a fine viewpoint inland to the Tablelands in Kahurangi National Park (see p217).

To the east of Ngarua Caves is Hawkes Lookout. A short walk leads to a platform perched over a precipitous 500-m (1,640-ft) drop to the forest at Riwaka Resurgence.

**Ngarua Caves**
**Tel** (03) 528 8093. **Open** summer: daily; winter: school hols.

## ⓰ Takaka

**Road map** D4. 🚹 1,230. ✈ 6 km (4 miles) N of town. 🚌 🛈 Willow St, (03) 525 9136. 🌐 nelsonnz.com

Takaka is the main shopping and business area for the Golden Bay region and an access point to Abel Tasman National Park (see pp218–19). The townspeople are a mix of "alternative life-stylers" and farming folk. Dairy farming is one of the largest industries in the region. The **Golden Bay Museum** is excellent, and best known for its displays on Abel

Tasman and the story of Golden Bay's many mining ventures. Several galleries operate in the area and many artists near Takaka show their work – painted gourds, pottery and wood or stone sculptures – to visitors.

At **Bencarri Farm Park & Café**, home to tame eels and farm animals, rare species such as yaks, llamas and alpacas are bred. Riverside walking and picnics in a valley at the park are other attractions.

**🏛 Golden Bay Museum**
Commercial St. **Tel** (03) 525 6268. **Open** 10am–4pm daily. **Closed** Sun in winter, public hols.

**Bencarri Farm Park & Café**
McCallum's Rd. **Tel** (03) 525 8261. **Open** summer: daily. **Closed** 25 Dec. limited.

**Environs**
Beyond the beach at Pohara, 10 km (6 miles) from Takaka, is a memorial to Dutch navigator Abel Tasman, with a lookout platform and display. After the memorial, the road leads to **Wainui Bay**. Several coastal walks and one to Wainui Falls (see p218) begin there. Beyond Wainui Bay the road climbs to Abel Tasman National Park, descending finally to the sea and golden sands of Totaranui. A camp ground and visitor centre with a shop operate here over the summer.

Painted gourd

Llamas at Bencarri Farm Park

The clear waters of Waikoropupu Springs Scenic Reserve

## ⑰ Waikoropupu Springs Scenic Reserve

Road map D4.

Seven km (4 miles) north of Takaka on State Highway 60, a turnoff leads to the Waikoropupu Springs Scenic Reserve. The waters here at New Zealand's largest freshwater springs are exceptionally clear, coming from an underground cave system that is connected to the features on Takaka Hill and at Riwaka Resurgence (see p220). The springs are best viewed using a large fixed periscope set on a viewing platform, reached by an easy walk through beautiful forest. Swimming is prohibited as the water is considered sacred.

Beyond the springs (at the end of the road), the Pupu Walkway is a track that follows the line of a water race built to serve a gold mining claim. An impressive piece of engineering, the water race was later used (and still is) to generate electric power. The walk is about 3 km (2 miles) long.

## ⑱ Collingwood

Road map D4. ⛰ 500. 🚌

A quiet village at the mouth of the Aorere River, Collingwood was designated a port of entry in the 1850s gold rush and was considered as the site for New Zealand's capital city. Despite several devastating fires, the courthouse, post office, original cemetery and Anglican St Cuthbert's Church remain to remind visitors of the town's fleeting moment of glory.

Collingwood acts as a base for tours to Farewell Spit and for buses serving the Heaphy Track in Kahurangi National Park (see p216).

### Environs
Within 20 km (12 miles) of Collingwood is the beautiful Kaituna Track with river views and lush forest, the Te Anaroa Caves, a 350-m (1,148-ft) limestone cave system with glowworms and shellfish fossils, and the Aorere, New Zealand's first major gold field. Quartz, silver and gold were mined here. The workings can be explored by a walking track with views over the valley.

## ⑲ Farewell Spit

Road map D4. 🛈 Farewell Spit Information Centre (03) 524 8454. **Open** daily. 🚫 💻 📷

At the northern tip of the South Island, a 35-km (22-mile) sandspit sweeps eastward into the sea. Farewell Spit is a nature reserve with restricted access and has been designated a Wetland of International Importance.

In late spring, tens of thousands of migratory waders arrive from the northern hemisphere, joining the year-round residents before returning home in autumn to breed. Black swans, Canadian geese, Australasian gannets, Caspian terns, oystercatchers, black

Early gold workings at Aorere, near Collingwood

shags and eastern bartailed godwits are amongst the species to be seen in summer. As the region is a protected area, the only way to visit the spit is on a guided tour with one of the licensed tour operators based in Collingwood.

### Environs
Immediately to the west of the spit is **Puponga Farm Park**, with walking tracks and viewpoints. Visitors can also participate in the activities on a working farm. A short walk from the Farewell Spit visitor centre and café leads to Fossil Point on the wild ocean beach. Further west is the easy climb to Pillar Point lighthouse and the Old Man Range, while at the end of the road a short track crosses a series of dunes to Whariariki Beach, with rock pools, birds, seals and the towering Archway Islands nearby.

🏞 **Puponga Farm Park**
Collingwood–Puponga Main Rd.
**Tel** (03) 525 8026. **Open** daily. 💻

Tourists climbing the sand dunes at Farewell Spit

# CANTERBURY AND THE WEST COAST

Canterbury and the West Coast, stretching from the Tasman Sea in the west to the Pacific Ocean in the east, is characterized by sharp and sudden distinctions of geology, flora and climate. The combined area contains four national parks and New Zealand's highest mountain. Christchurch, the largest city in the South Island, is an ideal base from which to explore the various subregions.

When large-scale European settlement of Canterbury began in 1850, both Canterbury and the West Coast were dominated by the Ngai Tahu tribe. By 1860, the bulk of the tribe's land had been acquired by the government in a series of dubious sales transactions, leaving the Ngai Tahu impoverished and unable to participate equally in the new settler economy. It was not until 1997 that the Ngai Tahu received compensation from the New Zealand Government.

While pastoral farming was the key to the development of Canterbury in the 1850s, it was the discovery of gold in the 1860s that brought European settlement to the West Coast. Today, "the Coast" retains a rustic mystique, a product of its mining heritage, powerful landscapes of rugged mountains and glaciers, lush rainforest, rushing rivers and sombre lakes, as well as its isolation from the rest of New Zealand. The West Coast climate is wet, with prevailing westerly air-flows bringing frequent heavy rain as moisture-laden air is forced up and over the Southern Alps. By contrast, Canterbury is relatively dry, with warm, blustery winds commonly sweeping down the eastern side of the alps and over the Canterbury Plains.

The plains are carved into a patchwork of grazing and crop paddocks, backed by tussock vegetation and forest-covered mountain ranges. They merge to the north and south with rolling farmland, interspersed with wide, braided rivers. The inland region is a large, dry, open basin of austere beauty, over which New Zealand's highest mountains loom.

Climbers on the summit of Aoraki/Mount Cook

◀ Scenic view of Maruia River from Lewis Pass

# Exploring Canterbury and the West Coast

Canterbury and the West Coast's distinctive landscapes are dominated by the Southern Alps through which there are only two roads and one railway line. To get the best out of the region, and particularly to appreciate the beauty of its varied geology, flora and fauna, a willingness to don sturdy shoes and set out on foot is necessary. For the independent outdoor enthusiast, the opportunities are enormous, and for those who prefer to be guided through the wilderness, commercially run adventure tourism activities are available at most key locations.

Inner-city tram in Christchurch

## Sights at a Glance

1 Christchurch pp226–33
2 Port Hills
3 Lyttelton
4 Banks Peninsula
5 Akaroa
7 Hanmer Springs
8 Lewis Pass
9 Reefton
10 Karamea
11 Westport
12 Paparoa National Park
13 Greymouth
14 Hokitika
15 Westland National Park pp242–3
17 Arthur's Pass
18 Arthur's Pass National Park pp246–7
19 Mount Hutt
20 Rakaia
21 Ashburton
22 Geraldine
23 Timaru pp252–3
24 Lake Tekapo
25 Lake Pukaki
26 Twizel
27 Lake Ohau
28 Aoraki/Mount Cook National Park pp256–7

### Tours

6 Waipara Vineyards
16 Arthur's Pass

## Top Outdoor Activities

The places shown here have been selected for their recreational activities. Conditions vary depending on the weather and the time of year, so exercise caution and, if in doubt, seek local advice.

| | Fishing | Golf | Mountain Biking | Mountain Climbing | Skiing/Heli-Skiing | Tramping | Walking | White-Water Rafting |
|---|---|---|---|---|---|---|---|---|
| Arthur's Pass National Park | | | | ■ | ● | ■ | ● | |
| Banks Peninsula | ● | ■ | ● | | | ■ | ● | |
| Franz Josef Glacier | | | | ■ | ● | ■ | ● | ■ |
| Hanmer Springs | ● | ■ | ● | | | ■ | ● | ■ |
| Hokitika | ● | ■ | | | | | ■ | |
| Karamea | ● | ■ | ● | | | ■ | ● | |
| Lake Ohau | ● | ■ | | | ● | | ● | |
| Lake Tekapo | ● | | | | ■ | ● | ● | |
| Lewis Pass | | | ● | ■ | ● | ■ | ● | |
| Aoraki/Mount Cook | | ■ | | | ● | | ● | |
| Mount Hutt | ● | | | ■ | ● | ■ | ● | |
| Paparoa National Park | ● | | | | | ■ | ● | |
| Port Hills | | | ● | | | | ● | |
| Rakaia | ● | ■ | | | | | ● | ■ |
| Reefton | ● | | ● | | | ■ | | ■ |
| Westport | ● | ■ | | | | | | ■ |

For additional symbols see back flap

Abut Head

Whataroa

Franz Josef Glacier

Fox Glacier

WESTLAND NATIONAL PARK

AORAKI/MOUNT COOK NATIONAL PARK

Mount Cook 3755m

Haast

Mount Ward 2644m

Mount Huxley 2499m

Obau Forest

Ben Ohau Range

LAKE TEKAPO

LAKE PUKAKI 25

Mount C

LAKE OHAU 27

8

26 TWIZEL

Clay Cliffs

Omarama

Queenstown

83

Map legend (partial):

torway
or road
or road
nic route
or railway
or railway
ional border
mit

**KARAMEA** ⑩

*Karamea Bight*

*TASMAN SEA*

Seddonville

Granity

Waimangaroa

Cape Foulwind

⑪ **WESTPORT**

*Nelson*

*Butler*

Charleston

Inangahua

**PAPAROA NATIONAL PARK** ⑫

Punakaiki

Cronadun

⑨ **REEFTON**

Ikamatua

Springs Junction

⑧ **LEWIS PASS**

Runanga

OUTH ⑬

Paroa

*WEST COAST*

Ngahere

Shantytown

Moana

*Lake Brunner*

*Mount Ajax 1834m*

*Lake Sumner*

⑦ **HANMER SPRINGS**

*Kaikoura*

Waiau

Culverden

Rotherham

⑭

Kaniere

*Lake Kaniere*

Kumara

Otira

**ARTHUR'S PASS**

⑱

**ARTHUR'S PASS TOUR**

⑰

⑯

**ARTHUR'S PASS NP**

Waikari

Scargill

Waipara

⑥ **WAIPARA VINEYARDS TOUR**

Amberley

*Pegasus Bay*

Porters Pass 945m

**Rangiora**

Springfield

Oxford

Sheffield

*Rakaia Gorge*

Darfield

Kaiapoi

**CHRISTCHURCH**

① ②

**PORT HILLS**

③ **LYTTELTON**

Rolleston

*BANKS PENINSULA*

④

Okains Bay

**MOUNT HUTT** ⑲

Methven

Lincoln

*Lake Ellesmere*

Little River

⑤

**AKAROA**

Mt Somers

**RAKAIA** ⑳

Mayfield

Southbridge

*Canterbury Plains*

*Peel Forest*

ANTERBURY

㉑ **ASHBURTON**

Hinds

㉒ **GERALDINE**

Temuka

*Canterbury Bight*

ant Point

㉓ **TIMARU**

Pareora

Makikihi

*Dunedin*

Studholme

| 0 kilometres | 40 |
| 0 miles | 20 |

**Getting Around**

Numerous bus operators link all parts of the region, but the most convenient way to get around is by car. The roads are good, although care is needed in winter on the alpine routes, and some sights are accessible only via gravel roads. Many areas are easily visited by day trips from Christchurch, including Banks Peninsula, Hanmer Springs, Arthur's Pass and mid-Canterbury's ski fields. The four and a half hour trip from Christchurch to Greymouth on the TranzAlpine railway is a relaxing way to see the region's diverse scenery.

Lake Tekapo, a popular venue for water sports

# ❶ Christchurch

Canterbury's provincial capital, Christchurch, is the largest city in the South Island and the principal gateway to its scenic wonders. Laid out as the capital of the Canterbury Settlement in 1850, the city has many notable buildings and monuments that recall its colonial heritage, as well as many parks and gardens. It is often thought of as a conservative city, a reflection of its origins as a Church of England settlement modelled on 19th-century English society. During the 20th century the city became increasingly industrialized and is today a centre for IT. A rebuilding programme is underway to repair the damage caused by earthquakes in 2010 and 2011.

Old Government Building, built in Italian Renaissance style, now a Heritage Hotel

### 🏛 Cathedral Square

In the heart of the city, amid the worst of the earthquake devastation, Cathedral Square is still dominated by the ruins of Christchurch Cathedral. Other historic buildings include the sturdy Old Government Building (1911), which survived relatively intact, as well as the Renaissance-style Old Chief Post Office (1897) and the ornate Edwardian Regent Theatre (1905), both of which are likely to be torn down. Completely demolished is the Gothic Press Building, which housed the city's daily newspaper. The 1867 statue of Robert Godley, which used to face the cathedral, was removed after the 2011 earthquake and is now in the Re:Start Mall *(see p229)*. The cathedral steps once attracted eccentrics and street performers. Now this precinct is out of bounds, but the fenced-off ruins still draw crowds of tourists and well-wishers.

### 🏛 Christchurch Cathedral

Cathedral Square. 🈺 (03) 366 0046. **Closed** due to earthquake damage.

Begun in 1864 and completed in 1904, Christchurch Cathedral was built as the focal point of the new Anglican settlement of Canterbury and remains the city's most important landmark, particularly following the earthquakes. It was designed by English architect George Gilbert Scott in the Gothic Revival style. Noted local architect Benjamin Mountfort supervised the completion and also had considerable influence over the design. Built of Canterbury stone and native timbers, this impressive building had many notable features, including detailed wood and stone carvings around the high altar and main pulpit.

The cathedral had survived the earthquake of September 2010 with only minor damage, but during 2011's quake the iconic spire toppled into Cathedral Square, leaving the main entrance surrounded by deep drifts of broken masonry. The final fate of the cathedral ruins has yet to be decided and a new church may be built.

## Godley and the Canterbury Settlement

John Robert Godley (1814–61) is regarded as the founder of Canterbury although he spent only three years in the new province. With Edward Gibbon Wakefield, founder of the New Zealand Company *(see p53)*, he formed the Canterbury Association in 1848, which then purchased 1,210 sq km (470 sq miles) of land for the creation of a Church of England-dominated province in New Zealand. A slice of England was to be transplanted on Canterbury's far shores. English newspapers commented on the "respectability" of the so-called "Canterbury Pilgrims" who set sail on four ships, the *Randolph*, *Charlotte Jane*, *Cressy* and *Sir George Seymour*, in September 1850. Within three years of its founding, Canterbury was governing itself as one of New Zealand's six provinces. Godley returned to England in 1852.

Statue of John Robert Godley

### Key

🟦 Street-by-Street: Christchurch *pp228–9*

– – Inner-city tram route

0 metres 500
0 yards 500

A transitional 700-seat Cardboard
Cathedral, designed by architect
Shigeru Ban, opened in 2013
on Latimer Square. A steel- and
timber-clad A-frame structure
supported by 90 cardboard
tubes, it is expected to have
a lifespan of at least 50 years.

Punting on the Avon River in Christchurch

### Avon River
Cashel St & Oxford Terrace.
The Avon River, which gently
meanders through the city, is
Christchurch's greatest natural
asset and one of its main
attractions. Its grassy banks,
weeping willows, old oak trees,
ducks, and bridges linking the
city's main streets lure office
workers and visitors alike to its
banks in summer. A walk along
the Avon River bank from
Victoria Square to the Bridge of
Remembrance takes visitors past
the Law Courts, the Floral Clock,
the Provincial Council Buildings
and a 1917 statue of Antarctic
explorer Robert Scott sculpted
by his widow, Kathleen.

Another great way to enjoy
the river is to take a boat trip.
Punts operate from various
landings along the river,
including near the Town Hall
(*see p228*) and Antigua
Boat Sheds.

### Victoria Square
Victoria Square is a beautifully
landscaped expanse of green
north of Cathedral Square. Focal
points are the Floral Clock (*see
p228*), statues of Queen Victoria
(1901) and James Cook (1932),
and the much photographed
Bowker and Ferrier fountains.
The Town Hall, built in 1972,
was badly damaged in the
earthquakes and is being
repaired. A block away, on
Victoria Street, is the
Christchurch Casino,
recognizable by its stylized
roulette wheel façade.

## Christchurch City Centre

① Cathedral Square
② Christchurch Cathedral
③ Cardboard Cathedral
④ Victoria Square
⑤ Avon River
⑥ Provincial Council Buildings
⑦ Bridge of Remembrance
⑧ Antigua Boat Sheds
⑨ Arts Centre
⑩ Canterbury Museum
⑪ Christchurch Art Gallery
⑫ Christ's College
⑬ *Botanic Gardens pp232–3*
⑭ Hagley Park
⑮ Mona Vale

Victoria Square, a park north of
Cathedral Square

**For keys to symbols** *see back flap*

# Street-by-Street: Christchurch

The streets surrounding Cathedral Square are laid out in a grid pattern bordered by four broad avenues. The formality of the layout is broken by the quaint Avon River which winds serpentine through the inner city and adjacent parks. Christchurch's many Gothic Revival and Edwardian buildings, pretty parks and landscaped river bank support the oft-repeated description of Christchurch as the most English of cities outside England. As a result of earthquake damage, many of the city's buildings are facing demolition and a programme of rebuilding is ongoing.

**New Regent Street**
This charming pedestrian-only area was built in the Spanish Mission style in 1932.

**Floral Clock**
Established in 1955, the clock was destroyed in the earthquake, but should be replaced in 2014.

**Victoria Square**, with its Avon River boundary, clipped lawns, formal plantings and many trees, is a peaceful oasis in the city.

**The Town Hall**, built in 1972 by noted local architects Warren and Mahoney, was badly damaged in the earthquakes, and is being repaired.

New Regent St

OXFORD TERRACE

COLOMBO STREET

ARMAGH STREET

Parkroyal Hotel

Law Courts

### Earthquake Damage

Many notable Christchurch structures suffered extensive earthquake damage and are closed for repairs. These include: Bridge of Remembrance; Provincial Council Buildings; and the Town Hall. Those damaged beyond repair include: Christchurch Cathedral; Edwardian Regent Theatre; Gothic Press Building (demolished); Old Chief Post Office; and Oxford Terrace, replaced with Re:START Mall, but being rebuilt.

**★ Provincial Council Buildings**
These buildings, built 1858–1865, feature fine stained-glass windows, a ridge-and-furrow ceiling and mosaic tile work. They suffered extensive earthquake damage but will be repaired.

*For hotels and restaurants in this region see pp302–7 and pp314–25*

**★ Christchurch Cathedral**
Built between 1864 and 1904 and severely damaged in the 2011 earthquake, the ruined cathedral has remained the city's most important landmark. It is likely that a new church will one day be built here.

Old Government Building

**Christchurch Tram**
A fleet of restored vintage trams takes passengers on a scenic route past many significant city centre sights (see pp226–7).

**City Mall**, a pedestrian-only precinct spanning parts of High and Cashel streets, is a diverse complex including a department store (Ballantynes), shopping arcades and fashion boutiques.

COLOMBO STREET

HEREFORD STREET

CITY MALL

WORCESTER

OXFORD TERRACE

STREET

**Key**

— Suggested route

| 0 metres | 100 |
| 0 yards | 100 |

Avon River

**Bridge of Remembrance**
The bridge's stone archway commemorates the gunners from Canterbury who served in World Wars I and II and subsequent conflicts.

**Re:START Mall**
At the site of the former Oxford Terrace, which was devastated in the earthquakes, these brightly coloured shipping containers house quality retailers, food outlets and entertainment venues.

Stone legislative chamber of the Provincial Council Buildings before the earthquakes

### 🏛 Provincial Council Buildings

Cnr of Armagh & Durham sts. **Tel** (03) 941 7680. **Closed** until further notice for repairs to earthquake damage.

Designed by Christchurch architect Benjamin Mountfort, the Provincial Council Buildings are claimed to be the finest example of secular Gothic Revival architecture in New Zealand. The buildings were constructed in three stages. The first two, from 1858 to 1861, saw the creation of a mainly wooden building. The third involved the construction of a stone council chamber, completed in 1865, the high point of the complex.

All of the buildings were severely damaged in the earthquakes, but their status as a UNESCO World Heritage Site ensures that they will be fully repaired and rebuilt.

### 🏛 Bridge of Remembrance

Cnr of Cashel St & Oxford Terrace.

A commemoration of New Zealand soldiers who served in various arenas of war, the bridge stands at the head of City Mall, the city's central shopping area. Structurally damaged during the earthquakes, the Bridge of Remembrance will be under repair until the end of 2016.

### 🏛 Canterbury Museum

Rolleston Ave. **Tel** (03) 366 5000. **Open** Oct–Mar: 9am–5:30pm daily; Apr–Sep: 9am–5pm daily. **Closed** 25 Dec. 🖼 donation. ♿ 🇼 canterburymuseum.com

Built between 1869 and 1876, Canterbury Museum is considered to be one of Mountfort's most successful adaptations of the Gothic style for secular purposes. The museum has a comprehensive selection of genuine Antarctic relics as well as one of the finest mounted bird displays in the southern hemisphere. Other halls feature oriental art, a reconstruction of a 19th-century Christchurch street, and a Maori cultural section, including displays of the extinct moa and the bird's early Polynesian hunters.

### 🏛 Christ's College

Rolleston Ave. **Tel** (03) 366 8705. **Open** daily. **Closed** during school hols. 📷 by arrangement. ♿ partial.

At Christ's College, a modern-day reminder of Christchurch's English heritage, the sons of Canterbury's élite are educated in black and white striped blazers along English public school lines amid Gothic Revival buildings dating back to 1863. There are tours of the grounds and buildings.

### 🏛 Arts Centre

Cnr of Rolleston Ave & Worcester Boulevard. **Tel** (03) 363 2836. **Closed** until further notice due to earthquake damage; check website for latest information. 🇼 artscentre.org.nz

Located in the old University of Canterbury buildings, the Arts Centre was Christchurch's art and crafts hub until it sustained substantial damage during the 2011 earthquake. The complex housed more than 40 galleries, studios and shops, as well as theatre, film and ballet venues and eateries. Construction of the Gothic Revival-style buildings began in 1877. It was designed by a succession of architects, including Mountfort, who was responsible for the Clock Tower building, Great Hall and Classics block.

The Clock Tower building was the early focus of earthquake repair work, but the entire complex is expected to be eventually repaired and rebuilt.

Moa skeleton, Canterbury Museum

Canterbury Museum, housed in a beautiful stone building in Gothic Revival style

*For hotels and restaurants in this region see pp302–7 and pp314–25*

### 🏛 Christchurch Art Gallery (Te Puna o Waiwhetu)

Corner of Montreal St & Worcester Blvd. **Tel** (03) 941 7300. **Closed** for earthquake repairs until 2015. 🏛 for some exhibitions. ♿ 🅿 🛒 📷
🌐 christchurchartgallery.org.nz

Situated close to Cathedral Square, this is the city's principal art gallery. It houses a collection of 5,000 New Zealand and international works of art, which are complemented by touring exhibitions. The gallery's large, permanent display features Dutch, French, Italian and British paintings, drawings, prints, sculpture and ceramics.

The New Zealand collection, especially of Canterbury works, is one of the most comprehensive in the country. The collection displays works by Canterbury landscape artist William Sutton (see p36), as well as other prominent New Zealand painters, including Doris Lusk, Colin McCahon, Rita Angus, Charles Goldie, Frances Hodgkins, Dick Frizzell and Seraphine Pick.

### 🚣 Antigua Boat Sheds

2 Cambridge Terrace. **Tel** (03) 366 5885. **Open** daily. **Closed** 25 Dec.
📷 🛒 🌐 boatsheds.co.nz

The Antigua Boat Sheds, on the banks of the Avon River, have been providing people with river recreation since 1882. Here, canoes, punts and paddle boats can be hired for trips through the city or upstream to the Botanic Gardens. They are the only surviving commercial boat sheds of the five or six that once offered boats for hire.

### 🏛 Mona Vale

63 Fendalton Rd. **Tel** (03) 348 9660. **Closed** for repairs to earthquake damage; check website before visiting. 🌐 monavale.co.nz

Mona Vale, one of Christchurch's historic homes, built between 1899 and 1900, is situated among sweeping lawns, mature trees and landscaped gardens to the northwest of Hagley Park. The Avon River meanders through the property. Visitors are invited to stroll through the gardens and feed the ducks.

Antigua Boat Sheds

The imposing homestead was almost demolished in the 1960s, but a public appeal for funds led to its purchase by the city. Mona Vale suffered substantial damage in the Christchurch earthquakes and is closed until further notice.

### 🚣 Hagley Park

**Tel** (03) 941 6840. **Open** daily. ♿
Hagley Park, a vast green expanse in the heart of Christchurch, serves as the city's lungs. Within its boundaries are a golf course, sports grounds, tree-lined walking and cycling tracks, artificial lakes, and the Botanic Gardens (see pp232–3). When the early colonists laid out the site for their new town, they set aside 2 sq km (0.80 sq mile) for a public park, and in 1856 an ordinance was passed declaring it "reserved forever" for public recreation and enjoyment. By the early 1870s, the settlers had replaced the park's native flora with European plants, grasses and trees.

### 🏛 International Antarctic Centre

38 Orchard Rd. **Tel** (03) 353 7798. **Open** daily. 📷 ♿ 🛒 📷 🌐 iceberg.co.nz

About 20 minutes from the city centre, near the airport to the west, is the International Antarctic Centre, the base for the New Zealand, United States and Italian Antarctic programmes. Its visitor centre has a range of exhibits on the exploration and geology of Antarctica. Visitors can also take rides on Antarctic vehicles.

### 🚠 Christchurch Gondola

10 Bridle Path Rd. **Tel** (03) 384 0700. **Open** daily. 📷 ♿ 🚫 🛒 📷 🌐 gondola.co.nz

Southeast of the city, the Christchurch Gondola takes passengers from a terminal in the Heathcote Valley to the rim of an extinct volcano at the top of the Port Hills. From the top there are amazing 360-degree views of the city, Banks Peninsula, Canterbury Plains and the distant Southern Alps.

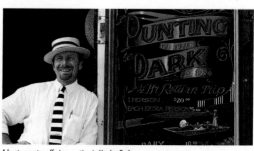

A boat operator offering punting in Hagley Park

# Botanic Gardens

The Botanic Gardens, founded in 1863, include conservatories, rose and bulb beds, rock and water gardens, English lawns and woodland, all largely enclosed in the loop of the Avon River. Trees damaged during the 2011 earthquake have been replanted and the gardens restored to their former glory, but some buildings, including the café, are still closed for repairs. The area fringing the eastern side of the Botanic Gardens is Christchurch's creative and artistic heart. The city's museum, civic art gallery, ballet company, professional theatre and Arts Centre are located here.

★ **Conservatory Complex**
Cuningham House (1923) and the complex's five other glasshouses remain closed for ongoing earthquake repairs.

★ **Water Garden**
This is enclosed by herbaceous perennials and exotic trees and shrubs, creating a cool and tranquil setting.

## KEY

① **The Rose Garden** is a formal garden in front of the Conservatory Complex. Roses are symbolic of the city's English heritage.

② **In the New Zealand Garden** native plants are displayed in an authentic mixed forest setting.

③ **The Cockayne Memorial Garden** has specimen plantings of native trees and shrubs.

④ **Children's Playground**

⑤ **The Victoria and Albert lakes**, both artificial, attract large numbers of ducks and other bird life, including shags and swans, and are often used for model boat racing.

⑥ **Christ's College** (see p230)

⑦ **Rolleston Avenue**

**Daffodil Woodland and Bandsmen's Memorial Rotunda**
The area surrounding the rotunda was planted with 16,000 bulbs in 1933, and in spring is a blaze of yellow. The rotunda itself is closed due to earthquake damage.

**The Canterbury Museum**
Founded in 1868 by geologist Julius von Haast, this museum includes notable permanent collections on early Antarctic exploration and traditional Maori society *(see p230)*.

## VISITORS' CHECKLIST

**Practical Information**
Rolleston Ave (main entrance).
W **ccc.govt.nz** *i* (03) 941 8666. **Open** 7am–1 hour before sunset daily. **Closed** 25 Dec. ♿ 🅿 summer only. 🚻 📷 🏛 🎦 Summertimes Festival (Dec–Mar).

**Transport**
🚍 Worcester Boulevard.

**Peacock Fountain**
This ornate cast-iron fountain plays amid formal flower beds at the eastern entrance to the gardens.

0 metres 100
0 yards 100

⑤

⑥

⑦

**Arts Centre**
Christchurch's arts and cultural hub was severely damaged during the 2011 earthquake and remains closed *(see p230)*.

**For keys to map symbols** *see back flap*

Sign of the Takahe, on Dyers Pass Road above Christchurch

## ❷ Port Hills

**Road map** C6. 🚍

The Port Hills separate Christchurch from Lyttelton Harbour, and were formed as the result of the eruption of the now extinct Lyttelton volcano. Their tussock-covered slopes and volcanic outcrops flank the southern part of the city. Because of their proximity to the city they are extremely popular with walkers, runners, rock climbers and mountain bikers.

The Port Hills are also easily accessed by car, thanks to the work of early 20th- century conservationist and politician Harry Ell, who strove for the creation of a road across the hills. The first stretch of the Summit Road was opened in 1938.

Ell's vision included the construction of a series of rest houses along the Port Hills, the most impressive of which is the Sign of the Takahe, completed in 1949 and now home to a restaurant. Nestled in the hill suburb of Cashmere, this imposing Gothic building was also the most cherished of his projects. Another Ell legacy, the Sign of the Kiwi, is a popular resting place for people travelling along the Summit Road who stop off here for ice creams and other refreshments.

The many tracks on the Port Hills provide striking views of Lyttelton Harbour, the Canterbury Plains and the Southern Alps. The rim of the crater can also be accessed via the Christchurch Gondola, which runs from Heathcote Valley (see p231).

## ❸ Lyttelton

**Road map** C6. 🏔 4,000. 🚍
ℹ️ 20 Oxford St, (03) 328 9093.

Lyttelton was the landing place of the Canterbury Pilgrims in 1850, and was named after Lord Lyttelton, the chairman of the Canterbury Association. In 1867, a rail tunnel was drilled through the volcanic rock of the Port Hills to provide a link between Lyttelton's port and Christchurch, and a road tunnel was completed in 1964.

The **Lyttelton Museum** has interesting displays of local maritime history and relics from the colonial past, as well as a small section on Antarctic exploration. The museum suffered extensive damage from the 2011 earthquake, with some collections moved to storage.

The historic Lyttelton Timeball Station stood sentry over the town from its construction in 1875 until 2011, when it was dismantled following irreparable damage during the earthquakes of 2010 and 2011. The large black ball hanging from its tower once signalled Greenwich Mean

Time to the ships in the harbour. It is hoped that the timeball mechanism can be salvaged and reused in a possible reconstruction of the building, which had been one of only five working timeball stations in the world.

A ferry service across the harbour to Quail and Ripapa islands and the small township of Diamond Harbour operates from the Lyttelton docks.

🏛 **Lyttelton Museum**
Gladstone Quay. **Tel** (03) 328 8972.
**Open** Tue, Thu, Sat & Sun, pm only.
**Closed** 25 Dec. 🎟 donation.
♿ ground floor.

## ❹ Banks Peninsula

**Road map** C6.

Formed by numerous eruptions of the Lyttelton and Akaroa volcanoes, Banks Peninsula was, until some 25,000 years ago, an island. Reminders of this dramatic geological past are everywhere, including rocky volcanic outcrops, craggy headlands, deep valleys and precipitous bluffs. The Summit Road allows excellent views of this striking scenery.

The peninsula has been settled by Maori for 1,000 years, and until the 1820s was a place of prosperity and security for the Ngai Tahu tribe. That changed as a result of internecine and intertribal fighting, conflict which contributed indirectly to the decision taken by the British government to install a governor and sign the Treaty of Waitangi (see pp52–3).

Maori and Colonial Museum and meeting house at Okains Bay

Laverick's Bay, Banks Peninsula

Among the peninsula's many attractions are its beautiful bays and picturesque villages, including Pigeon Bay, Okains Bay, Laverick's Bay and Le Bons Bay. There are many walking tracks, including a 20-minute stroll through the Hay Scenic Reserve, which has one of the peninsula's best remaining stands of lowland podocarp forest; the five-hour Pigeon Bay Walkway; and the two- to four-day Banks Peninsula Track, which traverses private farmland and the coastline of many of the remote eastern bays. These remote areas can also be visited on the **Eastern Bays Scenic Mail Run**, a mail delivery service that invites up to eight passengers to join its four-hour mail run.

At Okains Bay is the **Maori and Colonial Museum** which houses an extensive collection of Maori artifacts, including an 1867 Maori *waka* (canoe) used during the Waitangi Day celebrations in February (*see p45*).

Also worth a visit is the boutique **Barry's Bay Cheese Factory**, which continues the peninsula's long tradition of cheese making.

**Maori and Colonial Museum**
146 Main Rd, Okains Bay.
**Tel** (03) 304 8611. **Open** daily.
**Closed** 25 Dec.

**Barry's Bay Cheese Factory**
State Hwy 75. **Tel** (03) 304 5809.
**Open** daily. **Closed** 25 Dec.

**Eastern Bays Scenic Mail Run**
19 Rue Renard. **Tel** (03) 304 7873.
**Open** Mon–Sat. **Closed** public hols.

## ❺ Akaroa

**Road map** C6. 580.
80 Rue Lavaud, (03) 304 8600.
akaroa.com

This attractive small town, nestled at the head of Akaroa Harbour, is the oldest town in Canterbury, and was founded by a small band of French settlers in 1840. The town boasts many French-influenced historic buildings, narrow streets and a beautiful harbourfront location.

Among the many reminders of Akaroa's French heritage is **Langlois-Eteveneaux House**, believed to have been prefabricated in France and erected in Akaroa in 1841. It is part of the **Akaroa Museum** complex, which also includes the town's old courthouse, opened in 1880. The museum exhibits cover natural and regional history and architecture. A self-guided walk through the town takes in 43 historic sites, including the 1880 **Akaroa Lighthouse**.

A good swimming beach lies at the centre of the town. Harbour cruises operate from the main wharf, and visitors may see Hector's dolphins, penguins and seal colonies. A number of walking tracks lead up to the surrounding volcanic saddles and peaks, affording panoramic views of the harbour. Akaroa also boasts an active art and crafts community, and many shops and galleries.

**Langlois-Eteveneaux House and Akaroa Museum**
71 Rue Lavaud. **Tel** (03) 304 1013.
**Open** daily. **Closed** 25 Dec.
ground floor.

**Akaroa Lighthouse**
**Tel** (03) 304 7325. **Open** weekends, public hols & by arrangement.
ground floor.

### Jean François Langlois

The man primarily responsible for Akaroa's French heritage was whaler Jean François Langlois. In August 1838, he conceived the idea of a French colony and attempted to buy most of the peninsula from the local Ngai Tahu people. The following year he returned to France to gain support for his plan, and formed the Nanto-Bordelaise Company as the vehicle for his colonizing ambitions.

French navy captain Charles Lavaud was dispatched to provide protection for the 57 colonists who landed at Akaroa in August 1840. However, French ambitions were thwarted by the British who, in the interim, had signed the Treaty of Waitangi and, upon hearing of the settlers' impending arrival, rushed to appoint two magistrates to Akaroa. Despite the assertion of British sovereignty, the settlers stayed, although by 1842 Langlois was back in France. The Nanto-Bordelaise Company was bought out by the New Zealand Company in 1849, opening the way for large-scale British migration to the settlement.

Langlois-Eteveneaux House

# ⊙ Waipara Vineyard Tour

The Waipara district's first vineyards were planted only in the 1980s. However, this wine-growing region has emerged quickly as a promising area, and many of its vineyards have won awards for their wines. Canterbury has more than 30 vineyards, but Waipara, about 65 km (40 miles) north of Christchurch, is the area of most rapid development. Wine-tasting tours can be arranged through the Christchurch i-SITE visitor information centre *(see p227)*.

**① Pegasus Bay**
This winery crushed its first grapes in 1991 and has since won many awards. Its wine-tasting venue has a charming garden setting overlooking the surrounding countryside.

**⑨ Black Estate**
Planted in 1993, Black Estate handcrafts artisan Pinot Noir, Chardonnay and Riesling. There is a tasting room and an eatery.

**⑧ Mountford Vineyard**
Mountford produces top-of-the-range Chardonnay and Pinot Noir. A beautiful homestead overlooks the small vineyard.

**⑦ Waipara Springs**
With its first vines planted in 1982, Waipara Springs is one of the oldest vineyards in the district, and has won many awards. Its popular wine-tasting venue is set in pleasant gardens.

0 kilometres  3
0 miles  3

*Hanmer Springs*

Mackenzies Road

Glenmark Drive

Church Road

**Waipara**

*Waipara River*

Mt Cass Road

Georges Road

Stockgrove Road

*Waipara River*

Glasnevin Road

↓ *Christchurch*

**④ Terrace Edge**
Set in a dramatic landscape, this family-owned vineyard and olive grove produces organically grown, award-winning wines and olive oil. Vineyard tours are given on request.

**⑤ Torlesse Wines**
Torlesse uses both Waipara and Marlborough grapes to produce a wide range of wines, including Gewürztraminer, Cabernet Sauvignon, Sauvignon Blanc and Chardonnay.

**⑥ Waipara River Estate**
Formerly named Glenmark Wines, the district's first winery, Waipara River Estate's wines have won many awards, and can be tasted in a pleasant, rustic setting.

Kaikoura

ihi Road          Reeces Road

**Waipara Hills**
pened in 1994, Waipara Hills pecializes in aromatics and is istinguished by a huge stone inery building.

**Fiddlers Green**
ddlers Green produced its rst vintage in 1998. Its Riesling nd Sauvignon Blanc wines ave won awards.

**ey**

■ Tour route
 Other roads
 River

Hot pool complex at Hanmer Springs

## ⓞ Hanmer Springs

Road map C5. 🏔 800. 🚌
ℹ 42 Amuri Ave, (03) 315 0020.
🌐 www.visithurunui.co.nz

This small alpine village, 385 m (1,260 ft) above sea level, is best known for the vast **Hanmer Springs Thermal Pools & Spa**. Although hot springs were first discovered in the area in 1859, they were officially opened only in 1883. Today, the complex has 15 thermal and freshwater pools of varying temperatures, as well as private pools and a children's waterslide and activity area.

Surrounding the hot pools is a 168-sq-km (65-sq-mile) forest park, which offers activities such as mountain biking and walks, ranging from the short Conical Hill walk (one hour return) to the longer Mount Isobel walk (five to six hours return). At the Waiau Ferry Bridge, 5 km (3 miles) from the village, tourist operators offer bungy jumping, jet-boating and rafting down the Waiau River.

**🏊 Hanmer Springs Thermal Pools & Spa**
42 Amuri Ave. **Tel** (03) 315 0000.
**Open** daily. **Closed** 25 Dec. 🅿 ♿
📷 🌐 hanmersprings.co.nz

## ⓞ Lewis Pass

Road map C5.

Lewis Pass marks the crossing point on State Highway 7 over the South Island's Main Divide. The surrounding 183-sq-km (70-sq-mile) Lewis Pass National Reserve offers a range of unguided outdoor

activities, including tramping, fishing and hunting. Just over the pass, **Maruia Springs Thermal Resort** has a small complex of outdoor hot pools in a natural setting, with views of the surrounding bush and mountain peaks.

**🏊 Maruia Springs Thermal Resort**
State Hwy 7. **Tel** (03) 523 8840.
**Open** daily. **Closed** 25 Dec. 🅿 ♿ 📷

## ⓞ Reefton

Road map C5. 🏔 1,000. 🚌
ℹ 67-69 Broadway, (03) 732 8391.

Founded in 1872, Reefton takes its name from the gold-bearing quartz reefs in the area. The town's gold-mining heritage is evident in the many historic remains of the 1870s boom dotted around the region, especially in the beech forest-clad Victoria Forest Park. A network of tracks provides opportunity for exploration on foot or on mountain bike.

A heritage walk around Reefton takes in many historic buildings, including the **School of Mines**, which operated from 1887 to 1970 as part of a network of similar schools around New Zealand. Two km (1.2 miles) from Reefton, the **Black's Point Museum** exhibits relics from the gold-mining era.

**🏛 School of Mines**
Shiel St. **Tel** (03) 732 8391.
**Open** by arrangement. 📷 📷

**🏛 Black's Point Museum**
State Hwy 7. **Tel** (03) 732 8391.
**Open** Wed–Sun. **Closed** 25 Dec.
📷 ♿

## ⑩ Karamea

**Road map** C4. 🅜 700. 🚍
ℹ️ Market Cross, (03) 782 6652
🎭 Whitebaiters Ball (Oct).
🆆 karameainfo.co.nz

Settled by Europeans in 1874, Karamea is an isolated farming community that lies at the northern end of the West Coast's State Highway 67. Nestled in a basin dominated by dairy farming and fringed by the Kahurangi National Park, Karamea is best known as the exit point for the Heaphy Track, which after following the coast from the Heaphy River ends 15 km (9 miles) to the north. Several short walking tracks are based around the Heaphy exit point, including the 40-minute Nikau Loop and the 90-minute Scotts Beach walk.

About 26 km (16 miles) to the northeast of Karamea is the **Oparara Basin**, featuring impressive limestone formations and a 15-km (9-mile) system of caves enveloped by dense forest. Much of the gravel road to the basin is narrow and winding, but can be undertaken in a 2WD vehicle. The highly fragile Honeycomb Caves system, first explored in 1980, is accessible only with a guide, and contains the remains of about 50 species, including the extinct moa and New Zealand eagle. Areas that can be explored without a guide are the Oparara Arch, 43 m (141 ft) high and 219 m (719 ft) long,

Cows, cabbage trees and beach near Karamea

which is reached after a 20-minute walk on a good track through the forest, and the Box Canyon and Crazy Paving caves. It is essential to carry a good torch. For the highly adventurous visitor, local tourist operators run grades four and five white-water rafting trips down the Karamea River.

Karamea is also a base for walkers using the popular three- to five-day Wangapeka Track. The Fenian Track is an historic gold-miners' route, and the four-hour return walk leads to the former mining settlement of Adams Flat.

### 🏕️ Oparara Basin
State Hwy 67. **Tel** (03) 782 6652.
🕳️ Honeycomb Caves. 📷 obligatory at Honeycomb Caves.

## ⑪ Westport

**Road map** C5. 🅜 5,000. ✈️ 5 km (3 miles) N of town. 🚍 ℹ️ 1 Brougham St, (03) 789 6658. 🆆 westport.org.nz

Although Westport's origins lie in the gold rush of the 1860s, coal has been its lifeline for much of its history. Until 1954, coal from mines in the surrounding mountains was shipped out through the town's once busy port at the head of the Buller River, but today the bulk is taken by train to Lyttelton on the east coast (see p234). The **Coal Town Museum** at Westport has extensive exhibits reconstructing aspects of the region's coal-mining heritage. Westport is a base for a number of outdoor activities,

including jet-boating and jet-skiing on the river. Among the most popular activities is underground rafting in the Nile River Canyon area. This can be done only with a guide and involves floating in inner tubes through glowworm grottos and caverns before emerging into the open to float down the Waitakere River rapids and Nile River Canyon. The Metro Cave, which has dramatic limestone stalactite and stalagmite formations, can be explored on foot. Westport's North Beach and Carter's Beach are both popular swimming and surfing spots, as is the scenic Tauranga Bay. On the Cape Foulwind Walkway at the edge of Tauranga Bay is a breeding colony of fur seals (see p197). The walkway, which takes three hours return, crosses rocky granite bluffs, grassy downs, swampy streams and sandy beaches.

### 🏛️ Coal Town Museum
Queen St South. **Tel** (03) 789 8204.
**Open** daily. **Closed** 25 Dec. 📷 ♿

Seals at Tauranga Bay, near Westport

Nikau Loop at the exit to the Heaphy Track

# Coal-Mining Heritage

Coal was first discovered on the West Coast by explorer Thomas Brunner in 1848. The largest of the early mines were on the Denniston and Stockton plateaus, north-east of Westport, where large-scale exploitation began in 1878. The task of extracting coal from the rugged, mountainous terrain was hazardous, and necessitated some striking feats of engineering. The most famous was the Denniston Incline, a gravity-powered rail system under which laden coal trucks were lowered 520 m (1,700 ft) down the mountainside on a steel cable. Empty wagons were pulled back up by the weight of full wagons. The incline closed in 1967, but during its 87 years of operation it carried 13 million tonnes of coal off the Denniston Plateau. The coal industry continues to be important to the West Coast economy, with over 2 million tonnes exported from the coalfields each year.

**Coal wagon** on steel tracks for transporting coal in and out of the mine.

**The entrance**, carefully reinforced to prevent collapse.

### Early Mining Towns

Several mining settlements sprang up in the 19th century to support the coal industry, but they are little more than ghost towns today. The 120-km (75-mile) self-guided Buller Coalfields Heritage Trail leads through many mining relics, including the once thriving towns of Denniston, Stockton and Millerton. Information on the trail is available at the i-SITE Visitor Centre in Westport.

Coal miners at the entrance to the Rewanui coal mine

**Coal wagons** like this one in the Coal Town Museum were used to bring coal down from the mountainous coalfields.

**This aerial ropeway** is used to lower coal from the opencast Stockton mine down to the coastal settlement of Ngakawau, where it is loaded onto trains bound for the port of Lyttelton on the east coast.

**Among the many** relics that remain at Denniston, the marshalling point for coal from all over the plateau, are retaining rock walls where coal would be screened before being lowered down the incline, and parts of machinery.

## ⑫ Paparoa National Park

**Road map** C5. 🚌 ℹ️ State Hwy 6, Punakaiki, (03) 731 1895.

Founded in 1987, this 300-sq-km (115-sq-mile) park contains varied and dramatic scenery, most famously the Pancake Rocks and blowholes near the small coastal settlement of Punakaiki. Bands of limestone, separated by thin bands of softer mudstone, which has been worn away by thousands of years of rain, wind and sea spray, have created the layered formations of the Pancake Rocks. Over hundreds of thousands of years, caverns have also been formed as carbon dioxide-bearing rain-water has gradually eaten into cracks in the limestone. During high seas, these subterranean caverns become blowholes as the waves surge in under huge pressure and explode in a plume of spray. The Pancake Rocks and blowholes are easily accessible from the main highway via the short Dolomite Point walk. Wheelchair access, if assisted, is also possible.

Other short walks as well as longer tramps are available in the park, including the 15-minute Truman Track through subtropical forest to a wild coastline featuring caverns, a blowhole and waterfall, and the two-hour walk to a huge limestone structure known as "the ballroom overhang". A two- to three-day tramp through the heart of the park follows a pack track, built in 1867 to avoid dangerous travel along the isolated and rugged coastline.

Left Bank Art Gallery

## ⑬ Greymouth

**Road map** C5. 🏔️ 13,500. 🚆 🚌 ℹ️ Cnr Herbert & Mackay sts, (03) 768 5101. 🌐 **west-coast.co.nz**

The largest town on the West Coast, Greymouth occupies the site of what was once Mawhera Pa. Although colonial government agents purchased the majority of the West Coast in 1860 for £300, the land under modern Greymouth remained a Maori reserve. Greymouth was laid out in 1865. Around this time, gold was being found in large quantities in the area, and coal had been discovered 17 years earlier. When the gold boom ended, coal mining ensured the district's continued survival. However, the Grey River mouth, which has served the town as a port, has also delivered misfortune. Repeatedly throughout its history, Greymouth has been submerged by flood waters, including twice in 1988. Since then a flood wall has been erected, popularly called "the great wall of Greymouth".

Greymouth's **History House Museum** has a large collection of historical photographs giving insight into the town's heritage. The **Left Bank Art Gallery** features an important greenstone collection, crafted in both contemporary and traditional designs, and hosts a major exhibition every few years. It also displays local art works.

Like other West Coast towns, Greymouth offers a range of adventure tourism activities, including floating through the Taniwha Caves on inflated tubes, and dolphin watching. The Grey River system is known for good fishing.

🏛️ **History House Museum**
Gresson St. **Tel** (03) 768 4028.
**Open** summer: daily; winter: Mon–Fri
**Closed** 25 Dec. 🖼️ ♿

🏛️ **Left Bank Art Gallery**
1 Tainui St. **Tel** (03) 768 0038.
**Open** summer: daily; winter: Tue–Sat
**Closed** 25 Dec, 1 Jan. 🖼️ ♿ 🎥 by arrangement. 📷

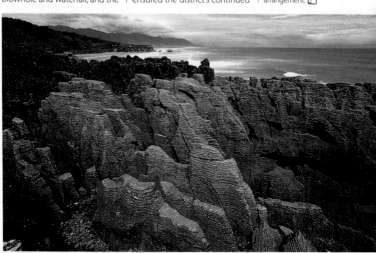

Pancake Rocks at Dolomite Point, Punakaiki

Street in Shantytown, a replica gold-mining town

## Environs
One of Greymouth's most popular attractions is **Shantytown**, 11 km (7 miles) south. This elaborate replica gold-mining town includes a 1913 steam train which travels through native bush to a working sawmill and gold claim where visitors can try gold panning and perhaps find a few specks of gold.

**Lake Brunner**, a restful, scenic spot surrounded by bush-clad mountains 42 km (26 miles) from Greymouth, is excellent for fishing, boating and water sports. The lake area is serviced by the small town of Moana, located at the northern end of Lake Brunner. There is a daily bus between Moana and Greymouth and the TranzAlpine scenic train, which leaves daily from Christchurch, is rated amongst the world's best scenic routes.

### Shantytown
Rutherglen Rd, Paroa, Greymouth. **Tel** 0800 742 689, (03) 762 6634. **Open** daily. **Closed** 25 Dec. 🦽🖥📷

## 🟤 Hokitika
**Road map** C5. 🏔 3,600. ✈ 2 km (1.2 miles) N of town. 🚌 ℹ 36 Weld St, (03) 755 6166. 🎪 Wildfoods Festival (Mar). 🖥 **hokitika.org** and 🖥 **wildfoods.co.nz**

With its wide streets, notable historic buildings and excellent local craft studios, Hokitika is perhaps the West Coast's most attractive town. Little more than a shanty town in 1864, by 1866 Hokitika had become a thriving commercial centre thanks to gold. Its river port bustled with ships bearing miners flocking from the goldfields of Australia, but it was a treacherous harbour where a ship went down every 10 weeks in the years 1865 and 1866. The wreck of one such ship is on the self-guided Hokitika Heritage Trail, which includes 22 historic buildings and sights. The most impressive of these is the 1908 Carnegie Library, now the home of the town's information centre and the **Historic Carnegie Complex and Museum**. The museum has displays on gold-mining and an audiovisual display of the town's history. It also houses a collection of rare books about the West Coast.

The **National Kiwi Centre** is a small wildlife centre specializing in kiwi, tuatara, giant long-finned eels and the tiny whitebait for which the West Coast's rivers are renowned. The remarkable Glowworm Dell, on the northern edge of the town, is worth a visit after dark. The best time to view the lights exuded by these carnivorous larvae is on a wet night.

### 🏛 Historic Carnegie Complex and Museum
Carnegie Centre, Cnr Tancred & Hamilton Sts. **Tel** (03) 755 6898. **Open** daily. **Closed** 25 Dec. 🦽♿

### ⛨ National Kiwi Centre
64 Tancred St. **Tel** (03) 755 5251. **Open** daily. **Closed** 1 Jan, 25 Dec. 🦽♿📷

## Environs
There are a number of scenic areas around Hokitika. **Lake Mahinapua**, 10 km (6 miles) south, and **Lake Kaniere**, 20 km (12 miles) east of the town, are peaceful retreats, popular for boating, fishing, swimming and bush walking. The Lake Kaniere Walkway is 13 km (8 miles) and takes about four hours. **Ross** township, 28 km (17 miles) south of Hokitika, has a small local museum devoted to its colourful gold-mining history. Walks take visitors past old gold mine workings. New Zealand's biggest gold nugget was discovered here in 1909, and the area – said still to contain many millions of dollars worth of gold – is again being mined.

Hokitika clock tower

## Greenstone
Nephrite jade (pounamu), locally known as greenstone, is a hard, opaque, emerald stone. Formed in alpine fault lines under intense heat and pressure, greenstone boulders are eventually flushed from the eroding mountains into West Coast rivers. Greenstone holds great spiritual significance for Maori. Long before European colonization, tribes sent missions to search for the precious stone, later bartering it for food and other items. It was the hardest material known to Maori and was used for making tools, weapons and items of personal adornment. In 1997, ownership of the greenstone resource on the West Coast was handed back to the South Island Ngai Tahu tribe as part of a major Treaty of Waitangi settlement (see p57).

Artisan at the Mountain Jade Greenstone Factory

# ⓯ Westland/Tai Poutini National Park

Stretching from the top of the Southern Alps in the east, where it shares a common boundary with Aoraki/Mount Cook National Park, to the Tasman Sea in the west, this 1,270-sq-km (490-sq-mile) national park is renowned for its mountain peaks (which reach a height of 3,500 m or 11,500 ft), dramatic glaciers, dense rainforest, coastal lagoons and beautiful lakes. Despite the intrusions of the West Coast gold rush of the 1860s and pastoral farming on the river flats, the area has remained largely unspoiled.

**Guided Glacier Tours**
This is one of the best ways to experience the glaciers in the park. Ski-plane and helicopter tours also allow stunning views.

★ **Lake Matheson**
On clear, still mornings, Aoraki/Mount Cook and Mount Tasman are reflected in the lake, which is enveloped by forest.

0 kilometres    6
0 yards         6

## KEY

① **The Copland Valley Track**, accessible from State Highway 6, is popular with trampers. For experienced climbers, the track continues over the Copland Pass and ends at Mount Cook village.

② **Gillespies Beach**, a historic gold-mining settlement 20 km (12 miles) from Fox Glacier, offers walks along an early miners' track and to a fur seal colony along the beach.

③ **Okarito Lagoon**, one of New Zealand's largest wetland areas, is home to abundant birdlife, including the rare white heron (see p197).

④ **Lake Mapourika**, at the northern end of the park, is a favourite spot for picnickers.

⑤ **Aoraki/Mount Cook and Mount Tasman**, New Zealand's two highest peaks, stand behind Fox Glacier.

## Key

▬▬ State highway
▬▬ Minor road
▬ River
- - Walking track
—•— Park boundary

*TASMAN SEA*

Gillespies Point

Gillespies Cook River Road

Cook River

*KARANGARUA FOREST*

Karangarua River

*COPLAND RAN*

Copland Track

Copland Ri

*ROCKY RANGE*

*HOOKER*

**Lowland rainforest**
The park's extremely high rainfall (5,000 mm or 200 inches a year at Franz Josef village) supports lush, densely ferned lowland podocarp forest, featuring local species.

## VISITORS' CHECKLIST

**Practical Information**
Road map B6. **w** doc.govt.nz
**i** Franz Josef Glacier village:
(03) 752 0796; Fox Glacier village:
(03) 751 0044. **Open** daily. **Closed**
25 Dec. obligatory on glaciers.

**Transport**

★ **Franz Josef Glacier**
A two-hour or so walk up the Waiho
River from the Franz Josef Glacier
village leads to the terminal face.

★ **Fox Glacier**
Because of the risk of rock and ice falls, it is safe for
visitors to walk only with a guide on the Fox Glacier,
the largest glacier in the park.

## Movement of a Glacier

A glacier is a large body of ice that forms on land
and moves slowly downhill at a rate of about
1.5 m (5 ft) a day. Glaciers are fed by snow
accumulating in high-altitude basins (névés)
where it condenses to form bluish ice. This ice
field flows downhill under its own weight,
cracking into a jumble of deep crevasses and
collecting moraine (debris) which scours the
mountain sides to form U-shaped valleys. The
glacier ends at a terminal where the ice melts.
The Franz Josef Glacier 11 km (7 miles) long and
Fox Glacier 13 km (8 miles) long, are unique in
that they descend from regions of perpetual
snow to rainforest close to the coast.

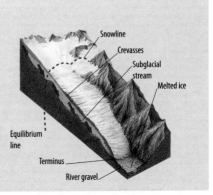

Snowline
Crevasses
Subglacial
stream
Melted ice
Equilibrium
line
Terminus
River gravel

Cave Stream, Arthur's Pass ▶

# ⓰ Arthur's Pass Driving Tour

Arthur's Pass road is the highest and most spectacular highway across the Southern Alps. From Springfield, the road climbs steeply to the 945-m (3,100-ft) Porters Pass before travelling through wide, tussock-covered basins hemmed by mountains and past dramatic limestone outcrops. Entering the eastern flank of Arthur's Pass National Park, the road is enveloped by mountain beech forest. It then climbs to the 920-m (3,017-ft) Arthur's Pass summit, before descending steeply on the western side of the Southern Alps.

### ① Porters Pass and Lake Lyndon
This area is characterized by distinctive dryland native fauna. Lake Lyndon is a good bird-watching spot in summer and a natural skating rink during the winter months.

### ② Porters Ski Field
This is the closest ski area to Christchurch and one of six ski fields along State Highway 73. Other than Porters, all are small fields run by local ski clubs where visitors are welcome.

Kumara Junction

Lake Brunner

Taramakau River

Hokitika

Otira

Arthur's Pass National Park

Arthur's Pass

### ⑩ Jacksons Pub
This is all that remains of what was once a busy railhead and staging post.

Cass

Bealey

### ⑨ Otira Viaduct
Completed in 1999, this section of State Highway 73 spans the rugged Otira River.

### ⑧ Beech Forests
The forests on the eastern side of the park are dominated by a canopy of mountain beech, and thus are dramatically different from the dense and varied forests on the western side.

**Key**

▬ Tour route
⎓ Other road
═ River

### Castle Hill

The large limestone rock formations of Castle Hill are eerily impressive, and very popular with rock climbers. The area has historical significance to Maori as a seasonal food-gathering spot and as part of the route used by Maori to reach the West Coast.

### Craigieburn Forest Park

The beech-covered hills in the park are popular spots for walking, picnicking and mountain biking.

**⑥ Lake Pearson**
Lake Pearson and nearby Lake Grasmere are both good trout fishing spots. Lake Pearson is also known for its beautiful mountain reflections.

**⑦ Bealey Spur**
A rustic cluster of holiday homes marks Bealey Spur, at the fringe of Arthur's Pass National Park.

**Springfield**

0 kilometres        20
0 miles             20

**Tips For Drivers**

**Tour length from Springfield to Kumara Junction:** 160 km (100 miles). This is an alpine route that is sometimes closed after snow, and drivers should check conditions.
**Stopping-off points:** There are many scenic viewpoints and lay-bys along the route. Arthur's Pass is the only township offering services between Kumara and Springfield, although there are hotels at Jacksons and Bealey.

### ④ Cave Stream

This 360-m (1,180-ft) limestone cave takes about two hours to navigate, and requires sturdy footwear, warm clothing and a good torch.

The road to Arthur's Pass

## ⑰ Arthur's Pass

**Road map** C5. 🚶 50. 🚌 🚉 ℹ️
Dept of Conservation, State Hwy 73, Arthur's Pass, (03) 318 9211.

The tiny village of Arthur's Pass is nestled in a valley about 5 km (3 miles) east of the summit of Arthur's Pass. It was originally the camping site of contractors engaged to push the road through from Christchurch to the West Coast in 1865–6. In 1908, workers at Arthur's Pass village and at Otira, on the western side of the Main Divide, began construction of the 8-km (5-mile) Otira rail tunnel. In 1912, the population of Arthur's Pass had swelled to about 300, comprised mainly of tunnel workers. It took 10 years for the two ends of the tunnel to meet, and another 5 years before the first train travelled through it. A number of tunnellers' cottages remain in the village, now used as private holiday homes.

Since the 1920s, the village has been a base for day-trippers from Christchurch and Greymouth, walkers, trampers, and mountaineers, as well as skiers who enjoy the splendid views and low-key atmosphere of the nearby Temple Basin ski field. It is also the headquarters of Arthur's Pass National Park (*see pp248–9*).

An original tunneller's cottage at Arthur's Pass village

# ⑱ Arthur's Pass National Park

Straddling the Southern Alps 153 km (95 miles) from Christchurch and 98 km (60 miles) from Greymouth, the 1,147-sq-km (443-sq-mile) Arthur's Pass National Park, the seventh largest in the country, is a place of huge geological and climatic contrasts. On the western side of the alps, where the rainfall is high, the park is clad in dense and varied rainforest through which steep, boulder-strewn rivers rush; on the drier eastern side, mountain beech forests and tussock-covered river flats predominate. Sixteen mountain peaks in the park exceed 2,000 m (6,560 ft). The park offers the well-equipped outdoor enthusiast superb mountain climbing and tramping opportunities, as well as many shorter walks suitable for people of all ages and fitness levels.

**★ Dobson Nature Walk**
This 30-minute walk on the Arthur's Pass summit gives an excellent introduction to the area's alpine and subalpine plants, which bloom from November to February.

Otira Track
*Otira River*

ARTHUR'S PASS
920 m (3,017 ft)                     Upper

▲
MOUNT ROLLESTON        *Bealey River*
2,275 m (7,462 ft)

Bridal
Walk

▲ MOUNT LANCELOT
2,112 m (6,927 ft)

Scotts Track

AVALANCHE PEAK ▲
1,833 m (6,012 ft)        Avalanche
Peak Track

*Crow River*

MOUNT BEALEY
1,836 m (6,022 ft)

*Waimakariri River*

**Bealey Valley**
A walking track leads from State Highway 73 through mountain beech forest to the beautiful Bealey Valley. It takes about three to four hours' return to complete the walk.

**★ Devil's Punchbowl Waterfall**
Although the top of this 131-m (430-ft) waterfall can be seen from the main road, a one-hour walk from Arthur's Pass village takes visitors to the base of the falls.

**Kea**
These cheeky, inquisitive alpine parrots are sometimes seen in Arthur's Pass village, pecking the rubber from around car windscreens.

**For additional map symbols** *see back flap*

## VISITORS' CHECKLIST

**Practical Information**
Road map C5. **W** doc.govt.nz
**i** Arthur's Pass village, (03) 318
9211. **Open** daily. **Closed** 25 Dec.
**d** in village only; not on tracks.

**Transport**

**Temple Basin**
Campers can enjoy great views
of Temple Basin's mountains and
valleys. In winter, the ski field is
accessible only by foot.

## Flora and Fauna in Arthur's Pass National Park

As well as the impressive mountain beech forests in the east and
mixed rainforest in the west, the park contains a wide variety of
alpine and subalpine plant species,
including tussock, snow grass,
alpine daisies and herbs, sedge and
ourisia. The park is also rich in
birdlife, and species such as the
paradise shelduck, bellbird, silvereye,
fantail, kea and rifleman are often
seen or heard. The area is home to a
number of rare species, including
the alpine rock wren, blue duck and
great spotted kiwi.

Blue ducks

**MOUNT TEMPLE**
1,913 m (6,274 ft)

**MOUNT OATES**
2,041 m (6,694 ft)

**MOUNT AIKEN**
1,859 m (6,097 ft)

**MOUNT WILLIAMS**
1,718 m (5,635 ft)

*Otis River*

*Edwards River*

0 kilometres          5

0 miles               5

### Key

▬ State highway

▬ Minor road

— River

- - Walking track

— Tranz Alpine Express route

– – Tunnel

**Waimakariri River**
The sinuous strands
of this mighty river
transport rock and
shingle from the
Southern Alps
*(see p195).*

Klondyke Corner

*Waimakariri River*

**BEALEY SPUR**
920 m (3,017 ft)          Bealey Spur

**Bealey Spur Village**
Tussock-covered valleys give
way to tall, craggy hills as the
road approaches Bealey Spur.

## Tips for Walkers

The valleys, alpine passes and
scree- and tussock-covered
mountainsides of the park offer
a range of graded walks, from
short, easy strolls to demanding
climbs. However, the climate in
the park is highly changeable and
many routes rudimentary, so it
is important for tramping and
climbing parties to register their
intentions with the visitor centre
at Arthur's Pass village.

Mount Hutt ski field with Lake Coleridge in the distance

## ⓲ Mount Hutt

**Road map** C6. 🚍 ℹ️ 121 Main St, Methven, (03) 302 8955. 🎿 New Zealand Walking Festival (Apr).

Mount Hutt, in the foot hills of the Southern Alps, is Canterbury's largest ski field, and claims to have the longest ski season in Australasia (early June to mid-October). The ski field is served by nine lifts and tows, as well as artificial snow-making facilities. From the 2,075-m (6,808-ft) mountain, there are excellent views over the Canterbury Plains.

**Environs**
The town of **Methven** serves as Mount Hutt's après-ski centre in winter, and reverts in summer to a typical New Zealand farming town. The 42-sq-km (16-sq-mile) Mount Hutt Conservation Area, 14 km (9 miles) west of the town, has a number of short walking tracks through native forest dominated by mountain beech. The Rakaia Gorge, about 16 km (10 miles) north of Methven, is popular for jet-boating. A 5-km (3-mile) walkway traverses its edge.

## ⓳ Rakaia

**Road map** C6. 🚶 800. 🚍 🎣 Rakaia Salmon Fishing Competition (end Feb).

Located on the southern bank of the Rakaia River, the small farming settlement of Rakaia claims to be "the salmon capital of New Zealand". A large

fibreglass fish in the middle of the township celebrates the excellent salmon and trout fishing to be had at various spots along the river.

Bridge over the Rakaia Gorge, a popular place for jet-boating

## ⓴ Ashburton

**Road map** C6. 🚶 16,000. 🚂 🚍 ℹ️ The Green, East St, (03) 308 1050. 🎡 Wheels Week (May).

Ashburton straddles the Ashburton River and is the principal town in the farming district of mid-Canterbury. The town was named after Lord Ashburton, a member of the Canterbury Association, which settled the province in the 1850s. Although originally dry and tussock covered, irrigation has allowed agriculture to flourish. The well-laid out town has historic brick buildings and many mature trees, including some in the Ashburton Domain. **Ashford Village** produces and

sells a variety of high quality craft work and has a museum housing spinning wheels.

### 🏛 Ashford Village
427 West St. **Tel** (03) 308 9085. **Open** daily. **Closed** 1 & 2 Jan, Good Fri, Easter Mon, 25 & 26 Dec. 🎟 in factory. ♿ 🅿️ required in factory. 🖥 📷

## ㉒ Geraldine

**Road map** C6. 🚶 2,000. 🚍 ℹ️ Cnr of Cox & Talbot sts, (03) 693 1006. 🎡 Geraldine Arts and Plants Festival (Nov). 🌐 southcanterbury.org.nz

This attractive small farming town is a popular stopover for travellers heading south to the Mackenzie Country. First known as Talbot Forest, then Fitzgerald and finally Geraldine, in 1866, it began as a sheep run and base for sawmillers. Talbot Forest now refers to the lowland podocarp forest which provides a backdrop to Geraldine. The town still has many historic buildings, such as the 1908 Post Office, which can be seen on a self-guided walking trail.

Locally produced juices and condiments can be sampled at **Four Peaks Plaza**. The **Vintage Car and Machinery Museum** has cars dating from 1907 to 1953 and tractors from 1874 as well as a large amount of early agricultural machinery.

### 🏞 Four Peaks Plaza
76 Talbot St. **Tel** (03) 693 9727. **Open** daily. **Closed** 25 Dec. ♿ 📷

### 🏛 Vintage Car and Machinery Museum
178 Talbot St. **Tel** (03) 693 8756. **Open** daily in summer; weekends only in winter. **Closed** 1 Jan, 25 & 26 Dec. 🎟 ♿ 🅿️ by arrangement.

**Environs**
The town is a good base for exploring the forests and rivers of Canterbury, including Peel Forest, 22 km (13 miles) north of Geraldine, as well as the Mount Somers Conservation Area, 47 km (29 miles) north, and the Orari, Waihi and Te Moana gorges, 15 km (9 miles) north, which are good spots for rafting, swimming and picnicking.

# High Country Farming

When the "Canterbury Pilgrims" arrived in 1850 to establish their new settlement, they quickly saw the potential of pastoral farming, and the runholders – the farmers who grazed Canterbury's extensive plains, downs, interior and high country – soon became a powerful economic and political force. Although land reform in the late 19th century saw the great estates broken up, large high country stations, where much of the land is leased, have remained a feature of farming in New Zealand, particularly in Canterbury. Good roads and modern communications have reduced the isolation and harshness of station life, but it remains a unique existence defined by the climate and the topography of the high country and the annual cycle of farming.

### The Annual Cycle

Stock graze the tussock-covered mountainsides over the summer, and are mustered down to lower ground before winter. This task takes several days and is carried out on horseback or on foot with the aid of teams of highly trained sheepdogs. As shearing, lambing and weaning are completed, stock are released back to the high country for the summer.

Mustering sheep

**Selling and buying sheep** is a serious business at local livestock auctions as sheep farmers seek to buy stock that will improve the quantity and quality of their wool and meat production.

**Shearing** is done by skilled teams of contractors, often using manual blade shears which leave a protective layer of wool on the sheep's back. The dominant breed farmed on high county farms is the fine-woolled and hardy merino.

**Fodder crops**, such as hay and silage, are grown on the farms as supplementary feed for sheep during the cold winter months.

**Roast lamb** served with vegetables such as baked potatoes, carrots and peas is a favourite traditional meal.

**Merino wool** from the high country farms of the South Island is very fine, and is used to make luxury knitwear and fine suiting fabrics.

# ㉓ Timaru

About halfway between Christchurch to the north and Dunedin to the south is Timaru. It is built on rolling hills marking the edge of the Canterbury Plains and is the largest town in South Canterbury. Its name derives from Te Maru, meaning "a place of shelter", denoting its historical importance as a safe haven for Maori canoes travelling the coast. It was a whaling station from 1838. The town centre is built on 0.5 sq km (0.2 sq mile) of land acquired by early settlers George and Robert Rhodes, although settlement did not begin in earnest until 1859. Today, Timaru has the appearance of a sturdy and well-appointed regional capital, with many notable buildings gracing its commercial heart.

![Aigantighe gallery with new extension and grounds]

Aigantighe gallery with new extension and grounds

## 🏖 Caroline Bay

From 1877, when Timaru's artificial port was first created, the white sand of Caroline Bay accumulated beside it to form a safe and popular swimming beach. The port flanks the southern end of the beach. Behind the beach is an extensive grassed area with a children's playground, an aviary, tennis courts and a mini-golf course. Large-scale redevelopment has added a seaside boardwalk, viewing platforms, volleyball courts and other recreational facilities. The Piazza, a series of staircases and platforms and a lift, links the bay with the central city on the hill above. To the north of the bay are the Benvenue Cliffs and the 1877 Timaru Lighthouse.

## ⛪ Basilica of the Sacred Heart

7 Craigie Ave. **Tel** (03) 684 4263.
**Open** daily. 🏛 daily. ♿
Arguably the most impressive of the many distinguished buildings in Timaru, Basilica of the Sacred Heart was designed by Francis William Petre and built in 1910–11. Its twin towers and large dome overlook the main route south through the city, and house an equally majestic interior featuring stencilled ceilings, large white pillars and stained-glass windows. Petre also designed the Catholic cathedrals in Christchurch and Dunedin.

## 🏛 Aigantighe

49 Wa-iti Rd. **Tel** (03) 688 4424. **Open**
Tue–Sun. **Closed** 1 & 2 Jan, 25 & 26 Dec. 🚻 ♿ 📷 by arrangement.
This charming museum, pronounced "egg and tie" ("at home" in Scottish Gaelic) is housed in a 1908 building bequeathed to the city by Alexander and Helen Grant, Scottish immigrants who had farmed in the Mackenzie Country. It opened as an art museum in 1956, with much of its fascinating collection donated by the Grant family. Its permanent collection includes works by New Zealand and British painters, as well as English and continental china. The well laid out gallery sits amid a restful garden, which features a permanent exhibition of stone sculptures.

## ⛪ St Mary's Anglican Church

Church St. **Tel** (03) 688 8377.
**Closed** until further notice for earthquake reinforcement.
The foundation stone for St Mary's Anglican Church was laid in 1880, and its nave was consecrated in 1886. The interior of the church features high ribbed ceilings, many fine stained-glass windows, intricate wooden carvings and sturdy columns.
Many of the art pieces and plaques in the church bear the names of influential colonial families in South Canterbury. Steps in the tower can be climbed for an excellent view of the city.

### Richard Pearse

Inventor, aviator and farmer, Richard Pearse (1877–1953) has for decades been at the centre of debate about who was the first to achieve powered flight. Pearse was born near Temuka, north of Timaru, and although ridiculed in his lifetime, has been posthumously recognized as an inventive genius. In his farm workshop he constructed a monoplane of bamboo, aluminium, wire and canvas. His first flight in the aircraft is said to have covered 46–91 m (150–300 ft), ending with a crash into a hedge. No records were kept of the flight, but there is some eyewitness evidence that it occurred on 31 March 1903 – about nine months before the 13 December 1903 flight of Orville and Wilbur Wright, officially regarded as the first in the world. Some people even put the date at 1902.

Replica of Pearse's monoplane

Roses in the Timaru Botanic Gardens

## 🌿 Timaru Botanic Gardens

Queen St. **Tel** (03) 687 7200.
**Open** daily. ♿

Opened in 1864, the gardens comprise 19 ha (50 acres) of undulating landforms and water features. Notable highlights include a 1913 statue of Scottish poet Robert Burns, a cabbage tree believed to date from pre-European times and a 1911 band rotunda. The gardens also boast a fine rose collection as well as many rare and threatened plants. The conservatory complex houses desert, tropical and subtropical collections.

## 🏛 South Canterbury Museum

Perth St. **Tel** (03) 684 2212.
**Open** Tue– Sun. **Closed** 1 Jan, 25 & 26 Dec. ♿

This octagonal-shaped museum, opened in 1966, is the main regional museum. Its collections cover the natural history of the area, local Maori history, the early whaling industry and European settlement. The development of the city is shown in a series of photographs. A highlight is a replica of the airplane built by Temuka farmer Richard Pearse, who is believed to have successfully flown in 1903, possibly before the Wright brothers in the US. The plane is suspended from the ceiling at about the height at which Pearse is thought to have flown.

### Environs

**Temuka**, about 18 km (11 miles) north of Timaru, is the service centre for a rich farming hinterland, and is also the home of the well-known Temuka Homeware, which makes a wide range of high-quality household ceramics. Although the factory is not open to the public, there is a separate factory shop on the State Highway 1 bypass in Temuka.

State Highway 8 to Tekapo passes through the small

township of Pleasant Point, where the **Pleasant Point Museum & Railway** retains a 2-km (1.2-mile) section of the old Timaru to Fairlie line, built in 1875 and closed in 1968. Two steam locomotives ply the track on school and public holidays. The road winds through rolling green farmland and passes through the small towns of Cave, Fairlie and Kimbell, and the turn-off to Mount Dobson Ski Field, before reaching Burkes Pass, which is the entrance to the Mackenzie Country.

## 🚂 Pleasant Point Museum & Railway

Main Rd. **Tel** (03) 614 8323.
**Open** variable. ♿ 🚻

## Timaru City Centre

① Caroline Bay
② Aigantighe
③ St Mary's Church
④ South Canterbury Museum
⑤ Basilica of the Sacred Heart
⑥ Timaru Botanic Gardens

0 metres  500
0 yards   500

**For keys to symbols** *see back flap*

Lupins on the shores of Lake Tekapo

## ❷❹ Lake Tekapo

**Road map** B6. 🏔 300. 🚌 ℹ️ Kiwi
Treasures, State Hwy 8, (03) 680 6686.
🌐 mtcooknz.com

Lake Tekapo is a place of
exceptional beauty and clarity.
The remarkable blue of the lake
is caused by "rock flour" – finely
ground particles of rock
brought down by the glaciers at
the head of the lake and held in
suspension in the melt water.
The lake is a very popular venue
for fishing, boating, kayaking,
swimming and hang-gliding.

On the lake front stands the
Church of the Good Shepherd.
The foundation stone of this
stone-and-oak church was laid
in 1935 by the Duke of
Gloucester. The front window
of the church creates a perfect
frame for a view of the lake.
Next to the church is a bronze
statue of a sheep dog, erected
in 1968 as a tribute to the
important role played by these
animals in the development of
high country farming.

Because of the purity of the
atmosphere above Lake Tekapo,
the University of Canterbury has
an observatory atop Mount
John to the west of the
township. There is a popular
walkway to the top of the
mountain (about three hours
return). Cowan's Hill Track (about
two hours) also provides good
views of the lake and mountains.

Lake Tekapo Village is a good
base for skiing at Mount Dobson,
Roundhill and Ohau, about 30 km
(18 miles) away, while the town's
small tourist airport is also a
base for scenic flights over
Mount Cook. Lake Alexandrina,
10 km (6 miles) from Tekapo, is
renowned for its trout fishing.

🏛 **Church of the Good Shepherd**
Pioneer Drive. **Tel** (03) 680 6516.
**Open** daily. **Closed** 25 Dec, weddings.
🕐 variable. 🎫 donation. ♿ 📷

## ❷❺ Lake Pukaki

**Road map** B6. ℹ️ State Hwy 8, (03)
435 3280. 🌐 mountcooknz.com

Like Lake Tekapo, Lake Pukaki is
a place of majestic scenery.
State Highway 8 hugs the
southern tip of the lake, and a
large and popular lay-by and

picnic area allows stunning
views of Mount Cook and the
Southern Alps. The lake is fed
by the Tasman River, which
flows off the Tasman Glacier. It
has been artificially raised as
part of the Upper Waitaki
hydroelectricity network and is
linked by canals to Lake Tekapo
and Lake Ohau. On a clear day,
Mount Cook is reflected in the
waters of the lake.

**Mount Cook Alpine Salmon**
is a farm on the Pukaki–Tekapo
canal. It sells fresh salmon and
offers tours.

**Glentanner Park Centre**,
about 20 km (12 miles) south
of Mount Cook village, on the
shores of Lake Pukaki, is a major
base for flightseeing over
Mount Cook. Other activites run
from the centre include horse
trekking, mountain biking, boat
trips, hunting and fishing. The

Glentanner Park Centre, backed by the Southern Alps

centre is set amid Glentanner Station, a 182-sq-km (70-sq-mile) high country farm. Occasional short tours of the farm allow visitors to see sheep shearing and sheepdog demonstrations.

**Mount Cook Alpine Salmon**
Canal Rd. **Tel** (03) 435 0085.
**Open** daily. 🅿 ♿ 📷 🏠

**Glentanner Park Centre**
State Hwy 80. **Tel** (03) 435 1855.
**Open** daily. 🅿 for activities. ♿ some activities. 🔵 **glentanner.co.nz**

## ㉖ Twizel

**Road map** B6. 👥 1,500. 🚌 ℹ
Twizel Events Centre, Market Place, (03) 435 3124. 🔵 **twizel.com**

Twizel was built in 1969 as a construction town for the Upper Waitaki hydro-electric development scheme. Once the hydro scheme was completed, the local people successfully fought to retain the town, and began to exploit its proximity to excellent fishing and boating lakes, and to Mount Cook 61 km (37 miles) away.
Lake Ruataniwha, a man-made lake just south of Twizel, is popular for water sports. It has an international standard rowing course and is the site of national rowing events every year. From Lake Ruataniwha, a sealed back road leads to Lake Benmore, a 75-sq-km (29-sq-mile) hydroelectric dam that has also become a favourite boating destination.

One of Twizel's most important attractions is the **Kaki Visitor Hide**. The kakī, or black stilt, is one of the rarest wading birds in the world, and the species has been subject to intensive conservation management since 1981 *(see p196)*. Visitors can take tours to view captive breeding birds from specially designed hides.

**Kaki Visitor Hide**
Twizel Events Centre, Market Place.
**Tel** (03) 435 3124. 📷 daily (except 25 Dec). 🅿 ♿

Clay cliffs at Omarama

### Environs
South of Twizel, on State Highway 8, lies the small town of **Omarama**. The town has a worldwide reputation for gliding because of its strong northwest thermal updraughts. Various gliding records have been set from Omarama.

About 10 km (6 miles) west of the town are the **Clay Cliffs**, a set of steep, high pinnacles separated by deep, narrow ravines. The cliffs are believed to have been frequented by early Maori travelling into the Mackenzie Country to hunt. Although privately owned, the cliffs are protected by covenant, and are accessible to the public.

Kaki/Black stilt

**Clay Cliffs**
Henburn Rd. **Tel** (03) 438 9780.
**Open** daily. 🅿

## ㉗ Lake Ohau

**Road map** B6.

About 30 km (18 miles) to the west of Twizel, Lake Ohau is a popular swimming, fishing, skiing and boating spot. The six native forests which surround the lake – the Ohau, Temple, Dobson, Huxley, Hopkins and Ahuriri – also provide excellent tramping and walking opportunities. Many huts are scattered in the forests for the use of more experienced trampers.

The Ohau ski field, overlooking the western side of the lake, is a commercial ski field serviced by basic facilities, such as a T-bar and platter lift.

### Upper Waitaki Hydro Development Scheme

The power stations of the Upper Waitaki and Mackenzie Country provide about one-third of New Zealand's hydro-electricity. The idea of harnessing the water resources of the region was first mooted in 1904, and today the vast scheme includes the Tekapo A and B power stations, Ohau A, B and C stations, and Benmore, Aviemore and Waitaki stations. An important feature of the scheme is 58 km (36 miles) of man-made canals, which pool the resources of Lakes Tekapo, Pukaki and Ohau, along which there is an attractive scenic drive. The lakes created by the hydro scheme have become popular venues for water sports.

Lake Benmore from the adjacent hills

# ㉘ Aoraki/Mount Cook National Park

Aoraki/Mount Cook National Park takes its name from Aoraki/Mount Cook, which at 3,754 m (12,316 ft) is New Zealand's highest mountain. It is sacred to the Ngai Tahu tribe of the South Island, and Maori legend has it that the mountain and its companion peaks were formed when a boy named Aoraki and his three brothers came down from the heavens to visit Papatuanuku (Earth Mother) in a canoe. The canoe overturned, and as the brothers moved to the back of the boat they turned to stone. The 700-sq-km (270-sq-mile) area was designated a national park in 1953 and includes 19 peaks over 3,000 m (9,842 ft). Glaciers cover 40 per cent of the park.

**Flightseeing**
Scenic flights operate from Glentanner Park Centre and Mount Cook Airport. They fly a range of routes over the park, and many include a landing on a glacier.

**★ Aoraki/Mount Cook**
A premier mountaineering destination, Aoraki/Mount Cook was first climbed in 1894 by New Zealanders Tom Fyfe, George Graham and Jack Clarke.

**DOUGLAS PEAK**
3,085 m (10,120 ft)

**MOUNT TASMAN ▲**
3,498 m (11,475 ft)

**MOUNT HICKS ▲**
3,198 m (10,492 ft)

**MOUNT DAM**
3,440 m (11,2

**AORAKI/MOUNT COO**
3,754 m (12,316 ft)

HOOKER GLACIER

MOUNT COOK RANGE

TASMAN

Hooker ①

Valley Track

**THE FOOTSTOOL**
2,764 m (9,068 ft)

**MOUNT SEFTON**
3,151 m (10,838 ft)

MUELLER GLACIER

SEALY RANGE

Mount Cook

Hooker River

Tasman Valley Road

Tasman River

SH 80

80

**The Hermitage**
First built in 1884 at White Horse Campground, then rebuilt and expanded over the years, The Hermitage is a major hotel in Aoraki/Mount Cook National Park *(see p306)*.

**KEY**

① **Copland Pass** is a high-altitude mountaineering route across the Southern Alps. From the pass the route travels down the Copland River through Westland/Tai Poutini National Park *(see pp242–3)* before emerging on State Highway 6.

② **The Godley River** can be reached from Lake Tekapo along a 4WD vehicle track.

**★ Tasman Glacier**
The Tasman Glacier, the largest in New Zealand, is 27 km (16 miles) long and up to 3 km (1.8 miles) wide. Heli-skiing is a popular way to experience the glacier.

## VISITORS' CHECKLIST

**Practical Information**
Road map A6. **W** doc.govt.nz
**i** Bowen Drive, Mount Cook
village, (03) 435 1186. **Open** daily.
**Closed** 25 Dec. **&** limited on
tracks. 🚻 🛒 🏨

**Transport**
✈ 5 km (3 miles) S of village. 🚌

**Tasman Saddle Hut**
This is one of 16 alpine huts and
shelters in the park for the use of
trampers and climbers.

HOCHSTETTER DOME
2,822 m (9,258 ft)

DE LA BECHE
2,950 m (9,678 ft)

TASMAN SADDLE
2,435 m (7,988 ft)

TASMAN GLACIER

MALTE BRUN
?9 m (10,495 ft)

MALTE BRUN RANGE

MURCHISON GLACIER

GODLEY GLACIER

Godley River

chison River

LIEBIG RANGE

2

LAKE TEKAPO

**Murchison Glacier**
The Murchison, along with the
Mueller, Hooker, Tasman and
Godley glaciers, dominate the
valley pattern in the park.

### Key

━━━ State highway

━━━ Minor road

〰〰 River

– – Walking track

— • Park boundary

0 kilometres    6

0 miles    6

## Walks From Aoraki/Mount Cook Village

There are several walking tracks in the
vicinity of Aoraki/Mount Cook village which
are well formed and signposted. They are
suitable for people who do not have any
climbing experience.

Kea Point and Governors Bush are short
walking trips which focus on the park's
vegetation and birdlife. Longer walks from
the village include the Sealy Tarns, Hooker
Valley and Red Tarns tracks. Although these
tracks are well marked, the ground is rough
in places and it is advisable to wear stout
shoes or boots and to carry a walking stick.
A warm sweater or jacket is needed for
places exposed to the wind, even
during summer.

Brochures on the walks, giving descriptions and walking times, are available at
the visitor centre in the village.

COPLAND PASS

MUELLER GLACIER

Sealy Track

WHITE HORSE HILL
3,050 m (10,004 ft)

Valley Track

Hooker River

FOLIAGE HILL
793 m (2,601 ft)

Kea Point Nature Walk

Hooker Valley Road

The Hermitage
Aoraki/Mount
Cook Village

Governors Bush Walk

SH 80

Red Tarns Walk

Hooker Corner

Tasman Valley Road

**For additional map symbols** *see back flap*

# OTAGO AND SOUTHLAND

With its high, snow-capped mountains, lush rainforests, dry tussocklands, deep glacial lakes, spectacular beaches and rugged coastlines, the Otago and Southland region is one of extreme natural beauty. Set among the area's untamed wilderness and historic settlements is Queenstown, a world centre for adventure sports and one of New Zealand's foremost tourist destinations.

Before the arrival of the first Europeans, Maori settled in coastal areas where seafood was plentiful, although they also hunted, and collected greenstone (*pounamu*), in the rugged interior. The first Europeans also looked to coastal areas for an environment that would be easy to tame. Members of the Free Church of Scotland were the first to settle the area in an organized way, making Dunedin the centre of their new land. Hopes of an idyllic enclave were dashed in the early 1860s with the discovery of gold.

Gold-miners poured into the inhospitable lands of what is now known as Central Otago, in search of an elusive fortune. The money gold brought to the region saw it leap ahead, and for a time Dunedin became New Zealand's commercial capital. The legacy of the gold mining era lives on in the humblest of stone cottages on remote and rugged landscapes as well as in the splendid buildings that adorn the streets of Dunedin. The region's natural legacy also lives on in many areas, such as the Mount Aspiring and Fiordland national parks, which remain relatively untapped. They are beautifully complemented by other natural attractions, such as Stewart Island and the Catlins area on the southeast coast, while the farmlands that have been tamed provide an attractive contrast. Such is the variety on offer, that each corner of the region provides its own attractions, making exploration very rewarding.

The Octagon in the heart of Dunedin

◀ Mountain view from Glenorchy Lagoon Walkway

# Exploring Otago and Southland

The geography, climate and scenery of the Otago and
Southland region vary greatly over relatively short distances.
To the west, the land rises steeply from the coast through
thick rainforest to 3,000-m (9,900-ft) high mountain peaks in
the space of only 40 km (25 miles) – features that make the
Fiordland and Mount Aspiring national parks so spectacular.
To the east of these peaks, the ranges and valleys of Central
Otago provide a stark contrast. The interior is dry and
rugged. Vivid blue lakes nestle among tussock-covered hills
and snow-capped mountains to create the scenery and
adventure playground that has made resorts such as
Queenstown so popular. From the lakes, the land drops
down to the eastern and southern coasts and hinterland
where extra rainfall has produced fertile farmland to
feed the cities of Dunedin and Invercargill.

White-water rafting, Shotover River,
Queenstown

## Sights at a Glance

1. Dunedin pp262–3
2. Otago Peninsula
3. Moeraki Boulders
   Scenic Reserve
4. Oamaru pp272–3
5. Lindis Pass
6. Lake Hawea
7. Wanaka
8. Mount Aspiring National
   Park pp276–7
9. Haast
10. Queenstown pp280–81
11. Glenorchy
12. Arrowtown
13. Cromwell
14. Kingston
15. Fiordland National
   Park pp284–5
17. Invercargill pp290–91
18. Gore
19. Bluff
20. Stewart Island pp 292–3

### Tours

16. Doubtful Sound
21. Catlins

TASM
SE

George
Sound    Su

Secretary
Island

DOUBTFUL 16
SOUND

Breaksea
Sound

Resolution
Island

Dusky
Sound

West
Cape

Chalky
Inlet

Puysegur
Point

Manapo
Power Stat

Mon

Lake
Hauroko

Lake
Pote

FIORDLAND NATION

Cameron Mountains

## Top Outdoor Activities

The places shown here have been selected for their recreational activities. Conditions vary depending on the weather and the time of year, so exercise caution and, if in doubt, seek local advice.

| | Aerial Sightseeing | Bungy Jumping | Jet-boating | Paragliding | Skiing | Tramping/Walking | White-water Rafting | Wildlife Watching |
|---|---|---|---|---|---|---|---|---|
| Catlins | | | | | | ● | | ● |
| Dunedin | ● | | | | | ● | | ● |
| Fiordland National Park | | | | | | ● | | ● |
| Haast | | | | | | ● | | ● |
| Invercargill | ● | | | | | ● | | ● |
| Milford Sound | ● | | | | | ● | | ● |
| Mount Aspiring National Park | ● | | | | | ● | | ● |
| Oamaru | | | | | | ● | | ● |
| Otago Peninsula | | | | | | ● | | ● |
| Queenstown | ● | ● | ● | ● | ● | ● | ● | |
| Stewart Island | ● | | | | | ● | | ● |
| Te Anau | ● | | ● | | | ● | | ● |
| Wanaka | ● | | ● | ● | ● | ● | ● | |

### Key

▬▬ Motorway
▬ Major road
═══ Minor road
▬ Scenic route
—— Minor railway
▬▬ Regional border
▲ Summit

**For additional map symbols** see back flap

The bright blue Lake Hawea, one of the
largest southern lakes

## Getting Around

Road travel is the main means of getting around the region.
There is a range of bus services along the main routes, and
for those who choose to drive the state highways are good
and generally not too busy, apart from peak holiday
periods. Some roads, such as State Hwy 94 to Milford,
require care because of the mountainous terrain. There are
international airports at Dunedin and Queenstown, while
the airport at Invercargill handles domestic flights.

# ● Dunedin

One of the joys of exploring Dunedin is that there is a great deal to see in a relatively small area. Its buildings are among the most interesting and architecturally diverse in the country. Many that have survived from Dunedin's heyday following the 1860s gold rush, when the city was the country's commercial centre, are within walking distance of the centre. Others are to the north of the city (see pp268–9) in proximity to Dunedin's many beautiful parks and gardens. The relatively flat central city, which remains the retail hub, is surrounded by hills, which afford a splendid view of the city and harbour below.

St Paul's Cathedral

## ⬗ The Octagon

When the site of the settlement of "New Edinburgh" was first surveyed in 1846 by its Edinburgh-based surveyors, The Octagon was planned as the focal point. More than 150 years later, The Octagon continues to fulfil that role. It has watched over a passing parade of festivals, protests, parties and royal visits, as well as seeing sporting heroes waved off and welcomed.

This small oasis in the heart of the city – a popular lunchtime spot – is surrounded by a number of fine buildings. A large bronze statue of Scottish poet Robert Burns, erected in 1887, has a prominent place in front of St Paul's Cathedral. Burns' nephew, the Reverend Thomas Burns, was the spiritual leader for the first group of Scottish settlers to arrive in Dunedin in 1848.

## ⬗ Municipal Chambers

48 The Octagon. **Tel** (03) 477 4000. **Open** Mon–Fri. **Closed** public hols. ✉ inside. ♿ public areas.

Completed in 1880, the Municipal Chambers is an excellent example of the use of Oamaru stone (see pp272–3). It has undergone considerable restoration and refurbishment both inside and out. It is home to the Council Chambers, where city councillors meet, and features a number of reception and meeting rooms. It also houses the Dunedin Visitor Centre, incorporating the 450-seat Glenroy Auditorium and the 2,100-seat Town Hall.

## ⬗ St Paul's Cathedral

The Octagon. **Tel** (03) 477 2336. **Open** daily. ✝ daily except Sat. ♿ ✉ Summer.

Consecrated in 1919, the Anglican St Paul's stands high above The Octagon on an elevated site, with a broad staircase leading to its doors. It owes its prominent position in a predominantly Presbyterian settlement to the generosity of Johnny Jones, an early whaler and trader. The cathedral, which replaced a smaller church built on the site in 1863, has many fine architectural details, including a vaulted stone ceiling.

## ⬗ Dunedin Public Art Gallery

30 The Octagon. **Tel** (03) 477 4000. **Open** daily. **Closed** Good Fri, 25 Dec. 🅿 (special exhibitions only). ✉ ♿ ▭

This modern gallery was designed to harmonize with The Octagon's historic buildings and has one of the best collections of European art in the country. It also has sections on early and contemporary New Zealand arts, including various works by the world-renowned artist Frances Hodgkins (see p36).

Entrance foyer of the Dunedin Public Art Gallery

0 metres    300
0 yards     300

### Key

▨ Street-by-Street: Central Dunedin pp264–5

**For keys to symbols** see back flap

### 🏛 First Church
415 Moray Place. **Tel** (03) 477 7118.
**Open** daily. 🕐 Sunday only. ♿ 📷

The flagship of the Presbyterian Church in Otago, First Church, consecrated in 1873, is considered to be architect Robert Lawson's greatest contribution to Dunedin's rich architectural heritage. Of note are its beautiful rose window, wooden ceiling and 56-m (184-ft) high spire. The church

The Law Courts in Central Dunedin

has undergone considerable restoration work to repair its exterior. Its history is told at the church's heritage centre. Bell Hill, on which First Church stands, was lowered by about 12 m (40 ft) to improve the city's traffic.

### 🏛 Law Courts
41 Stuart St.

These were completed in 1902 to a design by government architect John Campbell. The building is distinguished by its combination of local Port Chalmers bluestone and lighter Oamaru stone. Standing just around the corner in complete contrast is the former red brick Dunedin Prison, built to another Campbell design which mimics many aspects of London's New Scotland Yard, although on a smaller scale. Completed in 1895, it also served as the

Dunedin Police Station until a new building was built in the mid-1990s.

### 🏛 Toitu Otago Settlers Museum
31 Queens Gardens. **Tel** (03) 477 5052.
**Open** daily. **Closed** Good Fri, 25 Dec.
📷 ♿ 🛍 📷 🌐 otago.settlers.
museum/

This museum focuses on the lives of the province's settlers from Southern Maori to Scottish pioneers and Chinese gold miners. The displays range from early photographs and household goods to implements and vehicles, including two large steam locomotives, one of which dates back to the 1870s. The museum is housed in two adjoining buildings, one a former art gallery, the other a former bus station. A public archive is accessible, as is an exhibition space.

### Robert Lawson

Many of Dunedin's finest Victorian and Scottish Edwardian-style buildings are attributed to architect Robert Lawson (1833–1902). The Scottish-born Lawson had trained as an architect in his home country before migrating to Melbourne, where he found little work, and instead made a living from gold-mining and journalism. He took up his profession again in 1861 and the following year won a competition for the design of First Church in Dunedin. Lawson moved to Dunedin and so began a successful association with the city. His list of credits includes the Municipal Chambers, Otago Boys High School (a handsome bluestone building completed in 1884) and Knox Church in George Street, which was consecrated in 1876. However, it was his initial Dunedin design, First Church, which many consider to be his masterpiece.

First Church

# Street-by-Street: Central Dunedin

Dunedin has close historical links with the Scottish city of Edinburgh. Not only is Dunedin the old Gaelic name for Edinburgh, but many of its street names are Scottish and several Scottish traditions have been preserved since the first Presbyterian settlers arrived in 1848. The Octagon, so-called because of its eight sides, gives the city a central focus. Surrounding it, and within a few blocks, are a number of Victorian and Edwardian public buildings, which are among the finest in the country. Visitors can also enjoy the many cafés and restaurants dotted around the area.

**St Paul's Cathedral**
St Paul's has the only vaulted stone ceiling in New Zealand *(see p262).*

**Stuart Street Terrace Houses**
Built around 1900 as town residences for country folk, these terrace houses are now popular locations for restaurants, boutiques and professional offices.

Dunedin Public Art
Gallery *(see p262)*

First Church *(see p263)*

MORAY PLACE

BURLINGTON STREET

CUMBER

0 metres 300
0 yards 300

Queens
Gardens

RATTRAY ST

**Otago Settlers Museum**
This tells the story of Otago and its settlers. One wing is dedicated to old forms of transport *(see p263).*

**Key**
— Suggested route

*For hotels and restaurants in this region see pp302–7 and pp314–25*

**The Municipal Chambers**
Built in 1880 at a time when Dunedin was revelling in the fortune brought by the gold rush, the building is topped by a 47-m (155-ft) high tower *(see p262)*.

## VISITORS' CHECKLIST

**Practical Information**
Road map B7. 120,000.
dunedinnz.com i-SITE,
20 Princes St, (03) 474 3300.
Dunedin Summer Festival
(3rd week of Feb); iD Dunedin
Fashion Week (Mar); Midwinter
Carnival (Jun); Dunedin Cadbury
Chocolate Carnival (Jul).

**Transport**
25 km (16 miles) S of city
centre. Limited international
flights to and from Australia.
Anzac Ave. Intercity,
St Andrew St.

**★ The Octagon**
The Octagon is a popular gathering place for small groups who lunch under the trees, and for bigger crowds during festivals and exhibitions *(see p262)*.

**The Otago Daily Times Building**, an interesting piece of 1930s Art Deco architecture, is the home of New Zealand's oldest newspaper.

Law Courts *(see p263)*

**★ Dunedin Railway Station**
Perhaps the finest stone structure in the country, the station has a 37-m (120-ft) high square tower, three huge clock faces and a covered carriageway *(see pp266–7)*.

# Dunedin Railway Station

Dunedin's Railway Station is one of New Zealand's finest historic buildings and one of the best examples of railway architecture in the southern hemisphere. Although not large by international standards, the station's delightful proportions lend it an air of grandeur. Opened in 1906, the Flemish Renaissance-style building was designed by New Zealand Railways architect George Troup, whose detailing on the outside of the building earned him the nickname "Gingerbread George".

**★ Exterior Stonework**
Beige Oamaru limestone *(see pp272–3)* detailing provides a striking contrast to the darker Central Otago bluestone on the walls and the finely polished Aberdeen granite of the columns

**New Zealand Sports Hall of Fame**
This features imaginative displays recounting the exploits and achievements of famous New Zealanders.

## KEY

① **A frieze** of cherubs and foliage from the Royal Doulton factory in England encircles the ticket hall below the wrought-iron bordered balcony.

② **Dormer windows** projecting from the sloping gable roof are typical Flemish architectural features.

③ **The turret** provides a visual counterbalance to the main clock tower.

④ **The roof** is covered with clay Marseille tiles from France.

⑤ **Finely carved sandstone lions** on each corner of the clock tower guard the cupola behind them.

⑥ **The clock tower** rises 37 m (120 ft) above street level.

⑦ **The platform** is the arrival and departure point for visitors taking the Taieri Gorge Railway *(see p268)*.

Main entrance

**Ticket Windows**
The ticket windows are ornately decorated with white tiles and a crest featuring the old New Zealand Railways logo.

★ **Stained-glass Windows**
Two imposing stained-glass windows on the mezzanine balcony depict approaching steam engines, lights blazing, facing each other across the ticket hall.

**VISITORS' CHECKLIST**

**Practical Information**
Anzac Ave. **Tel** (03) 477 4449.
**Open** 8am–6pm Mon–Fri,
9am–6pm Sat, Sun & public hols.
**Closed** 25 Dec. ♿ 📷

**Transport**
🚌 Octagon.

**Staircase**
Complete with wrought-iron balustrades and Royal Doulton mosaic tiled steps, a staircase sweeps up from the ticket hall to the balcony above.

★ **Mosaic Floor**
More than 725,000 Royal Doulton porcelain squares form images of steam engines, rolling stock and the New Zealand Railways logo.

# North Dunedin and Environs

Dunedin's city centre is enclosed by hills to the north and west, and by water – the Otago Harbour and Pacific Ocean – to the east and south. In the north of the city are several green areas, most notably the Botanic Gardens at the foot of Signal Hill, and several historic buildings. A road along the narrow, scenic harbour leads to lookout points providing panoramic views of the city, harbour and peninsula.

University of Otago clock tower

### ⛰ Signal Hill
Signal Hill Rd via Opoho Rd.
**Open** daily. 🔗

To the north of the city, the road up Signal Hill leads to a monument built in 1940 to mark 100 years of British sovereignty in New Zealand. From here visitors can get excellent views of the central city, upper harbour and parts of the Otago Peninsula.

### 🌳 Dunedin Botanic Gardens
Opoho Rd. **Tel** (03) 471 9275.
**Open** daily. 🔗 🚻 🚗 🏛 📷
Rhododendron Festival (late Oct).

Dunedin's extensive Botanic Gardens were the first to be established in New Zealand, in 1868. The area's varied topography and microclimates are used to grow a diverse range of plants. The flat lower gardens are home to the more formal displays – lawns interspersed with trees and native bush and formal flower gardens – and to the Edwardian Winter Garden, first opened in 1908. On the hill, the upper gardens include more than 3,000 rhododendron varieties in the world-renowned Rhododendron Dell. These provide a springtime feast for the eyes.

### 🏛 Otago Museum
419 Great King St. **Tel** (03) 474 7474.
**Open** daily. **Closed** 25 Dec. 🎟 donation. 🔗 📷 2pm Sat & Sun. 🚻 🏛
🌐 otagomuseum.govt.nz

The displays in the large, Classical-style Otago Museum, opened in 1877, introduce visitors to the region's human and natural history. There are halls dealing with pre-European Maori life, Pacific culture, marine life, and archaeology of the ancient world. The museum also houses one of New Zealand's leading maritime exhibitions and an authentic Victorian "Animal Attic". The interactive Discovery World science centre includes a tropical forest with 1,000 butterflies.

### ⛰ Tunnel Beach Walkway
Blackhead Rd. **Open** daily.
**Closed** Aug–Oct.

Located 7 km (4 miles) south of the city, Tunnel Beach is named after the tunnel cut through sandstone cliffs in the 1870s by Edward Cargill so that his family could get down to the pretty beach below. The short but steep walkway to the beach gives breathtaking views of the sandstone cliffs which have been spectacularly sculpted by wind and sea.

### 🏛 University of Otago
Leith St. **Tel** (03) 479 1100.
**Open** Mon–Fri. **Closed** public hols.
🔗 grounds & public areas.
🌐 otago.ac.nz

Founded in 1869, the University of Otago – New Zealand's oldest university – plays a crucial role in the life of the city. The bluestone clock tower registry building dates from 1878 (see p32), while the semi-detached houses close to its northern end were built in 1879 to house the university's first four professors. The grounds are a pleasant place to wander.

### ⛰ The Organ Pipes
Mount Cargill Rd.

Strange multi-sided basalt columns, known as "the organ pipes", are a reminder of Dunedin's volcanic past. Reaching them requires a walk of at least an hour from a signpost on Mount Cargill Road north of the city. The panoramic views are a bonus.

### 🚂 Taieri Gorge Railway
Anzac Avenue. **Tel** (03) 477 4449.
**Open** departs daily; additional departures during summer. 🎟 🔗
🚻 🏛 🌐 taieri.co.nz

Departing from Dunedin Railway Station, the train takes passengers on a 77-km (48-mile) four-hour return trip west of the city. Opened in 1879, the line passes through the greenery of Dunedin's coast then climbs through a steep-sided river gorge to the arid grasslands and rocky outcrops of the Strath Taieri. It cuts through ten tunnels, crossing bridges and viaducts up to 47 m (155 ft) above the Taieri River.

Rhododendrons in bloom in the Dunedin Botanic Gardens

# Olveston House

Olveston, a 35-room Jacobean-style mansion, was completed in 1906 for David and Marie Theomin and their children, Edward and Dorothy. Dorothy left the house and its contents to the city and it remains as it was when the family lived in it. Olveston's grand drawing room, dining room, library, billiard room and great hall contain fine furniture and many treasures collected by the Theomins, who were keen travellers.

**VISITORS' CHECKLIST**

42 Royal Terrace. **Tel** (03) 477 33 20.
**W** olveston.co.nz
**Open** daily. **Closed** 25 Dec. 
 ground floor.  obligatory;
hourly 9:30am–4:00pm

**The kitchen** is dominated by a kauri dresser filled with blue and white Delft ware and a kauri table.

Library

**Exterior Stonework**
The double-brick house gets its warm exterior colour from a cladding of Moeraki pebbles with Oamaru stone highlights *(see pp272–3)*.

**The Billard Room** has a full-size table and adjustable overhead lights.

**★ Dining Room**
Attractive features are the oak panelling, semicircular stained-glass windows and richly embossed wallpaper.

Card Room

Main entrance

**Dutch gables** and projecting windows add architectural interest to the exterior of Olveston.

**★ Great Hall**
A centre for receptions, the hall has oak joinery, printed hessian wall covering featuring acanthus leaves, and a collection of porcelain.

**The Drawing Room**, used for entertaining and music, has the only decorated ceiling in the house.

# ➋ Otago Peninsula

The 24-km (15-mile) long Otago Peninsula offers a wide variety of attractions, including rare and unusual wildlife, historic buildings, woodland gardens and spectacular harbour and coastal scenery. The 64-km (40-mile) round trip, taking the "high" Highcliff Road, which runs over the top of the peninsula, on the outward journey, and returning via the "low" Portobello Road along the coast, can take a full day. The Highcliff Road offers the best views of the surrounding countryside and coastline.

### 🎫 Larnach Castle

145 Camp Rd. **Tel** (03) 476 1775
**Open** daily. **Closed** 25 Dec. 🚫 🚫
inside. ⚹ ground floor. 📷 by
arrangement. ☐ 🏠 🅦
larnachcastle.co.nz

Located 14 km (9 miles) from central Dunedin along the "high" road, Lanarch Castle is New Zealand's only castle. Built between 1871 and 1885 by financier, businessman and politician, William J M Larnach for his wife Eliza, the grand stone mansion, set in 2 sq km (0.8 sq mile) of bush and gardens, is built along Scottish baronial lines. It has many fine features, including elaborately carved and decorated ceilings and a large, hanging staircase. Its magnificent interior was created by English and Italian artisans brought to Dunedin to work on the building. There is also a ballroom, added as a complete wing as a birthday present for Larnach's

daughter, Kate. Visitors can climb up the narrow stone steps for a view from the top of the tower. Accommodation is available next to the castle *(see p307)*.

In 1967 the Barker family bought the castle which was by then derelict and spent many years restoring it to its former glory. Margaret Barker has worked particularly hard to restore the gardens and grounds, and they now contain a fine collection of native and exotic plants.

### ⌖ Royal Albatross Centre

Taiaroa Head. **Tel** (03) 478 0499.
**Open** daily. **Closed** 25 Dec. 🚫
⚹ visitor centre only. 📷 except Tue
am; tours obligatory; booking essential.
☐ 🏠 🅦 albatrosses.org.nz

The prominent Taiaroa head-land at the mouth of Otago Harbour is home to the world's only mainland royal albatross colony. Opened in 1989, the

Black and white royal albatrosses at Taiaroa Head

centre contains excellent displays about these large birds. During the nesting period, guides take visitors to an observatory where the birds can be seen nesting and flying. A colony of Stewart Island shags is also visible from the observatory. Taiaroa Head's other main attraction is the Armstrong disappearing gun, a 15-cm (6-inch) diameter naval defence gun installed in 1886 during the "Russian scare". Designed to pop out of the ground, fire and then recoil back into its pit, it is the only one of its kind in the world still in working order in its original position.

Larnach Castle viewed from the gardens

Homestead in the Glenfalloch Woodland Gardens

### ⑥ Glenfalloch Woodland Gardens

30 Portobello Rd. **Tel** (03) 476 1775. **Open** daily. 🏛 donation. ⚐ lower gardens. 🖼 🍴 summer only.

On the "low road", 10 km (6 miles) from Dunedin, the Glenfalloch Woodland Gardens – glenfalloch is Gaelic for "hidden glen" – have been attracting visitors since the 1870s. An elegant homestead, built in 1871, tearooms (open in summer), and a pottery, where pieces that are made on the spot are sold, are sheltered in grounds containing mature trees, shrubs, and a stream. The gardens are ablaze with rhododendrons and azaleas in spring, and during the summer months they are noted for their colourful displays of fuchsias.

Visitors to Glenfalloch can enjoy several short walking tracks through the trees and woodland gardens.

### ⑦ New Zealand Marine Studies Centre

Hatchery Rd, Portobello. **Tel** (03) 479 5826. **Open** daily. **Closed** 25 Dec. 🏛 ⚐ 🖼 🎥 **W** marine.ac.nz

Portobello is a peaceful little harbourside settlement with shops and a tavern. Its main claim to fame is the Marine Studies Centre's aquarium, part of the University of Otago's marine research centre. Located at the end of a small peninsula near Portobello, the aquarium features the marine life of the region and a "touch tank" for children with starfish, crabs and sea anemones.

### ⑧ Otakou

Off Harrington Point Rd. **Open** daily. 🖼 inside.

Otakou is the site of one of the earliest Maori settlements in the area, and it was this word which was anglicized to Otago to give the surrounding province its name. The local church and meeting house were built to commemorate the 1940 centenary of the signing of the Treaty of Waitangi *(see pp52–3)*. What appear to be carvings are actually moulded concrete.

Maori church and meeting house at Otakou

### ⑨ Penguin Place

Harrington Point Rd. **Tel** (03) 478 0286. **Open** daily. 🏛 🎥 obligatory, bookings essential. 🖼

The road to Taiaroa Head passes Penguin Place, an award-winning venture to save the yellow-eyed penguin, the world's rarest species of penguin. Yellow-eyed penguins are found only on the Otago Peninsula and other isolated east coast areas of Otago and Southland. An ingenious system of camouflaged trenches at Penguin Place allows visitors to view nesting yellow-eyed penguins at close range without disturbing them. It is best to visit at dusk when the birds are most active.

### ❿ Moeraki Boulders Scenic Reserve

**Road map** B7.

The Moeraki Boulders, 78 km (49 miles) north of Dunedin on State Highway 1, have long been the subject of legend and curiosity. Almost perfectly spherical, with a circumference of up to 4 m (13 ft), the grey boulders lie scattered along a 50-m (164-ft) stretch of the beach. They were formed on the sea bed about 60 million years ago as lime salts gradually accumulated around a hard core.

Maori legend claims that the boulders were the food baskets or Te Kaihinaki of the Araiteuru canoe, one of the great ancestral canoes that brought Maori to New Zealand from Hawaiki. The canoe was wrecked while on a greenstone gathering trip. It is said that the *kumara* on board became rough rocks, the food baskets became smooth boulders, and the wreck turned into a reef.

It is not unusual to see small black and white Hector's dolphins playing in the surf near the boulders. A nearby café and restaurant service the flow of visitors.

The tiny, picturesque fishing village of Moeraki, a former whaling station established in 1836, is on the opposite side of the bay from the reserve.

Spherical boulders on the beach at Moeraki

# ❹ Street-by-Street: Oamaru

The main town of North Otago and service centre for a rich agricultural hinterland, Oamaru is a pretty town with wide, tree-lined streets, well-kept gardens, galleries, beaches, colonies of rare penguins, and the best preserved collection of historic public and commercial buildings in New Zealand. The buildings were fashioned in the 1880s from Oamaru stone, a local cream-coloured limestone which is easily cut, carved and moulded. Oamaru was the childhood home of the novelist Janet Frame (1924–2004), who had an international reputation, and a walking tour takes visitors past sites featured in her writing.

**★ Forrester Gallery**
Ornately carved Corinthian columns distinguish this 1882 building, which formerly housed the Bank of New South Wales.

**Courthouse**
Built in 1883, the Court-house features a Neo-Classical portico with Corinthian columns. It is no longer in use.

**Meeks Grain Elevator Building (1883)**

**National Bank (1871)**

HUMBER ST

ITCHIN STREET

THAMES ST

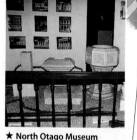

**★ North Otago Museum**
Exhibits in the museum, built in 1882, include displays on the quarrying and use of Oamaru stone.

**Oamaru's first Post Office**, a small Italianate building with a squat clock tower, was built in 1864.

**Colonial Bank (1878)**, now housing the Visitor Centre

**St Luke's Anglican Church** (1865–1913) contains fine interior woodcarving.

**Waitaki District Council**
Originally Oamaru's second post office (1883), the building's 28-m (92-ft) clock tower was added in 1903.

For hotels and restaurants in this region see pp302–7 and pp314–25

**Criterion Hotel**
Built in 1877, this hotel went "dry" in 1906 during prohibition. Now restored, it serves patrons in a Victorian pub atmosphere.

View of Oamaru and the harbour from Lookout Reserve

### Exploring Oamaru
Apart from its historic harbour precinct which features a number of boutique businesses, Oamaru has several scenic and natural attractions. The 1-km (0.6-mile) South Hill Walkway above the harbour leads to Lookout Reserve. Further on is Bushy Beach where a viewing hide allows visitors to see yellow-eyed penguins.

**Harbour Street**
At the heart of the port area, this street is lined with 19th-century warehouses, commercial buildings and grain stores.

**Harbour Board Office (1876)**

HARBOUR STREET

TYNE STREET

**Union Bank (1878–9)**

**Customs House (1884)**

**Tyne Street**, together with Harbour Street, contains over 20 buildings classified for preservation.

### 🐧 Oamaru Blue Penguin Colony
Waterfront Rd. **Tel** (03) 433 1195.
**Open** daily. **Closed** 25 Apr, 25 & 26 Dec. 🅿 🐧 no flash. ♿ 📷
🌐 penguins.co.nz
At Friendly Bay, in an old quarry at the end of Oamaru's harbour, visitors can see penguins leave to feed at sea, and return at dusk past a special viewing area. This is best viewed at dusk. From another viewing area, the penguins can be observed in their nesting boxes.

### 🌿 Oamaru Public Gardens
Chelmer St. **Open** daily, until sunset.
Established in 1876, these contain traditional features such as rose gardens, ponds, an azalea lawn and rhododendron dell. A band rotunda, summerhouse, aviary, peacock house and marble fountain are other attractions.

### 🏛 Totara Estate
State Hwy 1. ℹ (03) 434 7169.
**Open** daily. **Closed** end May–end Aug. 🅿 ♿ 📷
About 8 km (5 miles) south of Oamaru, this is where New Zealand's first shipment of frozen mutton to England in 1882 was processed, heralding the beginning of New Zealand's most important industry. Limestone buildings house displays on the industry's history.

**0 metres** 100
**0 yards** 100

**Key**
— Suggested route

★ **New Zealand Loan and Mercantile Warehouse**
This three-storey Victorian warehouse, built in 1882 for New Zealand's largest stock and station agency, was designed to hold up to 100,000 sacks of grain.

The Lindis Pass winding through tussock-covered hills

## ❺ Lindis Pass

**Road map** B6.

The main inland link between Otago and the Waitaki Basin, the Lindis Pass climbs through rocky gorges before reaching the tussock-covered hills of a Department of Conservation reserve near the summit. Early Maori, like today's holiday-makers, used the route in summer to get to Lakes Wanaka and Hawea.

In 1858, John McLean, the first European to settle in the area, established the 2,000-sq-km (772-sq-mile) Morven Hills Station. Many of the original buildings can still be seen about 15 km (9 miles) south of the summit. These include McLean's original homestead and a massive stone woolshed, built about 1880, which was capable of holding up to 1,500 sheep.

## ❻ Lake Hawea

**Road map** B6. 🏔 1,100. 🎪 Hawea Picnic Day & Races (Dec).

Tucked among hills and mountains, the bright blue waters of Lake Hawea make it one of the most beautiful of the southern lakes. The lake, which is 410 m (1,345 ft) deep in

places, is separated from the equally beautiful Lake Wanaka by a narrow, 35-km (22-mile) isthmus, known as "the neck".

Lake Hawea is a popular holiday haven. There are many free camping spots around its shores. It is also well known for its excellent trout and land-locked salmon fishing and for various boating activities. The small town of Hawea on the lake's southern shores is the main base for outdoor activities.

## ❼ Wanaka

**Road map** B6. 🏔 5,000.
🛈 100 Ardmore St, (03) 443 1233.
🎪 Wanakafest (Sep); Warbirds Over Wanaka (Easter, even-numbered years). 🌐 **lakewanaka.co.nz**

Located at the southern end of the lake, Wanaka is one of the country's favourite holiday spots. The willow-lined shores and bays of Lake Wanaka are popular in summer for boating, fishing and water-skiing, while in winter skiers and snowboarders flock to the local ski areas. Snow-capped peaks provide a beautiful lake setting, and these natural attractions also bring hikers and walkers to the many breathtaking tracks in the nearby Mount Aspiring National Park (*see pp276–7*).

Aside from the area's natural features, there is plenty to visit and see around the town. One of the chief attractions, the **New Zealand Fighter Pilots Museum**, located at Wanaka Airport, is home to a variety of World War II fighter aircraft, such as a Hawker Hurricane, Tiger Moth, Vampire, Chipmunk, a

replica of a SE5A and several rare Russian Polikar-povs. Illustrated displays explain the role of New Zealand fighter pilots and crews in several theatres of war. Visitors can also see aircraft being restored in the maintenance hangar. "Warbirds Over Wanaka", a major biennial airshow involving military aircraft, is held every second Easter in even-numbered years. It features aircraft from New Zealand as well as overseas in acrobatic displays and mock battles. Wanaka's open skies and dramatic alpine scenery provide a spectacular backdrop.

Next to Wanaka Airport is the **Wanaka Transport Museum**. Its large private collection of more than 13,000 items includes memorabilia, such as toys and models, as well as military vehicles and aircraft. A special exhibit is a huge Russian Antonov AN-2, the world's largest single engine biplane.

Stuart Landsborough's Puzzling World

**Stuart Landsborough's Puzzling World** is based around "The Great Maze", 1.5 km (1 mile) of three-dimensional wooden passages and under- and over-bridges. Other attractions include the incredible Illusion Rooms, a Hologram Hall, the Tumbling Towers/Tilted House, and the Puzzle Centre and Café where you can take a break and try to solve one of the many challenging puzzles on display.

Like many other parts of Central Otago, Wanaka's climate is proving ideal for grape growing. **Rippon Vineyard**, established in 1974 just 4 km (2.5 miles) from the centre of town, is one of the pioneering growers and wine makers of the region. The vineyard produces wines from a number of grape varieties.

Fishing on the shores of Lake Hawea

Rippon Vineyard on the shores of Lake Wanaka

**New Zealand Fighter Pilots Museum**
Wanaka Airport.
**Tel** (03) 443 7010. **Open** daily. **Closed** 25 Dec.
**W** nzfpm.co.nz

**Wanaka Transport and Toy Museum**
State Hwy 6. **Tel** (03) 443 8765.
**Open** daily. **Closed** 25 Dec.

**Stuart Landsborough's Puzzling World**
State Hwy 6.
**Tel** (03) 443 7489.
**Open** daily.
**W** puzzlingworld.com

**Rippon Vineyard**
Mt Aspiring Rd.
**Tel** (03) 443 8084.
**Open** daily. **Closed** May–June, 25 Dec.
wine tasting. Rippon Music Festival (biennial, even-numbered years in Feb).
**W** rippon.co.nz

**Environs**
Twenty-five km (16 miles) south of Wanaka is the tiny township of Cardrona, consisting of a few cottages and a hotel dating back to 1863.

The surrounding Cardrona Valley, a popular route for gold-miners in the 1860s, is now better known for the Cardrona Ski Field on the southeastern slopes of Mount Cardrona, and for cross-country skiing at the nearby Waiorau Snow Farm *(see pp198–9, 335)*.

The **Treble Cone Ski Area**, 20 km (12 miles) southwest of Wanaka, off Mount Aspiring Road, has uncrowded slopes which are great for skiers of all abilities *(see pp198–9, 335)*. Guided back country heli-skiing over the Harris, Richardson and Buchanan mountains is another option, flying you to some of the best out-of-the-way ski spots in the area.

## Wanaka's Outdoor Attractions

Wanaka is a recreational centre with a wide variety of outdoor pursuits in both summer and winter. Fishing is a popular activity on the lake shore, along rivers and from charter vessels. Waterborne adventures include kayaking, jet-boat and cruise boat trips, white-water sledging on small purpose-designed boards, and canyoning. There are several good walks which leave from or near the township, as well as longer hikes in the nearby Mount Aspiring National Park *(see pp276–7)* for more serious, well-equipped hikers. Horse riding, mountain biking and quad bike motorcycle tours are other ways of exploring Wanaka's back country areas.

Within easy distance of Wanaka lie two commercial downhill ski areas, Treble Cone and Cardrona, as well as the Waiorau Snow Farm cross-country ski area and heli-skiing in the surrounding mountains. From Wanaka Airport, flightseeing tours are available. or, for the more adventurous, acrobatic flights in Tiger Moths or World War II Mustangs.

Skiers on a chairlift at Treble Cone Ski Area, southwest of Wanaka

# ➑ Mount Aspiring National Park

New Zealand's third largest National Park after Fiordland and Kahurangi, Mount Aspiring National Park enjoys World Heritage status as part of the Te Wāhipounamu/Southwest New Zealand World Heritage Area, which stretches from Aoraki/Mount Cook to the southern tip of Fiordland. Within the park's 3,555-sq km (1,373-sq mile) area, the scenery ranges from snow- and glacier-clad mountains to rugged rock faces, spectacular forested valleys and picturesque river flats. The park, close to the tourist centres of Queenstown and Wanaka, is a popular walking, tramping and climbing destination.

**Exploring the park**
Opportunities to explore the park on foot are varied, and range from short walks from the road to back country circuits for fit trampers.

★ **Mount Aspiring/Tititea**
Because of its pyramid shape, Mount Aspiring/ Tititea is often described as New Zealand's "Matterhorn of the South".

## KEY

① **The Rees-Dart Track**, a challenging four- to five-day loop track reached from the head of Lake Wakatipu, offers outstanding scenery but requires a high level of fitness and the proper equipment.

② **The Olivine Wilderness Area**, which constitutes the core of the park, is maintained in an undeveloped state for wilderness recreation and has no tracks or huts.

## Birdlife in Mount Aspiring National Park

**Rock wren**

This park is known for its abundant birdlife. Some 59 species, 38 of them native, inhabit the valley floors, riverbeds, forests, subalpine scrub and high alpine regions. Especially symbolic of the park are the kea, rock wren and blue duck. The kea, whose call may be heard echoing through the valleys, is an inquisitive bird well known for its interest in trampers' equipment and food. The hardy little rock wren lives high in the hills in one of the harshest environments in the park, while pairs of blue ducks can be seen feeding on vegetation and insects in the park's swift mountain streams, especially in the hanging valleys.

Okuru

Jackson Bay • Waiato

HAAST RANGE
Arawhata River
Waiatoto River
MAIN DIVIDE

② MOUNT ASPIRING
3,033 m (9,948 ft)

OLIVINE RANGE

Lake Wilmot

Mount Aspiring Hut

ROB ROY GLACIER
Rob Roy Valley Walk

Matukituki Valley Walk

Rees-Dart Track

①

▲ MOUNT EARNSLAW
2,820 m (9,249 ft)

**Matukituki Valley**
A track up the west branch of the river from the end of the road takes trampers to the head of the valley and to some challenging climbing in the Mount Aspiring area.

★ **Gates of Haast**
At the Gates of Haast bridge, the Haast River roars down a steep-sided gorge strewn with boulders.

**Mount Brewster**
Accessible from State Highway 6, Mount Brewster is a popular climbing and camping spot.

★ **Thunder Creek Falls**
A short forest track from State Highway 6 leads to the 30-m (98-ft) falls which drop from a notch in a rock.

### Key

━━ State highway
━━ Minor road
▱▱ River
= = Walking track
▬ ▬ Park boundary

0 kilometres   10

0 miles            10

## VISITORS' CHECKLIST

**Practical Information**
**Road map** A6. **Wanaka**
🛈 Department of Conservation, Ardmore St, (03) 443 7660.
**Open** summer: daily, winter: Mon–Sat. **Closed** 25 Dec. 📷
**Makarora** 🛈 State Hwy 6, (03) 443 8365. **Open** summer: daily. **Closed** winter, 25 December. 📷
**W** doc.govt.nz

**Transport**
🚌 Ardmore St.

## ❾ Haast

**Road map** B6. 🚹 300. 🛈 Dept of Conservation, cnr State Hwy 6 & Haast–Jackson Bay Rd, (03) 750 0809.

A tiny community on the coast where the broad Haast River meets the sea, Haast is little more than a stopover and supply point for people travelling between the West Coast and the southern lakes, although it does offer good surf and river fishing. The visitor centre provides information on walks and tracks in the area, as well as maps, souvenirs and visitor publications. The staff can also advise on track and weather conditions in this high rainfall area. Fill up with fuel here before driving over the pass to Wanaka.

### Environs

The road south to the fishing village of **Jackson Bay** provides a number of walking and sightseeing opportunities, such as the Hapuka Estuary Walk, the Cascade Viewpoint and the Smoothwater Bay track at Jackson Bay itself. The Wharekai Te Kau Walk leads to the Okahu Wildlife Refuge.

There are several places of interest north of Haast, such as the Dune Lake Walk through dense coastal forest stunted by wind at Ship Creek, and the stunning Knights Point viewpoint.

Further on, past **Lake Moeraki**, the Monro Beach Walk passes through luxuriant coastal forest to a remote beach where (from July to December) Fiordland crested penguins are sometimes seen. The road carries on to trout-filled **Lake Paringa** where a 15-minute walk passes through native trees such as silver beech, rimu and kahikatea.

Jackson Bay, surrounded by swamp, bush and mountains

Kawarau River and Lake Wakatipu ▶

# ⑩ Queenstown

Situated on the northeast shore of Lake Wakatipu, backed by the mountain range called The Remarkables, Queenstown enjoys one of the most scenic settings in the world. Since the 1970s, it has developed from a sleepy lakeside town into a leading international resort and a world centre for adventure sports, including bungy jumping *(see pp198–9)*. Like most towns in the area, Queenstown was established during the 1860s gold rushes. Although the pace of development in Queenstown has been dictated by the demands of tourism, it still has the feel of a small town and proudly maintains its links with the days of the gold boom.

TSS *Earnslaw* on Lake Wakatipu

### 🎣 Lake Wakatipu

There is no mistaking Lake Wakatipu's glacial origins, although Maori legend has it that the lake was formed by the imprint of a sleeping demon burnt to death by the lover of a beautiful Maori girl captured by the demon.

Because his heart did not perish and still beats, the level of the lake rises and falls as much as 7 cm (3 inches) every five minutes. Lake Wakatipu, which is the second largest of the southern glacial lakes, after Te Anau, is up to 380 m (1,246 ft) deep in places.

The steep, rugged slopes of the Remarkables drop down to the lake's edge, leaving downtown Queenstown snuggled on one of the few pieces of relatively flat land in the area. Most private residences and many hotels have been banished to the surrounding hills. During the mining boom, the lake was the principal means of communication, but today it is a focus for recreational activities.

### 🌳 Queenstown Gardens

Park St. **Open** daily. ♿

Set on a glacial moraine peninsula, the Queenstown Gardens are within walking distance of the town centre. They are surrounded by stands of large fir trees and contain broad lawns and rose beds. The gardens provide a quiet oasis in an otherwise busy tourist town, and are particularly attractive in autumn. An ice skating rink, sporting greens, frisbee golf course, skate park, tennis courts and a walkway around the point are other attractions.

### 🚢 TSS Earnslaw

Steamer Wharf. **Tel** 0800 656 503.
**Open** daily. 🅿️ ♿ main deck. 📷 📺

The TSS (Twin Screw Steamer) *Earnslaw* is a wonderful relic of the mining boom when paddle steamers and other craft plied Lake Wakatipu as the principal means of transport. Launched in 1912, the 51-m (168-ft) vessel, affectionately known as "the lady of the lake", is still powered by its original twin 500-hp coal-fired steam engines. Its interior is finished with wood and brass.

A number of cruises depart from Queenstown all year round, from 90-minute cruises to four-hour dinner cruises in the warmer months. Visitors can also take daytime or evening excursions across the lake to the **Walter Peak High Country Farm**. Here they can enjoy refreshments at the Colonel's Homestead Restaurant, go horse trekking or mountain biking, or see displays of high country activities, such as sheep shearing and sheep dogs in action.

---

### Adventure Capital of New Zealand

Queenstown offers a range of adventures, from outdoor experiences to total adventure packages *(see pp198–9, 334–9)*. Many activities are centred around the lake and on the several rivers nearby, in particular the Dart, Shotover and Kawarau,

White-water rafting on the Shotover River

where jet-boat trips and white-water rafting offer exciting rides through narrow, rocky canyons. In winter, two ranges within 30 km (19 miles) of Queenstown – the Remarkables and Coronet Peak – provide great skiing. The town's reputation as New Zealand's adventure capital, however, rests on its many airborne activities: bungy jumping, ranging from the 43-m (141-ft) high Kawarau Bridge to the 134-m (440-ft) high Nevis highwire bungy; hang-gliding from the area's mountainous terrain; tandem parapenting from Bob's Peak; and tandem skydiving.

### 🞖 Underwater Observatory

Maintown Pier. **Tel** (03) 442 8538.
**Open** daily. 🞖 🞖

Built beneath the Maintown
Pier, Underwater Observatory
provides a unique opportunity
to see life below the surface of
the lake. From a viewing lounge
5 m (16 ft) under the water,
visitors can observe brown and
rainbow trout peacefully
swimming alongside enormous
New Zealand long-finned eels,
which are often joined by diving
black teal ducks.

### 🞖 The Mall

The best way to enjoy and
get to know Queenstown is
on foot and probably the best
place to start is at The Mall,
which is a popular meeting
place for visitors and a
pedestrian-only street
dominated by a variety of
restaurants, cafés and pubs,
as well as numerous souvenir
shops. The Mall leads directly
down to the Maintown Pier
from which boats and jet boats
regularly depart for cruises
on the lake.

A number of interesting old
colonial buildings, such as the
former bank, remain in The Mall.

### 🞖 Skyline Gondola

Brecon St. **Tel** (03) 441 0101.
**Open** daily. 🞖 🞖 🞖 🞖 🞖
🇼 skyline.co.nz

The gondola up to Bob's Peak is
synonymous with Queenstown.
It rises 450 m (1,476 ft) in just
730 m (2,400 ft) and provides
breathtaking panoramic views
of The Remarkables, Lake
Wakatipu and Queenstown
from the observation deck at
the top. Visitors can eat at the
restaurant or café, take walks
in the area, watch parapenters
float down from the peak or
take a ride downhill on the
luge – a short, raised toboggan.

Skyline Gondola

## VISITORS' CHECKLIST

**Practical Information**
Road map A6. 🞖 7,500
🇼 queenstownnz.co.nz
🞖 Cnr Camp & Shotover sts,
(03) 442 4100; 0800 668 888.
🞖 Winter Festival (Jul).

**Transport**
🞖 6 km (4 miles) E of town.
🞖 Steamer Wharf.

### 🞖 Kiwi Birdlife Park

Brecon St. Tel (03) 442 8059.
**Open** daily. **Closed** 25 Dec. 🞖 🞖
Kiwi House. 🞖 one house. 🞖 🞖
🇼 kiwibird.co.nz

Queenstown's Kiwi Birdlife Park,
below the gondola terminal, is
home to several kiwis and other
endangered native birds. The
birds are either part of national
breeding programmes for
release into the wild, or are
being rehabilitated after injury.

A major attraction is the
nocturnal Kiwi House where
visitors can see this flightless
bird. Other species on view in
natural, parklike surroundings
include native owls, large alpine
parrots known as kea, parakeets,
and the black stilt – a rare
wader (see p255).

## Queenstown Town Centre

① Lake Wakatipu
② Queenstown Gardens
③ TSS *Earnslaw*
④ Underwater Observatory
⑤ The Mall
⑥ Kiwi Birdlife Park
⑦ Skyline Gondola

| 0 metres | 400 |
| 0 yards | 400 |

**For keys to map symbols** *see back flap*

# ⓫ Glenorchy

**Road map** A6. 🏘 360. 🛈 Cnr Mull & Oban sts, (03) 441 0303.

Glenorchy is a small, tranquil township at the head of Lake Wakatipu, 44 km (27 miles) or 45 minutes' drive from Queenstown. The town stands in the shadow of snow-capped peaks with names such as Mount Chaos and Mount Head which rise steeply above the Rees and Dart river valleys.

The town is the transit point for trampers entering the valleys, which are part of the Mount Aspiring National Park (*see pp274–5*), and which are among New Zealand's Great Walks. For the serious tramper, there is a 77-km (48-mile) loop track which connects both valleys via the 1,447-m (4,747-ft) Rees Saddle. Although it takes four to five days and requires proper equipment, it is possible to enjoy a few hours' return walk up either valley. A variety of outdoor activities are also available at Glenorchy.

# ⓬ Arrowtown

**Road map** B6. 🏘 2,000. 🛈 49 Buckingham St (in museum), (03) 442 1824. 🎌 Autumn Festival (Apr).

Nestled at the foot of rugged hills 21 km (13 miles) from Queenstown, Arrowtown is the most picturesque and best preserved gold-mining town in the area. In 1862, a small band of miners, including William Fox and John O'Callaghan, discovered gold in the Fox River and within weeks they had recovered 113 kg (250 lb) of the precious metal. Arrowtown's

Lake Hayes near Arrowtown

population peaked at more than 7,000 and is one of the few boom towns not to have either become a ghost town or been overrun by more modern development. The main street, partly lined with deciduous trees, has many old colonial shops and buildings at one end and, at the other, tiny miners' stone cottages dating back to the 1860s and 1870s.

Chinese miners played a big part in Arrowtown's history after 1865, when they were invited to fill the vacuum created by European miners who had left for the West Coast gold rush. Their legacy is Arrowtown's **Chinese Village** with its preserved and restored stone buildings, including tiny cottages, an outhouse and a store.

Stone cottage at the Chinese Village

The **Lakes District Museum** chronicles both Arrowtown and Queenstown's past, focusing on gold-miners and their innovations. It includes a display on New Zealand's first hydroelectric plant, built in 1886 in what is now the ghost town of Bullendale. Other displays cover local geology, agriculture, sawmilling and domestic life of the gold rush period. The museum doubles as Arrowtown's visitor centre.

🏛 **Chinese Village**
Buckingham St. **Tel** (03) 442 1824. **Open** daily. ♿ assisted.

🏛 **Lakes District Museum**
49 Buckingham St. **Tel** (03) 442 1824. **Open** daily. **Closed** 25 Dec. 🎫 ♿ 🎁 📷

## Environs
Near to Arrowtown is the much-photographed **Lake Hayes**, at its best in autumn. The back road from Arrowtown to Queens-town passes the access road to Coronet Peak which heads 7 km (4 miles) up to great views from the ski area. **Macetown** is a popular destination for 4WD vehicles. A 26-km (16-mile) return journey from Arrowtown takes visitors up a steep, gold-bearing gorge. Ghost town relics include the remains of old stone buildings and a gold stamping battery.

**Gibbston Valley Wines** is a good example of vineyards in the area (*see pp40–41*). European varieties thrive in the hot summer days and cool evenings. Gibbston's wine is stored in a cool underground cave, and tours and wine tastings are available.

🍷 **Gibbston Valley Wines**
State Hwy 6. **Tel** (03) 442 6910. **Open** daily. **Closed** most public hols. ♿ 🎫 🎁 cave. 📷 📷

The main street of Arrowtown

## ⑬ Cromwell

**Road map** B7. 🗺 4,080.
ℹ 47 The Mall, (03) 445 0212.

Cromwell survived the gold era to become a service town in one of New Zealand's leading fruit growing areas. In the 1980s, an electricity generating dam built down river created nearby Lake Dunstan, flooding much of Cromwell's quaint and historic main street, although several of the more notable buildings were relocated stone by stone to a new site. Cromwell now makes its living from farming, horticulture, viticulture and tourism.

### Environs

Gold-mining relics in the area include **Bendigo**, a ghost town 4 km (2 miles) off State Highway 8, the main road between Cromwell and Lindis Pass. By 1866 Bendigo was all but deserted until a rich gold-bearing quartz reef was found, and mined for more than 50 years.

A loop track above Bendigo leads to **Logantown** and **Welshtown**, two associated settlements deserted in the 1880s. It is wise to keep to the tracks because there are many old unmarked mine shafts throughout the area.

The **Goldfields Mining Centre** in the Kawarau Gorge, 5 km (3 miles) from Cromwell, offers visitors working exhibitions of gold-mining techniques.

🏛 **Goldfields Mining Centre**
Kawarau Gorge, State Hwy 6. **Tel** (03) 445 1038. **Open** daily. **Closed** 25 Dec.
🅿 ♿ ⏷ 🖭 📷

### The Gold Rush

The Otago gold rush began with the discovery of gold in Gabriel's Gully in 1861, near the present-day town of Lawrence, 92 km (57 miles) west of Dunedin. A tent town sprang up and prospectors soon began pushing further inland. Finds in the Dunstan area around Cromwell and Alexandra followed in 1862, with discoveries in the Wakatipu region soon after. Tens of thousands braved hot, dry summers, cold, harsh winters and starvation in search of a quick fortune. New discoveries were made in other corners of the province,

but by the late 1860s the focus had shifted to the West Coast. With the main fields well picked over, more sophisticated methods, such as sluicing, dredging and quartz reef mining, were needed to extract gold. Gold-mining continued well into the 1900s and the development of modern methods has led to large-scale mining operations in the area.

Arrowtown miners at their claim in the 1860s

## ⑭ Kingston

**Road map** A7. 🗺 65. 🚉 ⛵ Kingston to Queenstown Yacht Race (Jan).

For a long time the little settlement of Kingston served as a railhead and steamer terminal for travellers heading towards Lake Wakatipu from the south. Nowadays, its main claim to fame is the **Kingston Flyer**, a restored vintage steam train with several coaches and staff in period costume which takes passengers on a 75-minute return trip.

🚉 **Kingston Flyer**
Kingston Railway Station.
**Tel** (03) 248 8848. **Open** Oct–Apr: daily. **Closed** 25 Dec. 🚫 🖭 📷

### Environs

To the south of Kingston, on State Highway 6, is **Lumsden**, well known for the trout-filled rivers which crisscross the countryside surrounding the town. Just before Lumsden, State Highway 94 branches west to Te Anau, Manapouri and Fiordland National Park, and east to the farming area of Gore.

The vintage steam train Kingston Flyer on a short "flight" from Kingston

# ⑮ Fiordland National Park

Fiordland National Park's 12,500 sq km (4,826 sq miles) make it the largest of New Zealand's National Parks, while its special geology, landscape, flora and fauna have earned it a place in the Te Wāhipounamu – Southwest New Zealand World Heritage Area. It is a region dominated by forest and water. Its 14 fiords and 5 major lakes – the work of Ice Age glaciers – flanked by steep mountains clad with thick, temperate rainforest, make the interior virtually impenetrable except along its 500 km (310 miles) of walking tracks. The park is also known for its wildlife, especially its marine mammals and native birds, including the Fiordland crested penguin.

**★ Doubtful Sound**
This fiord extends 40 km (25 miles) from the foot of the main mountain divide to the open waters of the Tasman Sea (see pp288–9).

## How the Fiords were Formed

Although named otherwise, Milford Sound/Piopiotahi, Doubtful Sound and the other sounds are, in fact, fiords. Sounds are flooded river valleys whereas fiords are valleys carved by the tremendous pressure and power of glaciers during successive Ice Ages, then later flooded by the sea as the ice melts and sea levels rise.

Rounded peak

V-shaped valley
**10 million years ago**, intense pressure in the earth's crust caused the most recent uplift in the area, forming peaks and V-shaped valleys.

Horn

Glacier
**2 million years ago**, the mountains were covered by glaciers. Ridges and peaks became sharper and valleys became U-shaped.

Hanging valley

U-shaped valley
**20,000 – 12,000 years ago**, the ice melted as the Ice Age receded, leaving the tributaries of rivers as hanging valleys above the main valley.

Flooded valley
**6,000 years ago**, at the end of the last Ice Age, the sea reached its present levels, flooding the valleys and leaving the peaks exposed.

DOUBTFUL SOUND

DUSKY SOUND

**Dusky Sound**
This sound can be reached by chartered cruise boat from Lake Manapouri via Doubtful Sound, or, for experienced climbers, via the 10-day Dusky Track.

### Key

- ▬▬ State highway
- ▬▬ Minor road
- ≈≈ River
- – – Walking track
- ▬ ▬ Park boundary
- – – Boat route

Lake McKerrow

Lake Alabaster

MILFORD SOUND

Bowen Falls ②

MITRE PEAK
1,492 m (4,893 ft)

Milford Sound

Hollyford River

Hollyford Track

Routeburn Track

Arthur River

Homer Tunnel

94

AN SEA

①

Sutherland Falls

Milford Track

Lake Gunn

③

Eglinton River

Te Anau Downs

Lake Te Anau

94

Kepler Track

Te Anau

napouri
wer
tion

Lake Manapouri

INVERCARGILL

Manapouri

Waiau River

④

⑤

Lake Monowai

TUATAPERE

CLIFDEN

Lake
teriteri

Lake Hauroko

p Ridge Track

ilometres        20
niles        20

## VISITORS' CHECKLIST

**Practical Information**
Road map A6.
🌐 fiordland.org.nz
ℹ️ Visitor Centre, Lakefront Drive, Te Anau, (03) 249 7924. **Open** daily.

**Transport**
✈️ Queenstown160 km (100 miles) from park. 🚌 Queenstown.

**★ Mitre Peak**
So-called because of its resemblance to a bishop's mitre, this is Milford Sound's most famous landmark (see pp286–7).

**★ Cleddau Valley**
The spectacular Cleddau Valley provides a natural route down to Milford Sound after emerging from the 1,200-m (3,940-ft) long Homer Tunnel.

**Lake Te Anau**
For most visitors, Lake Te Anau, with its backdrop of rich native forest and high mountain peaks, is their first view of Fiordland.

### KEY

① **Some of the best scenery** in New Zealand awaits visitors along the Milford Track and the other two Great Walks in the park (see pp286–7).

② **Bowen Falls** tumble 160 m (530 ft) from a U-shaped hanging valley.

③ **Mirror Lakes**, famous for their mountain reflections, can be viewed from boardwalks off State Highway 94 (see p288).

④ **Green Lake**, to the north of Lake Monowai, gets its name from its emerald green waters.

⑤ **Lake Monowai**, a centre for recreational activities, lies in a beautiful bush setting. Further south, Lake Hauroko, the deepest lake in New Zealand, can be reached by unsealed road from Clifden.

**For additional map symbols** see back flap

# Exploring Fiordland National Park

With mountains rising 2,750 m (9,020 ft), sheer rock walls climbing 1,200 m (3,940 ft) from deep fiords, and waterfalls tumbling 160 m (530 ft), Fiordland's spectacular landscape attracts visitors from around the world. The Maori were the first to exploit the area's natural resources, then came sealers who from 1792 to the 1820s slaughtered hundreds of thousands of fur seals. Until 1953, when State Highway 94 (the Milford Road) was completed, the only way to Milford Sound was by boat or via the Milford Track. Today, visitors arrive by the busload, and those with the time, fitness and equipment can walk the famous tracks. Others visit the sound by boat or scenic flight.

Sheep drive on the road to Milford Sound

## Te Anau

**Road map** A7. ⚐ 1,800. ⛟ Miro St.
ℹ Lakefront Drive, (03) 249 2924.

The picturesque town of Te Anau, on the southeastern shore of Lake Te Anau, is the largest town in Fiordland and a good base for exploring Fiordland National Park. The lake, the largest in the South Island, is 61 km (38 miles) long and 417 m (1,370 ft) deep, the result of glacial action. It is a popular venue for boating and fishing.

## Te Ana-au Caves

ℹ Real Journeys Visitor Centre, Lakefront Drive, Te Anau. **Tel** (03) 249 7416. **Open** daily. ⚐ ⚐

At the Te Ana-au Caves, reached by a boat trip across Lake Te Anau, a combination of carefully formed walkways and small boats allow visitors to explore a series of magical limestone grottos. The caves are home to thousands of tiny New Zealand

glowworms, which use their tiny light – the result of a chemical reaction – to attract insects for food. Return trips, which depart several times a day, take two and a half hours.

## The Milford Road

The 121-km (75-mile) road to Milford Sound from Te Anau has earned World Heritage Highway status for its beauty and scenic variety. This includes lush lakeside forest, rugged mountains, cascading alpine rivers and picturesque walks. Although Milford Sound can be reached by road in two hours, there are many side trips possible along the way to make the drive more memorable.

Te Anau Downs, 30 km (19 miles) from Te Anau, is the departure point for the boat

Sheep warning sign, Milford Road

to the Milford Track. From here there is a 45-minute forest walk to Lake Mistletoe. Further on, the Mirror Lakes are a short five-minute walk from the road across a boardwalk. On a calm day, beautiful reflections of the surrounding scenery are visible in the lakes (see p258).

At Lake Gunn, about 46 km (29 miles) from Te Anau Downs, an easy 45-minute loop through beech forest is suitable for all ages and for people in wheelchairs. The Divide, a short distance away, marks the start of the Routeburn Track, which leads overland to the stunning Lake Wakatipu (note that the track does not actually reach the lake, but ends at the road that then leads to the lake 10–15 km (6–9 miles) away). A three-hour return walk to Key Summit gives rewarding views. The nearby Hollyford Valley also makes a scenic trip.

Nineteen km (12 miles) east of Milford Sound is the 1,200-m (3,940-ft) long Homer Tunnel, started in 1935 but not completed until 1954. Leaving the tunnel, the road slopes very steeply downhill to the Milford side where there are spectacular views along the Cleddau Valley. The Chasm, a few kilometres from the tunnel, can be reached by a 20-minute walk to where the Cleddau River drops 22 m (72 ft) through a series of unusual rock formations.

Te Ana-au Caves

## Milford Sound

Road map A6. 🗺 170.

Milford Sound, a 16-km (10-mile) long fiord, is Fiordland's best-known attraction. Its most famous landmark is Mitre Peak, a pyramid-shaped mountain rising 1,692 m (5,550 ft) straight from the deep fiord. Although scenic flights are available, the grandeur of Milford Sound can be best appreciated by boat. Trips pass unusual geological features, such as Lion Mountain, the Elephant and Copper Point, as well as waterfalls: the Bowen Falls drop 160 m (530 ft) into the water, and the Stirling Falls 146 m (480 ft). Fur seals, dolphins, and the occasional Fiordland crested penguin can be seen along the way.

An Underwater Observatory at Milford Sound allows visitors to see the unusual black coral, red coral, anemones, starfish and fish that live in the fiord. High rainfall means there is a 3–4 m (10–13 ft) layer of fresh water above the underlying salt water.

Apart from day trips in the Milford Sound, full-day and overnight cruises take visitors out of the sound to the open Tasman Sea, with stops at other sounds, such as Dusky Sound. Cruises often combine fishing, kayaking and diving.

## Great Walks in Fiordland National Park

Trampers on the Milford Track

Fiordland National Park is considered by many to be the best place in New Zealand for trampers. Its three major walking tracks – the Milford, Routeburn and Kepler (*see pp284–5*) – can be walked independently, or on the Milford in a guided group, all year round. Advance booking is essential for the Milford and Routeburn tracks (*see pp334–5*) during the peak tramping season, while all tracks require advance purchase of hut or camp-site passes. All three walks are suitable only for experienced, well-equipped parties.

The spectacular 55-km (34-mile) **Milford Track**, which takes four days, climbs through the Clinton Valley to the Mackinnon Pass. It passes the Sutherland Falls before dropping down to Milford Sound. The 39-km (24-mile) **Routeburn Track** usually takes three days. It climbs through forest to spectacular subalpine terrain before crossing the Harris Saddle and descending the Routeburn Valley towards Lake Wakatipu. The **Kepler Track**, a three-to four-day 60-km (37-mile) loop, skirts Lake Te Anau, then climbs to panoramic views from Mount Luxmore before descending to Lake Manapouri.

Typical alpine plant

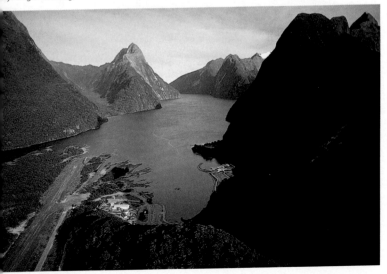

Aerial view of Milford Sound

# ⑯ A Trip to Doubtful Sound

Doubtful Sound was named by Captain James Cook in 1770, on his voyage to New Zealand when, looking at the narrow entrance to the sound, he was doubtful that he could safely get his vessel in and out. The 40-km (25-mile) long fiord is Fiordland's second largest and, at 421 m (1,380 ft), the deepest. It is a remote, unspoilt wilderness of mountain peaks, fiords and rainforest which supports a rich array of bird and marine life, including crested penguins, fur seals and bottlenose dolphins. Getting there is an adventure in itself, involving two boat trips and a coach ride over a mountain pass, with a side trip deep underground to the huge Manapouri Power Station generator hall.

① **Lake Manapouri**
The trip to Doubtful Sound begins at the Pearl Harbour marina on the Waiau River, which feeds into Lake Manapouri. The lake, which is forested to the shoreline, covers 142 sq km (55 sq miles) and is dotted with 34 islands.

*Tasman Sea*

*Thompson Sound*

*Secretary Island*

*Bradshaw Sound*

*Bauza Island*

*Malaspina Reach*

*Crooked Arm*

*Hall Arm*

⑩ **New Zealand Fur Seals**
Colonies of New Zealand's most common seal can be seen on the islands dotting the entrance to Doubtful Sound.

⑨ **Bottlenose Dolphins**
A resident pod of bottlenose dolphins may be seen playing in the waters at Malaspina Reach. They grow up to 4.5 m (15 ft).

⑧ **Commander Peak**
To the left at the head of Hall Arm, Commander Peak is one of many awe-inspiring bush-clad peaks that visitors see during a cruise of Doubtful Sound's flooded glacial valleys (see p284).

⑦ **Deep Cove**
The peaceful waters of Deep Cove hide the 10-km (6-mile) tunnel under the mountains from the Manapouri Power Station

## Manapouri Power Station

The Manapouri Power Station is a man-made wonder that takes advantage of the difference in height of the mountains between Lake Manapouri and Doubtful Sound to act as a natural dam. Water is chanelled through vertical penstocks into seven

generators housed in a huge underground room. The water then flows out of a 10-km (6-mile) tunnel to Deep Cove. The electricity generated is used to power the Comalco Aluminium Smelter 171 km (106 miles) to the south, at Bluff.

Underground machine hall

### ② Manapouri Power Station
Coaches take visitors down a 2-km (1.2-mile) spiral access tunnel to the machine hall which is carved out of solid granite 213 m (700 ft) under the mountains at West Arm.

### ④ Moss Gardens
Dozens of species of moss growing on a rock face show how plant life can get a foothold in all sorts of terrain in this high rainfall environment.

### ③ Wilmot Pass Road
The 22-km (13-mile) Wilmot Pass Road, completed in May 1965 to facilitate the building of the Manapouri Power Station tailrace at Deep Cove, cost more than $2 per cm ($5 per inch) to build.

### ⑤ Cleve Garth Falls
The 365-m (1,200ft) high Cleve Garth Falls make a breathtaking entrance from a mountain ridge high above the Wilmott Pass Road.

Kepler Mountains

Lake Te Anau

**Te Anau**

Waiau River

94

Gore

Lake Manapouri

South Arm

Hope Arm

**Manapouri**

Waiau River

Hunter Mountains

0 kilometres 5
0 miles 5

### ⑥ Wilmot Pass Summit
The 670-m (2,200-ft) summit is reached after a winding drive through cool temperate rainforest. The road then descends a one in five slope to Deep Cove.

**Key**
- - Boat tour route
▬ Coach tour route
═ Other roads
▬ River

# ⑰ Invercargill

New Zealand's southernmost city, and the commercial hub of Southland, Invercargill is a well-planned city with wide, tree-lined streets and many parks and reserves. Settled in the 1850s and 1860s by Scottish immigrants, the city's cultural links with Scotland are reflected in the streets named after Scottish rivers and in its many historic buildings. To the west of the city are several sheltered beaches and walking tracks.

## VISITORS' CHECKLIST

**Practical Information**
Road map A7. 🚗 54,000.
🔲 southlandnz.com 🛈 108
Gala St, (03) 211 0895. **Open** daily.
**Closed** 25 Dec. 🎭 Invercargill
Summer Festival (early Feb);
Shakespeare in the Park (Feb).

**Transport**
✈ 2 km (1.2 miles) W of city. 🚌

## 🏞 Queen's Park
Gala St. **Open** daily.
The best-known reserve in the city centre is the 0.8 sq km (0.3 sq mile) Queen's Park, a botanical reserve featuring formal gardens, including rose gardens and the extensive Steans Memorial Winter Garden. There is also a small wildlife park containing deer and wallabies, an aviary, and a challenging 18-hole golf course.

## 🏛 Southland Museum and Art Gallery
108 Gala St. **Tel** (03) 219 9069.
**Open** daily. **Closed** 25 Dec. ♿ 🎁 by arrangement. 📷 🚻 ♿ donation.
Apart from its three art exhibition galleries, the Southland Museum and Art Gallery, housed in a pyramid-shaped building near the entrance to Queen's Park, contains displays outlining the area's human and natural history. It also features a

Tuatara at the Southland Museum and Art Gallery

tuatarium where visitors can see several of New Zealand's "living fossils" *(see p28)* at close range. The "Roaring Forties Experience" at the Subantarctic Islands Interpretive Centre provides an introduction to New Zealand's five remote island reserves, which lie hundreds of kilometres to the south of Invercargill.

## 🏯 Water Tower
Leet St.
A distinctive landmark in the city, the 42-m (138-ft) high red brick water tower, completed in

1889 for the Public Works Department, is a fine example of Neo-Romanesque industrial design of the time.

## 🏢 Dee and Tay Streets
Invercargill's early prosperity resulted in the construction of many fine commercial buildings and churches. At the northern end of Dee Street lies the former Dee Street Hospital, the oldest public hospital buildings in New Zealand, and the quaint former Porter's Lodge, built around 1866 and reputed to be the oldest house in Invercargill. Nearby is St Paul's Presbyterian Church, whose square tower houses bells manufactured in Italy from captured guns. Further down, the 1901 red brick Alexander Building is noted for its eclectic style, while the Grand Hotel opposite has fine iron balconies.

## Invercargill City Centre

① Queen's Park
② Southland Museum and Art Gallery
③ Water Tower
④ Dee and Tay Streets
⑤ Anderson Park Art Gallery

0 metres          500
0 yards          500

For keys to map symbols *see back flap*

Anderson Park Art Gallery and gardens

At the intersection of Dee Street and Tay Street (Invercargill's main street) stands the impressive Troopers' Memorial flanked by three elegant bank buildings, erected between 1876 and 1926. In Tay Street is the imposing Renaissance-style Civic Theatre, completed in 1906, and St John's Anglican Church, noted for its stained-glass windows and timber barrel-vaulted ceiling. The Lombardy-style Romanesque First Presbyterian Church, also in Tay Street, features an unusual square 32-m (105-ft) tower.

### ⅏ Anderson Park and Art Gallery

91 McIvor Rd. **Tel** (03) 215 7432. **Open** 10:30am–5pm daily. **Closed** Good Fri, 25 Dec. 🐾 donation. 🖼 inside. ♿ ground floor. 📷 by arrangement.

Five km (3 miles) north of the city centre, this beautiful Georgian-style house built in 1925 and set in 0.2 sq km (0.08 sq mile) of gardens and native bush, houses a fine collection of New Zealand art.

First Presbyterian Church in Tay Street

## ⑱ Gore

**Road map** B7. 🏔 8,500. 🚍 ℹ Cnr Hokonui Drive & Norfolk St, (03) 203 9288. 🎸 New Zealand Gold Guitar Awards (May–Jun). 🌐 gorenz.com

Lying 66 km (41 miles) north of Invercargill, Gore has varied claims to fame: brown trout in the Mataura River and its tributaries (symbolized by a large trout statue in the middle of the town), sheep (the town is surrounded by fertile farmlands and thrives as an agricultural service town), moonshine whisky, and a reputation as the country music capital of New Zealand (country music fans come each May for the New Zealand Gold Guitar Awards).

The Gore Visitor Centre incorporates the **Gore Historical Museum** and the **Hokonui Moonshine Museum**. The latter covers the colourful period when whisky was made illegally in the Hokonui Hills.

The **Eastern Southland Art Gallery** (nicknamed the "Goreggenheim") features major works by New Zealand artists.

Fifteen km (9 miles) west of Gore on State Highway 94 is the **Croydon Aircraft Company**, which restores vintage aircraft and offers flights to visitors.

### ⅏ Gore Historical Museum and Hokonui Moonshine Museum
Cnr Hokonui Drive & Norfolk St. **Tel** (03) 203 9288. **Open** daily. **Closed** 1 Jan, Good Fri, 25 Dec. ♿ 📷

### ⅏ Eastern Southland Art Gallery
Cnr Hokonui Drive & Norfolk St. **Tel** (03) 208 9907. **Open** daily. **Closed** 1 Jan, Good Fri, 25–26 Dec. ♿ 📷

### ✈ Croydon Aircraft Company
**Tel** (03) 208 9755. **Open** daily. **Closed** 25 Dec. ♿ 📷 by arrangement.

## ⑲ Bluff

**Road map** A7. 🏔 2,000. 🚍 Gore St. 🚢 Stewart Island Wharf. 🎣 Bluff Oyster & Food Festival (May). 🌐 bluff.co.nz

Bluff is New Zealand's southernmost export port and the departure point for ferries to Stewart Island. It is also the base for fishing fleets which cruise the south and west coasts for fish, cray-fish and rock lobsters as well as the famous "Bluff oysters". Unique to New Zealand, the oysters are harvested during a limited season from March to the end of August.

Bluff has a long history of human occupation, with Maori settlement dating back to the 13th century. The town is named after the 265-m (870-ft) high Bluff Hill which overlooks Foveaux Strait towards Stewart Island, which lies 32 km (20 miles) away. Beneath the hill is Stirling Point – the end of State Highway 1 – where there is a much photographed international signpost. Several walks, including the Foveaux Walkway and the Glory Track, pass through native forest. A 45-minute climb up the hill gives panoramic views of the Foveaux Strait and inland areas.

The **Bluff Maritime Museum** traces the history of whaling, muttonbirding and oyster harvesting, as well as development of the port and the Stewart Island ferry.

### ⅏ Bluff Maritime Museum
241 Foreshore Rd. **Tel** (03) 212 7534. **Open** daily. **Closed** 25 Dec. 🐾 ♿ 📷 by arrangement. 📷

International signpost at Stirling Point, Bluff

*For hotels and restaurants in this region see pp302–7 and pp314–25*

# ⓴ Stewart Island

According to Maori legend, Stewart Island, New Zealand's third largest island, was the anchor of Maui's canoe (the South Island) when he pulled the great fish (the North Island) from the sea. Separated from the South Island by the 32-km (20-mile) Foveaux Strait, 85 per cent of Stewart Island became the Rakiura National Park in 2002. Its unspoilt inlets and beaches, bush-clad hills, rugged coastline and native birdlife combine to make the 1,746-sq-km (674-sq-mile) island a naturalist's paradise. First settled by Maori in the 13th century, Europeans arrived in the 1820s. Today's small population makes a living from fishing and tourism.

Paterson Inlet from Observation Rock

## Oban

Oban, Stewart Island's only settlement, sits snugly around the picturesque, protected shores of Halfmoon Bay. It is easy to explore the town on foot but a 90-minute bus tour along Oban's 28 km (17 miles) of road takes visitors past the main points of interest.

From Oban many short tracks lead through beautiful bush to places of scenic or historic interest, and to lookouts with stunning views, including Observation Rock, which provides splendid views over Paterson Inlet towards Ulva Island. On a clear, summer evening it is easy to see why Maori named Stewart Island "the land of the glowing skies". Several beautiful beaches also lie within walking distance to the north and east of the town.

The island offers a range of accommodation options, such as backpacker inns, beach houses, motels, bed and breakfasts, and the century-old South Sea Hotel.

The Rakiura Museum in Ayr Street, which is open daily, provides a fascinating insight into Stewart Island's past, such as Maori settlement, its seafaring history and relics of whaling, sealing, tin mining and timber milling.

Boat charters are also available from Oban, catering for a whole range of interests, including fishing, sightseeing and wildlife spotting. For the more active visitor, diving, kayak hire and guided sea kayak excursions are among the many exciting activities which are on offer. For those who are even more adventurous, cage-diving

South Sea Hotel on the shores of Halfmoon Bay

with great white sharks is one thrill-seeking option that allows participants to get close to these amazing creatures.

### 🐚 Paterson Inlet

Over the hill from Halfmoon Bay, the 16-km (10-mile) long Paterson Inlet, which extends deep into the hinterland. Charter boats and a water taxi can be hired in Oban and Golden Bay for sightseers, divers and those wanting to catch their own fish. These trips are also a great opportunity to view various seabirds, including yellow-eyed and little blue penguins and mollymawks, as well as seals and dolphins. The remains of an old sawmill and whaling station are also accessible from the inlet.

### 🐦 Ulva Island

Located in the centre of Paterson Inlet, Ulva Island is a 10-minute trip by water taxi from the wharf at Golden Bay. The island is predator-free, creating a sanctuary where visitors can get a close look at native New Zealand birds. Walks on the island range from 15 minutes to 3 hours.

*Dog Bay*

*Muttonbird Islands*

## Stewart Island

① Oban
② Paterson Inlet
③ Ulva Island
④ Big Glory Bay
⑤ Ocean Beach
⑥ Titi Islands
⑦ Codfish Island

## Ocean Beach

"Kiwi spotting" (viewing kiwis at night in their natural habitat) is an experience unique to Stewart Island. Licensed tour operators take small groups by boat to the Neck in Little Glory Bay, then on foot through the bush to Ocean Beach where the Stewart Island brown kiwi can be seen feeding as darkness falls.

## Big Glory Bay

Salmon and mussel farming have become important industries in Paterson Inlet. A boat trip takes visitors to a salmon farm at Big Glory Bay, past seal colonies and shag rookeries, with a stopover at Ulva Island on the way.

## Titi Islands

Muttonbirds, or sooty shearwaters, breed on Stewart Island's many offshore islands after a round-the-world migration. Long a source of food, young birds are harvested each April by descendants of the Rakiura Maori. By day, Ackers Point lighthouse gives panoramic views of the islands, and at night during the breeding season (October to April), visitors can hear the muttonbirds returning to land. Some tour operators are licenced to take visitors to the islands to view the birds from the boat.

Muttonbird (sooty shearwater) leaving its burrow

## Codfish Island/Whenua Hou

Codfish Island, about 3 km (2 miles) off the northwest coast of Stewart Island, has been cleared of introduced fauna and is now a protected sanctuary for some 60 species of birds, including the rare and endangered kakapo, a large, flightless, nocturnal parrot. Visitors are not allowed to visit the island.

---

MOUNT ANGLEM
980 m (3,215 ft) ▲

th-West Circuit

RUGGEDY MOUNTAINS

Foveaux Strait

THOMSON RIDGE

Freshwater River

Southern Circuit

Duck Creek

MOUNT RAKEAHUA
681 m (2,234 ft) ▲

AMS HILL
m (1,316 ft)

DOUGHBOY HILL
446 m (1,463 ft)

TIN RANGE

Rakeahua River

Heron River

Lords River

Gorge Creek

Kopeka River

Pegasus

BLUFF

Port William

Rakiura Track

Horseshoe Point
Ackers Point

Carter Passage

① ✈ ℹ

② ③ ⑥

④ ⑤

0 kilometres        10
0 miles            10

**Key**
≈≈≈ River
– – Ferry route
■ ■ Walking track

## Walking the Island

Stewart Island has a number of tracks that take visitors into some of New Zealand's most beautiful bush. From Oban, a three-hour return walk through coastal forest to Ackers Point Lighthouse goes past one of New Zealand's oldest buildings, Ackers Cottage, built in 1835. The Ryan's Creek Track is a three- to four-hour loop through coastal forest above Paterson Inlet. For the fitter visitor, there is the Rakiura Track, which is a popular three-day circuit that climbs a high, forested ridge and traverses the sheltered Paterson Inlet.

There are also 10- to 14-day North-West and Southern Circuits, for which hut and camp passes must be obtained from the visitor centre in Oban. For further information on any of the walks call (03) 219 0002.

Tramper on the Rakiura Track, north of Oban

*For hotels and restaurants in this region see pp302–7 and pp314–25*

# ㉑ Tour of the Catlins

Natural curiosities and beauty combine to make this southeastern corner of the South Island a scenic treasure. Fossilized trees, beautiful waterfalls, golden beaches, high cliffs and secret caves are all part of a unique mix of attractions in this area, commonly referred to as the Catlins after one of the early landowners of the 1840s. A varied coastline of cliffs and golden sand surf beaches provides a home to a wide range of wildlife, from rare Hector's dolphins to penguins, seals and sea lions. The area is made all the more spectacular by the ancient forests of rimu, matai, totara, beech and miro which reach almost to the sea, and which are filled with the sounds of native birds.

**② Curio Bay**
The fossilized remains of a 160 million-year-old forest from the Jurassic period can be seen on a rock platform at low tide.

**① Waipapa Point**
A picturesque spot but the site of New Zealand's worst shipping disaster when the SS *Tararua* ran aground on a hidden reef in 1881, with the loss of 131 lives.

**⑨ Nugget Point**
A lighthouse, built in 1869, stands sentry on a headland overlooking a series of wave-like pinnacles. The area is home to seals, sea lions, gannets, shags, penguins and shearwaters.

*Waikawa River*

Fortrose

Niagara

Haldane · Waikawa

Otara

③

②

①

| 0 km | 5 |
| 0 miles | 5 |

## Tips for Drivers

**Tour length:** 172 km (107 miles) from Invercargill to where the tour rejoins State Hwy 1 at Balclutha. It is well worth allowing at least a day to complete the journey because of the number of side tracks and walks taking visitors to the many sights.
**Stopping-off points:** Most accommodation on this route is on a small scale. There are motels at Papatowai and Owaka, and camping grounds, backpackers hostels and homestays dotted around the area. If an overnight stay is planned, it is wise to book ahead. Food and refreshments are available at several places along the route.

**⑧ Jack's Blowhole**
Sea water surges through a subterranean tunnel before spraying out of this 60-m (197-ft) deep blowhole, located in the middle of cliff top pastures.

### ③ Porpoise Bay
Little black and white Hector's dolphins are often seen playing here in the surf as the waves break along this long, curving beach.

**Balclutha**

**Romahapa**

**Otekura**

**Owaka**

*Catlins Forest Park*

*Catlins Lake*

**Ratanui**

*Tahakopa River*

**Maclennan**

**Papatowai**

...slands

### ④ McLean Falls
A 30-minute forest walk leads to the McLean Falls where the Tautuku River makes an impressive drop of 22 m (72 ft).

### ⑤ Cathedral Caves
The caves, accessible only at low tide, can be reached after a 40-minute walk through forest and along a beach. The opening of the largest cave is 30 m (98 ft) high.

### ⑥ Lake Wilkie
This small forest lake is only a short distance from the road but there is a 20-minute loop walk around it with some good examples of the large tree species found in the area.

### ⑦ Purakaunui Falls
A ten-minute walk through beech and podocarp forest leads to a viewing platform overlooking these attractive waterfalls where the river drops 20 m (65 ft) over a series of wide terraces.

**Key**

▬ Tour route

▭ Other road

〜 River

# TRAVELLERS' NEEDS

# WHERE TO STAY

A variety of accommodation to suit all budgets is available in New Zealand. At the top end of the range, five-star hotels and wilderness lodges provide luxury accommodation. Mid-range hotels, motels and motor lodges, self-catering apartments, country pubs, farmstays, and bed and breakfasts (B&Bs) cater for travellers on a more modest budget. For those on a very tight budget, camping grounds and backpacker hostels offer good value. Away from the larger cities and resorts, the choice of accommodation can be limited, although there are motels and backpacker hostels in virtually all locations. The listings on pages 302–307 give descriptions of the different types of accommodation throughout New Zealand to suit all budgets.

The beautiful setting of Eagles Nest villas in Russell *(see p303)*

## Gradings and Facilities

The country's accommodation grading system, Qualmark, was established in 1994 and now serves as New Zealand tourism's official quality mark. All businesses carrying the Qualmark name have been independently assessed against a set of national quality standards. Accommodation is graded on a star system. One star indicates the place meets the basic standards of comfort, cleanliness and hospitality; five stars denotes that the facility is superior in every way. The Qualmark system is voluntary, however, and many establishments choose not to participate in it.

Many of the large chain hotels are air-conditioned, but the New Zealand climate does not generally warrant air-conditioning. Hot showers and heating are provided in all types of accommodation. Linen is also provided in hotels and motels. In backpacker hostels and camping grounds, linen is not always provided but can usually be hired for a reasonable fee.

## Prices

Luxury lodges start at about NZ$650 a night, while a room in a backpacker hostel can be as low as NZ$20 a night. Most motels are in the range of NZ$100 to NZ$180 per unit, while B&Bs cost between NZ$50 and NZ$100 per person. Many B&Bs, however, offer rooms for a set price, rather than charging per person. Off-season discounts are often available, and it is a good idea to ask about these when making bookings.

## Bookings

It is advisable to book accommodation in advance, especially at peak holiday times (December to February). During winter (June to August), hotels and motels in ski resort towns are often fully booked during school holidays (two weeks in both early July and late September to early October). Bookings can be made directly, through travel agents or at one of New Zealand's 100 visitor information centres.

In most cases, a credit card number will be requested when a booking is arranged. It is wise to ask about cancellation policies when making bookings as some premises will debit the credit card for one night's accommodation if a cancellation is made

Edwardian façade of the Scenic Hotel, Dunedin *(see p307)*

◀ Sperm whale mural in a restaurant in Kaikoura

Huka Lodge on the banks of the Waikato River *(see p304)*

at short notice. For additional services, such as children's cots, inform the hotel when making a booking.

## Children

Travelling with children in New Zealand is easy, with cots and baby-sitting services generally available on request. However, children are not welcome at some exclusive lodges and guesthouses. The definition of a "child" among hotels varies, ranging from under 12 to 17 years. Children enjoy special rates only if they are the third or subsequent occupant of a room and do not request an extra bed. A useful website to look at is www.kidsnewzealand.com, which lists events as well as child-friendly places to visit, to eat and to stay.

## Disabled Travellers

New Zealand law requires all new buildings as well as old buildings undergoing major renovation to provide "reasonable and adequate" access for the disabled. Many facilities have wheelchair access, but it is best to check in advance.

## Luxury Lodges

Often located near a lake, river or beach, luxury lodges provide breathtaking scenery, elegant surroundings and

high-quality service for a limited number of guests at any one time. Many lodges specialise in fishing, hunting and other outdoor activities, and their hosts often have extensive knowledge of the local area. Tariffs at the most exclusive lodges range from NZ$1,500 to NZ$10,000 a night, including meals and alcohol.

## Chain Hotels

Several international luxury hotel chains, including the **Hyatt**, **Millennium**, **Novotel**, **Sofitel** and **Sheraton**, are represented in New Zealand. Other chains include the **Copthorne**, **Scenic Hotel Group**, **Heritage** and **Best Western NZ**, which offer a reliable standard of accommodation in the main cities and resorts of New Zealand. Chain hotels offer a full range of services, including a television, minibar telephone and en suite bathroom in all rooms, as well as room service and restaurants. Some hotels

also have sports, business and conference facilities. For hotel listings, see pp302–307.

## Motels and Motor Lodges

Motels are the most common form of visitor accommodation in New Zealand, and even small towns have at least one. They are particularly suitable for large families or groups because they are spacious and have their own cooking facilities. They usually contain one or two bedrooms, a lounge, kitchen and bathroom, and have a television set, radio, telephone and off-street parking. Smaller units, where guests sleep in the lounge or on a small mezzanine, are called studios. Larger motels and motor lodges are similar to hotels, with swimming pools, laundry facilities, restaurants and room service.

Travellers can save money by purchasing a motel accommodation pass for one of the local chains such as **Best Western NZ** or **Golden Chain NZ**.

Kauri Cliffs lodge, surrounded by lush forests *(see p302)*

Alpacas grazing in the sprawling grounds of Pete's Farm Stay, Rangiora *(see p306)*

## Farmstays, Homestays and B&Bs

Farmstays offer visitors the chance to gain an insight into everyday farming life. Guests stay either in the farmhouse or in separate quarters, and may share meals with their hosts. Bathroom facilities may be either shared with the family or separate in some cases. In many places, guests can participate in some farming activities if they choose to.

Homestays are located in both urban and rural areas, and, like farmstays, guests stay in the family home or in adjacent quarters and often share meals with their hosts. Tariffs for homestays and farmstays can range from NZ$100 to NZ$400 for a double room per night.

B&B's are also more pocket-friendly options and can be easily found throughout New Zealand. **The New Zealand Bed and Breakfast Book** has details about B&Bs across the country.

## Backpacker Hostels and Youth Hostels

New Zealand has more than 250 backpacker hostels in scenic locations. **Budget Backpacker Hostels New Zealand** and **VIP Backpacker Resorts New Zealand** have a comprehensive list of hostels. Hostels are also clearly signposted along the main roads. They offer clean and inexpensive accommodation, and are excellent places to meet other travellers and exchange up-to-date information. However,

they usually tend to attract younger clientele, so noise-averse travellers should be wary. Prices can be as low as NZ$20 per person for a shared room and NZ$30 for a single room.

Another option for low-budget travellers is the **Youth Hostel Association** (YHA), which has a chain of 56 hostels in strategic locations. Despite the name, youth hostels cater for travellers of all ages. They usually offer separate male and female dormitories, as well as twin, double and family rooms for those wanting more privacy. Linen and blankets are also provided. Youth hostels have well-equipped communal kitchens and comfortable lounges for relaxation. Bathroom facilities in most hostels are shared.

It is not necessary to be a member of the Youth Hostel

Accommodation sign in Marlborough

Association to stay at a hostel. However, non-members incur a surcharge of NZ$3–4 a night in addition to the regular fee.

## Camping Grounds

Camping grounds (also called holiday parks and motor camps) offer a cheap way to travel. **Top 10 Holiday Parks** has a list of these. Some contain sites for tents and caravans only, while others have basic cabins fitted with bunk beds, or tourist flats with full cooking and bathroom facilities. Many have kids' play-grounds and games rooms, and are located beside beaches, lakes or rivers in scenic locations. Camping grounds have shared washing and laundry facilities, and fully equipped communal kitchens. Some have shops that sell basic foodstuffs and supplies. Advance booking is advisable during the holiday period, from Christmas to the end of January. Most camping grounds charge about NZ$7 a night per person for a camp site and from about NZ$30 for a double cabin.

## Campervans

A popular way to see the country is in a self-drive campervan. Two-, four- and six-berth vans are available, complete with amenities *(see p359)*. Rental charges vary according to the season. Generally, campervan travellers stop for the night at camping

Campervan travellers taking a break by the sea

The Boatshed, a small luxury hotel on Waiheke Island, Auckland *(see p302)*

grounds where they can hire a site with electric power. In remote locations, travellers can park in a rest area near the roadside. Many camping grounds have "dump stations" for the disposal of sewage effluent.

Typical motor camp sign

## Recommended Hotels

New Zealand is a beautiful island destination where the dramatic coastline is never far away, and the plethora of accommodation options makes great use of sea and mountain views and stunning, awe-inspiring locations, right from luxurious top-dollar luxury residences down to more modest camping grounds and cabins.

The establishments that have been listed on pages 302–307 stand out from the crowd in their respective categories:

budget, bed and breakfast, chain, apartment, motel, luxury and boutique. They are listed by price within each area.

These lodgings have been featured for their excellent value, exceptional comfort, wide-ranging facilities, superb service, stunning location or unique character, or a combination of these.

Throughout the listings certain establishments have been highlighted as DK Choice. These offer a particularly special and memorable experience.

## DIRECTORY

### Luxury Lodges

**New Zealand Lodge Association**
41 Towey St, Oamaru.
**Tel** (03) 434 7939.
W lodgesofnz.co.nz

**Southern Crossings**
Private Bag 93-236, Parnell, Auckland.
**Tel** (09) 309 5912.

### Chain Hotels

**Best Western NZ**
W bestwestern.co.nz

**Copthorne**
W mckhotels.co.nz

**Heritage**
W heritagehotels. co.nz.com

**Hyatt**
W hyatt.com

**Millennium**
W mckhotels.co.nz

**Novotel**
W novotel.com

**Scenic Hotel Group**
W scenichotelgroup. co.nz

**Sheraton**
W sheraton.com

**Sofitel**
W sofitel.com

### Motels and Motor Lodges

**Best Western NZ**
**Tel** 0800 237 893.
W bestwestern.co.nz

**Golden Chain NZ**
**Tel** (03) 358 0821, 0800 465 336.
W goldenchain.co.nz

### Farmstays, Homestays and B&Bs

**The New Zealand Bed & Breakfast Book**
PO Box 6843, Wellington, 6141. **Tel** (04) 385 2615.
W bnb.co.nz

**Rural Holidays**
PO Box 2155, Christchurch, 8140
**Tel** (03) 355 6218.
W nzaccom.co.nz

### Backpacker and Youth Hostels

**Budget Backpacker Hostels New Zealand**
208 Kilmore St, Christchurch.
**Tel** (03) 379 3014.
W bbh.co.nz

**VIP Backpacker Resorts New Zealand**
PO Box 60177, Titirangi, Auckland.
**Tel** (09) 816 8903.
W vipbackpackers. com/nz
hostelworld.com/nz

**Youth Hostel Association of New Zealand**
PO Box 436, Christchurch.
**Tel** (03) 379 9970, 0800 278 299.
W yha.co.nz

### Camping Grounds

**Top 10 Holiday Parks**
PO Box 9088, Tower Junction, Christchurch.
**Tel** 0800 867 836.
W top10.co.nz

# Where to Stay

## Auckland

**Best Western President Hotel** $
Budget                    Map E2
*27–35 Victoria St West, 1010*
**Tel** *(09) 303 1333*
W presidenthotel.co.nz
A hotel with comfortable rooms,
a gym and internet services.

**The Quadrant** $
Apartment                 Map E2
*10 Waterloo Quadrant, 1010*
**Tel** *(09) 984 6000*
W vrhotels.co.nz
Studio, one- and two-bedroom
apartments have kitchens,
balconies and free Wif-Fi.

**YWCA** $
Budget                    Map E2
*103 Vincent St, 1010*
**Tel** *(09) 377 8763*
W akywca.org.nz
A friendly hostel, with several
women-only floors, cooking
facilities and café. No alcohol.

**Heritage Hotel
Auckland**                $$
Boutique                  Map E2
*35 Hobson St, 1010*
**Tel** *(09) 379 8553*
W heritagehotels.co.nz
In a former department store, this
comfortable hotel has several
pools and a great restaurant.

**The Langham** $$
Chain                     Map E2
*83 Symonds St, 1140*
**Tel** *(09) 379 5132*
W auckland.langhamhotels.co.nz
Old-world charm and elegance
with a five-star rating. Great spa.

**The Old Church Cottage** $$
Bed and Breakfast         Map E2
*1 Hastings Parade, Devonport, 0624*
**Tel** *(09) 445 9826*
W oldchurchcottage.co.nz
Charming B&B in a former 1909
Salvation Army Citadel.

**Rydges** $$
Chain                     Map E2
*59 Federal St, 1010*
**Tel** *(09) 375 5900*
W rydges.co.nz
Modern hotel with friendly staff
and an excellent restauraunt.

**SKYCITY Hotel** $$
Chain                     Map E2
*Cnr Federal and Victoria St, 1010*
**Tel** *(09) 363 6000*
W skycityauckland.co.nz
This hotel offers spacious rooms
and many restaurants and cafés.

**The Boatshed** $$$
Bed and Breakfast         Map E2
*Cnr Tawa and Huia sts, Little Oneroa,
Waiheke Island, 1840*
**Tel** *(09) 372 3242*
W boatshed.co.nz
Luxury accommodation in a sun-
drenched bay on Waiheke Island.

**The Great Ponsonby
Arthotel**                $$$
Bed and Breakfast         Map E2
*30 Ponsonby Terrace, Ponsonby, 1011*
**Tel** *(09) 376 5989*
W greatpons.co.nz
A historic villa crammed with
New Zealand art. Friendly staff.

### DK Choice

**Hilton** $$$
Chain                     Map E2
*Princes Wharf, 147 Quay St, 1010*
**Tel** *(09) 978 2000*
W auckland.hilton.com
Perched 300 m (985 ft) out on
Princes Wharf with panoramic
views of the marine playground,
the Hilton boasts suites shaped
like the bow of a ship. It also has
celebrated chef Simon Gault's
aptly named FISH restaurant.

**Latitude 37** $$$
Apartment                 Map E2
*20 Pakenham St E, 1010*
**Tel** *(09) 377 5649*
W www.latitude37.co.nz
Boutique-style serviced apartments
surrounded by ponds and trees.

**Penthouse 64** $$$
Apartment                 Map E2
*Viaduct Harbour, 1010*
**Tel** *0800 100 444*
W touchofspice.co.nz
Luxury apartment with a designer
kitchen, media room and spa pool.

Elegant lobby at the Colonial-style Kauri
Cliffs, Matauri Bay

**Penthouse 3** $$$
Apartment                 Map E2
*148 Quay St, Central Auckland, 1010*
**Tel** *(09) 377 5301*
W 148quay.com
Two-bedroom luxury apartment
with amazing views of the harbour.

**Wainui Country Retreat** $$$
Bed and Breakfast         Map E2
*990 Wainui Rd, Wainui, North
Auckland 0933*
**Tel** *(09) 420 4567*
W wainuicountryretreat.co.nz
This self-catering boutique farm
stay has a private waterfall.

## Northland

**KERIKERI: Aroha Island Kiwi
Lodge**                   $
Budget                    Map E1
*177 Rangitane Rd, Kerikeri, Bay of
Islands, 0294*
**Tel** *(09) 407 5243*
W arohaisland.co.nz
Comfortable eco-lodge set in
native forest.

**KERIKERI: Pagoda Lodge** $
Budget                    Map E1
*81 Pa Rd, Bay of Islands, 0230*
**Tel** *(09) 407 8617*
W pagoda.co.nz
Chinese-themed 1930s lodge in
beautiful gardens.

**KOHUKOHU: Kohukohu
Treehouse**               $
Budget                    Map D1
*168 West Coast Rd, RD1,
Hokianga, 0491*
**Tel** *(09) 405 5855*
W treehouse.co.nz
Cabins in subtropical gardens.
Shared kitchen/bathroom facilities.

### DK Choice

**MATAURI BAY: Kauri Cliffs** $$$
Luxury                    Map E1
*Matauri Bay Rd, 0478*
**Tel** *(09) 407 0010*
W kauricliffs.com
This complex of a Colonial-style
lodge and cottages has access
to beaches, waterfalls and forest
with 2,000-year-old kauri trees.
Great vista of the Pacific Ocean.

**OPUA: Crows Nest Holiday Villas** $$$
Luxury · Map E1
*20 Sir George Back St, Bay of Islands, 0200*
**Tel** *(09) 402 7783*
W crowsnest.co.nz
Two exclusive villas overlook the bay. Private and secluded.

**PAIHIA: Scenic Hotel** $$
Boutique · Map E1
*Cnr MacMurray and Seaview rds, Bay of Islands, 0200*
**Tel** *(09) 402 7826*
W scenichotels.co.nz
Set amid subtropical gardens, this hotel has spacious rooms.

**RUSSELL: Eagles Nest** $$$
Luxury · Map E1
*60 Tapeka Rd, Russell, Bay of Islands, 0202*
**Tel** *(09) 403 8333*
W eaglesnest.co.nz
Five luxury villas with balconies and sublime sea views. Fabulous resident chefs and spa.

**WAIPU: The Stonehouse** $
Budget · Map E1
*641 Cove Rd, 0582*
**Tel** *(09) 432 0432*
W stonehousewaipu.co.nz
Cottage by the sea, with dinghies and canoes in which to explore the lagoon and bird sanctuary.

**WHANGAREI: Little Earth Lodge** $
Budget · Map E1
*85 Abbey Caves Rd, 0175*
**Tel** *(09) 430 6562*
W littleearthlodge.co.nz
Cosy hostel with Balinese decor next to the Glowworm caves.

# The Central North Island

**COROMANDEL: Why Worry Bed and Breakfast** $
Bed and Breakfast · Map E2
*150 Huihana Lane, Long Bay RD1*
**Tel** *(07) 866 8221*
W coromandelaccommodation. net.nz
This hospitable B&B offers large rooms with panoramic sea views and a spa.

**COROMANDEL: Beachside Resort** $$
Boutique · Map E2
*20 Eyre St, Whitianga, 3510*
**Tel** *(07) 867 1356*
W beachsideresort.co.nz
Self-contained one-bedroom apartments with a tennis court and pool. Close to the beach.

A deluxe villa at Eagles Nest, Russell, with stunning sea views

**COROMANDEL: Grand Mercure Puka Park Resort** $$
Boutique · Map E2
*Pauanui Beach, 3546*
**Tel** *(07) 864 8088*
W pukapark.co.nz
Private chalets set along the forested slopes of Mt Pauanui.

**COROMANDEL: Brenton Lodge** $$$
Luxury · Map E2
*2 Brenton Place, Whangamata, 3691*
**Tel** *(07) 865 8400*
W brentonlodge.co.nz
Luxury suites in a peaceful garden with sea views and a pool.

**COROMANDEL: Waihi Waterlily Gardens** $$$
Luxury · Map E2
*441 Pukiekauri Rd, Waihi, 3682*
**Tel** *(07) 863 8267*
W waterlily.co.nz
These pretty self-contained cottages offer a romantic atmosphere in waterlily gardens

**GISBORNE: Portside Hotel** $
Boutique · Map F3
*2 Reads Rd, 4010*
**Tel** *(06) 869 1000*
W portsidegisborne.co.nz
The suites at this homely hotel are spacious and modern.

**HAMILTON: Shailers** $
Bed and Breakfast · Map E2
*1447 Kakaramea Rd, RD 10, 3290*
**Tel** *(07) 825 2729*
W shailers.co.nz
Homestay with a dairy farm offering hearty food, warm hospitality and farm tours.

**HAVELOCK NORTH: Mangapapa Petit Hotel** $$$
Luxury · Map F4
*466 Napier Rd, Hawkes Bay, 4172*
**Tel** *(06) 878 3234*
W mangapapa.co.nz
A boutique hotel with a gourmet restaurant. Free Wi-Fi.

**NAPIER: Albatross Motel** $
Budget · Map F4
*56 Meeanee Quay, Westshore, 4110*
**Tel** *(06) 835 5991*
W albatrossmotel.co.nz
This motel has both studio and two-bedroom units, with views of the Ahuriri Wildlife Reserve.

**OHOPE: Beachpoint Resort** $
Apartment · Map F3
*5 West End Rd, Ohope Beach*
**Tel** *(07) 312 6100*
W beachpoint.co.nz
Private, fully equipped self-service beachfront apartments with a gym and covered parking.

**OTOROHANGA: Kamahi Cottage** $$$
Bed and Breakfast · Map E3
*229 Barber Rd, Rewarewa, RD5*
**Tel** *(07) 873 0849*
W kamahi.co.nz
Try the farm-fresh breakfasts at this romantic luxury cottage set in a country garden.

**ROTORUA: Alpin Motel** $
Budget · Map E3
*16 Sala St, 3010*
**Tel** *(07) 348 4182*
W alpin.co.nz
Four-star apartments with a private garden. Rooms have plunge hot tubs.

**ROTORUA: Cleveland Motel** $
Budget · Map E3
*113 Lake Rd, 3010*
**Tel** *(07) 348 2041*
W clevelandmotel.co.nz
A family-friendly motel set in large gardens with comfortable rooms and an outdoor heated pool.

**ROTORUA: Rydges Rotorua** $
Chain · Map E3
*272 Fenton St, 3010*
**Tel** *(07) 349 0099*
W rydges.com
Well-appointed rooms with balconies. Rooftop pool.

For more information on types of hotels *see pages 298–301*

The comfortable lounge at Huka Lodge, Taupo

**ROTORUA: Utuhina Hot Springs
Lodge** $
Bed and Breakfast   Map E3
*99 Lake Rd, 3010*
**Tel** *(09) 348 5785*
W utuhinahotsprings.com
A historic lodge set in tranquil
gardens with four geothermal
mineral pools.

**ROTORUA: YHA Rotorua** $
Budget   Map E3
*1278 Haupapa St, 3010*
**Tel** *(07) 349 4088*
W yha.co.nz
No-frills hostel with clean rooms
and free parking.

**ROTORUA: Blossom Cottage** $$
Bed and Breakfast   Map E3
*62A Sunnex Rd, RD6, 3096*
**Tel** *(07) 332 2720*
W blossom-cottage.com
Enjoy the old-world charm of
this luxurious, romantic B&B in a
tranquil setting.

**ROTORUA: Country Villa** $$
Bed and Breakfast   Map E3
*351 Dalbeth Rd, RD2, 3072*
**Tel** *(07) 357 5893*
W countryvilla.biz
A Victorian villa with magnificent
gardens and lake views, spacious
rooms, friendly service and
cooked breakfasts.

**ROTORUA: Malfroy Motor
Lodge** $$
Boutique   Map E3
*51 Malfroy Rd, 2010*
**Tel** *(07) 346 8053*
W malfroymotorlodge.co.nz
Eco-friendly family lodge with
modern facilities and a
geothermal mineral pool in
lovely gardens.

**ROTORUA: Paradise Valley
Lodge** $$
Boutique   Map E3
*1099 Paradise Valley Rd, RD2*
**Tel** *021 538 311*
W paradisevalleylodge.co.nz
A charming lodge set in a large
expanse of lawns and gardens.
Family-friendly.

**ROTORUA: The Rising Trout** $$
Bed and Breakfast   Map E3
*15 Waana St, 3074*
**Tel** *(07) 362 4858*
W risingtrout.co.nz
Well-appointed rooms by a lake
that has trout fishing. Cooked
breakfasts and complimentary
happy hour drinks.

**ROTORUA: Peppers On The
Point** $$$
Luxury   Map E3
*214 Kawaha Point Rd, 3010*
**Tel** *(07) 348 4868*
W peppers.co.nz
This retreat in a historic property
offers individually designed
rooms, views of Mokoia Island
and a gourmet restaurant.

**DK Choice**

**TAUPO: Huka Lodge** $$$
Luxury   Map E3
*271 Huka Falls Rd, 3377*
**Tel** *(07) 3785791*
W hukalodge.co.nz
A tranquil refuge set within 6 ha
(17 acres) of pristine forest and
nature reserve, Huka Lodge
sits just 300 m (985 ft) upriver
from the mighty Huka Falls. This
exclusive 25-room hideaway is
close to fishing spots and
thermal attractions.

**TAURANGA: Sebel Trinity
Wharf** $$
Chain   Map E2
*51 Dive Crescent, 3110*
**Tel** *(07) 577 8700*
W trinitywharf.co.nz
This modern hotel, on the
harbour, has a private pontoon,
a pool and free Wi-Fi.

**TAURANGA: Casa del Mare** $$$
Luxury   Map E2
*35 Monticello Key, Palm Springs
Estate, Papamoa, 3118*
**Tel** *(07) 542 2996*
W casadelmare.co.nz
A romantic hotel with
Mediterranean-style rooms
and a private courtyard.

## Wellington and
## the South

**FEATHERSTON: Wharekauhau
Country Estate** $$$
Luxury   Map E4
*Western Lake Rd, Palliser Bay, RD3,
Wairarapa, 5710*
**Tel** *646 307 7581*
W wharekauhau.co.nz
This pretty Edwardian lodge
offers country hospitality.

**KAPITI COAST: Vista del Sol** $$$
Luxury   Map E4
*20 Derham Rd, 5581*
**Tel** *(06) 364 2173*
W vistadelsol.co.nz
Luxury lodge with views of sand
dunes and rolling farmland.

**WELLINGTON: Comfort Hotel** $
Budget   Map D5
*213–223 Cuba St, Te Aro, 6141*
**Tel** *(04) 385 2156*
W hotelwellington.co.nz
Historic Edwardian hotel with
double rooms and free Wi-Fi.

**WELLINGTON:
Hotel St George** $
Budget   Map D5
*124 Willis St, Te Aro, 6011*
**Tel** *(04) 470 7777*
W hotelstgeorge.co.nz
Comfortable rooms in an Art Deco
building. Shared kitchen facilities.

**WELLINGTON: Nomads Capital** $
Budget   Map D5
*118–120 Wakefield St, 6011*
**Tel** *(04) 978 7800*
W nomadsworld.com
This hostel has double rooms, en-
suite bathrooms and cable TV.

**WELLINGTON: Quest
Wellington** $
Apartment   Map D5
*Cnr Hunter and Lambton Quay, 6011*
**Tel** *(04) 916 0700*
W questapartments.co.nz
Boutique self-contained
apartments with kitchenettes.

**WELLINGTON: Bolton Hotel** $$
Boutique   Map D5
*12 Bolton St, Lambton Quay, 6011*
**Tel** *(04) 472 9966*
W boltonhotel.co.nz
This hotel offers luxurious, stylish
rooms, a pool, spa and sauna.

**WELLINGTON: Brandon
Village** $$
Apartment   Map D5
*22 Brandon St, Wellington
Central, 6011*
**Tel** *(04) 384 1070*
W villagegroup.co.nz
Luxury apartments with kitchen
and laundry facilities.

**For key to prices** *see page 302*

**WELLINGTON: Rydges Wellington** $$
Chain Map D5
75 Featherston St, Pipitea, 6011
Tel (04) 499 8686
W rydges.com
Apartment-style suites with kitchenettes and a pool.

**WELLINGTON: The Wellesley Boutique Hotel** $$
Boutique Map D5
2–8 Maginnity St, 6011
Tel (04) 474 1308
W wellesleyboutiquehotel.co.nz
Relax in the spacious, elegant rooms in this heritage building.

**WELLINGTON: Boulcott Suites** $$$
Apartment Map D5
5 O'Reily Ave, Te Aro, 6011
Tel (04) 384 1070
W villagegroup.co.nz
Spacious townhouses and luxury suites with laundry facilities and fully equipped kitchens.

**WELLINGTON: Intercontinental Hotel** $$$
Chain Map D5
2 Grey St, 6011
Tel (04) 472 2722
W intercontinental.com/wellington
Luxury hotel with a range of room types, gym, sauna and pool.

**DK Choice**

**WELLINGTON: Museum Art Hotel** $$$
Boutique Map D5
90 Cable St, Te Aro, 6011
Tel (04) 802 8900
W museumhotel.co.nz
Close to the waterfront, the Museum Art Hotel is brimming with original works of art. The rooms are luxurious and the Hippopotamus restaurant serves fine French-influenced cusine.

**WELLINGTON: Ohtel** $$$
Boutique Map D5
66 Oriental Parade, Oriental Bay, 6011
Tel (04) 803 0600
W ohtel.com
Designer chic with stunning decor. Cable TV and free Wi-Fi.

## Marlborough and Nelson

**BLENHEIM: Scenic Hotel** $$
Chain Map D5
5 Alfred St, 7201
Tel (03) 520 6187
W scenichotels.co.nz
This comfortable, friendly hotel has an outdoor pool.

**DK Choice**

**BLENHEIM: Old Saint Mary's Convent Vineyard Estate** $$$
Luxury Map D5
776 Rapaura Rd, 7273
Tel (03) 570 5700
W convent.co.nz
Once the Victorian-era home of the Sisters of Mercy, Old Saint Mary's Convent is now a beautifully restored refuge in 25 ha (60 acres) of gardens with vineyards, olive groves, a lake and abundant birdlife.

**BLENHEIM: Vintners Retreat** $$$
Luxury Map D5
55 Rapaura Rd, 7273
Tel (03) 572 7420
W vintnersretreat.co.nz
Set amid vineyards, these private, spacious and peaceful villas have fully equipped kitchens.

**KAIKOURA: Austin Heights** $$
Bed and Breakfast Map D5
19 Austin St, 7300
Tel (03) 3195836
W austinheights.co.nz
Enjoy lovely mountain and sea views from these self-contained apartments with kitchenettes.

**KAIKOURA: Seaview Motel** $$
Boutique Map D5
164 Esplanade, 7300
Tel 0800 456 000
W seaviewmotel.co.nz
Comfortable and private beachfront motel units with kitchenettes. Secured parking.

**KAIKOURA: Waves On The Esplanade** $$$
Apartment Map D5
78 Esplanade, 7300
Tel (03) 319 5890
W kaikouraapartment.co.nz
Two-bedroom beachfront apartments with private balconies and free Wi-Fi.

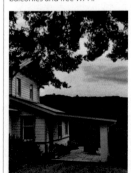
The historic McCormick House, Picton, surrounded by lush greenery

**MURCHISON: RiverSong Cottages** $
Boutique Map C5
30 Fairfax St, 7007
Tel (03) 523 9011
W riversong.co.nz
Tranquil cottages with private decks. Enjoy fresh fruit and vegetables from the gardens.

**MURCHISON: Lake Rotoroa Lodge** $$$
Luxury Map C5
Gowan Valley Rd, RD3, 7077
Tel (03) 523 9121
W lakerotoroalodge.com
A historic brown trout fishing lodge in a country house in a breathtaking forest location.

**MURCHISON: Owen River Lodge** $$$
Luxury Map C5
173 Owen Valley East Rd, Owen River, 7073
Tel (03) 523 9075
W owenriverlodge.co.nz
A five-star fishing lodge with contemporary decor in a picturesque setting.

**NELSON: Trailways Hotel** $
Boutique Map D4
66 Trafalgar St, The Wood, 7010
Tel (03) 548 7049
W trailwayshotel.co.nz
This hotel offers contemporary, stylish rooms. Excellent restaurant.

**NELSON: DeLorenzo's Studio Apartments** $$
Apartment Map D4
43–55 Trafalgar St, The Wood, 7010
Tel (03) 548 9774
W delorenzos.co.nz
Chic studio apartments with cable TV, free Wi-Fi and a pool.

**NELSON: Stonefly Lodge** $$$
Luxury Map D4
3256 Motueka Valley Hwy, Stanley Brook, 7096
Tel (03) 522 4479
W stoneflylodge.co.nz
A fishing lodge set on the riverbank in a private forest.

**PICTON: Cnoc na Lear** $$
Boutique Map D4
Queen Charlotte Track, Endeavour Inlet
Tel (03) 579 8444
W cnocnalear.co.nz
Peaceful lodge with comfortable suites and home-cooked meals.

**PICTON: McCormick House** $$$
Bed and Breakfast Map D4
21 Leicester St, 7220
Tel (03) 573 5253
W mccormickhouse.co.nz
Luxurious, beautifully furnished historic house. Gourmet breakfasts.

For more information on types of hotels see pages 298–301

Conservatory at Kapitea Ridge Hotel, Hokitika

**PORTAGE: Peppers Portage** $$$
Boutique     Map D4
*2923 Kenepuru Rd, 7282*
**Tel** *(03) 573 4309*
W portage.co.nz
This lovely wilderness retreat is
right on the waterfront.

## Canterbury and the West Coast

**AORAKI: The Hermitage** $$
Boutique     Map B6
*Aoraki Mt Cook Alpine Village, 8770*
**Tel** *(03) 435 1809*
W hermitage.co.nz
Cosy units with kitchenettes in an
incredible glacial setting.

**ARTHUR'S PASS: Wilderness
Lodge Arthur's Pass** $$$
Luxury     Map C5
*Arthur's Pass*
**Tel** *(03) 318 9246*
W wildernesslodge.co.nz
Set in a beech forest, this lodge
has well-appointed rooms.

**CHRISTCHURCH: Camelot Motor
Lodge** $
Budget     Map C6
*28 Papanui Rd, Merivale, 8014*
**Tel** *(03) 355 9124*
W www.camelot.co.nz
A wide choice of self-contained
rooms, a spa and pools.

**CHRISTCHURCH: Dorset House** $
Budget     Map C6
*1 Dorset St, 8144*
**Tel** *(03) 366 8268*
W dorset.co.nz
The sunny rooms have free Wi-Fi,
shared bathrooms and kitchen.

**CHRISTCHURCH: The Old
Country House** $
Budget     Map C6
*437 Gloucester St, Linwood, 8011*
**Tel** *(03) 381 5504*
W oldcountryhouse.co.nz
Hostel with spacious rooms and
an organic herb garden.

**CHRISTCHURCH: 315 Motel** $$
Boutique     Map C6
*315 Riccarton Rd, 8002*
**Tel** *(03) 982 9882*
W 315motelriccarton.co.nz
This motel has modern suites
with cooking facilities.

**CHRISTCHURCH: Country
Glen Lodge** $$
Motel     Map C6
*107 Bealey Ave, 8013*
**Tel** *(03) 365 9980*
W glenlodge.co.nz
The rooms here are well
appointed, with kitchens and
stylish furnishings.

**CHRISTCHURCH: Heartland
Hotel Cotswold** $$
Boutique     Map C6
*88/96 Papanui Rd,
Merivale, 8540*
**Tel** *(03) 355 3535*
W heartlandhotels.co.nz
Hospitable, Tudor-style hotel
with award-winning gardens.

**CHRISTCHURCH: Orari Bed
and Breakfast** $$
Boutique     Map C6
*42 Gloucester St, 8013*
**Tel** *(03) 365 6569*
W orari.co.nz
Spacious suites in a heritage
building with old-world charm.

**CHRISTCHURCH: Clearview
Lodge** $$$
Bed and Breakfast     Map C6
*8 Clearwater Ave, Northwood, 8051*
**Tel** *(03) 359 5797*
W clearviewlodge.com
Vineyard lodge offering suites
with balconies overlooking
peaceful gardens.

**FOX GLACIER: Heartland Hotel
Glacier Country** $
Boutique     Map B6
*39 Main Rd, 7859*
**Tel** *(03) 751 0847*
W heartlandhotels.co.nz
Hospitable hotel on the edge of
the Westland World Heritage Park.

**FRANZ JOSEF GLACIER:
Te Waonui Forest Retreat** $$$
Luxury     Map B6
*3 Wallace St, 7856*
**Tel** *(03) 752 0555*
W tewaonui.co.nz
Tucked away in the wilderness,
this hotel has large, quiet rooms.

### DK Choice

**HANMER SPRINGS: Heritage
Hanmer Springs** $$
Boutique     Map C5
*1 Conical Hill Rd, 7334*
**Tel** *(03) 315 0060*
W heritagehotels.co.nz
Just across the road from
Hanmer Springs Thermal
Reserve with its healing waters,
this well-appointed hotel in a
historic building offers a range
of accommodation options
from three-bedroom villas to
garden rooms. It has a restaurant,
outdoor pool and tennis courts.

**HOKITIKA: Shining Star
Beachfront Accommodation** $
Budget     Map C5
*16 Richards Drive, 7810*
**Tel** *(03) 755 8921*
W shiningstar.co.nz
Awe-inspiring ocean views, and a
choice of self-contained motel or
cabin accommodation.

**HOKITIKA: Kapitea Ridge
Lodge** $$$
Luxury     Map C5
*Chesterfield Rd, State Hwy 6*
**Tel** *(03) 755 6805*
W kapitea.co.nz
The suites here have gorgeous
rainforest and beach views.

**RANGIORA: Pete's Farm Stay** $$
Bed and Breakfast     Map C6
*45 Mairaki Rd, 7471*
**Tel** *(03) 313 5180*
W petesfarm.co.nz
Help feed the alpaca and sheep
at this family-friendly farm stay.

**ROLLESTON: Garden View Bed &
Breakfast** $
Bed and Breakfast     Map C6
*133 Lowes Rd, 7614*
**Tel** *(03) 347 9293*
W gardenviewbandbnz.com
Tranquil, well-appointed rooms
in a glorious garden setting full
of birdsong.

**TIMARU: The Grosvenor** $
Budget     Map C
*26 Cains Terrace, 7910*
**Tel** *(03) 688 3129*
W thegrosvenor.co.nz
There's a bohemian atmosphere
at this refurbished historic hotel.
Themed rooms and a great bar.

**For key to prices** *see page 302*

**WAIAU: The Gates Country Lodge** $$$
Boutique     Map D5
1 Gates Rd, North Canterbury, 7395
Tel (03) 315 6162
W thegateslodge.co.nz
Historic lodge in an idyllic farm setting with antique decor.

## Otago and Southland

**ARROWTOWN: Viking Lodge** $
Budget     Map B6
1 Inverness Crescent, 9302
Tel (03) 442 1765
W vikinglodge.co.nz
Self-contained chalets with kitchens, cable TV and a pool.

**DUNEDIN: Living Space** $
Budget     Map B7
92 Castle St, 9016
Tel (03) 951 5000
Comfortable, clean hotel housed in a former tannery.

**DUNEDIN: Scenic Hotel** $
Chain     Map B7
123 Princes St, 9016
Tel (03) 470 1470
W scenichotels.co.nz
The spacious rooms at this hotel have a stunning modern design.

**DUNEDIN: Brothers Boutique Hotel** $$
Boutique     Map B7
295 Rattray St, 9016
Tel (03) 477 0043
W brothershotel.co.nz
A charming heritage building with harbour views. Free Wi-Fi.

**DUNEDIN: Scenic Hotel Dunedin City** $$
Chain     Map B7
18 High St, 9054
Tel (03) 477 0752
W scenichotels.co.nz
Dunedin's largest hotel offers elegant rooms and superb service.

A plush room at Scenic Hotel Dunedin City

## DK Choice

**DUNEDIN: Camp Estate, Larnach Castle** $$$
Luxury     Map B7
100 Camp Rd, Larnach Castle, 9077
Tel (03) 476 1616
W larnachcastle.co.nz
A beautiful country house in the grounds of New Zealand's only genuine castle, Camp Estate has five spacious rooms decorated in Neo-Classical style with fireplaces and views of the surrounding countryside.

**DUNEDIN: Glendinning House** $$$
Bed and Breakfast     Map B7
222 Highgate, Roslyn, 9010
Tel (03) 477 8262
W glendinninghouse.co.nz
A heritage house with modern facilities and superb service.

**FIORDLAND: Possum Lodge** $
Budget     Map A6
13 Murrell Ave, Manapouri, 9679
Tel (03) 249 6623
W possumlodge.co.nz
Self-contained cottages, motel units, cabins and tent sites in an incredible natural setting.

**HAAST: Heartland World Heritage Hotel** $
Budget     Map B6
7844 State Hwy 6, 7886
Tel (03) 3775767
W heartlandhotels.co.nz
Tranquil hotel nestled in a world heritage park. On-site pub.

**MILFORD SOUND: Milford Sound Lodge** $
Budget     Map A6
State Hwy 94
Tel (03) 249 8071
W milfordlodge.com
Basic but comfortable dorm-style rooms, cabins and tent sites.

**QUEENSTOWN: Nomads Queenstown** $
Budget     Map A6
5/11 Church St, 9300
Tel (03) 441 3922
W nomadsworld.com
Hostel with dorms and some private rooms with en suite baths.

**QUEENSTOWN: YHA Queenstown Central** $
Budget     Map A6
48A Shotover St, 9300
Tel (03) 442 7400
W yha.co.nz
Busy backpacker hostel with a selection of private rooms with en suite baths.

**QUEENSTOWN: The Ferry** $$
Bed and Breakfast     Map A6
92 Spence Rd, 9371
Tel (03) 442 2194
W ferry.co.nz
Historic hotel for fishing and skiing enthusiasts set in English cottage gardens. Home cooking and great service.

**QUEENSTOWN: Heartland Hotel Queenstown** $$
Boutique     Map A6
27 Stanley St, 9300
Tel (03) 442 7700
W heartlandhotels.co.nz
Hotel offering charming, chalet-style rooms, friendly service and mountain and lake views.

**QUEENSTOWN: Oaks Shores** $$
Apartment     Map A6
327–343 Frankton Rd, 9300
Tel (03) 450 0005
W oakshotelsresorts.com
Spacious, stylish apartment-style rooms with modern decor, kitchens and balconies.

**QUEENSTOWN: Scenic Suites** $$
Apartment     Map A6
27 Stanley St, 9348
Tel (03) 442 4718
W scenichotels.co.nz
Spectacular mountain and lake views can be enjoyed from the hotel's elevated position. Luxurious suites.

**QUEENSTOWN: Azur Luxury Lodge** $$$
Luxury     Map A6
23 Mackinnon Terrace, Sunshine Bay, 9300
Tel (03) 409 0588
W azur.co.nz
Nine stunning open-plan villas offer peace and tranquillity. Spa treatments and attentive service.

**QUEENSTOWN: Queenstown Country Lodge** $$$
Luxury     Map A6
497 Frankton–Ladies Mile Hwy, 9371
Tel (03) 441 8548
W queenstowncountrylodge.co.nz
Lodge offering luxuriously appointed rooms, set in secluded gardens and farmland, and surrounded by mountains. Excellent service.

**QUEENSTOWN: Villa Forty Two** $$$
Luxury     Map A6
42 Man St, 9300
Tel (03) 450 0855
W touchofspice.co.nz
Immaculate three-bedroom apartment by the lake and mountains. Barbecue area and swimming pool.

For more information on types of hotels see pages 298–301

# WHERE TO EAT

New Zealand's restaurants and cuisine have both undergone a revolution in the past few decades. Whereas eating in restaurants was once reserved for special occasions and usually included a traditional European meal, such as roast lamb and vegetables, New Zealand now has a wide variety of eating places to suit all tastes and all budgets. Although plainer fare is still available, the country's multicultural population has meant that restaurants serving traditional food sit alongside those offering cuisine from almost every corner of the world. Influences from Asia and the Pacific have been particularly significant. New Zealand restaurants make good use of home-grown produce, such as fresh fish (including whitebait), oysters, mussels, cray-fish (rock lobsters), beef, lamb and venison, as well as vegetables and fruit. These can be enjoyed with a glass of New Zealand wine *(see pp312–13)*. A popular experience is a Maori *hangi*, where food is wrapped and cooked on heated rocks under the ground.

The lounge bar at Herzog Winery and Restaurant in Blenheim *(see p321)*

## Types of Restaurants

New Zealand's major cities have a vibrant restaurant scene ranging from formal dining to a multitude of casual cafés. Diners can experience haute cuisine or eat in a café offering cheaper, simpler food. Some eateries feature courtyard, garden or pavement seating. There is every type of ethnic restaurant imaginable, offering the cuisines of every continent, such as Chinese, Cambodian, Malaysian, Turkish and Greek. Some high-quality restaurants can be found in provincial and rural areas. Many vineyard restaurants serve ploughman's lunches with seating among the vines as well as more formal meals in picturesque restaurant settings. Pubs also offer food that can range from cheap and basic fare to more sophisticated, restaurant-quality dishes. A typical and very popular pub meal is a roast.

A meal in a café or ethnic restaurant can cost as little as NZ$15 for a one-course meal. Restaurant prices range from NZ$25 to more than NZ$100 per person for a three-course meal. A range of fast-food chains, such as McDonalds, KFC and Burger King, have franchises in New Zealand, and there are the traditional, local fish and chip shops as well as gourmet burger and pizza outlets.

## Eating Hours and Reservations

Many restaurants serve lunch from noon to 2pm and dinner from 6 to 10pm. Some establishments open earlier and serve increasingly popular "all day breakfasts". Late-night and 24-hour cafés are gaining in popularity.

Bookings are often necessary at more formal restaurants. Cafés and bars vary in their booking policies, with some taking reservations and others operating on a casual basis. It pays to ring and check to avoid disappointment.

## Paying and Tipping

The majority of restaurants and cafés accept credit cards, though it is a good idea to check when booking. Most restaurants will not accept personal cheques or traveller's cheques. Government taxes are included in the menu prices and there are no service charges. Tipping is not standard

Exquisite views from the restaurant at Cable Bay Vineyards *(see p315)*

Tables outside a café at Mount Maunganui

procedure, although a tip will be appreciated for very good service. Patrons can leave tips in cash on the table or a tip jar on the counter, or include them in credit card payments.

## Children

Most restaurants cater for children. If travelling with very young children, it is best to check with the restaurant to ensure that children are welcome. An option in busy cafés is to book early before large numbers of adult diners arrive. Chinese, Greek and other ethnic restaurants tend to have more relaxed attitudes towards children. Fast-food chains can be found in most cities and towns, and children usually enjoy a takeaway meal at the park or beach. Families staying in motels with equipped kitchens may find that a trip to a local supermarket provides a break from having to take small children to eat out in restaurants.

## Wheelchair Access

Government regulations require building owners to ensure that new and redeveloped buildings are accessible by wheelchair. Many restaurants provide toilet facilities for the disabled.

## Vegetarians

Many restaurants offer some vegetarian meals and will usually be happy to adapt menus, especially in areas where there is an abundance of home-grown produce. Many restaurants also have dairy-free and gluten-free options. Most Asian restaurants in New Zealand also offer vegetarian food on their menus. There are more than 50 vegetarian and vegan restaurants in Auckland alone. The Doctor Feelgood website (www.doctorfeelgood. co.nz) has a full lists of vegetarian establishments.

## BYO Restaurants

BYO means "bring your own" alcohol. Instead of a full liquor licence, restaurants may have a BYO licence that allows diners to bring their own alcohol. This is cheaper than buying alcohol on the premises, although a fee may be charged for corkage. Some fully licensed restaurants allow diners to bring their own wine, but corkage charges can add NZ$5–10 to the bill.

## Alcohol and Other Drinks

Licensed restaurants and bars serve a range of alcohol, including wine, beer and spirits. Many cafés are also fully licensed, but offer a more limited range of alcohol. Many restaurants and cafés highlight New Zealand wines and boutique beers. Restaurants in wine-growing areas usually specialize in wine from that region. Tap water is safe in all urban and town supply areas, and bottled still and sparkling water is available in all dining establishments.

## Dress

Dress in New Zealand is informal compared to many other parts of the world, especially when dining out for lunch. It is unlikely that a jacket or tie will be needed, although visitors may feel more comfortable if they are formally dressed at the more upmarket restaurants. Informal but tidy dress is appreciated at less formal restaurants. Street fashion is acceptable at inner-city cafés.

## Smoking

Along with most other indoor workplaces and on all public transport, restaurants, cafés and bars became smoke-free zones by law at the end of 2004. At present, the ban does not apply to outdoor dining areas, and where possible, restaurateurs make every effort to satisfy a customer's requirements. It is common for most restaurants in New Zealand to have dedicated gardens or gazebos for smokers to retreat to, away from other diners.

## Recommended Restaurants

The restaurants on pages 314–25 have been carefully selected to give a cross-section of the best options from across the country: from the smartest and most upmarket establishments to the best budget food vendors.

Many eateries boast spectacular rural locations and views of New Zealand's dramatic coastline, but some of the tastiest (and cheapest) meals are to be enjoyed in urban environments, especially in Auckland and Wellington, where there is a good selection of fantastic Asian restaurants.

The DK Choice category draws attention to the truly exceptional establishments: those that boast superb cuisine, beverages, presentation, service, atmosphere or location, or provide an outstanding overall experience.

# The Flavours of New Zealand

Cuisine in New Zealand is most likely to be characterized by its freshness and diversity and, as a relatively youthful nation, there is a willingness to experiment with food and flavours. Surrounded by clean ocean and with extremely fertile land, New Zealand offers food of the very highest standards, and many of its producers are certified organic, reinforcing its clean, green image. New Zealand's cuisine has been described as Pacific Rim, drawing inspiration from Europe, Asia, Polynesia and its indigenous people, the Maori. Chefs hailing from New Zealand are among the most sought-after in the world, due to their contemporary approach and passion for good ingredients.

Avocado oil

Flock of New Zealand's superb, pasture-fed sheep

## Meat

There are over 30 million sheep in New Zealand, all bred on natural, free-range pastureland. New Zealand lamb is world-famous and features on menus. It appears in a wide variety of dishes, ranging from a traditional rack of lamb to a Moroccan-style lamb tagine – and you can always expect to see more than a few chops on a barbecue. For a change from lamb, there are plenty of other meats available, such as beef, pork, chicken and cervena, which is a lighter, leaner style of farmed venison.

## Fish & Seafood

New Zealand has a plentiful supply of *kaimoana* (seafood), with many local varieties – in particular blue cod from the South Island and the Chatham Islands, oysters from Bluff, Southland, and the amazing green lip mussels of Havelock, Marlborough Sounds. Snapper *tarakihi* and *hapuku* (the Maori name for grouper) are the most common saltwater fish. There is also wonderful farmed salmon (wild salmon cannot

Mussels | Lobster | Samphire | Red snapper | Salmon | Clam | Whitebait

Selection of seafood found in the waters of New Zealand

### New Zealand's Varied Cuisine

Cuisine in New Zealand is very diverse. Fine dining often has a French influence with a modern edge, and you will also find great bistros serving classics such as *boeuf bourguignon* and *tarte au citron*. Cafés in New Zealand tend to have a more relaxed, Mediterranean approach. Most pubs serve a wide range of dishes, such as fish, salads, steaks and, of course, roast meats. There are increasing numbers of pubs serving restaurant-quality food. New Zealand is part of the Asia-Pacific region, and there is a vibrant Asian flavour to be found in many dishes. Look out for whitebait fritters on the West Coast from August to September, when the season is at its peak. Eating at one of the many wonderful vineyard restaurants is highly recommended, as is the chance to sample a genuine Maori *hangi*.

Manuka honey

**Kumara soup** Made with the native sweet potato, this soup is especially delicous topped with goat's cheese croutons.

Basket of yams in a local farmers' market

be sold commercially). Other popular fish include, John Dory, monkfish and blue warehau. As for shellfish, New Zealand has a native clam called *tuangi*, as well as bivalves called *tuatua* and *pipi*. Oysters, mussels and crayfish are also popular.

Upmarket fish and chips, best enjoyed outdoors by the sea

## Fruit & Vegetables

The almost perfect farming conditions in New Zealand mean that the enormous variety of produce cultivated is of a consistently high quality. All common vegetables are farmed here, alongside some native varieties. Kumara is a local sweet potato, and a traditional Maori food. They are often baked in their jackets, and also boiled, roasted, fried or scalloped (sliced, seasoned, and slowly cooked in milk). Other common root vegetables are parsnips and yams. The tamarillo (tree tomato), kiwi fruit and feijoa are all local fruits. During harvest time, look out for roadside stalls near farms, selling fresh vegetables and fruit cheaply. Honey from the native Manuka plant is popular worldwide for its woody, earthy aromas and supposed medicinal properties. Also gaining fame around the globe is the delicious and decadent avocado oil from the North Island.

## Dairy Produce

The conditions in New Zealand are perfect for dairy farming. Wonderful cheeses, yoghurt and ice cream, made by small producers can be found all over the country. Hokey-pokey ice cream is a New Zealand speciality – delicious vanilla ice cream loaded with caramel chunks.

### Maori Food (*Kai*)

New Zealand's abundant supply of food is explained in Maori legend as a gift from the gods. From Tane, god of the forest, come the game birds, from Tangaroa seafood, from Haumia wild plants, and from Rongo cultivated vegetables.

The main traditional method for feasting is the *hangi* (pronounced hung-ee). Men heat stones in a fire and dig an earth pit, while women prepare the meat and vegetables. The stones are placed in the pit with the food (covered in cloth), and earth is piled back into the pit. The food cooks slowly for up to four hours. The results of this laborious process are worth the wait – succulent, tender meat and smoky, delicious vegetables.

**Pan fried hapuka** Roasted shallots, pancetta and rocket give this popular fish a Mediterranean flavour.

**Grilled lamb** Simple, fresh flavours, such as polenta and red pepper sauce, complement this superb meat.

**Pavlova** Aussies and Kiwis disagree over who invented this delicious meringue, cream and fruit dessert.

# What to Drink in New Zealand

New Zealanders were until the 1960s a nation of beer drinkers and wine consumption was not that common. However, the meteoric rise of New Zealand's wine industry, which has scooped many international awards, means wine has enjoyed a dramatic rise in popularity since the early 1960s. New Zealand's temperate maritime climate is ideal for maximizing grape ripeness and the production of premium, intensely flavoured wines. There are almost 700 wineries throughout the country, many near the coast (see pp40–41). Guides on wines, vineyards and vineyard restaurants are available at larger book shops or can be found at www.nzwine.com.

Wine tasting at C J Pask Winery, Hastings (see pp154–5)

## White Wine

Sauvignon Blanc is regarded as New Zealand's most outstanding white wine, with critics naming

New Zealand Sauvignon Blanc as the world's finest. New Zealand's white wines, produced by both modern and traditional methods, are known for their fruit flavours. There is also a fascinating range of Chardonnays to choose from, ranging from cheaper Chardonnays fermented in stainless steel tanks and bottled young to more expensive Chardonnays fermented and aged

Huia
Sauvignon
Blanc

Palliser
Sauvignon
Blanc

in oak barrels. Riesling is growing in popularity, with New Zealand Riesling often described as similar to the light and elegant German style. Pinot Gris is also increasingly popular.

## Sweet White Wine

New Zealand sweet wines are also winning international recognition and awards. The most interesting of these sweet wines are made from botrytis-affected grapes, with the Marlborough region emerging as a leading producer of the finest wines (see pp210–11). However, the weather conditions needed to produce botrytis-type wines occur irregularly in New Zealand, and therefore prices for these luscious dessert wines tend to be somewhat higher than other wine varieties.

Cave cellar at Gibbston Valley Wines (see p282)

| Wine Type | Regions | Recommended Producers |
|-----------|---------|----------------------|
| Chardonnay | All key wine regions | Church Road, Clearview, Cloudy Bay, Corbans, Hunters, Morton Estate Wines, Vavasour |
| Chenin Blanc | Gisborne, Hawke's Bay | Collard Brothers, The Millton Vineyard |
| Gewürztraminer | Central Otago, Gisborne, Hawke's Bay, Marlborough | Brookfields, Chifney Wines, Dry River, Eskdale, Gatehouse, Lawson's Dry Hills, Stonecroft |
| Muller-Thurgau | Gisborne, Hawke's Bay, Marlborough | Corbans Gisborne Winery, Pleasant Valley Wines, Vidal of Hawke's Bay, Villa Maria |
| Pinot Gris | Canterbury, Marlborough | Brookfields, Dry River, Margrain, Martinborough Vineyard |
| Riesling | Canterbury, Central Otago, Hawke's Bay, Marlborough, Nelson, Wairarapa | Allan Scott Wines and Estates, Collards, Cooper's Creek, Corbans, Framingham Wine Company, Grove Mill, Martinborough Vineyard, Neudorf, Stoneleigh |
| Sauvignon Blanc | Canterbury, Gisborne, Hawke's Bay, Marlborough | Cloudy Bay, Grove Mill, Hunters, Jackson Estate, Nautilus, Palliser, Selaks, Villa Maria |
| Sémillon | Gisborne, Hawke's Bay, Marlborough | Collards, Huntaway, Kim Crawford, Pleasant Valley, Vidal of Hawke's Bay |
| Sweet wines | Central Otago, Gisborne, Hawke's Bay, Marlborough | Church Road, Cooper's Creek, Cottage Block, Dry River, Framingham Wine Company, Villa Maria |

## Sparkling Wine

New Zealand sparkling wines are world class and have won a number of awards. Deutz Marlborough Cuvée was voted "Sparkling Wine of the Year" in the Great Wine Challenge held in Britain in 1998 and has been awarded numerous medals since. Visitors should be aware that there are two types of sparkling wine. At the bottom end of the market, "bubblies" are carbonated wines and tend to be rather sweet. However, the middle and top ends of the market feature *méthode traditionnelle* labels made by bottle fermentation methods. Marlborough is regarded as the country's top region for bottle-fermented *méthode traditionnelle*, although other regions in the country are now also gaining a reputation for producing high quality products.

**Huia Marlborough Brut**

### Wine Regions of New Zealand

| Auckland | Cabernet Sauvignon, Chardonnay, Merlot, Pinot Noir |
| --- | --- |
| Northland | Cabernet Sauvignon, Chardonnay, Merlot |
| Waikato and Bay of Plenty | Cabernet Sauvignon, Chardonnay, Chenin Blanc, Sauvignon Blanc |
| Gisborne | Chardonnay, Muller-Thurgau, Muscat, Sémillon |
| Hawke's Bay | Cabernet, Chardonnay, Chenin Blanc, Merlot, Sauvignon Blanc, Sémillon, Shiraz |
| Wairarapa | Chardonnay, Pinot Noir, Riesling, Sauvignon Blanc |
| Nelson | Chardonnay, Pinot Noir, Riesling, Sauvignon Blanc |
| Marlborough | Chardonnay, Pinot Noir, Riesling, Sauvignon Blanc |
| Canterbury | Chardonnay, Pinot Gris, Pinot Noir, Riesling |
| Otago | Chardonnay, Pinot Noir, Riesling, Sauvignon Blanc |

### Red Wine

Although New Zealand is still primarily known for its white wines, its red wines are gaining in importance as wine makers discover better sites, perfect their viticulture methods and as vines mature, making them more stable. Pinot Noir is the most widely planted red variety, but Cabernet Sauvignon, Merlot and Cabernet Franc are also well suited to New Zealand's soil and climatic conditions. Wine makers frequently blend red wines from different areas and provinces.

**Alana Estate Pinot Noir**

Clearview Estate's popular seaside restaurant, Hawke's Bay *(see pp154–5)*

| Wine Type | Regions | Recommended Producers |
| --- | --- | --- |
| Cabernet Sauvignon | Auckland, Hawke's Bay, Northland, Waikato | Benfield, Brookfields, Church Road, Delamere Esk Valley, Goldwater, Morton Estate, Villa Maria |
| Merlot | Auckland, Gisborne, Hawke's Bay, Marlborough | Arahura, Babich, Church Road, C J Pask, Clearview Estate, Corbans, Delegates, Esk Valley, Villa Maria |
| Pinotage | Auckland, Gisborne, Hawke's Bay, Marlborough | Cottle Hill Winery, Kerr Farm Vineyard, Landmark Estate Wines, Ohinemuri Estate Wine, Pleasant Valley |
| Pinot Noir | Canterbury, Central Otago, Hawke's Bay, Marlborough, Nelson, Wairarapa | Ata Rangi, Black Ridge, Cloudy Bay, Cooper's Creek, Dry River, Martinborough Vineyard, Palliser, Rippon Vineyard |

## Beer

Beer remains a popular drink in New Zealand and beers such as Steinlager and Kiwi Lager have won international recognition. There are about 68 breweries in the country producing styles that range from light lagers to draft beers and malt ales. Beer is usually served chilled and is available on tap in bars and hotels. Low-alcohol beers as well as overseas bottled and canned beers are available in supermarkets, bottle stores, bars and restaurants.

**Steinlager**

## Other Drinks

New Zealand's climate, which ranges from subtropical to alpine, allows the cultivation of a large variety of fresh fruit for juicing, including its famous kiwifruit *(see p133)*. Its apples are made into cider. Other bottled drinks and mineral waters are also widely available. A speciality is Lemon and Paeroa, a lemon-flavoured carbonated mineral water originally from Paeroa on the Hauraki Plains. Coffee and tea are other popular drinks with New Zealanders.

**Kiwifruit**

# Where to Eat and Drink

## Auckland

### Art Gallery Café
Café                                  **Map** E2    $
*Kitchener St, CBD, 1010*
**Tel** *(09) 369 1149*
This daytime café has art-themed dishes, an "aspiring artists" menu for children and plenty of gluten-free, dairy-free and vegetarian options.

### Barilla Dumpling
Chinese                               **Map** E2    $
*571 Dominion Rd, Balmoral, 1446*
**Tel** *(09) 638 8032*
Come here for all sorts of dumplings – boiled, steamed or fried. They are fragrant, flavourful and inexpensive. Cash only.

### Bikanervala
Indian                                **Map** E2    $
*2 White Swan Rd, Mt Roskill, 1041*
**Tel** *(09) 630 1899*
Indulge in Bikanervala's extensive range of mouth-watering, spicy vegetarian meals, including an exquisite selection of *dosas* (rice batter and black lentil pancakes). There is also a sweet shop on site.

### Bird On A Wire
Rotisserie                            **Map** E2    $
*234 Ponsonby Rd, Ponsonby, 1011*
**Tel** *(09) 378 6369*
Succulent free-range rotisserie chicken that comes every which way – breaded, basted or in a burger bun.

### Eden Noodles
Chinese                               **Map** E2    $
*105 Dominion Rd, Mt Eden, 1024*
**Tel** *(09) 630 1899*        **Closed** *Sun*
Tiny, bustling restaurant with loyal patrons enjoying spicy Sichuan soup, noodles and dumplings. Extensive menu; no credit cards.

### Fish Market Wynyard Quarter
Seafood                               **Map** E2    $
*22 Jellicoe St, Westhaven, 1011*
**Tel** *(09) 303 0262*
A treat for seafood lovers, this restaurant is located on Auckland's wharf. Fish straight off the boats is cooked any way you want.

### Happy Japanese
Japanese                              **Map** E2    $
*4038 Great North Rd, Kelston, 0602*
**Tel** *(09) 813 1078*
This big, bustling establishment offers a wide range of à la carte dishes, set menus, sushi and even Japanese-flavoured burgers. Wash it down with some sake.

### Jai Jalaram Khaman
Indian                                **Map** E2    $
*570 Sandringham Rd, Sandringham, 1025*
**Tel** *(09) 845 5555*        **Closed** *Mon*
Sit down and savour vegetarian Gujarati and South Indian street food. Try the amazing *pau bhaji* (bread with a thick, tangy curry) and the spicy veggie burgers

### Jolin Shanghai
Chinese                               **Map** E2    $
*248 Dominion Rd, Mt Eden, 1024*
**Tel** *(09) 631 5575*
Head here for Chinese food on a budget. The marinated pork ribs and soupy dumplings are fantastic.

### Kati Grill
East Indian                           **Map** E2    $
*146 Karangahape Rd, CBD,1010*
**Tel** *(09) 302 5284*
Delicious Kati rolls, made with paratha (Indian flat bread), are stuffed with various fillings such as tandoor cooked chicken, lamb or spicy vegetables.

---

### Price Guide
Prices are based on a three-course meal per person, without drinks, and inclusive of taxes and service charges.

| | |
|---|---|
| $ | up to NZ$50 |
| $$ | NZ$50–NZ$150 |
| $$$ | over NZ$150 |

---

### Kokako
Café                                  **Map** E2    $
*537 Great North Rd, Grey Lynn, 1021*
**Tel** *(09) 379 2868*        **Closed** *Sun*
Daytime café where everything is fresh, organic and vegetarian. The salads are meals in themselves, and the coffee is divine.

### Mamak Malaysian
Malaysian                             **Map** E2    $
*Cnr Kitchener and Wellesley sts, CBD, 1010*
**Tel** *(09) 948 6479*        **Closed** *Mon*
Expect friendly, helpful service at one of Auckland's best Malaysian eateries. Don't miss the crispy, soft-shelled crab or the incredible *laksa* – spicy noodles with curry.

### Original California Burrito Company
Tex Mex                               **Map** E2    $
*8 Commerce St, CBD, 1010*
**Tel** *(09) 375 3061*
This is a franchise with multiple branches, but the food is hearty and reliable. Extensive menu.

### Sanchun Bamboo House
Korean                                **Map** E2    $
*9 Commerce St, CBD, 1010*
**Tel** *(09) 377 8377*        **Closed** *Sun*
The food at this small, charming restaurant is the next best thing to home-cooked Korean cuisine.

### Takapuna Beach Café
Café                                  **Map** E2    $
*22 The Promenade, Takapuna, 0622*
**Tel** *(09) 484 0002*
This excellent beachside venue offers delicious casual dining. Try the hand-made ice creams.

### Basque Kitchen and Bar
Spanish                               **Map** E2    $$
*61 Davis Crescent (entrance on Short St), Newmarket, 1023*
**Tel** *(09) 523 1057*        **Closed** *Sun*
This restaurant serves excellent Spanish tapas and wines.

### Café Hanoi
Vietnamese                            **Map** E2    $$
*Cnr Galway and Commerce St, Britomart, 1010*
**Tel** *(09) 302 3478*
Authentic Vietnamese dining with shared plates. Deft seasonings and free-range meat ensure a gastronomic treat.

Contemporary interior of Kokako, Auckland, known for its organic fare

**Casita Miro** $$
Mediterranean **Map** E2
*3 Brown Rd, Onetangi, Waiheke
Island, 1081*
**Tel** *(09) 372 7854*
Specializing in Spanish and
Mediterranean cuisine, the menu
here features delicious tapas as
well as larger plates to share.

**Coco's Cantina** $$
Italian **Map** E2
*376 Karangahape Rd, Newton, 1010*
**Tel** *(09) 300 7582* **Closed** *Sun & Mon*
Coco's is an Italian-style bistro:
casual dining, no bookings and
a great place to hang out. Try the
juicy steaks.

Cable Bay restaurant, Auckland, set amid sprawling grounds

---

**DK Choice**

**Depot Eatery and
Oyster Bar** $$
Seafood **Map** E2
*86 Federal St, CBD, 1010*
**Tel** *(09) 363 7048*
Fine dining in an informal
atmosphere features at this
award-winning restaurant.
Simple dishes using seasonal
produce are prepared over
charcoal or hard wood. Try a
selection of small plates. Swift
service. No reservations.

---

**The Engine Room** $$
Bistro **Map** E2
*115 Queen St, Northcote Point, 0627*
**Tel** *(09) 480 9502* **Closed** *Sun & Mon*
A fine dining restaurant, the
Engine Room has won a number
of awards for its classic bistro
dishes made with local produce.

**Moochowchow** $$
Thai **Map** E2
*23 Ponsonby Rd, Ponsonby, 1010*
**Tel** *(09) 360 6262* **Closed** *Sun*
This Thai restaurant offers
delectable, fragrant dishes that
delight the palate. The jasmine-
smoked salmon is a good choice.

**Antoine's** $$$
Fine dining **Map** E2
*333 Parnell Rd, Parnell, 1052*
**Tel** *(09) 379 8756* **Closed** *Sun*
Antoine's has been serving
delicious French-European
cuisine since 1973. Try the
timeless favourites such as roast
duck with Grand Marnier sauce.

**Botswana Butchery** $$$
Fine dining **Map** E2
*99 Quay St, CBD, 1010*
**Tel** *(09) 307 6966*
Slow-roasted lamb shoulder
and rib-eye steak count among
the specialities here in the
sumptuous historic Ferry Building
overlooking the harbour.

**Cable Bay** $$$
Vineyard **Map** E2
*12 Nick Johnstone Drive,
Oneroa, Waiheke Island, 1971*
**Tel** *(09) 372 5889*
Enjoy amazing views of the
Hauraki Gulf at this restaurant,
and a delicious à la carte menu
featuring fresh local produce;
alternatively, the adjoining wine
bar offers small plates.

**Cibo** $$$
Fine dining **Map** E2
*91 St Georges Bay Rd, Parnell, 1149*
**Tel** *(09) 303 9660* **Closed** *Sun*
Housed in an old chocolate
factory, the award-winning Cibo
offers seasonal dishes prepared
with flair. There is a coutyard for
alfresco summer dining.

**Clooney** $$$
Fine dining **Map** E2
*33 Sale St, Freemans Bay, 1010*
**Tel** *(09) 358 1702* **Closed** *Mon*
Winner of several awards,
including Metro magazine's
coveted Best Restaurant 2012 in
the greater Auckland area,
Clooney serves classic dishes
with a contemporary twist.

**Cocoro** $$$
Japanese **Map** E2
*56A Brown St, Ponsonby, 1021*
**Tel** *(09) 360 0927* **Closed** *Sun
& Mon*
Japanese cuisine with a
difference. The exquisite dishes
are a world away from takeaway
sushi. The octopus sashimi is a
popular choice.

**Euro** $$$
Contemporary **Map** E2
*Shed 22, Princes Wharf, Viaduct*
**Tel** *(09) 309 9866*
Euro boasts an exceptional,
diverse menu created under the
leadership of chef Simon Gault.
Try the pizzas or the Bluff oysters.
Lovely waterfront views.

**Sugar Club** $$$
Fusion **Map** E2
*90 Federal St, CBD, 1010*
**Tel** *(09) 363 6000*
In this fourth incarnation of the
iconic Sugar Club, chef Peter
Gordon expertly mixes and
matches Asian and European
cuisine 57 floors above Auckland
in the Sky Tower.

---

# Northland

**DARGAVILLE: Funky Fish Café** $
Café **Map** E1
*34 Sea View Rd, Baylys Beach, 0377*
**Tel** *(09) 439 8883* **Closed** *Mon*
A classic New Zealand fish 'n'
chips experience with a
difference: this is a restaurant,
café and bar in one with live
music, and nature on its doorstep.

**KAIPARA: Dragon's Rest Café** $
Café **Map** E1
*11 Oruawharo Rd, Topuni, 0975*
**Tel** *(09) 431 2893*
This country café, housed in
an old railway station, offers tasty
home-made fusion dishes and
live music at weekends. There is
also a deli section.

**KAITAIA: Bushman's Hut** $$
Steakhouse **Map** D1
*5 Bank St, 0410*
**Tel** *(09) 408 4320* **Closed** *Sun*
Casual dining in a rustic
atmosphere, often with
live music. The steak is legendary
and portions are generous.

**KERIKERI: Ake Ake Vineyard
and Restaurant** $
Vineyard **Map** E1
*165 Waimate North Rd, 0293*
**Tel** *(09) 407 8230*
This bistro-style restaurant uses
fresh local produce to create
fulsome flavours that complement
the organic wines.

Alfresco dining in the subtropical gardens at Food At Wharepuke

## DK Choice

### KERIKERI: Food At Wharepuke
Fusion $ **Map** E1
190 Kerikeri Rd, 0230
**Tel** (09) 407 8936 **Closed** Mon
Serving European and Thai-inspired dishes, Food At Wharepuke wins awards and critics' accolades year after year for its tasty concoctions made largely from the restaurant's own organic gardens. Its accent on Thai flavours complements the airy garden setting.

### KERIKERI: Posh Nosh Café $
Mediterranean **Map** E1
3 Homestead Rd, 0230
**Tel** (09) 407 7213 **Closed** Sun & hols
Mediterranean-oriented cuisine, including tapas, and excellent coffee, distinguish this relaxing venue. Try the cafe's house blend coffee.

### KERIKERI: Marsden Estate $$
Café **Map** E1
56 Wiroa Rd, 0293
**Tel** (09) 407 9398
Come here to enjoy exquisitely prepared fresh food with excellent wines on a terrace overlooking the vineyard and lake. A great experience.

### KOHUKOHU: Koke Pub and Café $
Café **Map** D1
1372 Kohukohu Rd, 0491
**Tel** (09) 405 5808
Hearty dishes, such as rich and creamy mushroom pies, fish 'n' chips, as well as great coffee, are served at this delightful open-air café in a remote village. The portions are generous and the prices reasonable.

### MANGAWAHI: Harvest Café $
Café **Map** E1
198 Molesworth Drive, 0505
**Tel** (09) 431 4111
A reliably great daytime café, Harvest is open til late Thursday to Saturday. It has an extensive menu and live music at nights. The eggs Benedict is a must.

### MANGAWHAI: Sail Rock Café $$
Café **Map** E1
12A Wood St, Mangawhai Heads, 0505
**Tel** (09) 431 4051 **Closed** Wed eve in winter
The Sail Rock Café is justifiably an iconic Mangawhai institution. Indulge in their signature dish, the incredible salt and pepper squid.

### MANGAWHAI: Sandbar and Grill $$
Pub **Map** E1
7 Wood St, Mangawhai Heads, 0505
**Tel** (09) 431 5587
The food at Sandbar and Grill is prepared with locally sourced produce, perfectly paired with local wines. The ambience is relaxed – a good place to enjoy a full meal or just linger over coffee.

### MANGAWHAI: Frog and Kiwi $$$
French **Map** E1
6 Molesworth Drive, 0505
**Tel** (09) 431 4439
An intimate, charming restaurant serving genuine Gallic dishes, the Frog and Kiwi invites patrons to linger. Good service.

### MANGONUI: Waterfront Café and Bar $
Contemporary **Map** D1
1A Waterfront Drive, 0420
**Tel** (09) 406 0850
Superb views of the waterfront, and excellent brunches featuring simple, fresh-cooked produce with a wine list to match, feature here. There is also a kids' menu.

### MATAKANA: Ascension Wine Estate $$
Bistro **Map** E2
480 Matakana Rd, 0982
**Tel** (09) 422 9601 **Closed** Sun
The famous Ascension vineyards offer The Larder menu, consisting of delicious deli-style fare to accompany fine wines.

### MATAKANA: Plume $$$
Fine dining **Map** E2
49A Sharp Rd, 0982
**Tel** (09) 422 7915 **Closed** Mon
A treat of fusion food made with local produce is served at this stunning restaurant with panoramic vineyard views.

### MOEREWA: Lori's Cookery $
Café **Map** E1
63 State Hwy 1, 0211
**Tel** (09) 404 1818 **Closed** Sun
This home bakery boasts a great selection of 18 different pie flavours and milkshakes to wash them down.

### OMAPERE: Bryers Room Restaurant $
Contemporary **Map** D1
State Hwy. 12, 0473
**Tel** (09) 405 8737
Housed in a hotel, this restaurant specializes in fresh crayfish and offers a great selection of Northland wines.

### OPUA: Marina Café $
Seafood **Map** E1
Opua Marina Bldg, Baffin St, 0200
**Tel** (09) 402 6991
This family-run venue specializing in seafood has great views of the Kawakawa river. There is live music in summer. Open till late.

### PAIHIA: Alfresco's Restaurant and Bar $
Contemporary **Map** E1
6 Marsden Rd, 0200
**Tel** (09) 402 6797
Enjoy inspired food, made with fresh produce, and waterfront views. A great place to relax.

Lunching on the terrace at Marsden Estate, Kerikeri

### PAIHIA: Jimmy Jack's
### Rib Shack $
American      Map E1
*9 Williams Rd, 0200*
**Tel** *(09) 402 5002*
An unpretentious eatery whose
speciality is prime rib platters.
Big portions, cooked just right,
for a reasonable price.

### RUSSELL: The Gables $$$
Fine dining      Map E1
Café
*19 The Strand, 0202*
**Tel** *(09) 403 7670*
Housed in a heritage building, The
Gables serves perfectly cooked,
fresh local cuts of beef and lamb
as well as a range of seafood.
Stunning waterfront views.

### WHANGAREI: Killer Prawn $$
Seafood      Map E1
*26–28 Bank St, 0110*
**Tel** *(09) 430 3333*    **Closed** *Sun*
A seafood-oriented delight,
Killer Prawn's menu includes
large seafood plates to share and
pizzas. It also has a busy bar.

## The Central
## North Island

### GISBORNE: Café Villagio $
Café
*57 Ballance St, Whataupoko, 4010*
**Tel** *(06) 863 3895*
Housed in an Art Deco building,
Café Villagio also offers outdoor
dining in the large courtyard. Try
their famous Big V breakfast.
Family-friendly.

### GISBORNE: Cantina Caliente $
Mexican      Map F3
*7 Oneroa Rd, 4010*
**Tel** *(06) 868 6828*    **Closed** *Mon*
A lively beachside Mexican
restaurant with famously large
portions and a selection of
rare tequilas.

### GISBORNE: Works Café $
Café      Map F3
*41 Esplanade, Kaiti, 4010*
**Tel** *(06) 868 9699*
Lovely pub food is offered in a
beautiful old brick building with
indoor as well as outdoor dining.
Extensive beer and wine selection.

### GISBORNE: Marina
### Restaurant $$
French      Map F3
*Vogel St, Whataupoko, 4010*
**Tel** *(06) 868 5959*    **Closed** *Sun*
*& Mon*
Fine French cuisine, cooked
by Michelin-trained chefs, is
served in an elegant setting –
a beautiful former ballroom
by the river.

Well-stocked bar at The Gables restaurant in Russell

### GISBORNE: Ussco Bar
### and Bistro $$
Bistro      Map F3
*16 Childers Rd, 4010*
**Tel** *(06) 868 3246*
Set in a historic shipping
company building by the inner
harbour, Ussco's award-winning
cuisine revolves around seasonal,
local produce.

### GISBORNE: Bushmere Arms $$$
Fine dining      Map F3
*Main Rd, Waerenga-a-Hika,
Gisborne, 4071*
**Tel** *(06) 862 5820*    **Closed** *Mon*
In an exquisite, country garden
setting, Bushmere Arms has been
awarded the New Zealand Beef
and Lamb Hallmark of Excellence
Award every year since 1999.

### GISBORNE: Colosseum Banquet
### and Bistro $$$
Mediterranean      Map F3
*10 Riverpoint Rd, 4071*
**Tel** *(06) 867 4733*    **Closed** *Mon*
*& Tue*
A large restaurant, Colosseum
offers Mediterranean-style cuisine
with New Zealand touches. All
ingredients are sourced from the
garden and local farms.

### HAMILTON: The River Kitchen $
Café      Map E2
*237 Victoria St, 3204*
**Tel** *(07) 839 2906*
This daytime café keeps winning
Best Café awards for its delicious,
fresh, organic food.

### HAMILTON: Vegan Buffet $
Chinese      Map E2
*148 Ward St, Hamilton Central, 3204*
**Tel** *(07) 838 0805*    **Closed** *Sat*
*& Sun*
Hamilton's Vegan Buffet is not
just popular with vegans
and vegetarians – many meat
eaters enjoy the tasty Chinese
dishes offered here.

### HAMILTON: Gothenburg
### Restaurant $$
Tapas      Map E2
*15 Hood St, Hamilton Central, 3204*
**Tel** *(07) 834 3562* **Closed** *Sun & Mon*
Specializing in tapas, this
restaurant also serves a small
selection of international main
dishes. It has a huge selection
of mostly Belgian beers and a
stunning cheese board.

### HAMILTON: Little Korea $$
Korean      Map E2
*643 Victoria St, Hamilton Central,
3204*
**Tel** *(07) 839 1600*    **Closed** *Sun*
A traditional Korean restaurant,
Little Korea serves its barbecued
meats steaming at the table. Try
the kimchi stew, a Korean staple.

### HASTINGS: Taste Cornucopia
### Organic Café $
Café      Map F4
*219 Heretaunga St East, 4122*
**Tel** *(06) 878 8730*    **Closed** *Sat*
*& Sun*
Winner of numerous awards, this
café aims to use locally grown
organic food. It has a kids' menu
and a play area.

### HASTINGS: Te Awa Restaurant
### and Winery $$$
Vineyard      Map F4
*2375 State Hwy 50, Rd 5 Hawkes Bay*
**Tel** *(06) 879 7602*    **Closed** *Mon*
*& Tue*
Try the seven-spice pork belly at
this long-established restaurant
in the heart of wine country.

### HAVELOCK NORTH: Deliciosa
### Tapas and Wine Bar $
Spanish      Map F4
*21 Napier Rd, Hawkes Bay, 4130*
**Tel** *(06) 877 6031*    **Closed** *Sun*
Customers are encouraged to
linger over and enjoy their food
at this tapas restaurant with
indoor and outdoor seating.

For more information on types of restaurants *see pages 308–309*

Scenic outdoor terrace at the Terrôir Restaurant at Craggy Range, Havelock North

### HAVELOCK NORTH: Namaskar India $
Indian                                Map F4
10 Joll Rd, Hawkes Bay, 4130
**Tel** (06) 877 7208
World-class Indian chefs mix spices by hand and use only the freshest ingredients to create a range of traditional favourite dishes here, all gluten-free.

### HAVELOCK NORTH: Terrôir Restaurant at Craggy Range $$$
Vineyard                              Map F4
253 Waimarama Rd, 4292
**Tel** (06) 873 0143
Enjoy delicious, French-style treats in an amazing setting at one of Hawkes Bay's most legendary wineries. The menu features seasonal offerings.

### NAPIER: Groove Kitchen Espresso $
Café                                  Map F4
112 Tennyson St, Hawkes Bay, 4110
**Tel** (06) 835 8530
The divine coffee alone makes this daytime café worth a visit, but the Groove Kitchen whips up great brunches as well, and, as the name implies, it plays the grooviest tunes.

### NAPIER: Indigo $
Indian                                Map F4
24A Hastings St, Hawkes Bay, 4110
(06) 834 4085
This restaurant boasts chefs trained at five-star hotels, an extensive wine list that includes local wines and authentic Indian food prepared in a traditional charcoal oven.

### NAPIER: Restaurant Indonesia $
Indonesian                            Map F4
409 Marine Parade, Hawkes Bay, 4110
**Tel** (06) 835 8303        **Closed** Mon
Since 1983 Restaurant Indonesia has been providing an inviting atmosphere and attentive service to accompany its authentic tapas-style dishes.

### NAPIER: Trattoria alla Toscana $
Italian                               Map F4
180 Emerson St, Hawkes Bay, 4110
**Tel** (06) 834 1988        **Closed** Mon
This beautifully appointed family-owned restaurant serves fine traditional dishes. The home-made pasta and salsa are the house specialities.

### NAPIER: Wild Roses Café $
Café                                  Map F4
10A West Place, Hawkes Bay, 4112
**Tel** (06) 844 6856
Great coffee and tasty food are served in a gorgeous, idyllic garden setting, surrounded by roses indoors and outside.

### NAPIER: Caution Dining Lounge and Shed 2 $$
Contemporary                          Map F4
56 West Quay, Ahuriri, 4110
**Tel** (06) 835 2202        **Closed** Mon
Housed in an elegant, historic building that was once a storage shed, this eatery offers harbour views, intimate dining booths and the best wood-fired pizzas in Napier. Classy cocktails.

### NAPIER: Crab Farm Restaurant $$
Vineyard                              Map F4
511 Main Rd, Bay View, 4104
**Tel** (06) 836 6678   **Closed** Mon–Wed
The small but delightful menu at this winery includes fabulous seafood platters. Seasonal specials made with fresh local produce are also on offer.

## DK Choice

### NAPIER: Mission Estate Restaurant $$$
Vineyard                              Map F4
198 Church Rd, Taradale
**Tel** (06) 845 9350
Inside a historic, elegant seminary building, this award-winning restaurant serves contemporary fine cuisine with a European influence using seasonal produce. Diners can enjoy distinguished wines with delicious cuts of beef and lamb while gazing out over vineyards that stretch to the horizon.

### NAPIER: The Old Church Restaurant $$$
Fine dining                           Map F4
199 Meeanee Rd, 4112
**Tel** (06) 844 8866
This restored former church in an exquisite vineyard setting houses a fine restaurant. Try the tasting menu.

### ROTORUA: The Pizza Library Co $
Italian                               Map E3
54 Springfield Rd, 3015
**Tel** (07) 349 2328        **Closed** Mon
A family-run, gloriously rustic pizza restaurant that takes you all the way to Italy. The amazing creations made by the skilled chefs have loyal fans.

### ROTORUA: Aorangi Peak Restaurant $$
European                              Map E3
353C Mountain Rd, Ngongotaha, 3015
**Tel** (07) 347 0036
Photo opportunities abound at this amazingly scenic location that also boasts reasonably priced, award-winning food.

### ROTORUA: Mokoia Restaurant $$$
Fine dining                           Map E3
77 Robinson Ave, 3010
**Tel** (07) 343 5100
Award-winning beef and lamb dishes are the highlights at this restaurant with lovely views of Lake Rotorua. Vegetarian and gluten-free options are available.

Eating outside at the Mission Estate Restaurant, Napier

Chic, modern interior of Satori Lounge, Tauranga

### TAURANGA: Satori Lounge $$
Japanese     Map E2
*309 Maunganui Rd,*
*Mt Maunganui, 3116*
**Tel** (07) 575 0979    **Closed** *Mon*
Satori Lounge is a unique combination of sushi and cocktail bar with resident DJs. The sushi is rolled fresh when you order.

### TAURANGA: Mount Bistro Restaurant $$$
Bistro     Map E2
*6 Adams Ave,*
*Mt Maunganui, 3010*
**Tel** (07) 575 3872    **Closed** *Mon*
The award-winning fusion food at Mount Bistro is made from fresh local produce.

### TURANGI: River Restaurant and Vineyard $$
Vineyard     Map E3
*2/134 Grace Rd, 3382*
**Tel** (07) 386 6704    **Closed** *Sun*
Its setting near the beautiful Tongariro river and the delicious platters and notable wines make this restaurant a real experience.

## Wellington and the South

### NEW PLYMOUTH: Flame $
Indian     Map D3
*151 Devon St East, Taranaki, 4310*
**Tel** (06) 758 0030
Friendly staff, generous portions of Indian favourites and a great selection of New Zealand wines characterize this restaurant.

### NEW PLYMOUTH: Sushi Ninja $
Japanese     Map D3
*89 Devon St East,*
*Taranaki, 4310*
**Tel** (06) 759 1392    **Closed** *Sun*
This authentic sushi restaurant is a casual dining experience by day and a sake bar at night.

### NEW PLYMOUTH: Gusto Restaurant $$
Contemporary     Map D3
*Ocean View Parade, 4310*
**Tel** (06) 759 8133
Perched on the port, Gusto offers sophisticated cuisine and lovely sea views.

### PALMERSTON NORTH: The Bean Café $
Asian     Map E4
*16 Broadway Ave, 4410*
**Tel** (06) 353 6556    **Closed** *Sun*
Good-value, cheerful eatery in a charming old building. This is the place for stone bowl garlic pepper chicken and bubble tea.

### PALMERSTON NORTH: Moxies Café $
Café     Map E4
*67 George St, 4410*
**Tel** (06) 355 4238
A daytime café, Moxies has a broad all-day breakfast menu, and separate menus for those with gluten or dairy allergies.

### PALMERSTON NORTH: Roma The Grand Fire Barbecue $$
Barbecue     Map E4
*44 The Square, 4410*
**Tel** (06) 952 5579    **Closed** *Sun & Mon*
Try the prime meat cuts in flavour-packed marinades at this restaurant in the Grand Hotel.

### PALMERSTON NORTH: Yatai Japanese Izakaya $$
Japanese     Map E4
*316 Featherston St, 4410*
**Tel** (06) 356 1316    **Closed** *Sun*
Enjoy authentic dishes to share and Japanese beers, cocktails or sake at this restaurant in a lovely old building.

### TARANAKI: Volcanoview Grand Café and Restaurant $
Family     Map D3
*1917 Egmont Rd, Inglewood, 4386*
**Tel** (06) 756 6112    **Closed** *Tue*
This alpine restaurant with endless menu options is attached to a kids' playground and camping site.

### WAIPAWA: Misty River Café $
Café     Map E4
*12 High St, Hawkes Bay 4210*
**Tel** (06) 857 8911    **Closed** *Mon & Tue*
Everything is made on the premises at this daytime café, which stakes its reputation on quality food and good service.

### WELLINGTON: Cinta Malaysian Kitchen $
Malaysian     Map D5
*119 Manners St, Wellington Central, 6011*
**Tel** (04) 385 8622
A local favourite, Cinta Malaysian Kitchen has basic decor but offers great food in huge portions.

### WELLINGTON: The Larder $
Café     Map D5
*133 Darlington Rd, Miramar, 6022*
**Tel** (04) 891 0354    **Closed** *Mon*
Flavourful, fresh and locally grown seasonal produce is used at this great café situated close to the town centre.

### WELLINGTON: Memphis Belle Coffee House $
Café     Map D5
*38 Dixon St, Wellington Central, 6011*
**Tel** (021) 244 8852
The food is fresh and healthy, but Memphis Belle is really about the coffee. Regular winner of "Best Café" plaudits.

### WELLINGTON: Saigon Taste $
Vietnamese     Map D5
*17 Majoribanks St, Mt Victoria, 6011*
**Tel** (04) 801 6866
Come here for reasonably priced authentic Vietnamese fare. Unpretentious venue and warm service.

### WELLINGTON: Ti Kouka Café $
Café     Map D5
*76 Willis St, Wellington Central, 6011*
**Tel** (04) 472 7682    **Closed** *Sun*
Expect fresh, organic dishes made with local ingredients, as well as great service, at the daytime Ti Kouka Café.

The garden at Turangi's River Restaurant and Vineyard

**For more information on types of restaurants** *see pages 308–309*

Busy bartenders at Wellington's Arbitrageur Wine Room and Restaurant

**WELLINGTON: Viva Mexico** $
Mexican  Map D5
210C Left Bank, Wellington Central, 6011
Tel (04) 382 9913  Closed Mon
This is a great restaurant for hearty, authentic Mexican food with both meat and vegetarian options, in a rustic dining room.

**WELLINGTON: Arbitrageur Wine Room and Restaurant** $$
European  Map D5
125 Featherston St, Wellington Central, 6011
Tel (04) 499 5530  Closed Sun
A fine-dining eatery without the sky-high prices, Arbitrageur matches its wines with the Mediterranean-inspired dishes.

**WELLINGTON: Arthur's** $$
Bistro  Map D5
272 Cuba St, Wellington Central, 6011
Tel (04) 385 7227  Closed Mon
Inside a lovely Edwardian building, Arthur's offers homely food such as perfectly cooked pies and roasts. Try the braised lamb shank.

**WELLINGTON: Boulcott St Bistro and Winebar** $$
Bistro  Map D5
99 Boulcott St, Wellington Central, 6011
Tel (04) 499 4199
This delightful informal bistro serves classic dishes with an innovative twist in a fabulous old villa. The roasts are recommended.

**WELLINGTON: Café Polo** $$
Bistro  Map D5
82 Rotherham Terrace, Miramar, 6022
Tel (04) 380 7273  Closed Sun & Mon
The accent here is on Slow Food cooking using local organic produce and free-range meat and eggs. The coffee is organic and fair trade.

**WELLINGTON: Capitol** $$
Italian  Map D5
10 Kent Terrace, Wellington Central, 6011
Tel (04) 384 2855
Classic Italian dishes are served with a New Zealand twist.

**WELLINGTON: The General Practitioner** $$
Pub  Map D5
100 Willis St, Wellington Central, 6011
Tel (04) 499 6001
A gastro-pub in a former doctor's residence, famous for "wild food". The dinner menu changes daily.

**WELLINGTON: The Green Man** $$
Pub  Map D5
25 Victoria St, Wellington Central, 6011
Tel (04) 499 5440  Closed Sun
This big gastro-pub is always busy. The super-spicy chicken wings are a speciality.

**WELLINGTON: Havana Bar and Restaurant** $$
Cuban/Spanish  Map D5
32a–34 Wigan St, Wellington Central, 6011
Tel (04) 384 7039  Closed Sun
A Cuban-themed eatery serving tasty tapas. There is live music most evenings.

**WELLINGTON: Hummingbird Eatery and Bar** $$
Bar  Map D5
22 Courtenay Place, Wellington Central, 6011
Tel (04) 801 6336  Closed Mon
Unpretentious, tasty food, good cocktails and an extensive wine list make this a popular venue.

**WELLINGTON: Muse On Allen** $$
Fusion  Map D5
16 Allen St, Wellington Central, 6011
Tel (04) 384 1181  Closed Sun & Mon
Local organic produce is used to prepare the New Zealand–European fusion dishes here.

**WELLINGTON: Ortega Fish Shack and Bar** $$
Seafood  Map D5
16 Majoribanks St, Wellington Central, 6011
Tel (04) 382 9559  Closed Sun & Mon
A popular restaurant for seafood lovers, Ortega has a relaxed, casual environment and serves quality dishes.

**WELLINGTON: Shed 5 Restaurant and Bar** $$
Seafood  Map D5
3 Queens Wharf, Wellington Central, 6011
Tel (04) 499 9069
A superb waterfront location, super-fresh seafood picked by the restaurant's own fishmonger and top New Zealand wines make this one of Wellington's leading seafood restaurants.

**WELLINGTON: Soi** $$
International  Map D5
305 Evans Bay Parade, Hataitai, 6021
Tel (04) 386 3830  Closed Mon
Situated on the edge of the harbour, Soi offers a modern diverse menu. Try the seafood chowder.

**WELLINGTON: Two Souls Bistro** $$
Bistro  Map D5
290 Wakefield St, Wellington Central, 6011
Tel (04) 803 3137
This restarant offers great-value and perfectly cooked dishes in a relaxed atmosphere. Excellent service too.

**WELLINGTON: Charlie Bill** $$$
Bistro  Map D5
241 Tinakori Rd, Thorndon, 6011
Tel (04) 499 8464  Closed Mon & Tue
An intimate, fine-food bistro serving wholesome dishes, Charlie Bill is the perfect venue for a romantic dinner.

The cosy Hummingbird Eatery and Bar, Wellington

Lavish interior of the award-winning Logan Brown restaurant, Wellington

**WELLINGTON:**
**Hippopotamus** $$$
European **Map** D5
*Museum Art Hotel 90 Cable St,*
*Wellington Central, 6011*
**Tel** *(04) 802 8935*
Enjoy breathtaking harbour views
and superb dishes in this quirky
French-influenced restaurant
inside the Museum Art Hotel
*(see p305)*. Booking essential.

## DK Choice

**WELLINGTON:**
**Logan Brown** $$$
European **Map** D5
*Cnr Cuba and Vivian sts,*
*Wellington, 6011*
**Tel** *(04) 801 5114*
Since it opened in 1996
Logan Brown has won many
awards. Contemporary dishes
containing fresh local produce
are prepared using classic
cooking methods. The elegant
but relaxed atmosphere,
extensive wine list and
excellent service make for an
exceptional dining experience.

**WELLINGTON: MariLuca**
**Ristoro** $$$
Italian **Map** D5
*55 Mulgrave St, Thorndon,*
*6011*
**Tel** *(04) 499 5590* **Closed** *Sun*
Dishes that emphasize freshness
and simplicity, including hand-
made pasta, are served here.

**WELLINGTON: Martin Bosley's**
**Restaurant** $$$
Fine dining **Map** D5
*103 Oriental Parade, Mt Victoria,*
*6011*
**Tel** *(04) 920 8302* **Closed** *Mon*
Owned by a celebrated local
chef, this award-winning
restaurant is a Wellington

institution. Come here for fresh,
beautifully prepared seafood and
panoramic views of the harbour.

**WELLINGTON: Portlander Bar**
**and Grill** $$$
Steakhouse **Map** D5
*75 Featherston St, Wellington*
*Central, 6011*
**Tel** *(04) 498 3762*
It is hard to argue with the
Portlander Bar and Grill's claim to
being the best steakhouse in
Wellington. The excellent food is
served in a relaxed environment.

**WELLINGTON: The White**
**House** $$$
Fine dining **Map** D5
*232 Oriental Parade, 6011*
**Tel** *(04) 385 8555*
The dishes at this award-winning
restaurant are made from local,
seasonal ingredients, some from
the restaurant's own rooftop
garden. The wine list includes
some rare vintages

# Marlborough and Nelson

**BLENHEIM: Raupo Riverside**
**Café and Restaurant** $$
International **Map** D5
*6 Symons St, 7201*
**Tel** *(03) 577 8822* Closed late Jun–
Aug
In an eco-friendly building
overlooking the river, this eatery
offers fresh innovative cuisine. Their
high teas are an indulgence.

**Blenheim: Twelve Trees** $$
Vineyard **Map** D5
*229 Jacksons Rd, Marlborough, 7273*
**Tel** *(03) 572 7123*
Located at the famous Allan
Scott vineyard, Twelve Trees is a
popular lunchtime destination

with a great seasonal menu.
The name refers to the original
walnut trees that lined the
winery's entrance.

**BLENHEIM: Wither Hills** $$
Vineyard **Map** D5
*211 New Renwick Rd,*
*Marlborough, 7272*
**Tel** *(03) 578 4036*
This beautiful restaurant, in
one of New Zealand's most
celebrated wineries, is named for
the Wither Hills range that forms
its backdrop. Everything on the
menu is handmade on-site.

## DK Choice

**BLENHEIM: Herzog Winery**
**and Restaurant** $$$
Vineyard **Map** D5
*81 Jeffries Rd, RD3 Marlborough,*
*7273*
**Tel** *(03) 572 8770* **Closed** *Mon*
A famous Marlborough
vineyard restaurant, but with
a difference – Herzog
specializes in a tasting menu
that is a multi-course offering
of flavours to complement
perfectly the accompanying
wines (there are over 500 wines
to choose from). There is a
charming Mediterranean-style
garden with views of the
vineyard for outdoor dining.

**HAVELOCK: Mussel Pot** $$
Seafood **Map** D4
*73 Main Rd, 7100*
**Tel** *(03) 574 2824* **Closed** *late Jun–*
*Aug*
This iconic seafood restaurant
specializes in green-lipped
mussels and has vegetarian and
gluten-free options. There are
different menus for breakfast,
lunch and dinner.

**KAIKOURA: The Whaler** $$
Bar **Map** D5
*49 West End, 7300*
**Tel** *(03) 319 3333*
Sample the tapas menu
or indulge in the huge steaks
washed down with local beers at
the Whaler Bar. The large upstairs
deck boasts gorgeous sea and
mountain views.

**MARLBOROUGH: East Coast Inn**
**Café & Bar** $
Café **Map** D5
*7364 State Hwy 1, Ward, 7285*
**Tel** *(03) 575 6414*
Simple, delicious home-
made dishes with a focus on
seafood and wild food are
served in a homely pub-type
atmosphere at the East Coast
Inn. Try the fish cakes.

Elegant table settings at Drylands, Marlborough

### MARLBOROUGH: Drylands $$
Vineyard     **Map** D5
*237 Hammerichs Rd, Rapaura, 7273*
**Tel** *(03) 570 5671*   **Closed** *Mon & Tue*
The best South Island produce paired with some of the finest Marlborough wines, and a superb view of one of New Zealand's oldest vineyards, makes for a perfect dining experience here.

### NELSON: East St Vegetarian Café Bar $
Café     **Map** D4
*335 Trafalgar Square, 7010*
**Tel** *(022) 238 1234*   **Closed** *Mon*
All the tasty dishes are freshly prepared at this vegetarian café and include vegan and gluten-free options.

### NELSON: La Gourmandise $
French     **Map** D4
*276 Hardy St, 7010*
**Tel** *(03) 546 6348*   **Closed** *Mon*
Only organic, local produce is used and half the menu is gluten-free at this friendly, unpretentious creperie. As well as sweet and savoury crepes there are also salads and sandwiches.

### NELSON: Morrison Street Café $
Café     **Map** D4
*244 Hardy St, 7010*
**Tel** *(03) 548 8110*
Winner of many café awards, the Morrison Street Café serves a variety of fusion dishes and excellent coffee. There are also two art galleries on site, with frequently changing exhibitions.

### NELSON: Café Olive $$
Mediterranean     **Map** D4
*136 Hardy St, 7010*
**Tel** *(03) 548 8755*   **Closed** *Mon*
Serving Mediterranean-inspired cuisine based on seasonal Nelson produce, this café has a diverse menu, ranging from salads and seafood starters to pasta and steaks. The atmosphere is warm and relaxed.

### NELSON: Ford's Restaurant & Bar $$
Fusion     **Map** D4
*276 Trafalgar St, 7010*
**Tel** *(03) 546 9400*
Housed in a historic villa and boasting a diverse tapas menu and European-style dishes with New Zealand influences, this family-run restaurant is a Nelson secret worth discovering. Open for breakfast, lunch and dinner.

### NELSON: Hopgoods $$
Contemporary     **Map** D4
*284 Trafalgar St, 7010*
**Tel** *(03) 545 7191*   **Closed** *Sun*
A casual fine-dining restaurant, Hopgoods mixes great service with a relaxed atmosphere. The seasonal menu consists of simple, well executed dishes made from locally sourced ingredients. Nelson wines feature strongly on the drinks list.

The bright, arty interior of Morrison Street Café, Nelson

### NELSON: Mint Dining Room $$
International     **Map** D4
*20 Harley St, 7010*
**Tel** *(03) 546 7092*   **Closed** *Sun*
Simple dishes with local ingredients are on the menu in this intimate 19th-century cottage setting. The wine list includes both local and international labels. Winner of the Best Restaurant in Nelson 2012 award.

### NELSON: Tides Restaurant & Bar $$
Seafood     **Map** D4
*66 Trafalgar St, 7010*
**Tel** *(03) 548 7049*
With an accent on seafood, this restaurant's diverse menu also includes game, beef and lamb, all locally sourced. There is also a children's menu. The balcony offers lovely river views.

### PICTON: Cortado Restaurant, Bar & Café $$
European     **Map** D4
*Cnr High Street & London Quay, Marlborough, 7220*
**Tel** *(03) 573 9100*   **Closed** *Mon–Tue*
Located on the waterfront promenade, Cortado offers European-inspired dishes, including seafood and Italian-style pizzas prepared with local produce, plus coffee and craft beers, in a relaxed atmosphere.

### PICTON: Le Café $$
European     **Map** D4
*12 London Quay, Marlborough, 7220*
**Tel** *(03) 573 5588*
Divided into formal and casual dining areas, Le Café combines great sea views with European-inspired dishes cooked with care and pride. There is regular live music in the evenings. Open for breakfast, lunch and dinner.

# Canterbury and the West Coast

**CHRISTCHURCH: Bamboozle Oriental Fusion**  $
Asian                          Map C6
*6 Wakefield St, Sumner, 8081*
**Tel** *(03) 326 7878*      **Closed** *Sun & Mon*
Chef Phillip Kraal's Asian restaurant offers traditional oriental dishes as well as some with fusion leanings, such as steamed buns filled with Caesar salad ingredients.

**CHRISTCHURCH: Beat Street Café**  $
Café                           Map C6
*324 Barbadoes St, 8011*
**Tel** *(03) 366 6324*
This café offers the best egg-laced breakfasts in Christchurch. All ingredients are sourced locally and the food is cooked in an open-plan kitchen.

**CHRISTCHURCH: Dimitri's Greek Food**  $
Greek                          Map C6
*79 Cashel St, 8011*
**Tel** *(03) 377 7110*
A bustling daytime restaurant that never skimps on meat or flavour. The decor is basic, but the food is great. Try the *souvlaki*.

**CHRISTCHURCH: Mum's 24 Restaurant**  $
Asian                          Map C6
*62 Manchester St, 8011*
**Tel** *(03) 365 2211*
This restaurant offers traditional, slow-cooked Korean and Japanese food with fresh spices and ingredients and no MSG.

**CHRISTCHURCH: The Thai Kitchen**  $
Thai                           Map C6
*239 Colombo St, 8023*
**Tel** *(03) 332 8280*
Fresh, flavoursome Thai fare, considered by many to be the best in Christchurch, is offered at The Thai Kitchen. The portions are generous, and there are vegetarian and gluten-free options too. Welcoming atmosphere.

**CHRISTCHURCH: Cook 'N' With Gas**  $$
Bistro                         Map C6
*23 Worcester St Boulevard, 8013*
**Tel** *(03) 377 9166*      **Closed** *Sun*
Housed inside a 19th-century villa, this celebrated Christchurch eatery is all about fine dining on a budget. The menu offers modern New Zealand cuisine and over 200 beers and wines.

**CHRISTCHURCH: Curator's House Restaurant**  $$
Spanish                        Map C6
*7 Rolleston Ave, Botanic Gardens, 8013*
**Tel** *(03) 379 2252*
Enjoy the view of the Botanic Gardens from this heritage building while dining on tasty Spanish-influenced dishes.

**CHRISTCHURCH: Edesia Restaurant and Bar**  $$
European                       Map C6
*12 Show Place, Addington, 8024*
**Tel** *(03) 943 2144*      **Closed** *Sun*
This spacious, stylish restaurant serves fine food with service to match. There is an extensive wine list.

**CHRISTCHURCH: 50 Bistro**  $$
Bistro                         Map C6
*50 Park Terrace, 8013*
**Tel** *(03) 371 0250*
Classic bistro dishes with a twist and a wine selection to match are served in a stylish interior and extensive outdoor area. The menu changes seasonally.

**CHRISTCHURCH: Flames Restaurant**  $$
Italian                        Map C6
*2 Soleares Ave, Mt Pleasant, 8081*
**Tel** *(03) 384 1309*      **Closed** *Sun & Mon*
This is one of Christchurch's most popular Italian restaurants, serving excellent home-made pasta, gnocchi, risotto and steaks accompanied by New Zealand and Italian wines.

**CHRISTCHURCH: Morgan's Vineyard Café**  $$
Vineyard                       Map C6
*355 Buchanans Rd, Yaldhurst, 7676*
**Tel** *(03) 348 8038*      **Closed** *Mon*
Boasting a lovely setting on the rural fringes of Christchurch, Morgan's Café is run by a father-and-daughter team. The food is wholesome, with a focus on traditional dishes.

**CHRISTCHURCH: The Station Restaurant**  $$
Korean                         Map C6
*1 Restell St, Papanui, 8053*
**Tel** *(03) 354 9003*
Enjoy spicy, mouth-watering Korean food, and a karaoke "train booth" in the garden.

**CHRISTCHURCH: Misceo Café & Bar**  $$$
Café                           Map C6
*Cnr Ilam & Clyde Rd, Ilam, 8041*
**Tel** *(03) 351 8011*
Buzzing upmarket pub-style food is served in this popular suburban eatery.

**CHRISTCHURCH: Pescatore Restaurant**  $$$
Seafood                        Map C6
*50 Park Terrace, 8011*
**Tel** *(03) 371 0257* **Closed** *Sun & Mon*
This premium restaurant offers contemporary fine dining and lovely views of Hagley Park.

## DK Choice

**CHRISTCHURCH: Rotherhams of Riccarton**  $$$
Fine dining                    Map C6
*42 Rotherham St, Riccarton, 8041*
**Tel** *(03) 341 5142*      **Closed** *Sun & Mon*
A multi-award-winning restaurant, serving classic European and New Zealand dishes in an elegant but cosy setting. The innovative menu includes five- and eight-course tasting menus and over 500 top wines to choose from.

**CHRISTCHURCH: The Old Vicarage Café, Restaurant and Bar**  $$$
Fine dining                    Map C6
*335 Halswell Rd, Halswell, 8025*
**Tel** *(03) 322 1224*
The warm and inviting Old Vicarage offers European and New Zealand dishes. Open for breakfast, lunch and dinner.

Modern, stylish dining room at Christchurch's Pescatore Restaurant

**For more information on types of restaurants** *see pages 308–309*

Marine-themed booths at Fishbone Bar & Grill, Queenstown

### CHRISTCHURCH: Saggio di Vino
Italian     $$$    **Map** C6
*179 Victoria St, 8014*
**Tel** *(03) 379 4006*
The Italian-inspired cuisine at this Christchurch institution is simple and refined, and the exquisite wines complement the dishes perfectly.

### FOX GLACIER: The Salmon Farm Café
Café     $$    **Map** B6
*State Hwy 6, Paringa River, Westland, 7834*
**Tel** *(03) 751 0837*
In a beautiful forest setting, this café at the remote South Westland Salmon Farm offers delectable, fresh fish dishes.

### HOKITIKA: Ocean View Restaurant
Seafood     $$    **Map** C5
*111 Revell St, Westland, 7810*
**Tel** *(03) 755 8344*
Enjoy the catch of the day while gazing at the panoramic view of the ocean at this restaurant in the Beachfront Hotel Hokitika.

### HURUNUI: The Mud House Winery Café
Vineyard     $$    **Map** C5
*780 Glasnevin Rd, Waipara, 7447*
**Tel** *(03) 314 6900*
Set among vines and rolling hills, The Mud House specializes in classic New Zealand fare such as game pies and fish 'n' chips.

### KARAMEA: Riverstone Karamea
Contemporary     $$$    **Map** C4
*2 Arapito Rd RD3, West Coast, 7893*
**Tel** *(03) 782 6640*
A varied, simple menu using fresh seasonal produce is served here in a wilderness setting with views of the Kahurangi National Park. Try the award-winning beef and lamb. Indoor and outdoor seating.

For key to prices *see page 314*

## Otago and Southland

### DUNEDIN: San
Cambodian     $    **Map** B7
*2 Dowling St, 9016*
**Tel** *(03) 479 0955*    **Closed** *Sun & Mon*
This authentic, reasonably priced restaurant serves fresh and tasty dishes.

### DUNEDIN: Salt Restaurant
International     $$    **Map** B7
*240 Forbury Rd, Saint Clair, 9012*
**Tel** *(03) 455 1077*    **Closed** *Tue & Wed*
A café by day and a bar and restaurant by night, Salt offers a diverse range of culinary options in a beautiful Art Deco venue.

### DUNEDIN: Speights Ale House
Southern New Zealand     $$    **Map** B7
*200 Rattray St, Dunedin, 9016*
**Tel** *(03) 471 9050*
One of New Zealand's oldest breweries, Speights Ale House features classics such as seafood chowder, blue cod, lamb shanks,

Freshly baked bread at Riverstone Kitchen, Oamaru

steak and venison. There are good vegetarian options. Package deals for groups include tours of the brewery.

### DUNEDIN: Luna Bar
Bar     $$$    **Map** B7
*314 Highgate, Roslyn, 9010*
**Tel** *(03) 477 2227*
Enjoy spectacular views of Dunedin, an extensive wine list and inspired dishes here. Relax in the bar or on the sunny deck.

### INVERCARGILL: Level One Restaurant and Bar
Southern New Zealand     $$    **Map** A7
*20 Kelvin St, 9810*
**Tel** *(03) 218 2829*
Situated on the first floor of the Kelvin hotel, Level One is a sophisticated restaurant with a diverse range of menu options. Try the lemon salted tempura scallops.

### OAMARU: Riverstone Kitchen
Southern New Zealand     $$    **Map** B7
*1431 State Hwy 1, RD5, 9493*
**Tel** *(03) 431 3505*
Famed chef Bevan Smith's "always seasonal, always local" fresh-produce dishes have won many awards. The daily-changing chef's tasting menu with seasonal ingredients is particularly recommended.

### QUEENSTOWN: Eichardt's Bar
Tapas     $    **Map** A6
*2 Marine Parade, 9348*
**Tel** *(03) 441 0450*
Fresh organic produce is served in an array of tapas-style platters at this bar, also famous for its cocktails. Comfortable sofas and a cosy fireplace give it a homely atmosphere .

### QUEENSTOWN: 1878
Tapas     $$    **Map** A6
*45 Ballarat St, 9300*
**Tel** *(03) 409 2178*
Located in a former courthouse, this restaurant offers tapas platters to share, as well as salads, burgers, steaks and a children's menu. There is a sunny courtyard for alfresco dining.

### QUEENSTOWN: Fishbone Bar & Grill
Seafood     $$    **Map** A6
*7 Beach St, 9300*
**Tel** *(03) 442 6768*
Choose from the freshest seafood, including signature dishes such as crumbed blue cod with tartare sauce. Fishbone sources only sustainable fish, and much of the produce is grown on their own farm.

### QUEENSTOWN: Lombardi    $$
International    Map A6
*10 Brunswick St, 9300*
**Tel** *(03) 442 4990*
In the Hotel St Mortiz, Lombardi has three dining spaces: tapas in the bar; pizzas in the dining room; and fine dining in The Library, all with lovely alpine and lake views.

### QUEENSTOWN: Birches Restaurant    $$$
Fine dining    Map A6
*146 Arthurs Point Rd, Queenstown-Lakes, 9371*
**Tel** *(03) 441 0288*
Part of the Distinction Hotel, Birches offers sophisticated dishes made with prime local produce. Stunning alpine views.

### QUEENSTOWN: The Bunker Restaurant and Bar    $$$
Fine dining    Map A6
*Cow Ln, 9300*
**Tel** *(03) 441 8030*
An intimate, rustic restaurant with an extensive wine and cocktail list, The Bunker serves New Zealand delicacies, including game and red meat. There is an excellent tasting menu .

### QUEENSTOWN: Gantleys Restaurant    $$$
Fine dining    Map A6
*172 Arthurs Point Rd, Arthurs Point 9371*
**Tel** *(03) 442 8999*
Housed in a historic stone building that was once a wayside inn for gold miners, Gantleys offers superb New Zealand cuisine.

### QUEENSTOWN: Rata    $$$
Fine dining    Map A6
*43 Ballarat St, 9300*
**Tel** *(03) 442 9393*
Michelin-trained star chef Josh Emmett is the talent behind Rata, with its emphasis on

Cosy interior of Gantley's Restaurant, Queenstown, in an old stone building

slow-cooked, full-flavoured dishes. It also has a courtyard for outdoor dining.

### QUEENSTOWN: Roaring Meg's Restaurant    $$$
Fine dining    Map A6
*53 Shotover St, Queenstown, 9300*
**Tel** *(03) 442 9676*    **Closed** *Mon*
This restaurant has won many accolades for its beef and lamb dishes. Try the award-winning rack of Canterbury lamb. The elegant Victorian decor and candlelit dining room give it a refined, romantic atmosphere.

### QUEENSTOWN: True South    $$$
Fine dining    Map A6
*377 Frankton Rd, 9300*
**Tel** *(03) 450 1100*
Located in the Rees Hotel, True South offers elegant dining with awe-inspiring views of lake and mountains, and a selection of wines so good that it wins international awards. A children's menu and vegetarian options are available on request.

### QUEENSTOWN: Wai Waterfront Restaurant    $$$
Seafood    Map A6
*Beach St, 9300*
**Tel** *(03) 442 5969*
In a spectacular location, this fine-dining restaurant has stunning lake views and an excellent wine list to match the food. The kitchen makes everything, including bread and pasta, on site.

### STEWART ISLAND: Church Hill Restaurant and Oyster Bar    $$$
Seafood    Map A7
*36 Kamahi Rd, Oban, Southland, 9846*
**Tel** *(03) 219 1323*
This amazing restaurant has a menu that focuses on local seafood, including the famous Stewart Island oysters.

### WANAKA: Amigos Mexican Grill    $
Mexican    Map B6
*71 Ardmore St, Queenstown-Lakes, Otago, 9305*
**Tel** *03 443 7872*
Family-owned Amigos offers a budget-conscious selection of traditonal favourites. The corn chips are cooked fresh everyday, and the margaritas are delicious. Children are very welcome and there is a Kids' menu, puzzles and games.

### WANAKA: Wanaka Bullock Bar – The Grill Restaurant    $$
Steakhouse    Map B6
*71 Ardmore St, 9305*
**Tel** *(03) 443 7148*
A meat lovers' delight, The Grill is famous for its 1 kg (2.2 lb) plate of BBQ ribs, juicy steaks and large range of local wines. It is very child-friendly, with high-chairs, a children's menu and even crayons and colouring sheets.

Façade of Wai Waterfront Restaurant, Queenstown

For more information on types of restaurants *see pages 308–309*

# SHOPPING IN NEW ZEALAND

New Zealand has a lot to offer the visiting shopper, including goods not available in most other countries. Such items range from traditional Maori bone and greenstone carvings to sheepskin rugs and handmade wool sweaters. Many small towns in popular tourist areas have galleries where local crafts people sell their goods, and Auckland, Wellington and Christchurch have major markets where artisans sell unique products. Because New Zealand is one of the most open economies in the world, with few tariffs and no import licensing, goods such as cameras and audio equipment are very reasonably priced. New Zealand's wines *(see pp312–13)*, meats, seafoods, dairy products and fruits are also well worth sampling.

Kirkcaldie and Stains, Wellington's leading department store

## Shopping Hours

Most shops in New Zealand are open from 9am to 5pm or 5:30pm, Monday to Saturday. Most stores are open on Sundays also for shorter hours. In big cities, late night shopping is usually available on Thursdays or Fridays, when stores stay open until 9pm.

Supermarkets and shopping malls in urban areas are open seven days a week, and many supermarkets stay open until 8pm or 9pm and some offer a 24-hour service. In towns, suburbs and rural areas, dairies stay open long hours.

## How to Pay

Credit and debit cards are accepted by most stores, usually with a minimum purchase limit. If your card is encoded with a PIN number, you can withdraw cash from one of the many automatic teller machines at banks and shopping centres. Identification, such as a passport or driver's licence, is required when presenting traveller's cheques. Personal cheques are accepted less and less now; shops prefer debit or credit cards. New Zealand shopkeepers are not accustomed to bargaining and many also prefer cash transactions.

All goods sold in New Zealand are levied a Goods and Service Tax (GST) of 15 per cent, which is included in the purchase price. GST is not refunded when you leave New Zealand.

## Rights and Refunds

The **Consumers' Institute** (04) 384 7963) can provide detailed information about your rights as a buyer. If the goods purchased are defective, you are entitled to a refund. If you decide you do not like an item, many shops will allow you to return or exchange it for something else. If you want to return or exchange an item, you will need to present the receipt.

## Department Stores

Each of the four main cities has a major department store selling high quality goods. In Auckland, it is **Smith and Caughey's**; in Wellington, **Kirkcaldie and Stains**; in Dunedin, **Arthur Barnett**, and in Christchurch, **Ballantynes**.

Farmers, Kmart and The Warehouse sell a wide range of lower priced goods, and have numerous branches throughout the country.

## Shopping Malls

Large indoor shopping malls are a feature of cities and larger towns. Most are located in the suburbs rather then central city areas, and usually include at least one supermarket plus a range of shops selling items such as clothing, sports equipment, household appliances and books. Many also have food halls selling a variety of inexpensive meals.

Shop assistant arranging a display of Zambesi fashion clothes

## Dairies

Dairies are small convenience stores that can be found in most towns and suburbs (though they are slowly disappearing). Hours of opening vary, but most are open seven days a week from about 7am until 8pm. They sell basic food supplies, snacks, drinks, newspapers and cigarettes.

## Roadside Stalls

Roadside stalls selling fruit and vegetables are common in major horticultural areas such as the Bay of Plenty, Marlborough, Nelson and Central Otago. Many orchards and berry farms encourage people to "pick their own", and may also sell the produce at a reduced price. Straw-berries can be found everywhere in late spring and summer; cherries in Marl-borough at Christmas; apricots, nectarines and peaches in Otago around January–February, and kiwifruit in the Bay of Plenty from April to September. Visitors should also look out for the many cheese factories in Waikato, Taranaki, Marlborough and Canterbury which sell delicious, locally made dairy products.

Roadside stall sign

## Markets

Most New Zealand markets specialize in crafts rather than foods, although Otara Market in South Auckland (see p95) specializes in Pacific foods. Farmers' markets, such as at Hastings and Dunedin, are also increasingly popular. Auckland, Christ-church and Nelson have craft markets. Opening times vary: in Auckland, the Victoria Park Market (see p95) is open daily; while Christchurch's Arts Centre market (see p228) and Nelson Market (see p215) are open at the weekend.

New Zealand-made crafts and souvenirs for sale in Blenheim

### Handicrafts

A wide variety of shops selling locally made crafts and souvenirs can be found in New Zealand's main cities, tourist towns and resorts. In areas where the local craft industry is particularly strong, such as Coromandel (see p131) and Nelson (see p217), small galleries maintained by individual artists and crafts people are dotted along the roadsides. Museum shops, such as at the **Museum of New Zealand Te Papa Tongarewa**, Wellington (see 170–71), and **Auckland War Memorial Museum** (see pp82–3), also sell top-of-the-range handcrafted products.

The variety and quality of New Zealand handicrafts is continually improving. Products worth buying are traditional Maori flax baskets, bone and greenstone jewellery and ornaments, *paua* (abalone) shell jewellery, ceramics, hand-blown glassware, wood products made from New Zealand's native timbers, and sheepskin and wool items (see pp328–9).

Colourful crafts for sale at Nelson's weekend market

### Designer Labels

New Zealand has a number of internationally successful fashion designers, whose clothing can be bought in boutiques in the main cities. Labels to look for are Trelise Cooper, Karen Walker, World, Zambesi and NomD. Top quality casual wool clothing is available under several labels, including Untouched World.

Quality outdoor clothing and equipment is available under the Canterbury, Heritage and Macpac brands (see p329). Arthur Ellis manufactures high quality Fairydown equipment. Icebreaker merino outdoor gear is very popular.

# What to Buy in New Zealand

New Zealand offers a wide range of unique goods. Some, such as bone and greenstone carvings and jewellery, and *harakeke* (woven flax) items, are reflective of the country's Maori heritage, while others, such as sheepskin rugs and wool garments, reflect its strong agricultural base. Other good buys are wood products made from New Zealand's native timbers, ceramics, outdoor equipment, and food and wine. Hundreds of gift and craft shops, as well as department stores and museum shops, make it easy to find New Zealand-made products to suit every budget.

Sheepskin floor rug with thick, combed wool

**Wool and sheepskin** products from New Zealand are major shopping attractions. Although most New Zealand wool is exported for use in carpets, merino wool is used locally for fine knitwear and suiting fabrics. Hand-knitted sweaters made from hand-spun, hand-dyed wool are widely available in department stores and souvenir shops, as are sheepskin rugs, car seat covers, jackets, boots, slippers, gloves, and souvenir items.

Sheepskin slippers

Hand-knitted sweater

Lamb's wool muff

Woollen gloves

Bowl made from the trunk of a tree

**Woodcrafts** fashioned from native timbers are well known for their attractive grains and fine work-manship. The most commonly used woods are rimu, kauri, matai and beech. Many crafts people also use recycled timber as well as exotic species such as macrocarpa.

Kauri timber trinket box

Wooden coasters with *paua* shell inlay

Carved Maori figure with *paua* shell eyes

Finely carved traditional Maori club

Pendant with perforated spiral design

**Greenstone** (or jade) is New Zealand's most precious stone. Artisans craft it into a wide range of jewellery and ornaments using both traditional Maori and contemporary designs *(see p241)*.

**Bone**, originally used by Maori to fashion fish-hooks, is now used mainly for decorative items. Stylized fish-hook pendants, embellished with delicate tracery, are popular purchases.

**Paua** (abalone) is a shellfish mollusc found around the New Zealand coastline, but it is treasured more for its iridescent inner shell than for its meat. It is used to make pendants and earrings, and for inlays in woodcrafts and traditional Maori carvings.

*Paua* shell and silver pendants and necklace

Box with inset *paua* shell

Hand-painted dish

Wine goblet

Red glass vase

**Ceramics and glassware** are widely available craft items in New Zealand. Ceramics range from rustic earthenware pieces to delicate ornamental works and top quality tableware. Hand-blown glassware is of high quality, and many artisans are happy to allow visitors to watch them at their work *(see p217)*.

Perfume bottle

Earthenware coffee mug

Cat-shaped coffee pot

**Outdoor equipment** made in New Zealand is among the best in the world. One of the leading brands is Macpac, which regularly tests its own equipment in the mountains of the South Island. The best places to buy such goods are specialist outdoor equipment shops in the main cities.

Tent in bag

Windcheater

Backpack

**Food and drink**, products of New Zealand's extensive farmlands, include excellent meats, fruit, dairy produce and wines. As well as lamb and beef, speciality meats such as ostrich and venison are available. Cheeses made by small boutique factories are worth trying, as is New Zealand's delicious ice cream and its honey from native plants. New Zealand wines have also gained a strong international reputation *(see pp40–41, 312–13)*.

Selection of Kapiti cheeses

Sauvignon Blanc from Marlborough

Kiwifruit flavoured chocolates

Jars of local honey

# ENTERTAINMENT IN NEW ZEALAND

From professional theatre, opera and ballet to Maori and Pacific Island culture, music and dance and "Down Under" rock music, New Zealand has a diverse entertainment scene. The liveliest places are the main cities, but even small provincial towns boast their own local bands and amateur performance societies.

New Zealand is on the itinerary of many international performers, although some of these venture no further than Auckland and Wellington. Maori culture is an important theme in New Zealand art, and is showcased at festivals and specialist venues, such as Te Puia, a Maori arts and crafts centre situated in Rotorua.

## Information Sources

**Tourism New Zealand** posts a yearly calendar of events around the country on its website *(see p331)*. Daily newspapers and magazines such as *North and South*, *The Listener* and *Metro* also provide details about current and upcoming performances.

THE EDGE, Auckland's main entertainment complex

## Major Venues

The major entertainment venues for the performing arts are located in New Zealand's four main cities. They include Auckland's **THE EDGE**, which comprises the Aotea Centre, Town Hall and Civic Theatre; Wellington's **Michael Fowler Centre** and **TSB Bank Arena**; Christchurch's **Town Hall** and **Isaac Theatre Royal**, and Dunedin's **Town Hall**.

## Booking Tickets

It is wise to book in advance for most live performances. The easiest way is to use the nationwide **Ticketek** and **Ticketmaster** systems, either via the Internet or by telephone through their many agencies around the

country. In many cases, tickets can also be purchased at the venue.

## Theatre

Professional theatre companies are restricted to the main cities, while the smaller provincial towns are served by amateur troupes. Wellington has the most vibrant theatre scene, with three professional theatre companies *(see pp160–61)*: **Downstage**; **Circa**, a co-operative established in the 1970s, known for its consistently excellent plays; and **Bats**, best known for experimental theatre performances. New Zealand's only national Maori theatre company, **Taki Rua**, specializes in indigenous ethnic drama and is based in Wellington, but also tours the country regularly with new productions. Other professional theatre groups

are the **Auckland Theatre Company**, which performs at the Maidment, Herald and Sky City theatres; the **Court Theatre** in Christchurch's historic Arts Centre; and the **Fortune Theatre**, located in Dunedin in an historic inner-city church.

## Classical Music, Opera and Dance

The **New Zealand Symphony Orchestra** is based in Wellington *(see pp160–61)* but tours the country regularly, covering about 50,000 km (31,000 miles) a year, making it one of the most travelled orchestras in the world. It sometimes performs outdoor city concerts in the summer.

New Zealand's regional professional orchestra companies are of a high standard and perform regularly.

New Zealand Symphony Orchestra at the Town Hall, Wellington

Saxcess, New Zealand's premier saxophone quartet

The principal opera company is the **New Zealand Opera**, which performs mainly at the Aotea Centre in Auckland and in Wellington. Canterbury is home to Southern Opera.

The **Royal New Zealand Ballet** is the oldest professional dance company in Australasia. It tours the country frequently with a wide range of work (see pp160–61).

**Footnote Dance**, New Zealand's only national contemporary dance troupe, also tours the country regularly, presenting productions created by New Zealand's own choreographers and composers.

## Rock, Jazz and Country

Kiwi rock music has a quirky charm that attracts fans worldwide. The Mutton Birds, Dave Dobbyn, Neil Finn and The Datsuns are among New Zealand's most internationally successful rock performers, and they occasionally perform in the country. Many local bands perform in pubs and popular venues such as Auckland's **THE EDGE**.

Events such as Wellington's International Arts Festival attract both local and international jazz performers (see pp160–61), as do regional festivals such as the Bay of Islands Jazz and Blues Festival each August.

Entertainment posters

Country and Western has a strong following in New Zealand and there are a number of excellent singers and bands. Lovers of traditional country music should make their way to Gore in Southland during May and June to watch the Gold Guitar Awards.

## Maori Music and Dance

Traditional Maori performing arts are showcased at a number of venues, including **Te Puia**, a Maori arts and crafts centre, at Rotorua (see pp142–3), and at the **Auckland War Memorial Museum** (see pp82–3), both staging daily concerts. The biennial three-day Aotearoa Traditional Maori Performing Arts Festival, held at different locations, features Maori culture, music and dance from around New Zealand. Tourist operators specializing in Maori heritage include music and dance in their programmes (see p339).

Maori cultural performance at an arts festival in Wellington

# DIRECTORY

# Film and Popular Music

New Zealand arts and entertainment are in the midst of a mini renaissance. Local music has benefited from a music commission that helps to market the industry both at home and overseas, so more New Zealand bands are now heard on the radio. The big theatres and cinema chains are found in the main centres (see p96), but many smaller towns also have vibrant entertainment venues, many of which play host during the international festivals.

## Film and Festivals

Although major New Zealand productions such as the *Lord of the Rings* trilogy have been making the headlines since 2001, for every Peter Jackson there are countless other filmmakers working on short films and digital feature films. New Zealanders love going to the cinema and advances in digital projection have prompted the revival of boutique suburban cinemas and an explosion of "small" big screen theatres that seat about 50 moviegoers in comfortable surroundings.

Alongside the growth in screen numbers there has been an explosion in the number of specialist film festivals. The biggest of them all is the **International Film Festival**, now in its 39th year. It presents a programme of critically acclaimed films from the international festival circuit alongside classics and director showcases, and includes world premieres of works by new and established New Zealand filmmakers. The festival travels the country starting in the main centres in July and takes in the provinces until the end of the year. The magnificently refurbished **Embassy Theatre** in Wellington is one beneficiary of the festival's popularity. Dunedin's arthouse cinema **Metro** and the **Academy Gold** in Christchurch also host festival showings.

Out Takes is a festival for gay and lesbian film that takes place in May and June in Auckland, Wellington and Christchurch, while The Date Palm Film Festival in September focuses on film from the Middle East. The Documentary Edge Festival takes place in February and March, with showings in both Wellington and Auckland, including at Auckland's independent **Academy Cinema**. The Italian Film Festival takes place in the main centres and provincial towns during October and November.

## Popular Music

There is no definitive New Zealand sound, but artists who are able to instil a local flavour to whatever genre they work in stand out from the crowd. The Wellington-based dub/soul/funksters Fat Freddy's Drop picked up a major New Zealand Music award in 2005 for their album *Based on a True Story*.

New Zealand hip hop is popular, with producer P Money leading the way, and MCs such as Scribe and Ladi 6 topping the charts. Local hip hop often fuses American gangster styles with Pacific Island rhythms and tales. Dub, roots and reggae are also popular, especially at summer festivals; The Black Seeds, Katchafire and Kora are leaders in these genres.

The Datsuns are a three-piece rock band from the provincial town of Cambridge who have exported their AC/DC style power chords to the rest of the world. Led Zeppelin bass player John Paul Jones produced their second album. Bands such as the Sneaks and the Checks are following in their wake. Stereogram, Pluto and Elemeno P are mainstream pop rockers who have benefited from commercial radio's current inclusive approach to local music.

Most of the live music action takes place in pubs and clubs, but established artists such as Neil Finn, Dave Dobbyn and Bic Runga now also play seated concerts in larger theatres such as the Opera House in Wellington and The Edge (see p78) in Auckland.

Jazz festivals are held in Wellington, Nelson and on Waiheke Island, and the national country music awards are held annually at the bottom of the South Island in Gore.

## Clubs, Bars and Cafés

The traditional New Zealand pub with at least three bars and accommodation is alive in the provinces, but in the cities it is rapidly being replaced by smaller bars and cafés offering good food and live entertainment as well as drinks. Many bars and cafés turn the lights down and the music up later in the evening, however, with the entertainment starting when the food stops. It is worth checking whether food is still being served when you arrive. Irish-themed bars, with Guinness on tap and Irish music, can be found in most reasonable sized towns.

It is often said Wellington has more bars, cafés and restaurants per head then New York City. That may or may not be true, but the most vibrant areas are in and around Courtenay Place and on Cuba Street. Bars cater for most musical tastes with **San Francisco Bathhouse**, **Mighty Mighty** and **Bar Bodega** flying the flag for live music while clubs like **The Garden Club** and **Sandwiches** cater for the dance crowd. **The Matterhorn**, **Good Luck** and **Lagerfield** are some of the many that offer good food and an eclectic selection of DJs.

Auckland's nightlife is more dispersed. Viaduct Basin (see p76) was developed in the late 1990s to cater for followers of the Americas Cup yachting regatta. The cup may have gone but bars such as **Soul Bar & Bistro** and **Chic Lounge** remain. The city's dance clubs are mainly found on High Street, Ponsonby Road and

Karangahape Road. **Rakinos** restaurant hosts live bands and DJs, and among the bars on High Street is **Cube**. **Occidental Belgian Beer Café** is an institution and Queen Street's **Khuja Lounge** is heading that way. Also on Queen Street is Auckland's home of underground dance music **Fu Bar**. Two main band venues are the **Kings Arms** and **Dogs Bollix**. **Galatos** has long been associated with reggae and dub. Karangahape Road is home to such clubs as **K'Road Ballroom**, **Eden's** and **Rising Sun**.

Christchurch is the home of New Zealand drum 'n' bass music. The premiere venue for live music is undoubtedly **Dux de Lux**, but **Zebedees**, **Creation** and **Foam Lounge** also play host to local and touring bands. **Ministry Nightclub** offers dance sounds and **Wunderbar** in nearby Lyttleton has live music.

Dunedin was the birthplace of some of New Zealand's more influential guitar bands such as The Chills and the Bats. **Arc Café** has carried on the tradition and often books guitar bands. The café is also the home of a record label that began recording Dunedin bands, but has since branched out and takes on acts from elsewhere in the country.

**Chicks Hotel** is a well-known haunt of a number of iconic Dunedin artists. It has a great atmosphere with locals and students converging to watch Dunedin music being performed. **Bath St**, a club named after its address, regularly hosts reggae and hip hop nights. The **Crown Hotel** and **10 Bar** both host DJs and live music.

## DIRECTORY

### Film and Festivals

**Academy Cinema**
City Library Building,
44 Lorne St, Auckland.
**Tel** (09) 373 2761.

**Academy Gold Cinema**
Arts Centre, 36 Colombo St, Christchurch.
**Tel** (03) 377 9911.

**Embassy Theatre**
10 Kent Tce, Wellington.
**Tel** (04) 384 7657.

**International Film Festival**
W nziff.co.nz

**Metro**
Town Hall, Moray Place, Dunedin.
**Tel** (03) 471 9635.

### Pubs and Bars

**10 Bar**
10 The Octagon, Dunedin.
**Tel** (03) 477 6310.

**Bar Bodega**
101 Ghuznee St, Wellington.
**Tel** (04) 384 8212.

**Chicks Hotel**
2 Mount St, Port Chalmers.
**Tel** (03) 472 8736.

**Crown Hotel**
179 Rattray St, Dunedin.
**Tel** (03) 477 0132.

**Dogs Bollix**
Newton Rd (K Rd End), Auckland.
**Tel** (09) 376 4600.

**Eden's Bar**
335 Karangahape Rd.
Auckland.

**Kings Arms**
59 France St,
Auckland.
**Tel** (09) 373 3240.

**Mighty Mighty**
104 Cuba St,
Wellington.

**Occidental Belgian Beer Café**
6–8 Vulcan Lane,
Auckland.
**Tel** (09) 300 6226.

**Rising Sun**
373 Karangahape Rd,
Auckland.
**Tel** (027) 559 7876.

**San Francisco Bathhouse**
171 Cuba St,
Wellington.
**Tel** (04) 801 6797.

**Southern Cross**
35 Abel Smith St,
Wellington.
**Tel** (04) 384 9085.

**The Twisted Hop**
6 Poplar St,
Christchurch.
**Tel** (03) 962 3688.

**Wunderbar**
19 London St,
Lyttelton.
**Tel** (03) 328 8818.

### Cafés

**Arc Café**
135 High St, Dunedin.
**Tel** (03) 477 7200.

**Dux de Lux**
28 Riccarton Rd,
Christchurch.
**Tel** (03) 366 6919.

**Good Luck**
126 Cuba St, Wellington.
**Tel** (04) 801 9950.

**Khuja Lounge**
3rd floor, 536 Queen St,
Auckland.
**Tel** (09) 377 3711.

**Lagerfield**
21 Blair St, Wellington.
**Tel** (04) 801 5212.

**Rakinos**
Level 1, 35 High St,
Auckland.
**Tel** (09) 358 3535.

**Soul Bar & Bistro**
Viaduct Harbour Ave,
Auckland.
**Tel** (09) 356 7249.

**The Matterhorn**
106 Cuba St, Wellington.
**Tel** (04) 384 3359.

### Clubs

**Bath St**
1 Bath St, Dunedin.
**Tel** (03) 477 6750.

**Chic Lounge**
201 Quay St, Auckland.
**Tel** (09) 377 5360.

**Creation**
105 Worcester St,
Christchurch.
**Tel** (03) 366 4009.

**Cube**
5 High St, Auckland.
**Tel** (09) 379 9091.

**Foam Lounge**
30 Bedford Row,
Christchurch.
**Tel** (03) 365 2926.

**Fu Bar**
4 Wolfe St, Auckland.
**Tel** (09) 309 3079.

**Galatos**
17 Galatos St, Auckland.
**Tel** (09) 303 1928.

**K'Road Ballroom**
214 Karangahape Rd,
Auckland.
**Tel** (09) 366 0340.

**Live Bar**
68 Hobson St, Auckland.
**Tel** (06) 307 5975.

**Ministry Nightclub**
90 Lichfield St,
Christchurch.
**Tel** (03) 379 2910.

**Sandwiches**
Cnr Kent Tce and
Marjoribanks St,
Wellington.
**Tel** (04) 385 7698.

**The Garden Club**
13 Dixon St, Wellington.
**Tel** (04) 381 2341.

**Zebedees**
479 Blenheim Rd,
Christchurch.
**Tel** (03) 341 5210.

# SPECIALIST HOLIDAYS AND ACTIVITIES

Lovers of the outdoors will find New Zealand an ideal place to pursue their interests, or to experience something they have never tried before. From quick thrills, such as bungy jumping, jet-boating and helicopter rides to mountain climbing, abseiling, white-water rafting and skiing, New Zealand offers a huge range of activities for outdoor enthusiasts. The best places to find out what is available are at the Department of Conservation (DOC) offices, visitor information centres (i-SITES) and travel agents.

### Tramping and Walking

With its 14 national parks, as well as many forest parks and protected natural areas, New Zealand offers immense opportunities for walking and tramping at all levels; tramping is the term New Zealanders use for trekking or hiking. A national network of walkways, ranging from short, well-graded paths to rudimentary alpine routes, thread their way throughout New Zealand, and every location boasts tracks and trails that allow visitors to experience the locality's finest aspects.

The best tramping routes are in the national parks, which are serviced by basic but comfortable huts costing between NZ$10 and NZ$45 per night. Nine of these tracks – world famous for their beauty – have been designated "Great Walks".

Tramping can be done with a guide or independently. In the latter case, trampers are required to be self-sufficient in food, suitable clothing and sleeping gear. Tramping huts vary in size and facilities, and it is wise to check with the DOC before setting off. It is also vital to check track and weather conditions with the DOC. Always sign in at the local DOC office or in intentions books provided at the beginning of major tracks. Although New Zealand has a sophisticated search and rescue system, it cannot operate if trampers do not leave a record of their whereabouts and expected date of return. On popular routes, such as the Abel Tasman Coastal Track and the Routeburn and Milford tracks, advance booking is essential.

Walkway signpost

### Mountaineering and Rock Climbing

With 30 peaks at heights over 3,000 m (9,840 ft), the South Island's Southern Alps provide climbers many opportunities for technically demanding mountain climbing. The principal climbing regions are the Aoraki/Mount Cook, Westland/Tai Poutini, Tititea/Mount Aspiring, Arthur's Pass and Fiordland national parks, while in the North Island the Central Plateau offers the best climbing. The main season is from November to March. Weather in the mountains can change extremely rapidly, and it is important that climbers get an up-to-date weather forecast, are adequately equipped, and post their intentions with the DOC before setting off. Experienced mountain guides, such as Aoraki/Mount Cook's **Alpine Guides (Aoraki) Ltd**, are available in many of the major climbing regions.

There is also plenty of scope for rock climbing. Among the best locations are the volcanic rock outcrops of Christchurch's Port Hills (p234) and the limestone formations of Castle Hill in Canterbury (see p246).

### Caving and Abseiling

New Zealand has extensive cave systems, among the most notable being the Waitomo Caves in the central North Island (see pp124–5) and the Takaka region in northwest Nelson (see p220). Some caves are easil

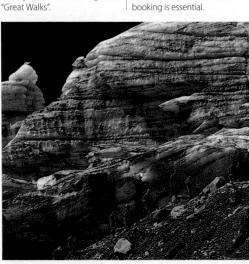
Guided walk on Franz Josef Glacier (see pp242–3)

Abseiling in the Mangapu Cave system, Waitomo *(see pp124–5)*

accessed, while others are more suited to experienced cavers. A popular way of experiencing New Zealand's cave formations is with the **Legendary Black Water Rafting Co™**. Participants float in rubber tubes through extensive cave systems illuminated by glowworms. Two of the best locations for this activity are Waitomo *(see p124–5)* and Westport *(see p238)*, where rafting operators run tours.

Both the North and South islands offer exhilarating abseiling. In the Waitomo area, tourists can descend down a 100-m (330-ft) hole into the "Lost World" *(see p125)* Mangapu Cave system with **Waitomo Adventures**.

## Cycling

Cycle touring on New Zealand's highways and back roads is a popular way of seeing the country. Among the many scenic roads suited to cycling are the Queen Charlotte Drive in the Marlborough Sounds *(see p206)* and State Highway 6 on the West Coast. The **Otago Central Rail Trail** offers three

Mountain biking in Rangataua Forest *(see p146)*

to five days cycling along a 150-km (93-mile) old rail line, upgraded specifically for cyclists. An extensive network of off-road tracks is also available for mountain bikers. Hanmer Springs *(see p237)* and Victoria Forest Park *(see p237)* are among the best mountain biking destinations.

## Skiing

New Zealand has numerous ski fields, ranging from highly commercialized fields to small fields owned by local ski clubs. Major fields are **Whakapapa Ski Area** and **Turoa Ski Resort** on the slopes of the North Island's Mount Ruapehu *(see pp146–7)*, the **Mount Hutt Ski Area** in Canterbury *(see p250)*, and **Coronet Peak**, the **Remarkables Ski Area**, **Cardrona Alpine Resort** and **Treble Cone** in Central Otago *(see pp198–9)*.

The ski season runs from mid-June to September. In the South Island, heli-skiing operators take skiers to untouched powder snow. Ski touring and cross-country skiing take place in many locations, including the **Waiorau Snow Farm** near Wanaka *(see pp198–9)*.

## DIRECTORY

### Tramping

**w** doc.govt.nz
provides information on "Great Walks" and how to make bookings.

### Mountaineering and Rock Climbing

**Alpine Guides (Aoraki) Ltd**
PO Box 20, Mt Cook Village. **Tel** (03) 435 1834.
**w** alpineguides.co.nz

**Mount Aspiring Guides**
99 Ardmore St, Wanaka.
**Tel** (03) 443 9422.
**w** mtaspiringguides. co.nz

### Caving and Abseiling

**Legendary Black Water Rafting Co™**
Private Bag 501,

Otorohanga. **Tel** (07) 878 6219, 0800 228 464.
**w** blackwaterrafting. co.nz

**Norwest Adventures**
182 Queen St, Westport.
**Tel** (03) 788 8168
**w** caverafting.com

**Waitomo Adventures**
PO Box 29, Waitomo Caves. **Tel** (07) 878 7788, 0800 924 866.
**w** waitomo.co.nz

### Cycling

**New Zealand Pedaltours**
PO Box 37-575 Parnell, Auckland.
**Tel** (09) 585 1338.
**w** pedaltours.co.nz

**Ohakune Mountain Ride**
16 Miro St, Ohakune.
**Tel** (06) 385 8257.

**Otago Central Rail Trail**
i-SITE Visitor Centre, 48 The Octagon, Dunedin.
**Tel** (03) 474 3300.

**Pacific Cycle Tours**
Unit 3, 14 Kennaway Rd, Christchurch.
**Tel** (03) 329 9913.
**w** bike-nz.com

### Skiing

**Cardrona Alpine Resort**
**Tel** (03) 443 7411.
**w** cardrona.co.nz

**Coronet Peak**
**Tel** (03) 442 4620.
**w** nzski.com

**Harris Mountains Heli-skiing**
**Tel** (03) 442 6722.
**w** heliski.co.nz

**Mount Hutt Ski Area**
PO Box 14, Methven.
**Tel** (03) 308 5074.
**w** nzski.com

**Remarkables Ski Area**
PO Box 359, Queenstown.
**Tel** (03) 442 4615.
**w** nzski.com

**Treble Cone**
PO Box 206, Wanaka.
**Tel** (03) 443 7443.
**w** treblecone.co.nz

**Turoa Ski Area**
**Tel** (06) 385 8274.
**w** turoa.com

**Waiorau Snow Farm**
Cardrona, Wanaka.
**Tel** (03) 443 7542.
**w** snowfarmnz.com

**Whakapapa Ski Area**
**Tel** (07) 892 3738.
**w** whakapapa.co.nz

Surfing at Whale Bay, Raglan
*(see pp120–1)*

## Water Sports

With a coastline 18,200 km (11,300 miles) long and an abundance of lakes and rivers, New Zealand offers plenty of opportunities for visitors to participate in water sports. From Auckland's Hauraki Gulf northwards is a yachting paradise where experienced sailors can hire boats for "bareboat" cruising *(see pp92–3)*. Skippered sailing is more common, however, as the country's gusty winds can test even the most capable "boaties".

Surfing is popular, especially in the North Island at beaches like Piha *(see p90)*, Raglan *(see pp120–1)* and in the Bay of Plenty *(see pp130, 132)*. The calm waters of the country's harbours and lakes are suitable for windsurfing, and

boards can be hired at many waterfront locations.

The Bay of Islands, Auckland's Hauraki Gulf, Nelson's Abel Tasman National Park, the Marlborough Sounds, Fiordland and Stewart Island are prime venues for sea kayaking. Tours can take as long as a week. Kayaks can also be hired for a few hours' paddling around the harbours of Auckland, Wellington and other coastal cities.

New Zealand's fast-flowing rivers are excellent for white-water rafting and kayaking. Among the most challenging rivers are the Motu *(see p136)*, Rangitikei and Tongariro in the North Island, while the South Island has dozens of rivers, from the Buller on the West Coast to the Clarence in Canterbury. Among the rivers suitable for the inexperienced is the Whanganui River, which winds its way through the historic Whanganui National Park *(see p183)*.

There are many good dive spots, including the network of marine reserves around the New Zealand coastline *(see pp30–1)*. Near Whangarei, the dramatic underwater caves of the Poor Knights Islands are rated as one of the world's top diving destinations *(see p103)*. Further north, the Greenpeace boat, the *Rainbow Warrior*, is a well-known underwater wreck. In Fiordland, a unique marine eco-system, tempered by huge quantities of freshwater run-off, attracts species nearer to the surface than in other areas.

## Hunting

Because many of the animals introduced into New Zealand by Europeans have no natural predators, they have become pests, and therefore hunting of big game is encouraged by the authorities. No licence is required, there is no restriction on the numbers killed and the season is generally open all year round.

Professional guiding companies operate throughout the country, many with access to extensive tracts of private land. Seven species of deer, wild pigs and goats are common in forests, while chamois and thar can be found in mountain areas of the South Island. The duck shooting season starts at the beginning of May and lasts eight weeks.

## Fishing

New Zealand is justly renowned for the quality of its sea and freshwater fishing. Lake Taupo and the rivers surrounding it (especially the famed Tongariro) are internationally regarded as the Mecca of trout fishing *(see p145)*, although there are good rivers throughout the country. The trout fishing season runs from October to May. The main salmon rivers are on the east coast of the South Island. A licence is compulsory in order to fish for trout and salmon, and tackle is readily available.

The Bay of Islands is the centre of deep-sea marlin fishing *(see pp106–7)*. The best

Kayaking over rapids on the Tongariro River

Fishing in the Waikato River near Huka Lodge *(see p299)*

deep-sea angling is found on the North Island's east coast, northwards from the Bay of Plenty. The best fishing months are from January to May and licences are not necessary.

## Ecotours

A long tradition of environmental activism in New Zealand has led to numerous ecotourism developments. There are many specialist nature tour operators to choose from, and guides working in the adventure tourism area, such as black-water rafting *(see p124)*, often have a good knowledge of local flora and fauna.

There are numerous opportunities for bird watching *(see pp196–7)*, including at the Royal Albatross colony on Otago Peninsula, ocean birds at Kaikoura *(see p213)*, the white heron colony at Okarito and the immense birdlife of Farewell Spit *(see p221)*.

Kaikoura is synonomous with whale watching *(see p213)*. During winter there is nearly a 100 per cent chance of seeing sperm whales. Dolphin watching tours operate from many areas, including Banks Peninsula, the Bay of Islands and Southland.

Whale Watch® tour at Kaikoura *(see p213)*

# DIRECTORY

## Rafting

**Queenstown Rafting**
35 Shotover St,
Queenstown.
**Tel** (03) 442 9792,
0800 723 8464.
W queenstownrafting.
co.nz

**Wet 'n' Wild Rafting Company**
2 White St,
Rotorua.
**Tel** (07) 348 3191,
0800 462 7238.
W wetnwildrafting.
co.nz

## Kayaking

**Abel Tasman Kayaks**
Main Rd, Marahau.
**Tel** (03) 527 8022.
W abeltasmankayaks.
co.nz

**Abel Tasman Wilson's Experiences**
265 High St, Motueka.
**Tel** (03) 528 2027.
W abeltasman.co.nz

**Fiordland Wilderness Experiences**
Sandy Brown Rd, Te Anau.
**Tel** (03) 249 7700.
W fiordlandseakayak.
co.nz

## Diving

**Dive! Tutukaka**
Marina Rd, Tutukaka,
Whangarei.
**Tel** (09) 434 3867.
W diving.co.nz

**Splash Gordon**
432 The Esplanade,
Island Bay,
Wellington.
**Tel** (04) 939 3483.
W splashgordon.co.nz

## Hunting and Fishing

**Chris Jolly Outdoors**
PO Box 1020, Lake Taupo.
**Tel** (07) 378 0623.
W chrisjolly.co.nz

**Mountain High Adventure Company**
C/- Snow and Stream
Lodge, 5–7 Farquhar
Place, Methven.
**Tel** (03) 302 8733.
W fishandhunt.co.nz

## Eco Tours

**Albatross Encounter**
96 Esplanade,
Kaikoura.
**Tel** (03) 319 6777.
W albatrossencounter.
co.nz

## Catlins Wildlife Trackers Ecotours
5 Mirren St, Papatowai,
RD2, Owaka. **Tel** (03) 415
8613. W catlins-
ecotours.co.nz

**Dolphin Discoveries**
PO Box 400, Cnr Marsden
& Williams rds, Paihia, Bay
of Islands. **Tel** (09) 402
8234. W dolphinz.co.nz

**Heritage Expeditions**
53b Montreal St,
Christchurch. **Tel** (03) 365
3500. W heritage-
expeditions.co.nz

**Whale Watch® Kaikoura Ltd**
Railway Station Rd,
Kaikoura.
**Tel** (03) 319 6767.
W whalewatch.co.nz

Paraglider near Queenstown

## Aerial Adventures

Hot-air ballooning, tandem parapenting (paragliding) and tandem skydiving are more adventurous ways of taking to the air than flying (see p199). Commercial operators offering all three types of aerial thrill exist in the main cities and major resorts (see p339). A hot-air balloon ride is a spectacular way to view the extensive Southern Alps and Canterbury Plains, while parapenting from Te Mata Peak in Hawke's Bay (see p153) and the Remarkables near Queenstown is a unique experience (see pp198–9). Check with local visitor centres or travel agents for details of available services.

Aerial sightseeing is also popular throughout the country, either in small planes, helicopters or float planes. Highlights in the North Island include flights over the volcanically active White Island (see p134) and volcanic Tongariro National Park (pp146–7). In the South Island, flights over Mount Cook, the Fox and Franz Josef glaciers (see pp256–7) and Fiordland (see pp284–5)

Flightseeing over Fiordland National Park (pp284–7)

are popular and readily available. Many flights touch down in spectacular locations, such as White Island and the glaciers of the Southern Alps.

Bungy jumping from the Kawarau Bridge, Queenstown (see p280)

## Bungy Jumping

Ever since A J Hackett used an historic bridge over the Kawarau River in Queenstown (see pp198–9) to launch the bungy jumping phenomenon in 1988, tourism operators have set up bungy jump sites in picturesque locations, usually on bridges above river gorges, in both the North and South islands.

Safety is a key issue in bungy jumping. Jumpers are weighed so that the correct length of bungy cord can be calculated for their jump. The cord is securely attached to their ankles before the jump from a bridge or platform.

## Jet-Boating

Bill Hamilton, a local engineer and farmer, perfected the design of the jet-boat so it is no coincidence that these highly manoeuvrable craft are so popular on the nation's waterways. In locations such as Waikato (see p144) and Queenstown (see pp198–9), jet-boat operators take tourists through narrow canyons, across the shallowest of water and whirl 360 degrees "on a sixpence". Some operators offer jet-boat safaris, taking visitors on longer trips into the scenic back country. Mandatory life jackets are supplied.

## Golf

There are more than 400 golf courses in New Zealand, more per head of population than virtually any other country. Green fees can be as low as NZ$5 for a club in rural areas. Even the more exclusive city courses charge no more than NZ$50. Weekends are often reserved for members, although a number of clubs have reciprocal membership with overseas clubs, allowing visitors to play at any time. Major clubs have carts and clubs for hire.

## Four-Wheel Drive Touring

In the high country and rural areas of New Zealand are hundreds of rough tracks, many of which were created to provide access to farms, timber mills, gold mines and mining settlements. A four-wheel drive vehicle offers a physically undemanding way to explore these locations. Numerous tour operators exist throughout the country, offering both day trips and longer safaris through varied terrain.

## Horse Trekking

The wide open spaces of the country encourage horse riding and there are many operators who offer horse trekking through forests, high country trails or along one of the many beaches. Options range from half-day or all-day treks to multiday camping safaris. Some

Horse trekking at Hanmer, North Canterbury

operations are conveniently located close to cities. Most operators cater for a range of riding abilities and provide all equipment.

## Spectator Sports

New Zealanders are passionate about rugby. It is worth visiting a match during the rugby season from March to October *(see pp42–3)*. The Super 14 and Air New Zealand Cup are the major competitions. Matches generally attract large crowds, as do one-day cricket test matches. Highly entertaining, the atmosphere is

best at the day–night matches which begin in the afternoon and are played through the evening under lights.

Horse racing is a national passion, and a number of big race meetings are held between November and April *(see pp42–3)*. Netball also has a large following, with the most exciting games often involving the national team, the Silver Ferns.

Tickets for sports events can be obtained from Ticketek *(see p331)*.

## Maori Heritage Tours

Tour companies offering genuine encounters with Maori heritage operate in a number of locations. Tours may include a visit to a *marae*, where participants share a *hangi* (a traditional feast) and learn about Maori protocol, myths and legends, dance and art. One such operator near Rotorua, **Te Urewera Treks**, offers a range of eco-cultural treks and guided tours through the Urewera country, spiritual home to the Tuhoe people.

Waikato supporters at a provincial rugby match

# DIRECTORY

## Aerial Adventures

**Air Safaris**
PO Box 71,
Lake Tekapo.
**Tel** (03) 680 6880.
[W] airsafaris.co.nz

**Aoraki Hot Air Balloon Safaris**
PO Box 75,
Methven.
**Tel** (03) 302 8172,
0800 256 837.
[W] nzballooning.com

**Fiordland Helicopters**
PO Box 180,
Te Anau Airport.
**Tel** (03) 249 7575.
[W] fiordlandhelicopters.co.nz

**Sky Trek**
16 Lake Ave,
Frankton,
Queenstown.
**Tel** (03) 442 3992.
[W] skytrek.co.nz

## Bungy Jumping

**A J Hackett Bungy**
PO Box 488,
Queenstown.
**Tel** (03) 442 4007.
[W] ajhackett.com

**Taupo Bungy**
202 Spa Rd,
Taupo.
**Tel** (07) 377 1135,
0800 888 408.
[W] taupobungy.com

## Four-Wheel Driving

**Eco Wanaka**
59A Brownston St,
Wanaka.
**Tel** (03) 443 2869.
[W] adventure.net.nz

**Nomad Safaris**
Cnr George Rd &
Industrial Pl,
Queenstown.
**Tel** (03) 442 6699.
[W] nomadsafaris.co.nz

## Jet-Boating

**Huka Jet**
Wairakei Park, Taupo.
**Tel** (07) 374 8572.
[W] hukajet.co.nz

**Shotover Jet**
PO Box 189, Queenstown.
**Tel** (03) 442 8570.
[W] shotoverjet.co.nz

## Horse Trekking

**Alpine Horse Safaris**
Waitohi Downs,
Hawarden, Canterbury.
**Tel** (07) 314 4293.
[W] alpinehorse.co.nz

**Dart Stables**
PO Box 47, Glenorchy.
**Tel** (03) 442 5688.
[W] dartstables.com

**Hurunui Trails and Adventures**
757 The Peaks Rd,
Hawarden, Canterbury.
**Tel** (03) 314 4500.
[W] riding-vacations.info

## Pakiri Beach Horse Rides

Rahuikiri Rd, Pakiri,
RD 2, Wellsford.
**Tel** (09) 422 6275.
[W] horseride-nz.co.nz

## Maori Heritage Tours

**Red Feather (Tia Raukura) Expeditions**
PO Box 60243,
Titirangi, Auckland.
**Tel** (09) 818 7770.
[W] ecotoursnz.com

**Tamaki Tours**
PO Box 1492, 1220
Hinemaru St,
Rotorua.
**Tel** (07) 346 2999.
[W] maoriculture.co.nz

**Te Urewera Treks**
421 Rerewhakaaitu Rd,
Rotorua.
**Tel** (07) 366 6055.

# SURVIVAL GUIDE

# PRACTICAL INFORMATION

Tourism is one of New Zealand's most important industries, attracting over 2.5 million overseas visitors a year. As the industry has grown, services and facilities have improved to keep pace with demand. Visitors are well served by a wide range of accommodation and restaurants (*see pp298–307, 308–25*). There is easy and free access to good quality information through the many i-SITE visitor centres, which are co-ordinated by Tourism New Zealand, the national tourism body. Many of the best attractions in New Zealand are free – particularly when enjoying the natural landscape of national parks, beaches, lakes and rivers. New Zealanders are friendly people who are generally willing to offer assistance to tourists, although it is advisable for visitors to have a basic grasp of English as few New Zealanders are fluent in other languages.

Enjoying the sun at Scorching Bay, Wellington *(see p173)*

## When to Go

Spring (Sep–Nov), summer (Dec–Feb) and autumn (Mar–May) are the most popular seasons for travellers, although the ski season is a major attraction during the winter months (Jun–Aug). Average summer temperatures range between 20 and 30° C (68 and 86° F), and winter between 10 and 15° C (50 and 60° F), but the weather in New Zealand is changeable: temperatures can drop 10–20° C (50–68° F) in a short space of time when a cold southerly front blows in.

**Resort signboard**

The climate has strong regional variations. The north of the North Island is subtropical, while the remainder of the country is temperate. The country also has a pronounced west–east climate: the west coasts are wet and humid, the east coasts drier and sunnier.

Snow in winter falls mainly in the mountains of the South Island, when temperatures can fall below 0° C (32° F).

## Visas and Passports

Visitors to New Zealand must have a passport valid for at least three months longer than the intended period of stay. Visas are not required for Australian or British citizens, who are issued with a six-month visitor permit on arrival, or for visits of up to three months by residents of any of the 50 countries with which New Zealand has a visa-waiver agreement. All visitors should check visa requirements prior to travelling on the New Zealand Immigration Service website: www.immigration.govt.nz.

A reciprocal working holiday scheme exists between New Zealand and a further 34 other countries, entitling 18–30-year-olds to travel and work in the country temporarily for up to a year. It is also possible to obtain a work permit if you have been offered a job or have skills that are in demand; plan to set up a business or invest; or are visiting the country as an artist or athlete participating in a performance or sporting event. For full details visit the New Zealand Immigration Service website.

## Customs Information

New Zealand relies heavily on its agricultural industries and the bio security of its native flora and fauna. Great effort is made to keep the country free of introduced pests and diseases. All plant and animal materials must be declared on arrival, including fresh foodstuffs. Failure to declare quarantine items can lead to a fine of NZ$100,000 or five years in jail. If in doubt about an item, declare it to the inspectors on arrival. Tents or shoes that have been used recently in the countryside should be declared. For other restrictions and allowances, visit the New Zealand Customs Service website: www.customs.govt.nz

Class A, B and C drugs are prohibited, as are firearms and weapons unless a permit is obtained from the New Zealand Police on arrival. The country is also party to an international convention designed to prevent trade in all endangered species, and various animal products, which include anything made of ivory, turtle shell, clam shells and whalebone.

Visitors can buy duty-free goods on arrival, departure and at duty-free stores in cities (see p94). For travellers over 17 years old, the customs allowances are: 200 cigarettes, 250 grams of tobacco or 50 cigars, or a mixture of all three weighing no more than 250 grams; 4.5 litres of beer or wine and up to three 1,125 ml (40 oz) bottles of spirits or other beverages.

Department of Conservation information centre, Totaranui

## Tourist Information

The official information service that most visitors have contact with is the **i-SITE** visitor centre network. Independently owned but coordinated by the central tourism body, **Tourism New Zealand**, there are over 80 i-SITE centres scattered throughout New Zealand, sporting a distinctive green and black logo. They provide information on local attractions and activities, sell maps and guidebooks, and book accommodation.

**Department of Conservation** visitor centres are the best source of information on national parks. They provide maps and information on conditions for walkers.

## Admission Charges

Admission charges to attractions vary. Many galleries and museums request a donation or modest entry charge. Entry into the national parks is free, although access to certain areas is possible only with an approved tour company or guide. There is also a charge for overnight stays in Department of Conservation huts. Private companies run the many adventure tourism ventures, and charges vary.

## Opening Hours

Most major tourist attractions are open seven days a week in season, but it is best to check in advance. Business hours are generally from 8:30am to 5pm. Shops open 9am–5:30pm Monday–Friday and Saturday morning, with late-night shopping on Thursday. Shopping malls may stay open all day Saturday and Sunday. Many supermarkets open until 10pm.

## Language

English is the main language in New Zealand, but Maori also enjoys official status. Government departments and agencies often have bilingual names. *Kia ora* is a traditional Maori greeting and *haere mai* means "welcome". *Wharepaku* is the word for "toilet" – *wahine* for women and *tane* for men. "Wh" is pronounced "f".

## Etiquette and Smoking

New Zealand is a relatively informal society. On the whole, people are friendly and easygoing, and are happy to assist tourists. Dress standards vary, but casual wear is the norm.

Smoking is banned in cafés, bars, restaurants, shops and on public transport. It is not acceptable to smoke in private homes without asking permission. If invited to a New Zealander's home for a meal, take a bottle of wine or an item of food to share.

## Accessibility to Public Conveniences

Public conveniences can be found in town centres and shopping malls, at public beaches and at roadside service stations. They are generally free to use, open 24 hours and serviced regularly. Many, though not all, are wheelchair-accessible. Cafés, bars and restaurants have toilets for customers. The New Zealand Automobile Association website (www.aa.co.nz) has a searchable map of public toilet locations.

## Taxes and Tipping

A Goods and Services Tax (GST) is charged on most goods and services in New Zealand at a rate of 15 per cent. GST is usually included in the quoted price, but may occasionally be added at the end. There is currently no GST refund scheme for tourists.

Tipping in restaurants and hotels is not obligatory, although it has become more widespread with the increase in overseas tourists. Many New Zealanders do not tip taxi drivers, bartenders and porters, but it is becoming more common to reward good service in a restaurant (about 10 per cent of the bill).

Visitor information centre, Viaduct Basin, Auckland (see p76)

New Zealand has much to offer families on holiday

## Travellers with Special Needs

Disabled travellers are well catered for in New Zealand. Every new or substantially renovated building is required by law to have adequate access for people with disabilities. As a result, most hotels, restaurants and tourist sites have wheelchair facilities, and guide dogs are welcome.

Airports provide staff to assist disabled passengers, but national trains and buses are often inaccessible without assistance. City transport is more accessible, but it is best to check with the operating companies. Avis car rentals, can supply cars with hand controls *(see p359)*. All major towns have taxis that carry wheelchairs.

**Accessible Kiwi Tours** offer tour packages for disabled and mature travellers. **Enable New Zealand** offers support and information to disabled visitors on how to get around. **CCS Disability Action** can help with parking concessions when supplied with a home mobility card and a medical certificate. **Accombility** provides information on accommodation suitable for disabled travellers.

## Travelling with Children

New Zealand is a safe place to take children for a holiday. Many top attractions, such as beaches and national parks, appeal equally to children and adults. Children are well catered for, especially in motels with family rooms and self-catering facilities. Restaurants often have children's menus and high chairs. Breastfeeding in public is accepted and changing facilities are available in most public toilets. Children under five years must be restrained in an infant car seat.

## Senior Travellers

New Zealand is a popular destination for retired people. Most sights and activities are accessible to senior travellers, but participation in extreme sports will depend on individual age, health and fitness.

Some travel insurance policies set age limitations and many exclude pre-existing medical conditions, but it is possible to find policies targeted at older travellers. Ask about discounts on transport, tours and admission charges when booking.

## Gay and Lesbian Travellers

New Zealanders are generally accepting of homosexuality, though this is more true in the liberal cities than in the rural hinterland. The Human Rights Act 1993 made it unlawful to discriminate on grounds of sexual orientation, and travellers are highly unlikely to face discrimination. The **Gay New Zealand** website provides useful information about the gay scene in New Zealand.

## Travelling on a Budget

Students with a valid ISIC (International Student Identity Card) or young people with an IYTC (International Youth Travel Card) can obtain substantial discounts on flights, coach travel, tours and car hire, and at hotels and hostels. Cardholders are also entitled to reduced charges at art galleries, museums and attractions. The ISIC card can be acquired only by school, college or university students. The IYTC can be purchased by anyone aged 12–26. To find out about special deals, go to www.isiccard.com.

New Zealand is well equipped for budget backpacker travel, with a network of backpacker hostels in all the main towns and resorts around the country. **Backpacker bulletin boards** online and at hostels are a great place to pick up budget travel tips before you go or whilst on the road.

Several companies offer cost-effective group coach tours. **Magic Travellers Network** and **Flying Kiwi Adventure Tours** are well-known operators offering packages that combine travel with activities.

An International Student Identity Card (ISIC)

## Time

New Zealand is 12 hours ahead of Greenwich Mean Time and 2 hours ahead of Sydney. Clocks are put forward 1 hour each October and back 1 hour in March.

## Electricity

The electrical current is 230/240 volts 50 hertz, although most hotels and motels provide 110 volt AC sockets for electric razors. For all other equipment, an adaptor is necessary, as power outlets accept only flat, two- or three-pin plugs.

## Responsible Tourism

New Zealand is proud of its clean, green image, encapsulated in its "100% Pure NZ" tourism brand. It has 14 national parks, protecting a third of the country's land, and its wildlife sanctuaries preserve the country's unique native flora and fauna.

New Zealand was one of the first countries to pledge a carbon-neutral future, with a number of tourism companies achieving CarboNZero certification. The New Zealand tourism industry recognizes environmentally sustainable tourism with Qualmark Enviro certification, awarded to operators and accommodation providers for high levels of environmental responsibility. Eco-lodges committed to a sustainable accommodation

can be found in the most beautiful and remote locations such as **Hapuku Lodge**, found

Hapuku Lodge & Tree Houses, Kaikoura

in the Kaikoura forests. Organic food and produce is available from farmers' markets and specialist health shops.

## Maori Tourism

Maori tourism has moved on from the once limited "cultural shows" involving a *kapa haka* performed by indigenous people in traditional dress. Today Maori-led tours, such as those by **Indigenous New Zealand**, combine hiking, kayaking or whitewater-rafting with storytelling and interpretation.

## DIRECTORY

### Embassies and Consulates

#### Australia
72–76 Hobson St, Wellington.
**Tel** (04) 473 6411.
Ⓦ australia.org.nz

#### Canada
Level 11, 125 The Terrace, Wellington.
**Tel** (04) 473 9577.
Ⓦ newzealand.gc.ca

#### United Kindgom
44 Hill St, Wellington.
**Tel** (04) 924 2888.
Ⓦ britain.org.nz

#### USA
29 Fitzherbert Terrace, Wellington.
**Tel** (04) 462 6000.
Ⓦ newzealand.usembassy.gov

### Tourist Information

#### Christchurch and Canterbury Tourism
Botanic Gardens, Rolleston Ave.
**Tel** (03) 379 9629.
Ⓦ christchurchnz.com

#### Destination Rotorua Tourism Marketing
1106 Arawa St, Rotorua.
**Tel** (07) 348 4133.
Ⓦ rotoruanz.com

#### Department of Conservation
Ⓦ doc.govt.nz

#### Hawkes' Bay Tourism
2nd Floor Civic Court, Napier. **Tel** (06) 834 1918.
Ⓦ hawkesbaynz.com

#### i-SITE
Ⓦ i-site.org.nz

#### Nelson Tasman Tourism
Cnr Trafalgar and Halifax sts. **Tel** (03) 546 6228.
Ⓦ nelsonnz.com

#### Positively Wellington Tourism
Level 28, Grand Plimer Tower, Wellington.
**Tel** (04) 916 1205.
Ⓦ WellingtonNZ.com

#### Tourism Auckland
Auckland Viaduct, Auckland.
**Tel** (09) 979 7070.
Ⓦ aucklandnz.com

#### Tourism Dunedin
193 Princes St, Dunedin.
**Tel** (03) 471 8042.
Ⓦ dunedinnz.com

#### Tourism New Zealand
157 Lambton Quay, Wellington.
**Tel** (04) 917 5400.
Ⓦ newzealand.com

#### Tourism West Coast
80 Tainui St, Greymouth.
**Tel** (03) 768 6633.
Ⓦ west-coast.co.nz

### Travellers with Special Needs

#### Accessible Kiwi Tours
Ⓦ toursnz.com

#### Accomobility
Ⓦ accomobility.co.nz.

#### CCS Disability Action
**Tel** 0800 227 225.
Ⓦ ccsdisabilityaction.org.nz

#### Disability Information Centre
**Tel** 0800 693 342.

#### Enable New Zealand
Ⓦ weka.net.nz

### Senior Travellers

#### Advocacy for older people
Ⓦ osc.govt.nz

#### Age UK
Ⓦ ageuk.org

#### Grey Power
Ⓦ greypower.co.nz

#### Saga
Ⓦ saga.co.uk

### Gay and Lesbian Travellers

#### Gay Caravan and Camping Club
Ⓦ gaycaravanclub.com

#### Gay New Zealand
Ⓦ gaynz.com

### Travelling on a Budget

#### Backpacker bulletin boards
Ⓦ backpackerboard.co.nz

#### Flying Kiwi Adventure Tours
Ⓦ flyingkiwi.com

#### Magic Travellers Network
Ⓦ magicbus.co.nz

### Responsible Tourism

#### Hapuku Lodge
Ⓦ hapukulodge.com

#### Korimako Lodge
Ⓦ korimako.co.nz

#### Organic Pathways
Ⓦ organicpathways.co.nz

#### Straw Lodge
Ⓦ strawlodge.co.nz

### Maori Tourism

#### Indigenous New Zealand
Ⓦ inz.maori.nz

#### Toi Maori Aotearoa Maori Arts New Zealand
Ⓦ maoriart.org.nz

# Personal Security and Health

New Zealand is one of the safest countries in the world to visit. New Zealanders have a reputation for being friendly and law-abiding, and the political and economic climate is stable. Crimes do occur in New Zealand as in any other society, and visitors need to take sensible precautions to protect themselves and their property. The greatest risks, however, are environmental; many tourists have been caught out on the water, or in the mountains or bush with inadequate food and clothing, having underestimated the dangers of the terrain and the speed with which New Zealand's weather can change.

Travellers should be aware that New Zealand is situated on the Pacific Rim of Fire. Big earthquakes are infrequent but they do happen – Christchurch suffered major earthquakes in 2010 and again in 2011, both causing widespread damage. The Ministry of Civil Defence website (www.getthru.govt.nz) gives details on what to do in the event of an earthquake.

## Police

The New Zealand Police force are professional and helpful. They are divided into 12 districts, which between them run more than 400 community-based police stations across New Zealand.

Police officers are identified by their dark blue uniforms with epaulettes indicating rank. Police are highly visible patrolling the cities' streets day and night, in a non-aggressive manner. It is common to see highway police at roadsides in most cities and in rural districts, carrying out breath-tests on suspected drunk drivers.

To report a crime, visit the nearest police station: addresses and contact details can be found at www.police. govt.nz or in the blue pages of the telephone directory under "police".

## What to Be Aware Of

There are few areas in New Zealand that are not suitable for tourists to visit. However, use common sense to ensure your personal safety. Streets are often deserted after dark and it is not advisable, particularly for women, to walk alone at night. Licensed taxis are readily available and are safe to use. Hitchhiking is not recommended, especially for women and lone travellers.

Road accidents are a major public health issue and tourists planning to drive should be aware of the rules of the road in New Zealand.

## In an Emergency

In an emergency, police, fire and ambulance services can be contacted by dialling **111**.

In the event of a non-emergency road traffic incident, call *555.

## Lost and Stolen Property

Travellers need to use common sense to safeguard their property in New Zealand. Theft from cars can occur so lock vehicles and make sure valuable items remain out of view. Passports and credit cards should be kept in a hotel safe deposit box, a money belt or a zipped bag. A comprehensive travel insurance policy is advisable.

Stolen property should be reported to the police, who will issue a report, which can be used to support an insurance claim. Local police stations are easily located in all towns and cities. Most airports, bus and train stations, and the public transport networks in the big cities, have lost property offices and it is worth checking with the service in case any lost items have been handed in.

## Hospitals and Pharmacies

Urgent medical treatment, including emergency dental care, can be received at hospital A&E departments or at 24-hour walk-in GP surgeries. New Zealand has an extensive network of pharmacies (known as chemists), which offer over-the-counter remedies and prescription drugs. Qualified chemists can provide free advice but a doctor must write out prescriptions. All major towns have chemists, that open 9am–5:30pm daily and later on Thursday and Friday. Contact details for hospitals, GP and dental surgeries and pharmacies are listed in the front of local telephone directories.

Police car

Fire engine

Ambulance

A Golden Bay chemist, Takaka

## Environmental Hazards

New Zealand poses few risks to the visitor, as long as sensible precautions are taken. Its changeable climate is probably the greatest threat, but the vast majority of accidents befall people who venture into the wilderness unprepared. The **New Zealand Mountain Safety Council** outdoor safety code advises that you: plan your trip, let someone know where you are going, be aware of the weather, know your limits and take enough supplies – food, warm clothes, first aid kit and a means of communication – even when going for a day's walk in the bush or mountains. Hypothermia can set in quickly and be fatal.

Many hikes involve river crossings, and water levels can rise rapidly after heavy rain. It is often necessary to take shelter and wait until rivers drop to a safe level.

Lifeguards patrol popular beaches, and red and yellow flags indicate areas where it is safe to swim. Patrols are run by individual clubs under the umbrella of **Surf Life Saving New Zealand**. However the New Zealand coastline is extensive and in areas where there are no lifeguards there may be dangerous rip tides.

Sunburn can occur quickly so a good hat and sun block with a rating of at least SPF 30 are essential in summer.

It is best to avoid drinking water from rivers, lakes or ponds without boiling or treating the water first.

The tiny sandfly bites exposed skin, causing an annoying itch. They can usually be kept at bay with insect repellent.

## Travel and Health Insurance

New Zealand has excellent medical services. Under its accident compensation scheme, **ACC**, visitors may be covered for the cost of treatment if they are injured. ACC does not cover continuing costs of injury-related rehabilitation or loss of earnings once visitors return home. The no-fault scheme precludes the option of suing for damages, so it should not be regarded as a substitute for medical insurance. Non-accident medical treatment is not free. Reciprocal publicly funded medical care is available for Australian and British citizens, but not for other nationalities. Visitors are strongly advised to take out travel insurance to cover medical care. No vaccinations are needed.

Surf rescue boat at Mount Maunganui *(see p132)*

## DIRECTORY

### In an Emergency

**AA Road Service**
Free call **Tel** 0800 500 222 (24 hours, all areas).

**Police, Fire and Ambulance**
Free call **Tel** 111 (24 hours, all areas).

**Search and Rescue**
Free call **Tel** 111 (24 hours, all areas).

### Lost and Stolen Property

**Auckland**
Lost Property & Baggage, Auckland Airport.
**Tel** (09) 256 8813.

**Christchurch**
Lost & Found, Travel & Tourism Centre, Christchurch Airport.
**Tel** (03) 353 7774.

**Wellington**
General Lost Property, Main terminal, Wellington Airport. **Tel** (04) 385 5124.

### Hospitals

**Auckland**
2, Park Road, Grafton.
**Tel** (09) 379 7440.

**Christchurch**
2, Riccarton Avenue, Addlington 8011.
**Tel** (03) 364 0640.

**Dunedin**
201, Great King Street.
**Tel** (03) 474 0890.

**Wellington**
Riddiford Street, Newton. **Tel** (04) 385 5999.

### Pharmacies

**Auckland**
**Tel** (09) 520 6634.

**Christchurch**
**Tel** (03) 366 4439.

**Dunedin**
**Tel** (03) 477 0890.

**Wellington**
**Tel** (04) 385 8810.

### Environmental Hazards

**New Zealand Mountain Safety Council**
w mountainsafety. org.nz

**Sunsmart**
w sunsmart.org.nz

**Surf Life Saving New Zealand**
w slsnz.org.nz

### Travel and Health Insurance

**ACC**
w acc.co.nz

# Banking and Currency

A large number of banking institutions operate in New Zealand, all of them foreign owned apart from government-owned Kiwibank, which is a subsidiary of New Zealand Post and operates from PostShops around New Zealand. Major banking chains include ANZ, ASB, Bank of New Zealand (BNZ), HSBC and Westpac. Branches can be found in the central business districts of the major cities and in suburban shopping centres. Foreign currency can be readily exchanged at banks and private bureaux de change. There is no restriction on the amount of foreign currency that can be brought in or taken out of New Zealand, although people carrying more than NZ$10,000 in cash must make a declaration to customs.

### Banks and Bureaux de Change

The New Zealand banking system is modern and efficient. However, electronic banking has led to a decline in the number of bank branches and some small rural towns no longer have a local banking service. Banks are generally open from 9:30am to 4:30pm Monday to Friday, and some also open on Saturdays.

Bureaux de change can be found at international airports, in city centres and in resort areas. They are generally open from 8am to 8pm on weekdays, and from 10am until early evening on weekends. Commissions and fees are higher than at banks.

### ATMs

ATMs are widely available in New Zealand and can be found outside banks in town centres. Travellers should check with their own bank whether there will be a charge for using their debit card to access cash through ATMs in New Zealand. It is possible to withdraw cash from an ATM using a credit or debit card with a PIN number: the "Plus" logo indicates this service is available to VISA card holders, while the symbol for MasterCard holders is "Maestro".

### Credit and Debit Cards

All major credit and debit cards are used in New Zealand. **Visa**, and **MasterCard**, **Diners Club**, and **American Express**, are the most widely accepted, and can be used to book and pay for hotels, rental cars and airline tickets, as well as to pay for entry to tourist attractions and purchases from shops. China UnionPay (CUP) cards are also increasingly accepted. Check with your bank regarding fees for using your credit or debit card abroad.

## Traveller's Cheques and Cash Passports

Traveller's cheques and Cash Passports are safe alternatives to travelling with a debit or credit card. Thomas Cook and American Express traveller's cheques are widely accepted in New Zealand. Foreign currency cheques can be cashed for New Zealand dollars at banks, American Express and Travelex branches, and bureaux de change. The Cash Passport is a prepaid, PIN-protected travel money card, which can be used at ATMs to withdraw cash. It can be topped up at Cash Passport offices or via the Internet.

## DIRECTORY

### Banks

**ANZ**
W anz.co.nz

**ASB**
W asb.co.nz

**Bank of New Zealand**
W bnz.co.nz

**HSBC**
W hsbc.co.nz

**Kiwibank**
W kiwibank.co.nz

**Westpac**
W westpac.co.nz

### Bureaux de Change

**Cash Passport**
Tel 0800 748 000.
W cashpassport.com

**Travelex**
W travelex.com/nz

### Lost Cards and Traveller's Cheques

**American Express**
Tel 0800 441 068.

**Diners Club**
Tel 0800 657 373.

**MasterCard**
Tel 0800 449 140.

**Visa**
Tel 0508 600 300.

An ATM, widely available throughout New Zealand's towns and cities

## Currency

The unit of currency in New Zealand is the New Zealand dollar (NZ$), divided into 100 cents (c). In 2006 a set of smaller coins came into circulation and prices for cash purchases were rounded up to the nearest 10 cents. These coins are now legal tender, replacing the 1 cent, 2 cent and 5 cent coins. Small shops, cafés and taxis may not be able to provide change for NZ$50 or NZ$100 notes, so it is advisable to carry cash in NZ$10 and NZ$20 notes. To make it more difficult for counterfeiters to operate and to ensure notes can stay in circulation for longer, plasticized notes have replaced paper ones.

### Bank Notes

*New Zealand's bank notes are issued in denominations of NZ$5, NZ$10, NZ$20, NZ$50 and NZ$100. Sir Edmund Hillary, the first man to climb Mount Everest features on the NZ$5 note, and 19th-century women's suffrage campaigner Kate Sheppard is on the NZ$10 note. The reverse sides feature native fauna.*

NZ$100 note

NZ$50 note

NZ$20 note

NZ$10 note

NZ$5 note

10 cents (10c)

20 cents (20c)

50 cents (50c)

### Coins

*Coins currently in use in New Zealand are 10c, 20c, 50c, NZ$1 and NZ$2. The 10c piece features a traditional Maori carving, while the NZ$1 coin showing the national icon, the flightless kiwi, brings reality to the colloquial term the "kiwi dollar".*

1 dollar (NZ$1)

2 dollars (NZ$2)

# Communication and Media

Despite serving a small, widely dispersed population, New Zealand's telecommunications industry has kept pace with the rest of the developed world. Mobile phones are ubiquitous, broadband Internet access has reached most areas and Wi-Fi is increasingly available in the cities, small town centres and popular tourist areas. Visitors can make cheap phone calls within and outside New Zealand by subscribing to one of the mobile networks or taking advantage of cheap calling card schemes. New Zealand's traditional media – newspapers, magazines, television and radio – are high quality, but the widespread use of the Internet has brought easy access to international media too.

### International and Local Telephone Calls

To make telephone calls within New Zealand, visitors may consider purchasing a pay-as-you-go mobile phone. Alternatively, public payphones, available in public spaces, are operated with phonecards, purchased at supermarkets, dairies (convenience stores), visitor information centres or PostShops. Some accept credit cards, but few accept coins. If using a payphone to make an international call, it is cheaper to use one of the discounted Telecom prepaid cards, such as the Yabba card, available from the same outlets as local phonecards. There is no charge for making emergency 111 calls.

Each region in New Zealand has a White Pages and a Yellow Pages telephone directory, listing residential and business numbers respectively. Both are available online at www.yellow. co.nz. In many regions the White Pages and Yellow Pages are in one directory but in larger regions, such as Auckland, Wellington and Christchurch, they come in separate volumes.

### Mobile Phones

New Zealand has analogue and GSM digital mobile phone networks, and mobile phones can be used throughout most of New Zealand, apart from remote and mountainous areas. International roaming is available with most providers,

but it may be cheaper to buy a pay-as-you-go phone or a New Zealand SIM card. New Zealand's main mobile phone providers are **Vodafone** and **Telecom**. Another option is **2degrees**, which offers competitive prepaid prices and rates for international texts and calls.

### Internet

Broadband Internet coverage now extends to most of New Zealand, apart from some of the very remote areas. Cybercafés still exist around the country, providing email and Internet services to travellers, but Wi-Fi hotspots can increasingly be found in cafés and public spaces such as libraries, museums and university campuses, especially in Auckland and Wellington. Many hotels and motels offer broadband or Wi-Fi facilities for

## Reaching the Right Number

- For long distance calls within New Zealand (STD calls), first dial the national access code **0**, then the area code and the number.
- For an international number (IDD call), dial **00** followed by the country code, then the area code and number.
- For local and national directory enquiries, dial **018** (charges vary).
- For international directory enquiries, dial **0172** (charges vary).
- For all internal operator-assisted calls, dial **010** (charges vary).
- For all international operator-assisted calls (credit card collect calls), dial **0170**.
- For price-defined international calls, dial **0160** instead of **00** at the beginning of the call. You will be charged a premium for **0160** and **0170** services.
- A free information service number (**123**) enables callers to find out the cost of an overseas call or reversing the charges.
- The prefixes **021**, **022**, **027** and **029** are mobile telephone numbers.
- **0800** numbers are toll free.
- See also Emergency Numbers, *p347*, or search for national numbers on yellow.co.nz/whitepages.

Cybercafés with Internet access are found all over New Zealand guests to check emails and access the Internet. Major hotel chains such as **Best Western** offer Internet access as a complimentary service.

Standard and FastPost boxes

## Postal Services

New Zealand's very efficient postal service is run by **New Zealand Post**. Letters and parcels can be sent through its PostShops, many of which are located in bookshops. Most are open from 9am to 5pm Mon–Sat. Stamps can be bought at supermarkets, dairies (convenience stores) and newsagents as well as at PostShop branches. There are two main classes of domestic mail: FastPost, which arrives the day after posting, and standard post, which takes two to three days to arrive.International airmail takes four to ten days to reach most countries.

The main post office in each town serves as a *Poste Restante*. You will need a passport or some other form of identification to claim *Poste Restante* mail.

New Zealand has several excellent domestic courier companies, offering same- or next-day delivery to anywhere in New Zealand. **Courier Post** is operated by New Zealand Post, and you can mail parcels using this service from their PostShops, found in all towns and cities. Or you can opt for one of the well-known international courier services, that ship parcels overseas such as **DHL**, **Fedex** or **UPS**. For all courier companies you will need to phone the 0800

number to arrange a pick-up or find the nearest depot. All companies offer an online tracking service for packages; a tracking number will be provided by the courier office.

## Newspapers and Magazines

Each of the main cities has its own morning newspaper. *The New Zealand Herald*, the country's largest, is published in Auckland. The Christchurch *Press* is the South Island's largest newspaper. The *Otago Daily Times* is published in Dunedin, the *Dominion Post* in Wellington and the *Southland Times* in Invercargill. Excellent weekend reading is contained in *The Sunday Star Times*, which is published nationally. The best current affairs magazines are *The Listener* and *North and South*.

Foreign newspapers and magazines are available in bookshops and at newsstands in larger towns, but can also be accessed via the Internet.

Newspapers and magazines for sale

## Televison and Radio

The three main free-to-air television channels are TV1 and TV3, which screen mostly local programmes, and TV2, which relies more heavily on US programmes. Pay channel Sky offers specialist channels, such as CNN and National Geographic. Maori Television broadcasts programmes nationally, often in *te reo Maori* (the Maori language), and can provide an insight into Maori culture.

The state-owned, non-commercial Radio New Zealand (similar to the BBC) is renowned for the quality of its broadcasting. Other stations provide regional news and traffic reports.

# TRAVEL INFORMATION

The vast majority of visitors arrive in New Zealand by air. Auckland is the busiest port of entry, followed by Christchurch. Once in New Zealand, many tourists use the domestic air network to get around, particularly to travel between the North and South islands. The coach network covers most major routes in the country. The rail network is limited, but travels through spectacular scenery. For visitors wanting to explore at their own pace, a car or campervan is the best way to travel. The roads are in good condition, but extra care is needed on alpine routes and back country roads.

### Arriving by Air

Despite New Zealand's clean, green image and attempts to make the cities less polluted, it is hard to reach the country in an environmentally responsible way. The country is also reliant on air travel for its domestic flight network (see pp354–5).

Around 15 international airlines fly into New Zealand daily. Others, such as **British Airways**, serve the country on a codeshare basis (sharing routes with a partner airline). The national airline, **Air New Zealand**, has an extensive international network, with links with more than 130 countries worldwide.

Air New Zealand and **Qantas** fly into New Zealand from the west coast of the United States, while **Cathay Pacific**, **Emirates**, **Japan Airlines**, **Korean Air**, **Malaysian Airlines**, **Royal Brunei**, **Singapore Airlines** and **Thai Airways** depart from major Asian airports for New Zealand. **Aerolineas Argentinas** flies direct from Buenos Aires to Auckland and **Lan Chile** direct from Santiago. Pacific Blue, a low-cost subsidiary of Virgin, flies from various Australian cities to Auckland, Hamilton, Wellington, Christchurch, Queenstown and Dunedin, and many other airlines fly via Australia.

New Zealand is a 3-hour flight from eastern Australia, 10 hours from Pacific Rim cities such as Singapore, Hong Kong and Tokyo, and between 13 and 16 hours from the USA and South America. Taking account of delays and transfers, a flight from Europe can be very taxing and it is worth making a stopover in Asia, the USA or on one of the Pacific Islands.

### Airports

New Zealand has two main international terminals. Auckland is the major gateway, accommodating international and domestic flights, followed by Christchurch, where flights arrive from Singapore, Bangkok and Dubai. This airport is known as the New Zealand's tourism gateway, due to its location on the south island close to major tourist sights. Wellington Airport, in the country's capital, is used mainly as a domestic hub and can only be reached direct from Australia or via a connecting flight from Auckland or Christchurch. Queenstown offers flights to and from Brisbane, Sydney and Melbourne in Australia as well as domestic in-land flights, while Hamilton links with Australia and some Pacific destinations. By international standards, none of the airports is congested and the airports are rarely affected by adverse weather conditions.

International signpost at Christchurch Airport

### Tickets and Fares

Air fares to New Zealand can be expensive, particularly during the peak season from December to February when airlines charge premium rates. The cost of flights also goes up during the northern hemisphere summer (July–August). Cheaper air fares are available during the "shoulder" season between the high and low seasons. Shop around and get several prices before making

The "City of Sails" design of Auckland International Airport

a booking. Online booking and Internet travel comparison sites make it easier to check ticket prices, but you may still save time and money by going through a travel agent. Air New Zealand may bundle in onward domestic flights with its international flights and sometimes offers cheap seats on www.grabaseat.co.nz. Always check the limitations and penalties before buying a cut-price ticket.

## On Arrival

During international flights to New Zealand, visitors are given a Passenger Arrival Card to complete and hand in on arrival, along with their passports. Travellers must declare any restricted items and items subject to agricultural quarantine *(see pp342–3)* and place fresh food in bins before the immigration area, where they will go through passport control, customs and bio security checks.

Auckland and Christchurch airports have a wide range of food and retail outlets, telecommunication services, visitor information and banking facilities *(see p348)*. Bookings can be made for further domestic air travel, if flights have not already been arranged in advance.

## Transport to and from the Airport

Transfer to the city centres from the airport is straightforward: taxis and shuttles (shared minivans with trailers for luggage) are available for door-to-door service, and buses run regularly. Taxis are an expensive option, with buses being the cheapest. Auckland is the only

Airport bus, a cheap option for reaching the city centre

Door-to-door shuttle with trailer to carry luggage

Airport taxi, an accessible way to reach the city centre

city to suffer from traffic congestion; it can take up to 1 hour to reach the city centre. Christchurch is a 15-minute drive from the airport.

## Departure Tax

An airport user fee is levied on passengers aged 12 and above departing from New Zealand's international airports. It is now included in the ticket price for departures from Auckland and Christchurch. Security checks are as stringent at New Zealand's airports as anywhere in the world. Make sure you pack restricted items such as liquid cosmetics or nail scissors in your checked baggage.

## Package Deals

Although New Zealand mostly attracts independent travellers, a range of package deals are on offer, from basic fly-drive deals to all-inclusive coach tours, backpacker and adventure tours, and ski/ snowboard packages. Alternatively, there are plentiful local tour operators who can plan activities on arrival. The Tourism New Zealand website *(see p345)* is an excellent place to start, as is www.destination-nz.com. **Discover New Zealand** offers a good selection of these tours and travel packages, which also includes coach and rail holidays.

## DIRECTORY

# Domestic Air Travel

New Zealand has an extensive domestic air transport network, linking all of the major and provincial cities as well as many smaller towns. Although it is a small country, New Zealand's long, thin shape means that land travel between major centres, such as Auckland, Wellington and Christchurch, is time-consuming. As a result, air services play a crucial transport role. The main domestic carrier is Air New Zealand, which also owns airline companies that operate services to provincial centres. A wide range of heavily discounted fares are always available, particularly on the Internet or if travellers are flexible and book well in advance.

Air New Zealand domestic flight arriving at Wellington airport

## Airports

Some 26 domestic destinations are serviced by scheduled flights that connect the main cities – Auckland, Wellington, Christchurch and Dunedin – with provincial centres. These include Nelson, Gisborne, Napier/Hastings, Taupo, Whangarei, Kaitaia, Hokitika and Timaru and tourist resorts such as Queenstown, Rotorua and the Bay of Islands, Mount Cook and Te Anau/Manapouri. It is also possible to fly from Invercargill to Stewart Island, from Auckland to Great Barrier Island, from Wellington to Blenheim, Picton or Nelson (as an alternative to the ferry) and from Wellington to Takaka in the South Island. Scenic flights over Mount Cook, Fiordland and other areas are also on offer.

Domestic flights within New Zealand save travelling time and the comprehensive network of airports and regular flights make every part of the country accessible.

## Domestic Airlines

**Air New Zealand** operates the main national network, incorporating the Air New Zealand Link carriers – Air Nelson, Mount Cook Line and Eagle Air – which service some provincial centres. All bookings for these services are made through Air New Zealand. **SoundsAir** operate across the Cook Strait, with up to eight return flights a day from Wellington to Picton, up to 20 return flights a week to Nelson and up to 12 return flights a week to Blenheim. **Golden Bay Air** flies the Wellington–Takaka route once a day out of season, two to four times daily in summer. **Steward Island Flights** fly three times a day between Invercargill and Stewart Island. **Great Barrier Airlines** fly from Auckland, North Shore, Coromandel and Whangarei to Great Barrier Island.

## Fly–Drive Deals

A convenient way to travel in New Zealand is to fly to a destination and then continue by car. Rental cars can be picked up and dropped off at different points; for example, it is possible to fly from Auckland to Queenstown, then drive from Queenstown to Christchurch. Air New Zealand and other airlines have links with car hire firms, which offer discounts to passengers travelling on those airlines (see p359).

A wide range of fly-drive packages operate from Auckland to the South Island during the ski season, including deals combining flights, car rental and ski lift passes. Travel agents offer a variety of special promotions, and it is best to shop around.

Fly-drive packages operate to Mount Cook Line ski-planes

## DIRECTORY

### Domestic Airlines

**Air New Zealand**
Tel 0800 737 000.
W airnewzealand.co.nz

**Golden Bay Air**
W goldenbayair.co.nz

**Great Barrier Airlines**
W greatbarrierairlines.co.nz

**SoundsAir**
Tel 0800 505 005.
W soundsair.com

**Stewart Island Flights**
Tel (03) 218 9129.
W stewartislandflights.com

### Domestic Airports

**Dunedin**
Tel (03) 486 2879.
W dnairport.co.nz

**Hamilton**
Tel (07) 848 9027.
W hamiltonairport.co.nz

**Invercargill**
Tel (03) 218 6367.
W invercargillairport.co.nz

**Nelson**
Tel (03) 547 3199.
W nelsonairport.co.nz

**Taupo**
Tel (07) 378 7771.
W taupoairport.co.nz

### Special Passes

**Star Alliance**
W staralliance.com

Passengers checking in at Christchurch International Airport

## Checking In

On domestic flights, airlines require passengers to check in at least 30 minutes before departure. This may be done at self check-in kiosks. All economy class passengers on domestic flights have a baggage allowance of 20 kg (44 lb) and a one bag limit, which is less than on international flights and is strictly enforced. If you are connecting with an international Air New Zealand flight, you should be able to check your baggage through from your domestic check-in point, and they may be more lenient about weight. The maximum weight for cabin baggage is 7 kg (11 lb). Personal articles, such as a coat, handbag, camera or laptop may also be carried into the aircraft.

## Air Fares and Special Passes

Standard domestic fares can be expensive, but airlines allocate a variety of fares to each flight. Even at short notice you can sometimes get a good deal: to find discounted last-minute fares on Air New Zealand flights, go to the website and click on the "grabaseat" option. It is usually cheaper to buy your first onward domestic flight along with your international flight booking. Various air passes allow visitors to make a number of single domestic flights for a set price. Air New Zealand offers a "South Pacific Airpass" to travellers flying in on any **Star Alliance** flight (Air New Zealand, Singapore Airlines and Thai Air). This entitles travellers to discounted airfares between New Zealand destinations and to Australia and the Pacific Islands. Fares are zoned by distance and range from NZ$98 to NZ$378 for flights within New Zealand. There are four domestic and four international (Australia and Pacific Islands) zones.

The air pass consists of three to 10 flight coupons. These coupons can be redeemed for tickets on any Star Alliance flight operating from New Zealand. Additional coupons may be purchased after arrival. All travel must be completed within three months of touching down in New Zealand.

## Principal Domestic Air Routes

Domestic flights operating between major cities, complemented by a host of connecting flights between smaller towns and tourist resorts, cover the country quite comprehensively. Flying is ideal for those with limited time to spend in the country.

**Key**

- – National Network
— Link Network

# Travelling by Coach, Train and Inter-Island Ferry

New Zealand's coach service is extensive and efficient, connecting most points throughout the country. Coaches cater for independent travellers as well as those who prefer guided tours. Although New Zealand does not have an extensive rail network, trains connect the main cities and passenger journeys are outstanding for their breathtaking scenery, some not visible from any road. The mountainous terrain has forced railway engineers to build spectacular viaducts and long tunnels. The North and South islands are connected by ferry, with several sailings each day.

Magic Bus coach

## Coach Travel

Coach travel is a safe, efficient and popular means of transport for tourists in New Zealand. Coach travellers can take regular scheduled services or use one of the travel pass options available to independent travellers. Most New Zealand cities and towns are linked by **InterCity Coachlines**, while **Newmans Coach Lines** offers tours. Discounts are available on scheduled services, subject to cancellation penalties. InterCity sometimes offers NZ$1 tickets.

**Magic Bus** offers a travel pass system, targeted at backpackers. Travellers buy a national coach pass, which is valid on selected routes at any time within 12 months of purchase. **Kiwi Experience** offers travel passes for backpackers and sightseeing tours.

## Tickets and Reservations

InterCity and Newmans coach tickets can be booked in advance by phone, online or from agents, based at i-SITE visitor centres (see p345) and independent travel agencies in most towns. InterCity offers a range of Travelpasses, valid for one to 14 days of travel on selected itineraries. They can be used over a 12-month period, and are priced from NZ$43 to NZ$1,249, according to the distance travelled and number of stops. The Flexipass, which is priced in blocks of time from 15 to 60 hours' travel and can be used over a 12-month period, is more flexible and costs NZ$443. Discounted back-packer rates are available.

Magic Bus passes range from NZ$290 to NZ$1,994, purchased at the Magic Bus office in Auckland or online.

## Travelling by Train

The New Zealand rail network is operated by a private company, **Tranz Scenic 2001 Ltd**, with choices of Tranz-Coastal, TranzAlpine and OverLander trains offering scenic rail journeys for tourists. Passenger rail services connect the major cities as well as a number of provincial centres, including Ohakune, Palmerston North, Picton, Kaikoura and Greymouth. In the North Island, the OverLander train connects Auckland to Wellington, and vice versa, and is mainly used by tourists.

The TranzAlpine journey from Christchurch to Greymouth crosses the Canterbury Plains before cutting dramatically through the Southern Alps via the Otira Tunnel (see pp246–7), and on through the rainforests of the West Coast. The TranzCoastal, which runs between Picton and Christchurch, is popular for viewing the Kaikoura coast scenery.

Otago has a privately-run excursion train: the Taieri Gorge Railway (see p268).

## Tickets and Reservations

Bookings for rail travel can be made through travel agents, by calling Tranz Scenic Reservations seven days a week from 7am to 9pm, or online. There is a multi-tier fare structure for both rail and ferry travel, and discounts of up to 50 per cent on standard fares are often available, especially during off-peak periods. Always ask for the best possible price when making a booking.

An economical and independent way to travel is to use the Tranz Scenic rail and ferry pass, similar to the passes available in the UK and Europe, where all travel must be completed by a certain date.

## Inter-Island Ferry Services

The main inter-island ferry service between Wellington and Picton is provided by the **Interislander** fleet, which carries passengers, cars and freight. The Interislander service operates five return trips a day, taking about 3 hours each way. The trip is one of the most scenic cruises

The TranzAlpine crossing Kowai Bridge near Springfield

A ship from the Interislander ferry service fleet

in the world, offering stunning views, and the three ships in the fleet are all comfortable, with a wide range of facilities on board, including restaurants, bars, cafés, children's rooms, observation decks and also "quiet rooms" for business people, which can booked when on board the ferry.

The **Bluebridge Cook Strait Ferry** runs twice daily and offers similar facilities to the Interislander ferries. A number of ferry companies operate services around Auckland Harbour.

### Tickets and Reservations

Bookings for Interislander ferries and Blueridge Cook Strait Ferry services can be made online, by telephone, at travel agents or at i-SITE visitor information centres *(see p345)*. It is advisable to book in advance particularly during school holidays and if you are taking a car across the strait. However, it is possible to buy tickets at the ferry terminals on the day, if they are not sold out. For joint rail and ferry passes, *see p356*.

*(see p345)* … *see p356*.

## DIRECTORY

### Rail Companies

**Tranz Scenic 2001 Ltd**
**Tel** (04) 495 0775.
W tranzscenic.co.nz

### Coach Companies

**InterCity Coachlines**
**Tel** (09) 913 6100.
W intercitycoach.co.nz

**Kiwi Experience**
**Tel** (09) 336 4286.
W kiwiexperience.com

**Magic Bus**
**Tel** (09) 358 5600.
W magicbus.co.nz

**Newmans Coach Lines**
**Tel** (09) 583 5780.
W newmanscoach.co.nz

### Ferry Companies

**Bluebridge Cook Strait Ferry**
**Tel** (04) 471 6188.
W bluebridge.co.nz

**Interislander**
**Tel** (04) 498 3302.
W interislandline.co.nz

## Principal Coach, Rail and Ferry Routes

In New Zealand, travel by the national coach network, the scenic rail network and the inter-island ferry services enables visitors to cover much of the country. Local bus companies service smaller towns. Note that the following rail services do not carry passengers: Wellington to Napier, Auckland to Tauranga, Auckland to Rotorua, and Christchurch to Invercargill.

0 kilometres 200
0 miles 200

**Key**

— Principal coach route
— Principal rail route

**For additional map symbols** *see back flap*

# Travelling by Car

Although the public transport system offers plenty of options for travelling between towns and cities, a car allows you to thoroughly explore New Zealand's scenic rural areas, and gives you the flexibility to stop at beaches, lakes, country cafés, wineries and restaurants, and other points of interest along the way, or pause to admire a view. Outside the main cities the roads are relatively uncongested. They are generally in good condition, but even major highways have winding, hilly sections. Multi-lane motorways occur on the approaches to the main cities and between Auckland and Hamilton.

State Highway 1 parallelling the railway line along the Kaikoura coast

between 7:30–9am and 4:30–6pm, especially in the main cities. Traffic reports and updates are regularly broadcast on local radio stations (see p351).

## Car Insurance

Car and campervan rental rates usually include insurance cover for collision damage and theft from the vehicle. However, policies often carry a very high excess payment. Many companies offer worthwhile "excess waiver" options. Personal accident plans are available, but this risk should be covered by comprehensive travel insurance. Insurance for drivers under the age of 25 is more expensive.

## Parking

Outside the main cities, parking in New Zealand poses few problems. In most town centres there is a combination of free and metered parking, and car parks. Parked cars must face the same direction as the flow of traffic. Parking is usually under the control of local councils and patrolled by wardens who can issue fines to vehicles that are parked illegally or that have expired meters.

Most cities have clearway zones and vehicles parked in these areas during certain times may be towed away. If this occurs, call the local traffic authority or police to find out where your car has been impounded.

## Driving in New Zealand

Holders of a current driving licence can drive in New Zealand for up to 12 months. If you do not hold a driving licence, you will need an International Driving Permit. All drivers must carry their licence when driving. New Zealanders drive on the left-hand side of the road. The speed limit is 100 km/h (60 mph) on the open road and 50 km/h (30 mph) in urban areas. Excessive speed is a major hazard and speeding drivers will be fined.

A yellow line down the centre of the road means it is illegal to overtake. Main highways have passing lanes at regular intervals. The confusing "right-hand rule" changed after years of debate, in early 2012, bringing New Zealand in line with the rest of the world: traffic crossing or approaching from the right now has to give way.

Drink-driving laws are strictly enforced in New Zealand. A driver may be required to give a breath test at any time. The legal blood alcohol level is 80 milligrams of alcohol per 100 millilitres of blood (30 milligrams for a driver under 20).

It is compulsory for the driver and passengers to wear a seat belt, and for children under five years to be in infant car seats, which are provided with car rentals.

It is illegal to use a mobile phone while driving. You may not make or answer calls, nor send or read text messages.

Traffic accidents involving injury must be reported to the police within 24 hours.

When driving in cities, an up-to-date street map is essential, especially for spotting one-way streets. Wherever possible, avoid peak traffic

One-lane
bridge ahead

## Fuel

The majority of New Zealand cars run on petrol, which is available in regular and premium unleaded. Most four-wheel drive vehicles and campervans use diesel, which is cheaper than petrol. Fuel is sold at service stations which stay open late or even 24 hours in cities, but may be closed in the evenings and at weekends in rural settlements. Rural service stations often have cafés and convenience stores for handy stop-off points.

Service station selling both petrol and diesel

## Breakdown Services

Car hire companies deal with breakdowns involving their own vehicles, and will arrange to provide a replacement if necessary. The **Automobile Association** (AA) is a nationwide motoring organization providing breakdown services. Members of most overseas motoring organizations, except AA UK and RAC UK, receive reciprocal services with the New Zealand AA. To benefit, take your home motoring organization card into any AA office in New Zealand.

New Zealand AA membership entitles you to six free breakdown call-outs a year, and discounted rates at some hotels and for car hire.

## Car and Motorcycle Rental

Rental cars are readily available with a range of companies to choose from. Large companies such as **Avis**, **Budget** and **Hertz** have nationwide networks. Smaller local companies may be cheaper, but offer less flexibility. Most rental companies will not hire to anyone under the age of 21. Companies are likely to ask for a credit card imprint as security against loss or damage.

Several companies offer specialized motorbike rental, guided motorbike tours or can help to plan routes, especially in the South Island. Try Christchurch-based **South Pacific Motorcycle Tours** for a fleet of bikes including BMWs, Triumph Thunderbirds and Harley Davidsons. **New Zealand Motorcycle Rentals**, with a fleet of mainly Japanese bikes, has bases in both Christchurch and Auckland, offering the option of picking up at one and dropping off at the other.

Rates start from about NZ$100 a day for a small bike, going up to about NZ$285 a day for a top-of-the-range bike. Rental should include a helmet and any other safety equipment, full insurance, breakdown cover, road maps and GPS hire.

## Campervan Rental

A popular form of transport with visitors is a campervan, motorhome or RV. Camping grounds can be found in beautiful locations around the country *(see p301)*. Campervans are available in a range of sizes and come with a refrigerator and gas cooker. Some have their own shower, toilet and microwave. One of the largest campervan rental companies in New Zealand, **Kea Campers** have gained CarboNZero certification for their campervans, which have engines that comply with EU standards, solar panels to heat water and self-contained waste, making them suitable for free camping.

Kea Campers, **Maui Rentals** and **Britz NZ** have depots in Auckland, Christchurch and Queenstown. You may be asked for a large deposit and the insurance excess may also be high. It is usually possible to pay a higher insurance premium to reduce or waive the excess and deposit.

Maui Rentals campervan parked near Auckland waterfront

## Road Conditions

The quality of New Zealand's roads is excellent. However, with few motorways, only a painted centre line separates opposing traffic on most roads, and winding stretches are common. Many back roads are unsealed and require extreme care as it is easy to lose control on the uneven surface.

Check road conditions with the Department of Conservation (www.doc.govt.nz) or AA before travelling on roads in the snowbound mountainous and inland areas of the South Island in winter, on any back roads leading to scenic areas. Take care on unsealed roads such as the one leading to the Oparara Basin north of Karamea *(see p238)*. These roads are often narrow and driving can be dangerous on the gravel surface or on verges.

*(see p301)* *(see p238)*

## DIRECTORY

### Breakdown Services

**Automobile Association**
Tel 0800 500 543 or 0900 33 222.
W aa.co.nz

### Car and Motorcycle Rental

**Avis**
Tel 0800 284 722.
W avis.co.nz

**Budget Rent A Car**
Tel 0800 283 438.
W budget.co.nz

**Hertz**
Tel 0800 654 321.
W hertz.com

**New Zealand Motorcycle Rentals**
W nzbike.com

**South Pacific Motorcycle Tours**
W motorbiketours.co.nz

### Campervan Rentals

**Britz NZ**
W britz.co.nz

**Kea Campers**
W keacampers.com

**Maui Rentals**
W maui.co.nz

# Getting Around Towns and Cities

Although rural New Zealand is very car-dependent, it is possible to get around the main towns and cities on foot and using public transport. Auckland, Wellington and Christchurch have a mix of suburban trains, buses and trams, which can be supplemented by taxis. Auckland is a sprawling city and some means of transport is necessary to travel between its suburbs, although the central business district can be traversed on foot. Central Wellington is compact, but its outlying districts are steep and hilly. Christchurch, by contrast, is flat and is ideally suited to touring by bicycle.

## Buses

Auckland has an extensive bus network. The **Britomart Transport Centre**, its downtown hub, has an information kiosk open daily. Alternatively, check Auckland Transport's MAXX website (www.maxx.co.nz) for route maps, timetables, fares and a useful journey planner.

In Wellington, the main bus routes traverse downtown. Buses are operated by several companies and information for all services can be found on the **Metlink** website.

Christchurch's **Central Bus Exchange** is the main bus service provider. Information is available on the Metro website. Leopard Coachlines run a fleet of biodiesel buses that run on animal fat, identified by a "biodiesel" tag.

Queenstown's **Connectabus** service links the resort centre to outlying areas.

Historic hop-on, hop-off tram, Christchurch

## Trams

Christchurch has a historic tram service which runs on a 2.5 km (1.5 mile) loop around the city centre. It offers a hop- on, hop-off service, with a two-day ticket costing NZ$17. Buy tickets from the **Christchurch Tramway** website, at the tram station or from the conductor.

Wellington has a system of trolleybuses that run on electric overhead cables.

## Tickets

Single bus tickets and day passes can be paid for as you board the bus, or cheaper 10-ride tickets can be bought at dairies (convenience stores) and newsagents. Single tram tickets, day passes or 10-ride tickets can be purchased at train stations or on the trams.

Both Auckland and Wellington offer a "top-up" Snapper Card, which gives a 20 per cent discount on bus travel. Cards can be bought from the **Snapper** website or at dairies. The card can also act a form of payment in some shops.

Christchurch has a prepaid Metrocard, offering users a 30 per cent discount on cash fares and can be purchased on the **Metro** website or at the Central Bus Exchange.

## Walking

Walking is an eco-friendly way to get around New Zealand's cities, offering the chance to take in the local architecture at a leisurely pace.

Sprawling Auckland, covering 100 sq km (39 sq miles), is not immediately conducive to walking, but the central business district is easily covered on foot, and suburbs such as Ponsonby, Newmarket and Parnell, as well as the city parks, are pleasant to walk around. The **Travelwise** website highlights the cost savings and health benefits of walking.

Wellington's scale is more walker-friendly, but its steep hills may be a deterrent to all but the keenest. To encourage walkers, **Greater Wellington Regional Council** offers a walking journey planner, which not only gives directions from A to B, but shows how hilly the trip will be and how many calories you will burn.

Central Christchurch is easily covered on foot, and has the advantage of being flat. Getting around Queenstown's central business district is likely to be an easy stroll for outdoor enthusiasts using the resort town as a base for arduous mountain hikes.

Bus en route to the railway station, Wellington

## Taxis

Taxis are readily available in all the cities, operated by private companies and licensed by the **New Zealand Transport Association** (NZTA). To find a taxi, look in the Yellow Pages of the telephone directory or ask at your hotel. Taxi ranks are found at airports, in city centres and near shopping malls. Wellington's **Combined Taxis** are New Zealand's first CarboNZero certified taxi company.

## Cycling

Cycling is a good way to get around Auckland, although cyclists have to contend with the traffic. Bikes can be rented from **BikeCentral** near the Britomart Transport Centre. The MAXX website (www.maxx.co.nz) has a cycle route map, making cyclists aware of crash hotspots and indicating the location of bike lockers and parking, cycle-friendly cafés and cycle repair shops.

Hilly Wellington offers a challenge to cyclists. Greater Wellington Regional Council offers an online cycle journey planner showing the hills. To rent bikes, go to **Mud Cycles** in Karori or **Dirt Merchants** in Brooklyn.

Central Christchurch is flat, compact and ideal for cycling, with on-road cycle lanes and off-road paths for cyclists. **Christchurch City Council** publishes a guide, with route maps and information for cyclists. The Metro website has a map of bus routes that carry bikes. Bikes can be hired from **City Cycle Hire**.

## Guided Tours

A host of tourism providers offer guided tours of Auckland and its environs, including the North Shore and West Coast beaches, with transport by car and minivan included. **NZ Tours & Travel** offer a wide range of full- and half-day tours.

Several companies offer guided walking tours of all the main sights in Auckland, Wellington and Christchurch. All can be contacted through the i-SITE Visitor Information Centre (see p345). **Walk Wellington** offers daily tours taking in the main downtown sights in a 2-hour walk. Evening walks are available in summer and personalized walks can be arranged. **Zest Food Tours** follow foodie trails around the city, which boasts that it has more cafés and restaurants per capita than any other in the world.

**Christchurch Tours** offer daily guided tours of the South Island city, beach and harbour by coach, departing from Cathedral Square.

Cycling on South island

## DIRECTORY

### Buses

**Britomart Transport Centre**
Queen Elizabeth Sq, Lower Queen St, Auckland. **Tel** 0800 10 30 80 or (09) 366 6400.
 britomart.co.nz

**Central Bus Exchange**
Cnr Colombo and Lichfield sts, Christchurch.
**Tel** (03) 66 88 55.
 metroinfo.org.nz

**Connectabus**
**Tel** (03) 3 441 4471.
 connectabus.co.nz

**Metlink**
**Tel** 0800 801 700.
 metlink.org.nz

### Trams

**Christchurch Tramway**
 tram.co.nz

### Tickets

**Metro**
 metroinfo.co.nz

**Snapper**
 snapper.co.nz

### Walking

**Greater Wellington Regional Council**
 gw.govt.nz

**Travelwise**
 travelwise.org.nz

### Taxis

**Combined Taxis**
**Tel** (04) 384 4444.
 taxis.co.nz

**New Zealand Transport Agency**
 nzta.govt.nz

### Cycling

**BikeCentral**
**Tel** (09) 365 1768.
 travelwise.org.nz

**Christchurch City Council**
 ccc.govt.nz/cycling

**City Cycle Hire**
**Tel** 0800 343 848 or (03) 377 5952.
 cyclehire-tours.co.nz

### Dirt Merchants
42/a Mitchell St, Brooklyn.
**Tel** (04) 831 1512.

**Mud Cycles**
**Tel** (04) 476 4961.
 mudcycles.co.nz

### Guided Tours

**Christchurch Tours**
 christchurchtours.co.nz

**NZ Tours & Travel**
 newzealandtours.travel

**Walk Wellington**
 wellingtonnz.com

**Zest Food Tours**
 zestfoodtours.co.nz

# General Index

# Acknowledgments

Dorling Kindersley would like to thank the many people whose help and assistance contributed to the preparation of this book.

## Contributors

Helen Corrigan is a Wellington-based writer, editor, researcher and publicist. She has a background in journalism and radio and since 2002 has been a parliamentary press secretary.

Roef Hopman is a public relations consultant and freelance writer in Auckland. Formerly Chief Editor of *Design Trends*, he organizes public relations projects for Pacific Rim countries and contributes to various publications.

Gerard Hutching is a freelance journalist who specializes in natural history and the environment. He has written several books, including *The Natural World of New Zealand* which won the 1999 Montana Book of the Year (environment).

Rebecca Macfie is an award-winning Christchurch-based journalist. She specializes in business and current affairs feature writing, and contributes to a range of New Zealand newspapers and magazines.

Geoff Mercer lives in Hastings. He has written for daily newspapers in Wellington and Hawke's Bay. He now compiles oral histories, writes and publishes biographies, and contributes articles to various publications.

Simon Noble lives in Nelson and has a long involvement in the region's natural, historic and scenic areas. He is the author of *The Treasured Pathway*, a guide to a heritage highway through northern Nelson and Marlborough.

Peter Smith is an Auckland artist, educator, writer and yachtsman, and former principal of Auckland College of Education.

Michael Ward is a chef who has worked in the food industry for some twenty years. Michael has a keen interest in promoting New Zealand food and wine.

Mark Wright is a Dunedin-based freelance writer whose work ranges from articles on travel, technology and health to classic cars. He has a background in radio and writes scripts for television and video.

## Additional Contributors

Georgina Palffy; Simon Vita

## For Dorling Kindersley

*Picture Research* Rachel Barber, Marta Bescos, Sumita Khatwani, Ellen Root
*Publishing Manager* Kate Poole
*Cartographic Editors* Casper Morris, David Pugh
*Production* Michelle Thomas
*Publishing Director* Gillian Allan
*Revisions Editor* Neil Lockley
*Revisions Designers* Mariana Evmolpidou, Supriya Sahai

## Indexer

Kay Lyons

## Additional Photography

Peter Bush, Louise Goossens, Gerard Hindmarsh, Ian O'Leary, Rough Guides/Paul Whitfield

## Design and Editorial Assistance

Emma Anacootee, Lydia Baillie, Stuti Tiwari Bhatia, Sheeba Bhatnagar, Frances Chan, Rhiannon Furbear, Jenn Hadley, Christine Heilman, Gerard Hindmarsh, Brendan Hutching, Zafar ul Islam Khan, Hayley Maher, Sam Merrell, Kate Molan, Rakesh Kumar Pal, Georgina Palffy, Helen Partington, Marianne Petrou, Rada Radojicic, Susana Smith, Roseen Teare, Conrad Van Dyk, Deepika Verma.

## Special Assistance

Debbie Ameriks and Amelia Manson, Office of Treaty Settlements, Wellington; Tim Amos, Department of Conservation, Wellington; Lane Ayr, Bay of Islands Swordfish Club; Kate Banbury, Waitomo Glow Worm Caves New Zealand, Otorohanga; Jennifer Beatson, Latitude Nelson; Black's Point Museum, Reefton; Hughie Blues and Amanda Turner, Waikokopu Café, Waitangi; Julia Bradshaw, Lakes District Museum, Arrowtown; Linda Burgess, Wellington; Dennis Buurman, Ocean Wings; Elizabeth Caldwell, Arts Council of New Zealand; Cathedral Church of St Paul, Wellington; Alan Cooper, Geology Department, University of Otago, Dunedin; C.P. Group, Auckland; Croydon Aircraft Company, Gore; Jo Darby, Tourism Industry Association New Zealand; Carol Davidson, New Zealand Festival 2000; Department of Conservation Visitor Centres; Jenny Dey, Photosource New Zealand Ltd; Richard Doyle and Lisa Hoffman, Christchurch City Council; Far North Regional Museum, Kaitia; Tammy Fromont and Nineke Metz, Destination Northland Limited; Dianne Gallagher, New Zealand Mountain Safety Council Inc.; Jane Gilbert, Film New Zealand; Gillooly family, Farewell Spit Safari, Collingwood; Donna Gray, Abel Tasman National Park Enterprises; Lesley Grey and Sharon Pasco, Stewart Island Promotion Association; Frank Habicht, Paihia; Haoni Waititi Marae, Auckland; Lee Harris, Fiordland Travel Limited, Queenstown; Tania Harris, Waitangi National Trust; Christine Harvey, Whale Watch®, Kaikoura; Cameron Hill, Air New Zealand, Auckland; Hillary Commission; Barbara Hinkley and Suzanne Knight, Museum of New Zealand Te Papa Tongarewa; InterCity Coachlines; Anne Irving, City Gallery, Wellington; Peter Jackson, Blenheim; Jean Johnston, Wellington City Council; Kapiti Cheese; Kelly Tarlton's Underwater World and Antarctic Encounter, Auckland; Michael Liao, Kiwfruit Country, Te Puke; Fay Looney, New Plymouth; Peter McCleavey Gallery, Wellington; Ruth McGirr, Robert McDougall Art Gallery and Annex, Christchurch; Bill and Joan MacGregor, Lake Hawea; Robert McGregor, Art Deco Trust, Napier; Annabelle MacKenzie and Cathy Muker, New Zealand High Commission, Kuala Lumpur; Cathy Maslin, Key-Light Image Library; Heather Mathie and Betty Moss, Alexander Turnbull Library; Darryl May, Oamaru; Montana Marlborough Winery; Anita Moreira, Air New Zealand, Kuala Lumpur; Morven Hills Station, Oamaru; Museum of Caves, Waitomo; Newmans Coach Lines; New Zealand Fighter Pilots Museum, Wanaka; Okarito Nature Tours, Westland; Old Mandeville Airport, Gore; Otago Early Settlers Museum, Dunedin; security staff, Parliament House, Wellington; Libby Passau and Nick Turzynski, Hodder Moa Beckett Publishers Ltd; Jacky Payne; Penguin Place, Otago Peninsula; Meng-Chong Phang, New Zealand Tourism Board, Singapore; Clive Ralph, Napier; Rewa's Village, Kerikeri; Chris and Phil Rose, Wairau River Wines; Royal Albatross Centre, Taiaroa Head; Russell Museum; Mary Sharrock, Ansett Airways, Australia; Jenny Shipley, MP, Wellington; Stone Store, Kerikeri; Annalese Taylor, New Zealand Tourism Board, Auckland; Judith Tizard, MP; Tourism Auckland Office; Tourism Industry Association New Zealand; Tranz Rail Ltd; Tom Van der Kwast, Picton; Andrew and Jeannie Van der Putten; Visitor Information Centres; Tim Warren, Visual Impact Pictures Ltd; concert staff, Whakarewarewa Thermal Village, Rotorua; Whangarei Museum of Fishes; Dr Rodney Wilson, Auckland War Memorial Museum; Jane Wynyard, The Royal New Zealand Ballet.

## Photography Permissions

The publisher would like to thank the following for their assistance and kind permission to photograph at their establishments.

Graham Abbott, Hanmer Springs Thermal Reserve; Art and Gourd Gallery, Golden Bay; Ashford Craft Village, Ashburton; Auckland International Airport; Auckland Zoological Gardens; Avis, Auckland International Airport; Babich Winery, Auckland; Grant Barron, Olveston House, Dunedin; Café de Paris, Hokitika; Canterbury House Vineyards, Waipara; Christ Church Cathedral, Christchurch; Dr Fiona Ciaran, Aigantighe Art Gallery, Timaru; Clapham Clock Museum, Whangarei; Coal Town Museum, Westport; Dargaville Maritime Museum; DFS Galleria, Auckland; Driving Creek Railway and Potteries, Coromandel; Dunedin Public Art Gallery;

Dunedin Railway Station; The Edwin Fox, Picton; Ana Foreman, Weta Shop, Coromandel; Gibbston Valley Winery, Queenstown; Lindsay Hazley, Southland Museum and Art Gallery, Invercargill; Helen and Ross Ivey, Glentanner Station; Kevin Judd, Cloudy Bay; Steve Jones, Science Centre, Manawatu Museum and Art Gallery, Palmerston North; Kauri Kingdom, Kaitaia; Stuart Landsborough's Puzzling World, Wanaka; Left Bank Art Gallery, Greymouth; Le Brun family, Blenheim; Malcolm McLaughlan and Peter Thornley, Icon Restaurant, Wellington; Maori Arts and Crafts Institute, Rotorua; Royce McGlashen, Nelson; Matakohe Kauri Museum, Dargaville; Mountain Jade Greenstone Factory, Hokitika; Mt Bruce Wildlife Centre, Wairarapa; Mountford Vineyard, Canterbury; Museum of Transport and Technology, Auckland; Museum of Wellington City and Sea; New Zealand Automobile Association; New Zealand Rugby Museum, Palmerston North; North Otago Museum, Oamaru; Nigel and Teresa Ogle, Tawhiti Museum, Hawera; Outdoor Heritage, Newmarket; Out of New Zealand, Auckland; Parnell Fire Service; Parnell Police Station; Pegasus Bay, Canterbury; Provincial Council Buildings, Christchurch; Queenstown Rafting; Rainbow's End Adventure Park, Auckland; Rippon Vineyards, Wanaka; St John's Ambulance; St Paul's Cathedral, Dunedin; Shantytown, Greymouth; Sheraton Auckland Hotel; Shotover Jet, Queenstown; Southward Car Museum, Paraparaumu; Stockton Mine, Westport; Thames School of Mines and Mineralogical Museum; Tramway Museum, Paekakariki; Waiau Waterworks, Coromandel; Waipara Springs, Canterbury; Whakarewarewa Thermal Village, Rotorua; Whale Watch®, Kaikoura; Whanganui Riverboat Centre; Zambesi, Wellington.

## Picture Credits

Key: a = above; b = below/bottom; c = centre; f = far; l = left; r = right; t = top.

The publisher would like to thank the following individuals, companies and picture libraries for permission to reproduce their photographs:

**111 Emergency**: Derek Quinn 346clb.

**Airbus Express**: 353tc; **AGL Aerial Imagery**: 43br; **Alamy Images**: Rafael Ben-Ari 1c; Jon Bower New Zealand 12bl; Greg Balfour Evans 13b; Carpe Diem - New Zealand 156; Cephas Picture Library 200; Douglas Fisher 4c; Paul Grogan 113tl; Paul Thompson Images 311tl; Douglas Fisher 311cl; frans lemmens 20; Vincent Lowe 12tr; Henk Meijer 346cl; UrbanZone 351cla; David Wall 62-63, 344tl; WinePix 211bc; **Arbitrageur Wine Room**: Sarah Hunter 320tl; **Art Deco Trust**: 150bl.

**Bay of Islands Swordfish Club**: 107tc, 107cla; **The Boatshed Hotel**: 301t; **Britomart Limited**: 74cla; **Peter Bush**: 37cr, 42clb, 42bl, 42br, 75tr, 123clb, 161bl, 331cr.

**Cable Bay Vineyards**: 308br, 315tr; **Christchurch City Council**: 222; **Christchurch International Airport**: 355tl; **City Gallery, Wellington**: 168tr; **Corbis**: All Canada Photos/Rolf Hicker 84-85; Peter Beck 310cl; Hulton-Deutsch Collection 8-9; Jami Tarris 180-181; Miz Watanabe 278-279.

**Department of Conservation, Wellington**: 195tr, 223b; **Destination Northland Limited**: 100cl, 107cra, 112bc; **Dreamstime.com**: Dirkr 11cr; Hugoht 15br; Light & Magic Photography 244-245; Lucidwaters 346bl; Millaus 24t; Christian Mueringer 14bl, 231tr; Cloudia Newland 2-3, 116; Mohd Nadly Aizat Mohd Nudri 258; Dmitry Pichugin 58-59, 148-149; Uros Ravbar 338tl; Alexey Stiop 222; Tupungato 13tr, 226tr, 230b; Mark Ward 15tc; **Drylands Restaurant**: 322t.

**Eagles Nest**: 298tc, 301t, 303tr.

**Fiordland Travel Limited**: 284tr, 288 -289 all; **Fishbone Bar & Grill**: 324tl; **Food At Wharepuke**: 316tl.

**The Gables**: 317tr; **Gantleys Restaurant**: 325tc; **Gareth Eyres, Exposure**: 43tl, 45bc, 46cr, 112c, 125r, 243cr, 275br, 287tr, 335tl, 336tl, 336b, 337t; **Getty Images**: Alexandre Cappi 361cr; Mark Daffey 25tr; Paul Kennedy 130tl; Doug Pearson 104-105; Darryl Torckler 103br, 190-191; Matthew Micah Wright 70; **Greater Wellington Regional Council**: 360bl. **Green Cabs**: 353bc.

**Hapuku Lodge & Tree Houses**: 345tl; **Herzog Winery & Luxury Restaurant**: 308cl; **Gerard Hindmarsh**: 274tl, 301c; **Hodder Moa Beckett Publishers Ltd**: 37bl; **The Huka Retreat**: 304tl.

**Interislander**: 357tl.

**Kapitea Ridge**: 306tl; **Kauri Cliffs**: 299br, 302bc; **Key-Light Image Library**: Andy Belcher 147crb; Nic Bishop 248bl, 277ca; Gary Bowering 41bc; Brian Chudleigh 198tr; Richard Cory-Wright 123br; Brian Enting Photography 171, 51bl, 68br, 146clb; Tim Hawkins 256bc; Caroline Hobbs 243cra; Warren Jacobs 26 -27, 30tr, 187br, 276cl, 339tl; Peter Laurenson 187crb; Geoff Mason 68tr, 199br, 251cl, 334bl, 354bc; Graham Meadows 38bc; Michael Pole 38tr; Graham Radcliffe 46bl, 177br, 356br; Andy Radka 30cl; Ron Redfern 335c; Peter Reese 294cl; Nick Servian 34br, 34–35c, 38br, 169tr; James White 38clb; **Kokako**: 314bl; **Kiwifruit Country**: 133tr.

**Lakes District Museum**: 283c; **Holger Leue**: 26br, 30cr, 31bl, 38cla, 38–39c, 53bc, 69cr, 69br, 72cl, 77clb, 78tl, 79bl, 81tr, 82br, 87bc, 93t, 96bl, 97tl, 107br, 117b, 124cl, 126bc, 131br, 134tr, 135crb, 147cra 194tr, 194cla, 198–199c, 231br, 236tl, 248br, 256tr, 256cla, 257tl, 271c, 276br, 281c, 282tr, 284br, 286tr, 286cl, 286bl, 287cl, 287b, 292cl, 292bc, 293br. **Logan Brown Restaurant & Bar**: 321tl; **Rob Lucas**: 28bl, 28bc, 28br, 29cla, 29bl, 29crb, 276tl, 287cr.

**Magic Travellers Network**: 356cla; **Marsden Estate**: 316br; **Maui, New Zealand**: 300br; **Darryl May**: 272tl, 272cla, 272clb, 273ca, 273ca; **McCormick House**: 305bc; **Robert McDougall Art Gallery and Annex**: 36bl; **Mission Estate Winery**: 318br; **Rod Morris**: 28clb, 28cb, 28crb, 29tl, 29tr, 29cl, 29cr, 29tl, 51cr, 93c, 196tr, 196tl, 196bl, 196br, 249cr, 255cl, 270tr, 276bl, 293cr, 295tl; **Morrison Street Café**: 322bc; **Museum of New Zealand Te Papa Tongarewa**: 33bl, 34bl, 35tl, 35cr, 37tl, 50tr, 50bc, 51cra, 55cb, 61bl, 170tr, 170cla, 170bl, 171tl; **NZTA**: 360c.

**Napier City Council**: 152tr; **National Party Office**: 57bc; **Nelson Tasman Tourism**: 14tr, 23b, 201b, 219tl; **New Zealand Festival 2000**: 160clb, 160–161c, 331tl; **The New Zealand Herald**: 22b, 57tr, 121bl, 161tc.

**Office of Treaty Settlements**: 57cl.

**Lloyd Park**: 27br, 39bl, 39bc, 194–195c, 195br, 251cra, 251cr; **Pescatore Restaurant**: 323br; **Pete's Farm Stay**: 300tl; **Photosource New Zealand Ltd**: 39cl, 39cr, 39clb, 42ca, 43clb, 43clb 44bl, 47c, 47b, 66cl, 113cra, 123bl, 125tl, 165cl, 186tr, 186bl, 197tr, 198br, 199tl, 242cl, 249tl, 257cr, 285cr, 339cr.

**River Restaurant and Vineyard**: 319br; **Riverstone Kitchen**: 324bc; **The Royal New Zealand Ballet**: 94c, 161br.

**Satori Lounge**: 319br; **SCENIC HOTEL GROUP**: 307bl; **Sky City Auckland Limited**: 78tl; **Stewart Island Promotion Association**: 292tl.; **SuperStock**: age fotostock 98, /Charles O. Cecil 184cl, /Ignacio Palacios 340-341; Travel Library Limited 208-209;

**Te Manawa Museums Trust**: Andrew Blayney 179 all; **Terrôir Restaurant at Craggy Range**: 318tl; **Tourism Auckland**: 75cr; **Tourism New Zealand**: 60bl, 61br, 64cla, 99b, 101tl, 193tr, 338bl, 359bc; **Tourism Transport Ltd**: 353cb; **Tourism West Coast**: 242tr Alexander Turnbull Library: 22c, 34tr, 35tr, 35b, 37br, 40cl, 48, 49bl, 50cl, 50bl, 50cla, 51tr, 51br, 52tl, 52cr, 52bl, 52br, 53br, 54tr, 54clb, 54bl, 55cc, 55bc, 56tl, 56clb, 66tl, 66bl, 66–67c, 67tl, 67cr, 89bc, 141br, 175br, 230cr, 239cl.

**Visual Impact Pictures Ltd**: 30bl, 31cr, 31br, 32tr, 39cra, 39crb, 39cla, 43ca, 44cr, 82tr, 107bl, 113crb,121cla, 127bl, 132bl, 146tr, 194clb, 195tl, 199bl, 218tr, 250tl, 295cr. **Wai Restaurant**: 325b; **Wairau River Wines**: 211cr; **Waitangi National Trust**: 45cr, 100br, 108cl, 108bl, 109tl, 109bl; **Wellington City Council**: 91br, 160br; **Dr Kim Westerskov**: 107crb, 153br, 197tl, 197cr, 197clb; **Westpac Limited**: 348cl; **Whale Watch®, Kaikoura**: 213cla; **Women's Golf New Zealand**: 43tr.

**Front Endpaper**: All special photography except **Alamy Images**: Carpe Diem - New Zealand Rtr; Cephas Picture Library Rcr, **Dreamstime.com**: Cloudia Newland Lcl; Mohd Nadly Aizat Mohd Nudri Rbr; Alexey Stiop Rbc; **Getty Images**: Matthew Micah Wright Ltl; **SuperStock**: age fotostock Ltc.

**Jacket** – Front and spine t: **4Corners**: SIME/Maurizio Rellini.

# Further Reading

## Art and Culture

*Contemporary Painting in New Zealand* Dunn, M., Craftsman House, Auckland 1996.

*Dream Collectors: 100 Years of Art in New Zealand* Wedde, I., Walsh, J. and Johnson, A., Te Papa Press, Wellington 1998.

*A History of New Zealand Architecture* Shaw, P., Hodder Moa Beckett, Auckland 1998.

*Looking for the Local: Architecture and the New Zealand Modern* Clark, J. and Walker, P., Victoria University Press, Wellington 2000.

*Mau Moko: The World of Maori Tattoo* Te Awekotuku, N. & Nikora, L.W., Penguin, Auckland 2007.

*New Zealand Pottery: Commercial and Collectable* Henry, G., Reed Publishing, Auckland 2007.

*Old New Zealand Houses 1800–1940* Salmond, J., Reed Publishing, Auckland 1998.

*100 New Zealand Craft Artists* Schamroth, H., Godwit, Auckland 1998.

*100 New Zealand Paintings* Brown, W., Godwit, Auckland 1997.

## Fiction

*Believers to the Bright Coast* O'Sullivan, V., Penguin, Auckland 1998.

*The Best of Katherine Mansfield's Short Stories* Mansfield K., Random House, Auckland 1998.

*The Best of Owen Marshall* Marshall, O., Random House, Auckland 1997.

*The Bone People* Hulme, K., Picador, Auckland 1986.

*Land of the Long White Cloud: Maori Myths, Tales and Legends* Kanawa, K.T. and Foreman, M., Penguin Auckland, 1997.

*Mister Pip* Jones, L., Penguin, Auckland 2006.

*The Matriarch* Ihimaera, W., Reed Publishing, Auckland 1996.

*Once Were Warriors* Duff, A., Tandem Press, Auckland 1990.

*100 New Zealand Poems* Manhire, B. (ed.), Godwit, Auckland 1994.

*Plumb* Gee, M., Penguin, Auckland 1981.

*Potiki* Grace, P., Penguin, Auckland 1986.

*Reconnaissance* Kassabova, K., Penguin, Auckland 1999.

*Season of the Jew* Shadbolt, M., David Ling Publishing, Auckland 1988.

*Skylark Lounge* Cox, N., Victoria University Press, Wellington 2000.

## Geography and Geology

*Aotearoa and New Zealand: A Historical Geography* Grey, A., Canterbury University Press, Christchurch 1995.

*Awesome Forces: The Natural Hazards That Threaten New Zealand* Campbell, H. and Hicks, G., Te Papa Press Wellington 1998.

*Contemporary Atlas of New Zealand* Kirkpatrick, R., David Bateman, Auckland 1999.

*Historical New Zealand Atlas* Malcolm McKinnon et al (eds.), David Bateman, Auckland 1997.

## History and Politics

*A Concise Encyclopaedia of Maori Myth and Legend* Orbell, M., Canterbury University Press, Christchurch 1998.

*The Discovery of Aotearoa* Evans, J., Reed Publishing, Auckland 1998.

*Historical Dictionary of New Zealand* Jackson, K. and McRobie, A., Addison, Wesley, Longman, Auckland 1996.

*Making Peoples: A History of New Zealanders from Polynesian Settlement to the End of the 19th Century* Belich, J., Penguin, Auckland 1996.

*New Zealand, the Story So Far: A Short History* Bohan, E., Harper Collins, Auckland 1997.

*The Oxford History of New Zealand* Oliver W.H. (ed.), Oxford University Press, Wellington 1981.

*Politics in New Zealand* Mulgan, R. Auckland University Press, Auckland 1997.

*Penguin History of New Zealand,* King, M., Penguin, 2003.

*The Treaty of Waitangi* Orange, C., Bridget Williams Books, Wellington 1991.

## Natural History

*A Field Guide to the Alpine Plants of New Zealand* Salmon, J., Godwit, Auckland 1999.

*Field Guide to the Birds of New Zealand* Heather, B. and Robertson, H., Viking, Auckland 1996.

*Game Animals of New Zealand* Roberts, G., Shoal Bay Press, Blenheim 1998.

*Ghosts of Gondwana,* Gibbs, G., Craig Potton Publishing, Nelson 2006.

*Kiwi: New Zealand's Remarkable Bird* Peat, N., Godwit, Auckland 1999.

*Native Trees of New Zealand* Salmon J., Reed Publishing, Auckland 1996.

*Natural History of New Zealand* Bishop, N., Hodder and Stoughton, Auckland 1992.

*The Natural World of New Zealand* Hutching, G., Viking, Auckland 1998.

## Outdoor Activities

*Bird's Eye Guide: Tramping in New Zealand* Barnett, S., Craig Potton Publishing, Nelson 2006.

*Classic New Zealand Mountain Bike Rides* Kennett, P., Kennett, S. and Kennett, J., Reed Publishing, Auckland 1998.

*Classic Walks of New Zealand* Potton C., Craig Potton Publishing, Nelson 1997.

*New Zealand: Pure Adventure* McLennan, C., David Bateman, Auckland 1999.

*A Tramper's Guide to New Zealand's National Parks* Burton, R. and Atkinson, M., Reed Publishing, Auckland 1998.

# Glossary

## Culture

**Aotearoa:** Maori name for New Zealand, literally "Land of the Long White Cloud", coined by the explorer Kupe's wife *(see p21)*

**haka:** war dance and song performed by males *(see p34)*

**hangi:** style of cooking food in an earth oven where the heat is provided by special stones or embers *(see p141)*

**hongi:** greeting by pressing noses together. When people *hongi*, their *hau* or life essence intermingles

**iwi:** tribe, people. A *hapu* is a subtribe and *whanau* an extended family

**kai:** food. Any word with *kai* in it relates to food, for example *kai moana* (seafood) *(see p113)*

**kete:** woven basket made from the fibre of flax, kiekie or pingao plants *(see p35)*

**mana:** authority, prestige, psychic power

**maori:** ordinary or usual, used by indigenous New Zealanders from the 19th century to distinguish themselves from *pakeha* (stranger or different)

**Maoritanga:** Maori culture

**marae:** gathering place, open courtyard in front of a village meeting house where important meetings, funerals and entertainment take place *(see p120)*

**mere:** flat greenstone war club, most highly valued of weapons *(see p204)*

**moko:** tattoos incised on the faces, buttocks and thighs of men and the lips and chins of women *(see p34)*

**pa:** fortified village or stockade *(see p54)*

**pakeha:** stranger, person of European descent

**poi:** ball made of leaves attached to a piece of string and used by women in graceful dances *(see p34–35)*

**tane:** man, male

**tangi:** funeral

**taonga:** treasures, cultural items such as carvings or woven cloaks passed down through the generations

**tapu:** holy, sacred, forbidden; taboo in English

**tiki:** from *heitiki*; prized greenstone figure worn around the neck. Debate continues over the origins and religious significance of this ornament *(see p34)*

**wahine:** woman, female

**waiata:** songs. There are many types, for example *waiata tangi* (laments) and *waiata aroha* (love songs)

**waka:** canoe. The masterpieces were elaborately carved 30-metre *waka taua* or war canoes *(see p51)*

**whare:** house. There are a number of different houses: *whare runanga* (meeting house) *(see p32)*; *whare whakairo* (carved house); *whare puni* (family sleeping house)

## Geography and Nature

**kauri:** huge forest tree growing in northern New Zealand *(see p28)*

**kea:** uncommon but inquisitive alpine parrot whose name is derived from its call *(see p29)*

**kiwi:** flightless, nocturnal indigenous bird which uses its long beak to probe in the earth for worms *(see p28)*

**koru:** the spiral, the principal motif used in Maori carving, inspired by the unfurling fern frond or *koru*; it signifies "awakening, the process of growth, joy" *(see p28)*

**kumara:** sweet potato, transported from Polynesia to New Zealand where it became a staple food *(see p49)*

**manuka:** shrubby plant popularly known as the tea tree with proven anti-bacterial qualities, source of honey and oils *(see p28)*

**paua:** black coloured shellfish known elsewhere as abalone, prized for its beautiful shell which is worked into jewellery *(see p329)*

**pohutukawa:** large spreading coastal tree covered in scarlet flowers during early summer, hence described as the "Christmas tree" *(see p29)*

**ponga:** tree fern

**pounamu:** greenstone or jade, the most precious stone used in jewellery and weapons, found in the South Island and traded with North Island tribes *(see p241)*

**Te Ika a Maui:** the fish of Maui, the North Island

**Te Wai Pounamu:** South Island

## Everyday Words and Phrases

**Haere mai:** Welcome

**Haere ra:** Goodbye (from the person staying to the one going)

**E noho ra:** Goodbye (from the person going to the one staying)

**Ka pai:** Thank you

**Kia ora:** Thank you, good luck, good health

**Tena koe:** Hello (to one person)

**Tena koutou:** Hello (to more than three people)

**Kei te pehea koe:** How are you?

**Kei te pai:** Very well, thank you

## Words Commonly Forming Place Names

**ao:** cloud

**atua:** spirit or gods

**awa:** river or valley

**hau:** wind

**ika:** fish

**iti:** small

**kai:** food

**kainga:** village

**kare:** rippling

**manga:** stream, tributary

**manu:** bird

**maunga:** mountain

**moana:** sea or lake

**motu:** island

**nui:** big

**one:** beach, sand or mud

**papa:** flat, broad slab

**po:** night

**puke:** hill

**puna:** water spring

**rangi:** sky, heavens

**roa:** long

**roto:** lake

**rua:** two, hole

**te:** the

**wai:** water

**wero:** challenge

**whanga:** bay or inlet

**whenua:** land or country

# Road Map of New Zealand

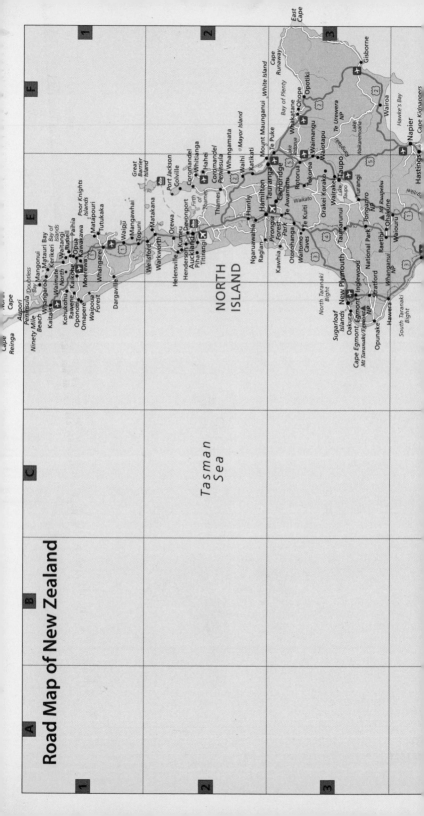

NORTH ISLAND

Tasman Sea